W9-AZO-140

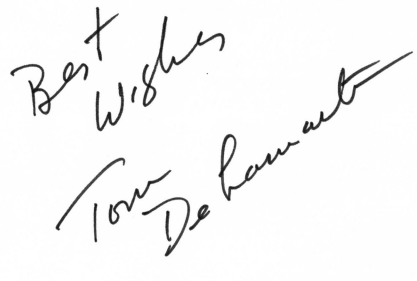

Best
Wishes

Tom DeLamater

BIG BLUE

BIG BLUE

IBM's Use and Abuse of Power

Richard Thomas DeLamarter

DODD, MEAD & COMPANY
NEW YORK

The material in Appendix H of this book is Copyright © 1986 by C.W. Communications Inc., Framingham, MA. 01701—reprinted from *Computerworld* magazine by permission.

Published by Dodd, Mead & Company, Inc.
79 Madison Avenue, New York, N.Y. 10016
Distributed in Canada by
McClelland and Stewart Limited, Toronto
Manufactured in the United States of America

Designed by Erich Hobbing

First Edition

1 2 3 4 5 6 7 8 9 10

Library of Congress Cataloging-in-Publication Data

DeLamarter, Richard Thomas.
   Big Blue: IBM's use and abuse of power.

   Includes index.
   1. International Business Machines Corporation. 2. Computer industry—
United States. 3. Monopolies—Government policy—United States. I. Title.
HD9696.C64I4835   1986   338.7′61004′0973   86–11635
ISBN 0–396–08515–6

This book is gratefully dedicated
to Patricia Dunne.

Contents

Acknowledgments

This has been a very difficult book to write—the technical, economic, and legal considerations are very complex, and the point of view is directly opposite to that generally held. At every stage I have benefitted from the assistance of others. Some helped in the actual analysis, others in the presentation, still others in dealing with the complexities of having a book published.

First, I owe a great deal to the many people with whom I worked at the Antitrust Division of the Department of Justice during its case against IBM. Their efforts to enforce this nation's laws have never been properly acknowledged. During the case, IBM portrayed itself as the underdog, asking, "Who are we against the vast resources of the U.S. Government?" In fact, IBM was, and still is, the most powerful corporation in the world and it fought tooth and nail for the continuation of that power. It spent lavishly on its defense, on a scale the government trial team was never able to match. Add to this the fact that IBM knew exactly the details of its abuse of power, details that we at the Justice Department had painstakingly to discover and prove, and one begins to appreciate how much my colleagues actually accomplished. This book, although different in argument and presentation from the government's case, is in a sense a continuation of their efforts.

I wish to recognize several individuals in particular. First, Lewis Bernstein, a long-standing fighter for competitive markets, who for many years led the Antitrust Division's case against IBM and who was for many of us a mentor. Others include the economists who directed our efforts, Drs. Alan McAdams, Leonard Wess, Hendrik Houthakker, and Lee Preston. Drs. Preston and Houthakker read a draft of this work and offered valuable comments. I learned much from working with them all.

My education was aided, too, by the many people working in the industry who stepped forward to contribute to the government's case. Too numerous to name individually, these busy executives and technicians patiently helped me grasp the intricacies of the computer market, the complexities of its products, and the methods of IBM's power. I am grateful to them all.

Following the end of the case, work on this book began. Once the main ideas were in place and supporting evidence was marshaled, John W. Verity joined the project. To him must go credit for making the material accessible not just to those technically trained in the complexities of computers, economics, and antitrust law, but also to the general reader.

During the many months of our writing collaboration, John's enthusiasm for the project proved invaluable. In addition, his intelligence in challenging and refining my ideas greatly helped the structure of their presentation. His willingness to engage in the frequent rewriting of the chapters in the book led to a much stronger, more persuasive argument than would have been the case otherwise. His considerable writing talents show on every page, and I am most grateful.

The book benefited from the encouragement and guidance of my agent, Maria Carvainis, and my editor at Dodd, Mead, Cynthia Vartan. Publishing a book is a complex venture and both have helped me and the project to its completion.

Finally, several individuals knowledgeable about aspects of the analysis have been generous with their time and encouragement. These include Connie Winkler, Richard Sharpe, Elie Noam, and Frederick G. Withington. All read early drafts of this material, as did my brother, William DeLamarter, and my brother-in-law, J. William Milne.

On a more personal level, there are many who have encouraged me throughout the completion of the book. I would like to mention particularly Mary-Clair Barton, Peter Weitz, Bill and Nancy Strong, Sarah Jackson, Dick Balzer, Lillian Voorhees, Doug Ross, Madeline Renkens, Nan Kilbourn and Jozef Tara, Mary-Ann Teed, Louise Hogg, Mike Mansour, Pierre and Marie-France Arcelin, Sally and Paul Vincent, and Honor Thacker. In particular, I am grateful to Mike Aiken for his patience at a critical earlier period. And finally, thanks to my children, Christopher and Andrew, and my parents, Ruth and Richard DeLamarter.

Any errors, naturally, are mine.

Introduction

It began for me on a cold morning in January 1974. For the first time, I went to the offices of the Department of Justice in Washington, D.C. I was looking for a job, and the Antitrust Division was looking for economists to help in its antitrust case against IBM. After the obligatory interviews with the members of the staff, I was escorted into the office of the chief lawyer in charge of the case, Raymond Carlson. We talked briefly. I seemed to pass, and he then very seriously informed me that if I were hired, I had to agree to stay for at least one year. I agreed, was hired, and stayed until the unfortunate end eight years later. At that time, the Reagan Administration's assistant attorney general in charge of the Antitrust Division, William Baxter, walked away from the case. In his opinion, our work was "without merit," and the case was withdrawn.

The case against IBM had begun with preliminary inquiries in 1964; the case was filed on January 17, 1969, and almost thirteen years later, on January 8, 1982, it was withdrawn. It was one of the longest and most complex court cases in history. I, as a senior economist for the U.S. government, had a ringside seat for most of it.

It was an interesting job, the pay was good, and I learned a great deal. I emerged from those eight years wiser in the ways of the world and the importance of power. I believe that Baxter was wrong in his hasty action, for IBM was and continues to be a monopolist—and a particularly threatening one at that.

Surprisingly, very little is known about IBM and how it has achieved its success. This is so because IBM has used its power, among other things, to cover its tracks. IBM has been seen as it wishes rather than as it is. In the end, Baxter was able to withdraw the case with little or no public outcry because the secret of IBM's great success remained hidden.

But, one may ask, does the opinion of one more Washington official concerning a case now over for more than four years really matter? I think it does. IBM is the single most powerful firm in the world today. If for no other reason, this means that it should be watched carefully. Moreover, the industry that it dominates is of all industries the single most important; it supplies the tools for processing information, and thus it increasingly underlies all others.

But, one may ask, is the decision to drop the IBM case really worth reconsidering now, almost five years after the fact? If there's no problem, don't fix it. Though not generally recognized, there is a problem with IBM, a major one, and Baxter singlehandedly stopped the process that could have effectively dealt with it. And what is that problem? It is that IBM monopolizes the computer business, which is arguably the most important industry in the world. IBM's power is such that all of its competitors, large and small, exist entirely at its sufference. IBM is nothing less than the most powerful corporation in the world and, thanks to Baxter's decision, it is now virtually unrestrained by the antitrust laws or meaningful public scrutiny.

Although simply stated, this conclusion is likely to be quite alien to most people, but then few enjoyed the opportunity to peek behind the veil and see IBM's inner workings. What I saw during the course of the trial helped explain IBM's astounding commercial success in a way that is quite different from the commonly accepted wisdom. I learned that it was not IBM's excellent management or its superior products that made it successful; rather, it was the clever ways in which the company has exploited an exclusive position of power.

Many people, including even some of those who acknowledge that the company wields extraordinary power, doubt that IBM would actually abuse its powerful position. They are only too willing, for a variety of reasons, to believe what IBM would like them to believe. But until we first answer the question, "How has IBM done it, how has it achieved such extraordinary success?", we shall have no chance of fixing the problem that currently dampens the health of the computer industry.

Answering that question and recognizing the true consequences of Baxter's decision, requires a thorough analysis of the computer's short but robust history. What is needed to truly understand the IBM phenomenon is not simply a recital of the computer's undeniably marvelous technological achievements, but a full and accurate description of the powerful forces that have driven this industry. This book tries to do just that.

The history presented here is based as much as possible on IBM's own documents, which were made public in large numbers during the government's antitrust case (and during the dozen or so private antitrust cases filed concurrently). When these documents are sifted through and understood in the context of the myriad technological, economic, and product changes that have taken place, they reveal an unprecedented exercise in sheer corporate power.

This book is an attempt to share with others what I saw. It is my report to those who paid the bill for the case—the people of America.

My analysis begins with a few facts about IBM today.

- In 1985, IBM was the most profitable company in the world. It earned almost $6.6 billion dollars in profit on over $50 billion in rev-

enues—more than Exxon, more than General Motors, more than any
other company.

- IBM continues to dominate the computer business and is well on its
  way to dominating everything that is connected to and/or operates
  with these computers.
- IBM faces no significant domestic or foreign competition that could
  threaten this dominance. It has such overwhelming political, financial, and technological power that what competition it faces exists at
  its sufferance.
- The antitrust laws, designed to police just such unequal competition,
  are of little use. The Reagan administration gives its actions a clean
  bill of health.

Thus, the future looks very bright for Big Blue. As computers continue to
grow in importance, IBM's position will grow, too. Sensing it is on a roll, IBM is
making the most of it. In the first year following Baxter's decision, IBM rose
three positions, from eleventh to eighth, in the annual *Fortune* magazine survey
of firms with the largest worldwide revenues. In the process of earning $34 bil-
lion in that year, it increased its 70 percent-plus share of the large computer
business and also expanded into new areas—areas where other firms already
had established positions. The company has, for example, quickly dominated
the personal computer market. Other firms long active in this market were left in
the dust, some even quit, as IBM muscled in. Ironically, IBM added this market
to its fiefdom with someone else's product; most of the parts for its personal
computer are made by others.

IBM's foreign competitors, following a string of costly but futile attempts to
get a significant share of the market, are weaker today than ever. The French,
the Germans, and the English, among others, have all tried and failed. What
foreign threat there is comes only from the Japanese; but IBM hypocritically
uses that threat to arouse us to support its dominant position. IBM would have
us believe that it is our defender. This is at the very least ironic since the largest
and most powerful computer company in Japan has long been IBM itself.
Nonetheless, because the Japanese have had success in other markets, we are
induced to fear the Japanese and ignore the fears of the Japanese themselves—
fears that are shared by the rest of the world. If the U.S. computer industry were
composed of firms more equal in size—with IBM having less power—the Japanese would not feel so compelled to take on IBM.

This foreign fear of IBM was expressed eleven years ago by British writer Rex
Malik in *And Tomorrow . . . The World? Inside IBM.*

> This book is about control. It is about a sham: an American company
> which masquerades as a multinational and has dozens of foreign subsid-
> iaries, each with a board packed full of local worthies and executive flun-

keys, but which in reality is a company, in all meaningful senses of the word, consolidated, and in which power is about as widely distributed as is power in the Kremlin.[1]

This image of IBM is different from and more ominous than the image held by most Americans. Is IBM the answer to foreign competition, or are IBM's size and power actually the root of the problem? Are there aspects of IBM that we, the proud parent country of this exceptional offspring, have been too close to recognize?

IBM's success is no accident, and neither is our benign view of it. Both are the result of a conscious and highly successful IBM policy. We believe about IBM what IBM wants us to believe, and IBM wants us to trust it and its substantial power.

Consider our image of IBM. We see it as:

- A class act—the very model of the enlightened corporation. Excellent in all that it does.
- Having managers that are wise, engineers that are geniuses, and a sales force that is the envy of its competitors.
- Offering products that are better than those offered by its competitors and at a lower price. These are the same products that have made us more productive with each passing year as computers assume more of the work of our economy.
- Having happy customers—customers that include not only the largest and most sophisticated organizations in the world but also small firms and just common folk using personal computers. These customers trust IBM because it always puts their interests before its own.
- Enjoying justified rewards derived from its status as number one in a wide-open, competitive business. Though IBM fights hard, it fights fair, and it would never engage in questionable actions or those that violate the law.
- Competing against firms that, though offering flashes of brilliance, are viewed as slightly tattered, somewhat second rate, and, when compared to IBM, very prone to make mistakes.

This image, although carefully constructed and widely believed, is wrong. Like its competitors, IBM is at times poorly managed, its products inferior, its customers unhappy, and its actions ruthless if not illegal. Yet its success has been indisputable, and its image is solid gold.

This book looks behind the image at IBM's record, and it explains the real reasons for IBM's success. Specifically, it shows that IBM's success is the result of a sophisticated strategy for exploiting its substantial power—power that its competition cannot match. As a result of its power, IBM's competitors cannot win. If they ever get close, IBM changes the rules in its own favor. This book presents the information we need to compare our image of IBM with the reality of how it achieved success.

Consider that each time IBM's corporate logo graces a cultural or a philanthropic activity, it reassures us that it has our best interests at heart, since it is willing to support things that make the world a better place.

Consider the advertising campaign for its popular personal computer. IBM chose to make its pitch using a Charlie Chaplin lookalike. That symbol represents good intentions, trust, honesty, and enough ineptitude to be nonthreatening. The reality, known well to its competitors who have felt the sting of its power if not to the general public, is just the opposite. IBM more accurately should be seen as efficient, highly organized, determined, and ruthless in dealing with all threats to its position.

Consider a final example, the popular book *In Search of Excellence.*[2] Their search quickly led the authors to IBM—a firm they claim to be excellently managed. Their opinion was based in part on IBM's stellar financial performance, which is explained by, among other things, the fact that IBM is action oriented and close to its customers; it encourages entrepreneurship, values its people, and sticks to its main business. According to the authors, IBM has benefited from a strong central philosophy that was originally laid down by its charismatic leaders, the Watsons. They present a simple, appealing model for IBM's success—excellence in management. But this view is dead wrong. IBM's success comes from the power of monopoly.

If in fact IBM is a monopolist and wins because of its power, then why has it been tolerated? There are, after all, antitrust laws that in theory are supposed to rid us of concentrated economic power. But there are problems, not so much in the laws themselves but in their enforcement. For decades IBM has been involved in a cat-and-mouse game with these laws, coming as close as possible to illegality without risking its commercial advantages. This book attempts to explain and document IBM's carefully choreographed dance around the edges of these laws, which define monopoly.

Once understood, the implications of IBM's monopolistic hold on the basic equipment of the information revolution are frightening. It is as if in the past, a single company had held a worldwide monopoly over the steam engine; or over the making of steel; or, later still, over automobile production. These were basic industries whose emergence had revolutionary impacts on the development of entire nations.

The basic tool of our Information Age is the computer; it offers tremendous advantages over all the other tools that manipulate information. IBM's expanding monopoly over the supply of this equipment means that it alone, and not the healthy interplay of competitive forces, will have the power to decide which information technology companies will succeed and which will fail. Every business that depends heavily on these powerful tools is vulnerable to IBM.

It is perilous to trust a single company with such power.

Amid all the excitement stirred up by the computer's amazing history of increasing capabilities and the economic benefits they have created, it is overlooked that this innovative machine is largely controlled by a single company. History shows that IBM uses its power for its own purposes, which are often quite different from those of the rest of us.

The hope for democracy is that one can speak truth to power, that complex issues can be explained and, once understood, acted upon constructively. The burden of this book is to speak such truth. Subsequent actions will require the involvement of many more than me.

BIG BLUE

Part 1

IBM Makes the Rules— A Game of Power

1. The Education of
T. J. Watson

The best way to kill a dog is to cut off its head.

—John Patterson, National Cash
Register chief, on how best to
deal with competitors

Few men have pursued the American Dream with as much zeal and attained as much lasting success as Thomas J. Watson, the legendary founder and for forty years the chief executive of International Business Machines. He was an extraordinarily talented salesman who, with his infectious, almost religious resolution, led regiments of blue-suited followers to great riches. His fixed and formidable fortitude was mesmerizing: "With Mr. Watson leading," they used to sing, "To greater heights we'll rise, And keep our IBM, Respected in all eyes."

The corporate anthems may be gone, and the dress code slightly loosened, but the chorus of praise for IBM continues to mount. Respect rings out from every quarter. The gullible, leading the more gullible, search for corporate "excellence" and say they find its epitome in IBM. They join politicians in gleefully championing the company as this nation's answer to the Japanese industrial machine. IBM is adduced both as *our* samurai warrior, defending U.S. interests in the global electronics market, and as a model, supposedly useful to others, of optimal industrial organization. Wall Street serenades the company as the bluest of blue chip stocks. As IBM moves, so moves the market. Finally, increasing numbers of professionals in every field find the company a valuable partner in establishing their lock on the "postindustrial" service—or information—economy. IBM suffers no lack of boosters these days.

As genuinely felt as this often-emotional public chorus of praise may be, it is misguided. In fact, IBM has very little to teach. Despite what the company or its supporters may claim, IBM's power has less to do with any twenty-first-century work ethic or with perseverance in the pursuit of sales quotas or with exotic technologies than it does with a crafty but hitherto unrecognized violation of the very spirit, if not always the letter, of antitrust law. By carefully controlling information about itself and deliberately obfuscating the matter when it has to, IBM has led the public to accept simplistic explanations for what are in fact subtle and complex abuses of its tremendous unchecked power.

The story of how IBM came to be so dominant a force in the world today begins in simpler times, a hundred years ago or so, when the lowly cash register, the fancy mechanical kind we see in antique shops, was the computer of its time. At first glance, there seems to be a world of difference between those majestically ornate machines of brass and today's computer, mass-produced of plastic and silicon. Where one boasted loudly of ratchets, gears, and bells, the other bleeps synthetically as its digits do a silent green dance.

As outwardly different as they are, though, the two machines are conceptual siblings, born of the same necessity. Each is a tool that helps the management of commercial enterprise by gathering and keeping track of vital business information. Each, in its day, has helped managers make better decisions. Yesterday's businessman, like today's, believed that the more perfect the data he collected, sorted, and shared with his subordinates each day, the better his decisions would be and the healthier his company. Although individual consumers often acquire things for intangible and even irrational reasons—status, enjoyment, guilt, and so forth—businessmen buy cash registers, typewriters, adding machines, telephones, and computers for one reason only: to increase their profits. They are presumed to make highly rational choices when buying such machines, for if they make a mistake, they can easily go out of business.

Businessmen—retailers in particular—used the cash register to keep track of coins and bills, to record total sales in different categories of goods, and to prevent sticky-fingered employees from stealing. The first cash registers combined a simple mechanical adding machine with an even simpler lock-box. Later models printed out receipts and sales totals. But even today's laser-scanning, voice-synthesizing models perform essentially the same task: they collect and aggregate information needed to run the business efficiently. The modern computer is a far more versatile machine than the cash register, applicable to a broader range of problems, but it, too, is basically a recorder and processor of data. Its primary customer, too, has been the businessman.

The appeal of both the cash register and the computer to the businessman is not the only reason for beginning an investigation into the computer giant's current power by describing the cash register marketplace of so many years ago. A more compelling reason is that, at a time when business ethics were not particularly high on corporate America's list of priorities, Thomas J. Watson discovered two things: that the cash register was a lucrative product to sell and that the monopoly was a uniquely lucrative form of company. Watson entered the business before the federal antitrust laws were instituted as a means to limit the actions of monopolists, but he later devised methods of evading those laws more successfully than anyone before or after.

Although IBM was never formally related to National Cash Register, the computer company's paternalistic management style, its legendary sales techniques, and its fundamental reliance on anticompetitive pricing stem directly from the experience and feelings that the humiliated Watson took with him in 1914 when he was ousted from NCR.

FIRST BLOOD

Watson's life has been widely recounted as a story of mounting ambition, evangelistic speeches, and plain old hard work. There is no doubt that Watson was a gifted businessman. He was a natural salesman whose cold-blooded instincts resembled those of a tiger chasing its prey. To go from his rural upbringing in New York State to his first job selling cash registers for NCR, to his rapid rise up through that company's echelons, to become heir apparent to the corporate throne took him only twenty years. But those cold-blooded instincts can just as easily be explained as the instincts of a hunted man, for during many of his first forty years and during many of the subsequent forty at IBM, Watson took on the law in a crafty game of stealth. How much can I get away with? he must have asked himself while peddling cash registers one year and more sophisticated business machines the next. How far can I go? What exactly is the limit of the law? Only once was he caught out at NCR, and only twice at IBM; his punishment each time amounted to a mere slap on the wrist. Between slaps, though, Watson and his faithful followers worked determinedly to further refine the methods of monopoly that he had seen administered so effectively, if not always so subtly, at NCR.

It was after a few rough years of traveling the back roads door to door that Watson in 1895 landed a job selling cash registers for NCR in the teeming port city of Buffalo. He quickly caught on to his employer's often brutish sales tactics, which amounted to outright warfare against any and all competitors. At the time, NCR was run by the domineering John Patterson, a man whose main passion in life was not merely to succeed in, but to dominate completely, the worldwide cash register business. Privately, Patterson viewed all challengers to his company's manifest destiny as just so many dogs to decapitate. Publicly, he was known for his strikingly paternal attitude toward employees.

Patterson's NCR operated during a time of anything-goes sales tactics in America. Salesmen then were a rather scruffy lot whose methods were unscrupulous if not completely dishonest. Rarely did they feel limited by any conventional notion of fair play. NCR's own strong-arm tactics were as reprehensible as any: sabotage of competitors' cash registers, slanderous character assaults, and barrages of nuisance lawsuits, to name a few. The nastiness of this street fighting, which often hurt customers as much as it served them, helped usher in the first antitrust laws, which were promoted as an attempt to channel this competitive zeal into socially useful business conduct. The new laws would be the bane of Watson for the rest of his life.

Salesmen, the infantry in this battle, were generally to be found in the seamier side of whatever town they happened to be working. They dressed poorly and drank heavily. The straitlaced Watson was fortunate enough to meet up with one exceptionally polished NCR salesman who showed him the benefits that were to be had from dressing well and at least putting on the airs of couth. It was from this early lesson that Watson formulated the strict IBM dress code that he became known for many years later.

Despite his rapacity, Patterson held to the belief that if NCR took care of its employees, they would work harder and take care of NCR in return. Workers in his well-lighted, safety-conscious Dayton factories enjoyed extraordinary benefits, and the NCR salesman was truly pampered. He was assigned an exclusive territory—unheard of at most other companies—and was paid generous commissions. Patterson motivated his sales force with evangelistic pep talks, which Watson would eventually copy, and with Hundred PerCent quota clubs. Patterson pushed his men hard, but they repaid him for his good treatment by dominating each of the markets he sent them after.

After great success in Buffalo and a four-year stint as district manager for Rochester, Watson was called to Dayton headquarters. There he was asked by Patterson himself, in a secret meeting, to take complete responsibility for an audacious, competition-smashing mission. Watson accepted, and he soon learned his first lesson in the prerogatives—and limits—of monopoly power. He learned that, by spending large amounts of cash, a monopolist can destroy legitimate but potentially damaging competition with little pain to himself. Whether it is called cross-subsidization, price discrimination, or just relying on deep pockets, this strategy calls for using the profits from an uncontested market area to subsidize below-cost prices in areas where competition is active and effective. It was corporate killing, plain and simple; the law called it predation, but for Patterson and NCR, it was just good business.

Watson's orders were to destroy not just a few individual companies but an entire sector of the market that was threatening to upset NCR's control. Marked to be destroyed were the many dealerships, all of them tiny compared to NCR but annoyingly prosperous, that specialized in secondhand cash registers. Headed by young, ambitious men like Watson, these dealerships had popped up in several large cities to sell perfectly usable secondhand machines at prices that undercut NCR's for new equipment. Chief among the trouble spots was New

York City, where Watson was sent first with a secret war chest of a million dollars.

After publicly pretending to quit NCR, his biographers write, Watson opened a used cash register store on New York's then fashionable Fourteenth Street, just a few doors down from a similar shop run by one Fred Brainin. NCR agent Watson quietly used his secret lode to buy used cash registers at prices so high that Brainin simply couldn't match them without suffering huge losses. It wasn't long before the legitimate dealer, distraught because his business had all but dried up, agreed to sell his entire stock to Watson. Brainin is said to have quibbled only about the price—he finally received $21,000—and to have not even blinked when Watson got him to agree in writing to leave the cash register business forever. Mission accomplished, Watson assigned a subordinate to take over the New York operation and moved on to Philadelphia for a similar clean-out. Then it was off to Chicago, and soon all the troublesome dealers were gone and with them the threat to NCR's control of the market.

It wasn't only used machines that bothered Patterson. Although cash registers were mechanical marvels in their time, they were not so complex that other companies couldn't design, manufacture, install, and service their own models. In fact, Yankee ingenuity had created a wide range of mechanisms that often made competitors' registers technically superior to NCR's. With NCR's entrenched power over the industry and its well-honed tactic of bashing competitors, its own engineering staff had little incentive to innovate. Complacent in their craft, they tended to fall behind their smaller, better-motivated competitors. Due to, among other factors, the hefty sales commissions Patterson paid, NCR's costs were comparatively high, and its prices were higher to compensate. So it was that about sixty different companies tried to enter the cash register business against NCR.

Elementary economics would say that, given free choice, customers would buy from suppliers that delivered better cash registers for lower prices. With relatively high costs, the theory has it, NCR would tend to lose market share and profits. But NCR lost no market share because it successfully denied the customers a free choice. Hardly any of its rivals even survived the turn of the century. Patterson retained a high market share and high profits against superior competition by setting his "competition department" loose on bothersome rivals. A veritable commando squad, ready to be thrown into action wherever and whenever it was needed, this group's tactics were often fatal to competitors.

A favorite trick of theirs, taught them by Patterson himself, was to bombard a competitor, and even its innocent customers, with outrageously inflated nuisance lawsuits, sometimes seventy-five at a time, so as to discredit the firm and plague it with bad publicity. The suits might charge an opponent with patent infringement—even as NCR's engineers in Dayton were stripping down the rival machine and unabashedly copying whatever innovations they could find in it.

Not only did such suits drain a competitor of precious cash, they made customers think twice about installing allegedly questionable machinery. The NCR salesmen would also slander a rival in local newspaper ads and leaflets. In cases where an order looked like it was already lost to a competitor, the NCR "knockers," as these scam artists were known, offered to pay legal fees for customers who broke contracts with the other supplier and installed NCR equipment instead.

Clearly more illegal was the competition department's practice of building "knockout machines"—cheap, lookalike copies of a competing product that were designed and built solely to discredit the original maker's reputation and ultimately ruin it altogether. A typical knockout machine was the one NCR built as a copy of the up-and-coming Hallwood register, which sold for $200. Disguised as Hallwood salesmen, NCR knockers sold their fake Hallwoods—which outwardly were almost perfect copies, but that contained purposely shoddy internal mechanisms—for the eye-catching price of $65. When the fake machine broke down, as it was meant to do, the knockers quickly publicized the failure as widely as possible as evidence of the Hallwood's unreliability. Then the Hallwood company would be pressed to repair or replace a machine it had never made or else suffer the further bad publicity that would be generated by an understandably irate customer.

If a knockout machine didn't do the job, then outright sabotage of offending equipment would. Or generous trade-in allowances on used machines would. Or vicious harassment of competing salesmen and their prospects. Or any of a long list of tactics available to the deep-pocketed monopolist, NCR.

NCR showed little respect for others' innovations. Patterson viewed the patent laws as just another means to bother competitors. A judge once ruled that in pressing patent infringement suits against rival manufacturers, NCR was interested more in sapping its opponents' time and cash resources than in actually protecting legitimately procured innovations of its own. Said Patterson on one occasion, "If a patent is granted to the Lamson Company, we will bring suit. If we lose, we will take it to the Court of Appeals. It will take five or six years of litigation and probably cost Lamson $100,000 before they would have a legal right to use their special key arrester and key coupler, and we would still have the right to go on using [it]."[1]

Patterson's hunger for domination seemed boundless. His knockout men themselves infiltrated—and hired others to infiltrate—the competition's ranks. A cash register maker might discover one day that its most loyal salesman also took payments from NCR for services rendered.

Patterson pointed proudly to the "Gloom Room" down the hall from his office: that was where his trophies, carcasses of machines that had succumbed to his knockout team, were piled high and left to rust in indignation.

LESSONS LEARNED

As illegal as they were, knockout tactics were highly effective. They ensured NCR great control over its markets. To the degree that NCR's operations against narrowly focused competitors (e.g., secondhand dealers) protected its larger, uncontested monopoly and enabled it to continue earning excessive profits, Patterson's knockout investments were well spent. Greedy he might have been, but he was not irrational.

This was the crucial lesson for Watson: Take over each narrow market segment as it emerges, for it might someday provide ground for an attack on the core business. Don't worry about initial losses, for the core business, where power and profits are greatest, must be protected at all cost. Once a monopoly is established, the monopolist can charge inordinately high prices to the bulk of its customers—those lacking alternatives—and can use the resulting profits to subsidize money-losing tactical operations against challengers in neighboring markets.

The key to this strategy is the ability to segment markets—that is, to create different product lines for different classes of customers in order to prevent low, anticompetitive prices in one sector from adversely affecting otherwise unchallenged profits in another sector. Power is easier to maintain in narrow, artificially isolated sectors than it is in a broad market where products are standardized and sold as commodities. Whether defined geographically or, as is predominantly the case in business machines, by product function, market segments created by a monopolist erect tough barriers against narrowly focused competitors.

Once the monopolist has gained control over a potentially threatening segment and has blocked inroads by competitors, it can control the prices there as well. Watson's undercover mission on Fourteenth Street, for instance, enabled NCR to become the only viable used cash register dealer in town. As the only supplier in that segment, it could easily get away with paying low prices for used machines and, after a little refurbishing, with selling them for high prices. In fact, the used cash register market grew to be highly profitable for NCR once it had the business to itself.

There were other reasons for Patterson's having Watson remove the secondhand cash register dealers than to provide cash for other anticompetitive actions. For one, customers would have to come to NCR for all their cash register needs—the machines themselves, extra rolls of paper, and maintenance services. NCR's control over its customers was greatly improved once other sources of these products and services were driven from the market.

Crushing competitors early also served notice to potential competitors that NCR was willing and able to use its power. Even established competitors, those with superior products and more efficient operations but lacking NCR's cash, would see the futility of their ways and sell out to NCR at low prices.

Watson also prevented the many small dealers from manufacturing new machines themselves. Using profits and technical knowledge gained from the used cash register market, the more ambitious of them might have banded together to build new gear. Their incentive would have been the high prices NCR charged for new machines. In effect, prospering secondhand dealers would have set an upper limit on the price NCR could safely charge for new gear—too high a price would draw new competition. Not particularly keen on any such limits, Patterson had the would-be challengers removed early.

On February 22, 1912, NCR's ruthlessness caught up with it. Patterson, Watson, and other top NCR executives became the first businessmen ever prosecuted under the newly legislated antitrust laws—laws passed to prevent just such conduct by a monopolist. After a nationally publicized three-month trial, they were declared guilty of criminal conspiracy in restraint of trade and of maintaining a monopoly. The prosecution's witnesses had included former NCR executives who had been forced out of the company by the increasingly paranoid Patterson; a long list of managers from competing cash register companies, some of which were now defunct; and customers who had seen firsthand the brutal effects of NCR's knockout operations. The trial revealed to the public the other side of NCR, which until then had been revered as one of the most enlightened companies of its time.

Watson, along with other NCR officials, was hit with the full sentence: a year in jail and a $5,000 fine. Released on bail, he waited for the appeals to begin, and he continued to work at NCR as the most likely heir to Patterson. It wasn't long, though, before the erratic Patterson turned on his loyal employee as he had on others: after months of being ignored, Watson was drummed into the street with no explanation.

He may have been bitter when he left, but by then Watson had learned something that Patterson in his fading years had never quite appreciated: that the basic NCR monopoly formula—dip into deep pockets as often as necessary to limit customers' choices—came closer to perfection when a salesman's behavior was guided by a little caution.

2. A Matter of Trust

Do right.

—Thomas J. Watson's perennial
advice to salesmen

It was 1914, and Watson was forty years old and recently married, and his wife
was expecting Thomas, Jr., any day. But Watson was out of work. Worse, he
and his NCR colleagues were close to becoming the first people ever to be jailed
under federal antitrust law. Humiliated, Watson vowed to take his revenge
in the way he knew best. He would build a company even bigger and more
powerful than NCR, and it would be under his complete control. Watson owed
much to Patterson, but he could do better. The former protégé would be sure to
avoid provoking close scrutiny of his activities, particularly by the antitrust
agencies.

Despite his notoriety in the NCR antitrust case, or perhaps because of it,
Watson was soon able to join forces with one Charles Ranlett Flint, a colorful,
energetic wheeler-dealer who was known best for building monopolies. With his
broad white mustache, vested pinstripe suits, and expensive hobbies—he sailed
the world's fastest steam yacht—Flint might easily be the model for that rascally
capitalist seen on Monopoly game cards. His fortune came from establishing a
series of conglomerate companies known as trusts. He combined into one corporation several small firms that had once competed with each other in some
market. The resulting trust could, by virtue of its large combined market share
and lack of competitors, set prices freely. Through clever manipulation of a
trust's stock, moreover, speculative investments could be turned into huge sums.
He was a master trust maker, and he spoke widely in their support and of their
supposed "economies of scale."

Flint claimed that these "industrial consolidations," as he preferred to call
them, inherently served customers better than smaller, freely competing companies would. A trust, he proclaimed, operated more efficiently precisely because of its larger size, which supposedly reduced overhead costs and helped it
produce goods at less expense. The "Father of Trusts," as a Chicago newspaper

dubbed him, oversaw the creation of some of the most prestigious companies in America, including the American Woolen Company, United States Rubber, and American Bobbin and Shuttle. More often than not, his "consolidations" dominated their markets because there was little competition left to challenge them. That fact, along with Flint's reputation as a successful deal maker, attracted many investors, including large banks and wealthy members of the Eastern establishment, to his companies. All counted on his ability to create a company whose stock value would rise quickly.

Flint recognized in Watson an executive who knew how to make the most of a monopoly, and he invited him to manage one of his latest creations. Watson said he wanted more than just a managerial post; he wanted a cut of the action, a salary and bonus that were pegged to the company's performance. Flint accepted this and, after persuading some of his partners to overlook Watson's still-pending conviction, made Watson general manager at the three-year-old Computing-Tabulating-Recording Company, based in New York City. Like Flint's previous arrangements, C-T-R was the product of a merger of several small outfits into one, but, uniquely, C-T-R's several component companies had never competed against each other. Each sold different products in different markets. The former Computing Scale of America, which itself had been organized from four small companies in 1901, sold scales and meat slicers to food merchants. International Time Recording specialized in clocks for factories, telephone companies, and railroads. Tabulating Machine Company, the forebear of IBM, made accounting machines for statistical work and bookkeeping.

The resourceful Flint's rationale for creating C-T-R was to build a company that would pay dividends during both good times and bad. C-T-R's diversity would be its strength, Flint reckoned, for it was structured to weather all but the worst of economic storms. If one division fared poorly—due, say, to a downturn in its market sector—chances were that the other C-T-R markets would be healthier and compensate. Although diversification as a way to insulate against business cycles is common practice these days, Flint was one of the first to create a company with that in mind.

IT'S IN THE CARDS

The most promising of C-T-R's products, Watson soon realized, was the tabulating machine. It had been invented for the U.S. Census Bureau, which in the 1880's had found itself fighting to stay afloat in the rising tide of demographic statistics pouring into its Washington, D.C., offices from across the burgeoning nation. But not only was the U.S. population increasing with the successive waves of immigrants; Bureau statisticians were busily concocting new categories of information to collect. The proud nation wanted to quantify scientifically its economic activities, its languages, the money its people earned, and the ways they lived.

To extract meaningful statistics from the mass of raw data that the Bureau collected every ten years required hundreds of workers to spend years laboriously processing stacks of paper forms. It wasn't long after the 1880 count was over that the Bureau realized that it would be time to begin the 1900 census well before the 1890 census results could be tabulated. Surely there ought to be a mechanical way to speed up the tabulation process, census takers thought. There was one indeed, and it came from the fertile mind of one Herman Hollerith, a brilliant engineer. Hollerith came up with an electromechanical tabulating machine that required information to be recorded as punched holes in stiff paper cards.

Inspired by the player piano and the Jacquard loom from France, both of which were controlled by similar forms of "software," Hollerith's tabulating machines could deal with virtually every sort of data. Holes punched in specific locations on the cards represented different numbers or categories of information. In the census, for example, a hole punched in one place might indicate the male sex while a certain group of holes in another place might indicate age. By carefully sorting the cards according to the patterns of holes in selected locations, it was possible to draw a detailed statistical picture of the American people.

With the statistical piano, as Hollerith's first tabulator was called, cards were processed one by one. An operator inserted each card into a frame and pulled down a waffle-iron-like device that pressed an array of needles against the card's surface. Wherever a hole was present, a needle passed through it and entered a small cup of mercury underneath, completing an electrical circuit. Depending on how it was arranged, the circuit triggered one or another of several clocklike counters.

Hollerith made a good dollar for himself by successfully automating the U.S. census, and before long he was renting his equipment (he never sold it) and services to czarist Russia and other nations. He was more an engineer than a marketeer, however, and before long his Tabulating Machine Company began losing market share to more aggressive competitors. Among them was the U.S. government itself, which wanted to avoid becoming dependent on the Hollerith monopoly; it built its own machines using by-then expired patents of Hollerith's. It awarded the 1910 census tabulation contract to the Powers Accounting Company, which then took the lead from Hollerith. Short of cash, Hollerith finally sold the Tabulating Machine Company to Flint; it became part of C-T-R.

Soon after, in May 1914, Watson came aboard C-T-R as general manager with orders to make the flagging business a success. It would be another decade,

however, before he was able to fully take control. His brand of pushy salesmanship at first didn't sit well with Hollerith, who had retired as manager but stayed
on with the company as technical consultant, but the two eventually managed a
peace of sorts.

Watson also had to contend with a board of directors who distrusted him for
his antitrust conviction. In fact, Watson had evaded punishment in that case on
a technicality. NCR's dramatically generous relief efforts during a 1913 flood in
its hometown of Dayton helped cast Patterson and his fellow monopolists in a
positive light. By the time an appeals court ruled that the original trial had been
procedurally flawed and would have to be held again, the antitrust agencies simply gave up and dropped the NCR-related charges. As Watson would later see
confirmed in his own career, the capriciousness with which the federal antitrust
laws are enforced tends in the long run to work to an accused's advantage. Since
the laws were worded ambiguously to begin with, it would only be a matter of
time before the political philosophy of those who were charged with enforcing
the laws would change, and the initial charges might be dropped altogether.

Watson did his best to revitalize C-T-R's various operations, concentrating
particularly on their sales and product development activities. If there was one
thing he knew how to do well, it was selling business machines and motivating
others to sell business machines. Taking a chapter out of NCR's book, he instituted generous commissions, exclusive territories, and quota clubs for his salesmen. In return, he demanded strict loyalty to C-T-R and made no bones about
what a good company man ought and ought not to do. His efforts evidently paid
off, because C-T-R's revenues doubled from $4.2 million in 1914 to $8.3 million
in 1917. Earnings grew even faster, tripling to $1.6 million. Thereupon the Hol-
lerith machines found widespread use during World War I: the arms industry,
the draft boards, and the busy railroads each used the machines to manage their
expanded operations. The war effort also caused the entire federal bureaucracy
to grow substantially and permanently, which further stimulated demand for
tabulating equipment. Once a faltering member of the C-T-R triumvirate, the
Tabulating Machine Company was turned around and gradually gained market
share.

By the end of the war, C-T-R had installed more than 650 tabulating machines, and it was selling blank punch cards at a rate of more than 80 million a
month. Just as IBM would later do until pressed to change, C-T-R never sold
tabulating machinery but only rented it. Renting gave C-T-R continuing ownership of the machines and, in fulfillment of what Watson had learned on New
York's Fourteenth Street, prevented a secondhand market from ever threatening its business. Customers liked the rental arrangement for its simplicity and security: C-T-R was entirely responsible for servicing or replacing tabulators
when they broke down, and there was never any worry about what to do with an

old tabulator once it was replaced by a newer, more powerful one. C-T-R owned it, C-T-R worried about it. Blank cards were another matter—they were consumables that a customer was bound by contract to buy from C-T-R. The company earned great profits from the cards, which it used to finance the hardware rentals.

Although the state of their technology was primitive in comparison with that of today's computers, punch card tabulating machines underwent many technical improvements by C-T-R and its rivals. New types of machines were brought out—a printer-lister in 1919, for instance, that printed out the information contained on a stack of cards—and gradually each was equipped with an electric motor to speed its operation.

During the economic recession of the early 1920s, tabulating machines became important to commerce, for they helped cut costs and trim excessive inventories. The rental of accounting machines proved to be relatively recession-proof, a quality that was later passed on to their successor, the electronic computer. Orders didn't drop off during a recession the way orders for hard goods did. In one sense, what C-T-R offered was not a hard good as much as a service: the service of processing, on rented machinery, vital corporate data stored on punch cards that the customer owned. It was during this period of growth that Watson, having finally gained total control of the company, molded C-T-R to reflect the full scope of his ambitious, worldwide vision. He expanded overseas operations by licensing manufacturing rights to several foreign companies. He rid C-T-R of most of its nontabulating businesses and changed its name. The International Business Machines Corporation was born in February 1924.

ACCOUNTING MACHINES COME OF AGE

Before the punch card machine, bookkeeping had been performed manually. Wearing a green eyeshade and garters to hold up his sleeves, an accountant sat on a high stool to pore over and pencil his books each day. Perhaps he had a few assistants to trot out the business information he needed and an adding machine to help with simple arithmetic, but his methods were limited by how much data he could personally look at each day. As commercial enterprises grew with the general expansion of the U.S. economy, so did the need for accountants. Before long, paying for their labor became a significant cost in running large businesses. Like cash registers, typewriters, and adding machines before them, tabulating machines of the kind IBM rented helped save the day for many firms by automating the tedious accounting chores and providing new forms of timely business information to managers.

Automating a set of accounting books, however, required machines that were flexible enough in the way they sorted and merged data to accommodate the extremely wide range of manual methods found from one company to another. Each company structured its bookkeeping differently from the next, depending on the business it was in, on the laws and regulations that applied to that business, and on the types of information it needed. In fact, the peculiarities of each customer's books make full-fledged accounting systems one of the most difficult tasks to automate even today. IBM's strength has always been—and continues to be—based largely on its understanding of how to automate just such critical tasks. IBM learned under Watson's guidance the patterns in which customers collected and processed data, and it developed ways to help them improve the overall efficiency of their businesses. In other words, IBM didn't merely drop off a few card punches, sorters, and printers to a customer and let him figure out how to use them effectively. Rather, it became intimately involved in the customer's business—a virtual partner in that business.

Although a customer's entire accounting operation was generally quite complex, very often there would be certain limited parts of it that lent themselves easily to automation. These were the areas in which a simple arithmetical task would be performed repeatedly on long lists of information—calculating electric bills for thousands of customers each month, say. As a result, it was public utilities, insurance companies, and railroads that became the earliest commercial users of punch card machines, for they dealt with vast quantities of records that required periodic updating and tedious sorting.

The first thirty years or so of IBM's growth, between the world wars, were crucial to the company's future success in electronic computers, for it was then that IBM established the basic commercial monopoly in the market for machines that process commercial data on a large scale that it still holds. Its punch card tabulating machines during that period became the standard tool that businesses and government agencies around the world used to process large quantities of data and, later, to perform large-scale scientific calculations. Not only did IBM install far more equipment and sell more blank punch cards than any other supplier, but it also learned more about the organization of accounting and data processing in large enterprises, the types of data customers wanted to record, and the ways in which they wanted to process them.

Although the cash register had provided much useful business data and had helped prevent pilferage, by no means had it solved all the businessman's accounting problems. In fact, it probably fueled the need for an even more powerful machine with which to process the data that it so successfully collected from shop floors. Once the cash was totaled, for instance, questions arose as to which items were selling best, how depleted the warehouse inventories were, and how much business each sales clerk handled. Moreover, as tax laws multiplied, information was needed on the state of unpaid bills, the sales of taxable items, and so forth. None of these questions was directly answerable by the cash register it-self, but that machine showed the way: there was a wealth of data in every com-mercial organization that was just waiting to be collected and profitably analyzed. Watson had just the machines for the job.

The punch card, or unit record, machine's advantage for the businessman was that it could economically aggregate and cross-tabulate huge amounts of nu-merical data in a way that was faster and more precise than was possible by hand. Once data were recorded on punch cards, it became simple to extract heretofore unseen information from them.

A typical commercial application might call for measuring the amount the business brought in each month by a group of salesmen working for the furni-ture manufacturer. Each time one of them made a sale, a new card would be punched with data showing the ID number of the chair or bed being purchased, its price, the customer's name and address, the date, and the salesman's ID num-ber. At the end of the month, the cards would be quickly and accurately sorted on a special machine according to any of these fields of information. Once sorted, each stack of cards would be processed using an accounting machine, which read the cards and tallied information on them to provide the different departments of the furniture maker with useful data. The sales manager could determine his own and individual salesmen's commissions, determine which salesman was performing best and was therefore entitled to a bonus, and deter-mine which type of product sold best. The warehouse could be provided with a list of items to restock, and the accounting department could get a total sales fig-ure so as to track cash reserves and tax liabilities. Once information was re-corded on the cards, a customer generally found many ways to sort and merge the cards to his benefit. The more profitably the cards could be used, the more quickly a customer's data processing investment would pay for itself.

IBM offered three basic types of accounting machines—card punches, sorters, and tabulators. The first recorded information; the second separated a deck of cards into new stacks that shared some specified attribute; and the third per-formed arithmetical calculations using data found on individual cards. All three types of machine evolved mechanically over the years; the most significant change was their motorization. The accounting machine, or tabulator, was the most complex device and underwent the greatest improvement, for it was typi-cally the heart of a customer's data processing operation. What had started out in Hollerith's day as a manually driven machine, able merely to count cards with holes punched in specified locations, had evolved into a sophisticated elec-tromechanical calculator capable of processing dozens of cards a minute and performing fairly complex arithmetic.

As IBM and its customers discovered the seemingly infinite variety of ways that data could be processed, IBM's product line expanded. Customers eagerly paid for each refinement for, as the equipment matured, once-manual functions became built into the machine. For instance, early tabulators could only add numbers. Subtraction called for the machine operator to calculate a special number in his head and add it to a subtotal; the result had been the same as if a direct subtraction had been performed. Later IBM tabulators performed subtraction automatically, thereby eliminating the operator's labor and skills. Still later, the machines performed multiplication and division automatically. Other improvements boosted the precision of the arithmetic: early IBM machines handled only eight significant digits; subsequent models could handle ten. Another improvement came when alphabetic letters as well as numerals could be read by the machines and acted upon: that enabled the printing of addresses as well as balances due, for instance. IBM also added printers and mechanical gang punches to its product line, each one making it possible for the overall assortment of machines to do more and better work for customers.

By the 1930s, many of the functions performed by IBM accounting machines were controlled by the wiring of a special control panel, the so-called plugboard, which resembled somewhat the panel used by old-time telephone operators. Changing the pattern of wires on this board altered the electrical and therefore the logical workings of the machines and determined, for instance, which numbers on a card were to be added together and into which columns the sum should be punched. Together with a series of switches on the accounting machine, the plug-boards formed the "software," such as it was, for these early IBM machines, though they hardly matched today's computer software in flexibility or detailed specification. Nevertheless, the plug-board caught on with customers, especially when it was made removable: then users could build collections of prewired boards with which to quickly reconfigure their accounting machines for different data processing tasks. Removable plug-boards also ensured that data could be processed exactly the same way time after time.

A KNACK FOR PRICING

The growing sophistication of unit record machines appealed to IBM customers' imaginations and drove them to employ the machines in an ever-widening circle of applications. IBM couldn't have been more pleased, of course, for each new application meant increased demand for more and faster machines, more sales of blank cards, and additional monthly charges to collect for the new functions it continually added to its equipment. The company priced its machine rentals in a way that illustrates in simple terms the company's growing power. It is what is known within IBM as *functional pricing*—setting a price according to the increase in function or performance as seen by the customer, not according to the actual cost of delivering that function.

One of the most popular of IBM's machines was a printer that listed the data stored on a stack of punch cards. The customer could choose from two models of this printer—let's call them A and B—that had different printing speeds and different monthly rental charges. Model B ran twice as fast as model A but, as an incentive for users to move up to the faster device, IBM priced B at a little less than twice the price of A. IBM informed its customers that their IBM serviceman could easily make the upgrade from A to B on the customer's premises—no complete change of machinery would be required.

So far, all seemed fair and square. The customer got what he paid for—twice the performance for not quite twice the price. However, IBM *never* let on to the customer that to double the printer's speed required only that a single rubber belt inside the machine be moved from one set of pulleys to another. Because IBM always rented its machines to its customers, it retained full ownership and could easily prevent others from tinkering with their mechanisms. When a field upgrade of this sort was ordered, the IBM serviceman hustled his customer out of the room and simply switched pulleys. The cost to IBM was trivial—no new parts and very little labor was required—but the customer saw his monthly printer bill almost double from then on. Naturally, profits from the faster machine—which was used mainly by customers with the greatest investment in punch cards—were substantially higher than those from the slower one, which was used primarily by new customers.[1]

The price of each IBM product, therefore, was set according to its performance relative to other IBM gear. It bore little relationship to the actual cost of providing that performance, as it might have in a competitive market where customers had a choice of suppliers. Functional pricing is certainly the clearest indication of IBM's power in the early data processing market. If it had faced effective competition, such pricing would have been impossible to maintain. At the very least, a group of consultants would have sprung up to sell their knowledge of how IBM machinery could be improved functionally, and customers would have done the necessary pulley-switching themselves. Customers' complete dependence on IBM, however, allowed IBM to price all its equipment functionally. Such pricing is only possible, in fact, when a supplier has no effective competition.

IBM gained market power largely from the nature of the investment its customers made in their individual data processing operations—their investment effectively limited their choices to IBM. It all began with the punch card itself. The millions of cards that a large customer typically acquired during a single year stored vital corporate data, all punched at a not-insignificant labor cost. As the customer expanded its data processing operations, its investment in cards and carefully specified procedures for processing them (including but not limited to the careful wiring of plug-boards) grew to the point where it was heavily dependent on IBM machinery to keep its daily business running smoothly. Suddenly IBM became an indispensable business partner, not merely a supplier of office equipment. Once a certain threshold had been crossed, a customer found it prohibitively expensive to switch to another tabulating machine supplier, for that would mean repunching masses of cards, retraining staff, and reworking operating procedures. Locked in to IBM this way, users were easily milked by the company.

IBM, by virtue of its market power, also made it impossible for a customer to buy punch cards from other suppliers, and it successfully discouraged the few competitors it did face from building machines that could process what would become its unique punch cards. IBM cards, for instance, developed rectangular holes arranged in a pattern of eighty columns. Remington Rand, which had acquired the Powers Company and shuffled along in IBM's shadow as its most viable competitor with only about 10 percent of the market, offered ninety-column cards with a continuation of the earlier round holes. Even if someone had come out with a machine that automatically translated from one card to the other, there would still have been major discrepancies in the way data were portrayed on the cards and in the way it was interpreted by the two vendors' machines. Quite simply, and by conscious design, IBM kept its accounting equipment and their cards strictly incompatible with Remington's and other vendors' machines.

This incompatibility provided protection for IBM, and to a lesser extent for Remington, too, which had agreed to a peace treaty of sorts with IBM and didn't seek to capture any IBM customers anyway. Once a customer had punched and processed a certain volume of cards each month, there was no turning back. The customer was locked in to IBM equipment and to IBM itself. This card lock-in worked to IBM's advantage in several ways, particularly, as later chapters will show, when the electronic computer emerged as a replacement for traditional punch card machines. The lock-in was subtle and seemingly unavoidable, and although customers were limited in their choice of supplier to IBM alone, most of them trusted IBM fully—after all, those men in the blue suits supplied equipment that made the customers unquestionably more effective than they would have been without it.

BRUSHES WITH THE LAW

As IBM prospered during the 1920s and into the Great Depression, so did Watson. His original deal with Flint had given him a salary and a share of company profits as high as 5 percent. In 1934, in the depths of the Depression, Watson claimed to be greatly embarrassed when he was declared the highest-paid executive in the nation—his take that year was $364,432. Not surprisingly, he spoke widely to the public and his own staff about rewards to be gained from pursuing the American Dream: hard work and dedication to business were all that mattered, he seemed to be saying. Little mention was made of the advantages of having a monopoly in bringing about such success.

And *monopoly* is the best word to describe IBM from then on.* Not only did disgruntled competitors, whose combined share of the tabulating machine market had dwindled to less than 10 percent by the early 1930s, call it that; so did the U.S. Justice Department. In 1932, just weeks after Watson saw his man Franklin D. Roosevelt swept into the White House, IBM was hit with a federal antitrust suit that charged it with abusing a dominant market position and engaging in anticompetitive tactics to maintain that position.

Watson, having faced similar charges before, was profoundly upset. To his mind, IBM's success had resulted entirely from his own superior management and from the hard work of his underlings in delivering superior products. He felt that the riches he and others at IBM now enjoyed were well justified. Moreover, to accuse IBM was to accuse Watson himself. He had worked his way up from the farm to enjoy the adulation of heads of state around the world, businessmen, journalists, and his own workers as one of the most enlightened businessmen of all time. Since so much of Watson's public esteem derived from his commercial success, the antitrust case seemed to throw the very legitimacy of that success into question. Watson is said to have always needed to feel that he was acting correctly and in a manner appropriate to the circumstances. His self-image did not allow him to see himself as a lawbreaker. He was unwilling to grant the government its position or voluntarily change IBM's business practices. He charged his lawyers with defending the company vigorously. They did, but to no avail, for IBM was convicted of being an illegal monopolist. Strenuous appeals failed in every court up to and including the U.S. Supreme Court.

The government's case centered on, among other things, a conspiracy that IBM had entered into with its chief competitor, Remington Rand, and on an IBM requirement that its tabulator customers buy all their blank punch cards from IBM. Under this scheme, Remington and IBM had managed to capture all but a few percentage points of the tabulating market—IBM had about 85 percent of the total—and privately they had agreed a few years before never to sell blank cards to each other's customers. By staying out of each other's hair this way, they found it easier to charge high prices for their respective cards. Except

---

* There may be some confusion over the use of the term *monopoly* to describe IBM. The derivation of the word—from **monos,** meaning "single" or "alone," and **polein,** meaning to sell—implies that for IBM to be a monopolist it must be the only seller. Since this is clearly not the case, some may object to calling it a monopolist. The precise definition of monopoly, however, requires that the firm meet two conditions. First, the firm must have the ability to control the prices within at least some of its markets, and second, it can, should it wish, drive away its competition. Since IBM, as this book attempts to show, passes both these tests, it can correctly be called a monopolist.

for the U.S. government, which was a large enough IBM customer to do as it pleased and made its own cards, customers had no alternative suppliers of cards, and they paid whatever their machine supplier wished to charge. Quietly, without all the potentially provocative noise caused by NCR's strong-arm methods, competition had been neutralized, and IBM could charge high prices with impunity.

Watson's lawyers defended the restriction on card suppliers as necessary to keep badly made cards out of the machines it owned and serviced. An improperly manufactured card could damage the machines and raise IBM's cost of maintaining them, the company argued. No, said the courts; customers, too, had a strong incentive to use only appropriate cards, and they would soon limit their purchases to reliable suppliers. IBM's actions and those of Remington Rand were plainly anticompetitive and impeded the proper functioning of the marketplace, the court ruled.

The restrictive card clause in IBM's contracts was deemed as supporting the illegal practice of a tie-in sale—a tactic IBM still employs to this day. A tie-in occurs when two separate products are offered only as a package with a single price. A customer who wishes to buy one of the products is forced to acquire the second whether he wants to or not.* If a company has substantial power in the market for one of the products, the tie-in sale can be strategically effective against less-powerful, more narrowly focused competitors in the other market. The major unfairness of the effective tie-in sale is its effect on specialized suppliers. They have to either overcome the obstacles of entering both markets or withdraw altogether from their original line of business. Entering the blank card business would not have been particularly difficult for, say, a well-equipped paper manufacturer, and many such firms would surely have done so just to take advantage of IBM's high prices there. But IBM's contract tied card pur-

---

* Distinguishing between an illegal tie-in sale—one that restrains trade and enhances a monopoly position—and the legal pricing of several products as a group is not always simple. For example, most people would not accept restrictions on where they could buy gasoline for their car, but car manufacturers might, absent the antitrust laws, agree among themselves to void warranties on any car that used gas from other than their own gasoline subsidiaries. Customers' choices would be limited and the car maker's gasoline would be priced inordinately high. Similarly, an electrical utility might write into its contracts a clause that prevented customers from plugging in any but utility-supplied appliances. The justification might be, as at IBM in the 1930s, that "foreign," improperly made appliances might damage the utility's network of wires and create trouble for other customers. This seems obviously unacceptable, and yet that was exactly the argument used for many decades by AT&T in limiting customers to using only Bell System telephone equipment in their homes and businesses. At the other extreme, most people would agree that a supplier without monopoly power should be able to aggregate pieces into a single product without separate pricing for each piece. Not every transistor in a television receiver, for example, need have its own price. Nor do laces have to be priced separately from the shoes with which they are packaged. When products are acquired in fixed proportions and are available from many effective competitors, a joint price is common and poses no antitrust concern.

chases to rental of its machinery and effectively locked out other card competitors. The only chance paper companies had to compete successfully under these conditions was to enter the tabulating machinery business themselves, but that was clearly out of the question. So IBM's deal with Remington along with the tie-in clause in its contracts helped IBM maintain a monopoly over both cards and machinery.

In its final ruling, the Supreme Court concluded that IBM had excessive market power and should be required to permit customers to buy their cards from the supplier of their choice. The court reported that by the end of 1935, IBM had installed 85.7 percent of the nation's tabulating-accounting machines, 86.1 percent of the sorting machines, and 81.6 percent of the key punches. It also sold about 3 billion blank cards each year. By tying-in its cards to this bulk of installed machines, IBM made it impossible for independent card manufacturers to compete.

Less than twenty years later, in 1952, the government was back at IBM's door with new charges of monopoly. Despite the changes IBM had agreed to make in 1936, there had been little actual change in the structure of the data processing business; Watson's company was still overwhelmingly dominant. IBM still would only rent its machines, and it still supplied most of the cards used in those machines—although with the legal tie broken, its card prices were now lower. But despite the lower prices, IBM's high-volume production and its control over certain technologies for making cards had enabled it to maintain its dominance there.

The 1952 suit was just as disturbing to the aging Watson as the one filed in 1932 had been, if only because this time, too, he had just finished helping into office the very administration, Eisenhower's, that filed it. The 1952 case was eventually dropped when IBM signed an agreement, the so-called 1956 Consent Decree, that called for it to begin selling its machines, to make its card-manufacturing technology available to competitors, and to drop its share of the card market to less than 50 percent by 1963. (The Consent Decree was to play an important role in the evolution of the computer industry. It became a great concern to IBM's lawyers as they advised its executives in devising strategies to maintain its monopoly. In addition, IBM's more daring competitors would try to use the restrictions the decree placed on IBM to compete with it—often to their own peril. Appendix A describes the decree's more important features.) Following the decree, competitors did in fact enter the card business, but IBM by then was starting to shift its attention to more lucrative markets. IBM's agreement to sell as well as rent its machines also had little effect until some ten years later, when computer leasing companies began taking advantage of IBM's suddenly vulnerable pricing on electronic computers.

During its first forty years, IBM earned high profits from the sale of blank cards that were tied in to the rental of its machines. Those profits helped finance not only Watson's high salary but the expansion of IBM's rental base of machines and its legendary corporate profits, which were shared among many enthusiastic investors. As it had been from the early days when cash registers defined the state of the art, the business machine market was lucrative, especially if pursued from the singular security of an overwhelming market share.

The antitrust episodes suggest that neither Watson nor IBM was incapable of changing its ways. The exuberant days of violently bashing NCR's competitors were long over, replaced by Watson's strict codes of conduct for all his employees and a squeaky-clean facade of we-can-do-no-wrong.

Yet Watson, it seems, could not accept the fact that what was good for IBM might not be good for society as a whole. Antitrust laws had been written to protect the larger public interest, to ensure that markets remained competitive and therefore beneficial to customers, and that companies with inordinate power did not abuse that power to eliminate lesser competitors or leverage their way into nearby competitive markets. After the antitrust laws were passed, it would no longer be sufficient that a monopolist's actions led to its commercial gain. Now these actions could be scrutinized in a court of law as to their fairness and their stifling effect on free competition.

Watson, and later his son as chief of IBM, had learned well Patterson's most important lesson: Always maintain the monopoly. Bend when possible and avoid strong-arming the competition too much, but don't under any circumstance lose dominance. When push comes to shove, when competition threatens to weaken the dominance, then you can break the antitrust laws and protect your market share. And when caught in such a violation, use your money to exploit all the complex ambiguity of the antitrust laws.

NCR had monopolized the cash register business for decades and had enjoyed the prerogatives and profits that came from that position. The embarrassments its executives suffered paled compared to the profits they enjoyed, and in the end they "beat the rap." A monopoly provides cash not only to crush competition but also to exploit the legal process, as Patterson well knew. IBM's revival of this strategy is summed up by an indiscreet admission of its longtime legal defender, the distinguished lawyer and ex-jurist Bruce Bromley. He explained his basic defense strategy against antitrust accusations thus: "Now I was born, I think, to be a protractor. . . . I quickly realized in my early days at the bar that I could take the simplest antitrust case . . . and protract it for the defense almost to infinity."[2]

Which is more than enough time to do the job. In the most recent antitrust case (filed in 1969), after thirteen years of prosecution by the Justice Department, a period spanning both Republican and Democratic administrations, IBM finally succeeded in wearing down the prosecution. Just before the judge was to make a ruling, Ronald Reagan's antitrust chief, William Baxter, dropped the case claiming it was "without merit." Interestingly, IBM's success in that case was masterfully choreographed by one Thomas Barr, a superb trial lawyer whose mentor at Cravaith, Swaine, Moore had been none other than Bruce Bromley himself.[3]

3. Enter the Computer

Never imply that you would be willing to sacrifice profit for market share.

—IBM's lawyers' advice to its
executives[1]

The 1950s opened with a bang for IBM. The first shot of the computer revolution was fired across its bow in 1951, when, with great fanfare, Remington Rand installed UNIVAC, the first electronic computer system to be offered as a commercial product. As IBM management was surely more aware than anyone, the digital computer posed the first serious threat that the IBM data processing monopoly had ever faced. Not only was the computer more powerful and more flexible than even IBM's latest punch card machinery, its technology was available to a potentially long list of competitors. Indeed, the following ten years saw over a dozen companies bring computers to market against IBM.

Rooted as heavily in the electromechanical age as it was and yet unable to ship a computer of its own for another two years, IBM might seem to have been in a fix. As this chapter will show, though, its monopoly provided advantages that enabled it to finish the decade unscathed and move aggressively to capture three-quarters or so of the market for the computers used by its most important customers, large business organizations. Despite the tumultuous shift from punch cards to computers, IBM's lock on commercial data processing remained secure in 1960 and beyond.

Like most American manufacturers, IBM had devoted its production capacity to the war effort in the years following the attack on Pearl Harbor. IBM factories had produced rifles and other armaments, while its accounting machines had helped manage the draft, coordinate arms manufacturing, and conserve natural and industrial resources. V-J day saw the company's share of the world's data processing business as solid as ever, and IBM soon reveled in the postwar boom. Reaching out to new geographic markets as well as to the expanding consumer economy at home, U.S. industry found IBM's machines indispensable for coherent management. IBM had the right goods at the right time.

The company, however, had been alerted during the war to the invention of the digital electronic computer. Developed independently in the United States, Britain, and Germany as a lightning-quick calculator, the computer had proven to be an enormously successful tool for grinding through tedious ballistics formulae, solving previously daunting atomic bomb equations, and quietly breaking Nazi codes. Although important technical developments before the war had paved the way for what we now know as the digital computer, it was only during wartime that that powerful machine was brought to fruition. Soon after, it became clear that the computer would eventually be useful not only as a simple arithmetic calculator but also as a general-purpose processor of all symbolic information. In other words, the computer would be able to help businessmen as well as scientists. It would easily process all those billions of punch cards IBM's customers were then cranking through accounting machines.

IBM was by no means surprised by the computer, for it had partially funded and worked on the pioneering Mark I computer project at Harvard, and it had developed close ties with those few government agencies that needed as big a calculator as they could find. IBM's accounting machines, in fact, had been specially modified in Los Alamos for precision arithmetic and were used extensively on the Manhattan Project there. It may be surmised that top IBM executives grew increasingly edgy that the fast-developing technology of electronic computing might sweep its lucrative empire of mechanical punch card machines into the junk heap. That fear increased when Remington Rand bought two small but brainy outfits, Eckert-Mauchly Computer Corporation and Electronic Research Associates, and backed their efforts to bring a computer, the UNIVAC, to market. IBM suddenly found it necessary to build its own computers, which meant a shift to manufacturing electronic as well as mechanical gear and to devising other, perhaps nontechnological means of holding competitors' computers at bay and removing their threat to its central data processing business.

The computer took its dazzling power from electronics, the technology of circuits made from vacuum tubes (or valves, as the British more accurately call them), which had been improved greatly during the war. The vacuum tube's ability to switch an electrical current on and off rapidly had been enhanced for combat radios and radar systems. Because the basic element of the digital computer was the flip-flop—a circuit that alternated between two basic electronic states that could represent the binary digits one and zero—the vacuum tube lent itself well to building computer logic circuits.

The electronic digital computer performed all the functions of IBM's standard punch card equipment—adding, sorting, and tabulating, among others—but at greater speed and with more accuracy. Most astonishing was the computer's versatility, which derived mainly from its ability to store programs, the basic logical instructions that controlled its behavior, in the same manner as it stored data: as

electrical signals that a computer program itself could move, modify, and duplicate. This stored-program feature endowed the computer with capabilities that
IBM's machines, controlled by static plug-boards and manual switches, could
never match. Because it could be reprogrammed so easily and in ways that were
simply not possible on accounting machines, the computer outperformed its
predecessor hands down. There was no question of IBM ignoring the computer.
The threat was real and growing from the moment UNIVAC performed its first
silent calculation.

WHAT MATTERS

Much has been written about the early days of the computer industry, but too
much of it has been merely anecdotal. There is a valid place for such literature,
but by concentrating on relatively minor incidents such as the date of certain
inventions, when products were first unveiled, and so forth, most of these discussions miss the forest for the trees. They take little notice of the economic structure of the data processing industry or of the relative sizes and strengths of the
companies active in the market then. There were indeed intense rivalries between different inventors and their companies, fateful technological choices that
doomed overconfident manufacturers to oblivion, and even brilliant entrepre-
neurs who won and lost fortunes. But the economic environment in which the
technological ferment took place was far more important historically than those
incidents themselves.

In fact, it was the structural factors that enabled IBM to enter the fast-paced
computer race with what would seem to be a serious handicap—a two-year period during which Remington had the computer market to itself—and yet still
manage to gain the supremely dominant market position that it has built on ever
since. The technological, organizational, and financial issues facing computer
makers during the formative postwar period must be understood in light of the
preexisting data processing industry's structure, not simply as a series of events
treated in isolation. The key decisions made by early computer manufacturers
were constrained by their individual strengths and weaknesses—their finances,
their research capabilities, and, more important than is generally recognized,
their previous involvement in data processing. One individual's decision to use a
certain technology one day bears far less on the industry's subsequent development than do the relative positions of IBM and its rivals at the outset. Indeed, it
will be argued here that because of its complete dominance in punch card
equipment, crucial prerogatives fell to IBM that all but guaranteed it success in
the commercial computer market, even as the pace of computer technology's advancement accelerated in the late 1950s.

For its part, IBM is not overly concerned that anecdotal evidence treated in isolation might lead to inaccurate conclusions about the industry's early history. Not wholly disinterested in historical interpretation, the company publicly articulated its views through the testimony of three top-class economists that it hired to defend itself during the long government antitrust trial that ended in 1982. Drs. Franklin M. Fisher, James W. McKie, and Richard B. Mancke all claimed to have examined the 100,000-plus pages of testimony accumulated during the thirteen-year trial; they concluded that "the knowledge and resources necessary to build primitive computer systems were widely held and therefore many firms were well positioned to develop and supply computer systems."[2]

Since no one company had a lock on computer knowhow, the IBM economists claim, many companies were "well positioned" to compete in the fierce computer race that began in 1950 or so. No company, not even IBM, had a head start over the others, they suggest. In fact, they write, IBM's success was due primarily to the "extent and depth of its commitment to the EDP [electronic data processing] business," a commitment that was "unique in the 1950s."[3]

In IBM's version of history, carefully worded to inform future historians as well as a trial judge, the many competitors that challenged IBM lost simply because they didn't try hard enough; they didn't show the willingness to spend cash and commit their resources as fully as IBM did. It was sufficient in those early years, IBM would have it, for a manufacturer merely to be able to build a primitive computer to be "well positioned" enough to compete in IBM's main territory, the data processing arena.

A casual observer might take IBM's word that it was on an equal footing with other manufacturers in the early 1950s if not for a surprisingly candid assessment of the situation that was made by an IBM official who must have known better than anyone else. That official was Watson's son, Thomas, Jr., who was given the IBM helm in 1956. In 1973 a reporter asked him, "What helped you take the lead [in computers]?" His reply:

"Traditionally, we had a big share of the punch card accounting machine market. So we had a large field force of salesmen, repairmen and servicemen. They were perhaps the only people in America who understood how to put in an automated bookkeeping system.

"The invention [of the computer] was important. But the knowledge of how to put a great big system on line, how to make it run, and solve problems was probably four times as important.

"We also had a cash flow that others didn't have to support a very expanded research and development program."[4]

So contrary to what the expert witnesses might insist later, the market advantages IBM alone possessed were "four times as important" as any "knowledge and resources necessary to build primitive computer systems." IBM had been able to dominate the nascent computer business because it had a monopoly over the punch card equipment market that gave it a large, trained field force and buckets of cash with which to "commit" itself to the emerging market.

IBM's size, profitability, and well-orchestrated public image have made the performance of its management the stuff of legend. Watson, Sr., and his well-groomed courtiers built a reputation during the 1930s, 1940s, and 1950s for establishing a new breed of executive who, with faith in catchwords like "Think" and some good old American salesmanship, demonstrated seemingly infallible wisdom in securing IBM's leading position amid a swirl of growth and technological change. Is this in fact the explanation of IBM's success? Was it their "excellence" in managing resources that enabled IBM managers to grab the lion's share of the rapidly expanding computer business?

IBM in the 1950s faced a simple choice between committing itself to the new computer technology on the one hand and watching its data processing monopoly erode away into insignificance on the other. The electronic computer, dealing as it did with generalized symbols and not just numbers and letters, offered a conceptual leap in capability and therefore could be sold to a potentially far greater market. Thus, the sooner the decision was made to enter the computer market, the more useful would be the punch card monopoly.

Both before and after the computer had proven itself viable as a product, IBM plotted its strategy from a singularly secure position. Given merely a reasonable level of competence, comparable to what other companies had at their disposal, IBM could not, in fact, have lost its hold on commercial data processing. Today its decision to enter the computer market seems only prudent and somewhat trivial, even if its timing and technological choices were the result of particularly insightful individuals.

But IBM's aim was not so much to enter the computer business as a profitable venture as it was to prevent the new technology from escaping its control and challenging its monopoly. Eventually it would have to move its monopoly from one technology, mechanical unit record machines, to another, electronic computers—and do so without losing market share. It is in relation to that goal that IBM should be judged.

IBM ensured its success during this process by using the basic strategy Watson had learned from Patterson at NCR and later refined on his own. It priced products selectively so that profits were maximized in secure market sectors and were virtually ignored in more competitive arenas. Sitting on huge reserves of cash earned from its extraordinarily profitable punch card machinery (IBM was about as secure as it could be, by then controlling upward of 90 percent of that market), the company effectively bought its way to the top of the emerging computer market through means that were wholly unavailable to any of its new competitors there.

This discriminatory pricing between secure and contested market sectors has been central to IBM's success in computers right from the beginning. If there is any brilliance among IBM's managers, it is in their successful but hidden adaptation of price discrimination to a market that has changed radically over time. IBM has repeatedly bested—and often broken—competitors that offered plainly better products at prices lower than its own. As it did so, it has lost little market share or profit and has continued to grow at rates that are the envy of industry worldwide. The following analysis will show that IBM's true craft is its ability to segment its product line and selectively set prices at levels precisely calculated to maintain control over the value customers perceive in their computer systems. To his credit, Watson, Sr.'s, followers have refined this strategy, embellishing it with ever-greater levels of complexity as the market for computer-based products expands. In the verbiage that exalts the computer's unquestionably unique and astounding record of technological progress (a record of change that itself makes the lasting success of IBM's strategy that much more remarkable), this most basic economic explanation of IBM's success has until now been either purposely hidden or simply overlooked.

MOVING THE MONOPOLY

In 1935, during the first government antitrust case, it was revealed that IBM had more than 4,100 card sorters, 8,400 card punches, and 4,300 calculators rented out to customers. Twenty-four years later, IBM's figures show, it had 61,000 sorters, 120,000 punches, and 143,500 calculators on rent. All together, in 1959, by which time the computer had established itself, IBM was collecting rent on 306,692 punch card machines of one sort or another. Its market share was almost 95 percent—up considerably from the 80 percent level measured during the Depression. If a corporation or government agency needed to process volumes of data during the 1950s, the customer generally went to IBM.

As these numbers attest, early computers did not replace IBM accounting machines but instead actually added greatly to their growth. The computer was at first just one more machine, albeit an extremely fast and versatile one, that used punch cards. Customers had to order even more traditional punch card equipment than they had had before. Additional punches, sorters, and printers, among other types of machine, were necessary to keep the speedy computer busy. It was practically impossible to install a computer during the 1950s without acquiring at least a card punch to prepare data and programs. If there was one IBM machine that the electronic computer replaced, it was the tabulator or accounting machine. Demand for the other machines actually rose with the advent of the card-hungry computer. But in the end, IBM was always the main source for card machines.

So as IBM and others began installing computers, only IBM enjoyed renewed demand for its bread-and-butter machines, which, thanks to the company's monopoly, earned extraordinarily high profits (Table 1).

Continued high profits, however, were not the only advantage IBM reaped from its strength in punch card machinery. It was also able, by virtue of its dominance, to dampen competitors' success by controlling their access to the card-reading machinery that was so vital to the efficient operation of their computers. IBM's patents and high manufacturing volumes had for many years made it the only economical source of card-handling machinery in the world.

So it happened that many of IBM's computer competitors humbly had to ask IBM for the punch card mechanisms they needed to complete their systems. Not surprisingly, IBM refused to cooperate. It was only the raw innards of the IBM punch card machines that the others needed, not the IBM gray box, not the IBM power supply, and, most of all, not the expensive IBM rental charge. But they had to take all those extras, for IBM deliberately provided its gear only in the form of complete machines, installed, serviced, and priced just the same way they were offered to its own data processing customers. With nowhere else to go, rival computer makers took what they could get. Because IBM still owned the

Table 1

Revenues, Profits, and Percent Profit From IBM's Unit Record Equipment, 1960–66 (in $ thousands)[5]

| | Unit Record Equipment | | |
YEAR	REVENUES	PROFITS	%
1960	636,363	249,611	39.2
1961	674,201	295,102	43.8
1962	660,562	273,488	41.4
1963	636,161	259,257	40.8
1964	631,271	267,648	42.4
1965	644,937	299,709	46.5
1966	640,660	296,578	46.3
Total	4,524,155	1,944,393	42.9

The increase in profit rate from 39.2 percent in 1960 to 46.3 percent in 1966 is not a mere 7.1 percent, as a subtraction of these two rates would seem to imply. To see this, consider $100 in revenues earned each year. This would produce $39.20 profit in 1960 and $46.30 profit in 1966. Thus, the overall rate of profit increased not 7.1 percent but rather 18 percent, or almost one-fifth, in these years.

rented card machines and it alone serviced them, its field people were free to foster strong ties with rivals' customers and help lure them to an IBM computer. Periodic service calls also enabled IBM to keep close tabs on the technical innovations of others' computer systems and on the new ways their customers were using them. More damaging to competitors, however, was that their costs now included the full rental price of IBM's card machines. Their profits were squeezed, particularly when they found themselves bidding IBM card machines against the very same machines proposed by IBM as part of its computer system.

Had the data processing market been more competitive and less under IBM's control, IBM would certainly have behaved differently. Had there been other manufacturers of viable card mechanisms, the company probably would have adhered to the standard electronics industry practice of offering stripped down mechanisms, not complete card machines, on the open market and with volume discounts. In a competitive market, IBM would most likely have offered all sorts of parts and subassemblies just as a means of maximizing manufacturing volumes and profits. But in withholding raw card mechanisms and offering no discounts on its complete card machines, the company calculated correctly that it could make marketing difficult for other computer makers and maximize its profits over the long run, even if it meant shipping a few less goods.

Pricing early computers for profitability was problematic for IBM's rivals for other reasons. Not only did they have to spend great amounts of money to design and manufacture their computers, but they had to successfully market them at a competitive price. Once an order was received, they had to install the machine, program it for the customer, and service it almost daily. But with a major part of their revenues flowing directly to IBM for card machinery, profits had to be made almost entirely on the one part of the system that wasn't under IBM's control, namely the computer system itself.

Given that situation, IBM made profits even harder for its competitors to generate by the way it priced its own first two computers: to lose money. Models 701 and 702, for scientific and commercial data processing respectively, were brought out in 1952 and 1953 with monthly rental prices that immediately lowered the going price for computers and set an upper price limit for those, like Remington, who were trying to crack the IBM monopoly with computers. The 701 was priced "arbitrarily at $15,000 [a month] per system (a known loss price—$30,000 was required)," recalled financial executive Hillary Faw several years later in a memo to top management. "We priced the 702 in error at $30,000 (some costs were not provided for)."[6]

Suddenly, after two years of having the computer market to itself, Remington faced a pair of IBM systems that were priced not to make a profit but actually to lose money for their manufacturer. Lacking IBM's deep pockets to subsidize comparable pricing of its own, Remington saw its share of the expanding market plunge irretrievably during the next few years as customers flocked to the IBM 701 and 702. In effect, IBM discriminated *against* its punch card machine customers, who paid its high prices because they were unable to take their business elsewhere, and *in favor* of its computer users, who were treated to low prices. Is there any wonder Remington's strength in computers immediately faded, leading many people (none of whom were likely to have been aware of IBM's no-profit pricing) to laugh condescendingly at Remington's having "snatched defeat from the jaws of victory" as a result of incompetent management and lack of "commitment"?[7]

IBM's early computer prices contradicted its own later antitrust guidelines,* which stated that "a seller may not sell its products at unreasonably low prices (e.g., below cost) for the purpose of destroying competition or eliminating a competitor."[8] From the very beginning of the computer industry, Watson's company was willing to engage in actions that only IBM with its unit record monopoly could afford and that arguably were illegal. These were young and exuberant days for the industry. Perhaps, in spite of its effect on competition, the below-cost pricing was not intended to "destroy competition." Perhaps it was just an accident. We shall see whether it happened again, when IBM was once more pressed by effective competition.

Like Remington, subsequent entrants in the computer race all lacked IBM's punch card technology and monopoly profits, and they paid IBM to dig their graves. IBM's profits from the card machines that its competitors' systems used helped subsidize the low prices of the very IBM computers they were competing against. It was a knockout move that Patterson would surely have applauded.

IBM went on to unveil several more computer systems during the 1950s (Table 2), including the scientific 704 and the commercial 705, in 1954; the 305, or RAMAC, which used a unique magnetic storage device, in 1956; and the sci-

---

* This book argues that IBM has acted unfairly against its competitors. But what is fair and unfair in the commercial arena? Determining such a standard has taxed the best efforts of judges, economists, politicians, and philosophers for years. Rather than wade deeply into these waters, I have taken an existing standard and confined the bulk of my efforts to applying it to the economic and technical complexity of the computer business. That standard is, of course, IBM's own *Business Conduct Policies: Responsibilities and Guide* (IBM-BCP), dated January 1, 1962. It is entirely reasonable to judge IBM's management and its actions by the same standards they required their own troops to uphold.

Though this IBM document is relied on throughout the book—the general sense of these instructions is well captured by Watson, Jr., himself in his statement. In considering a particular action Watson advised: "Turn the situation around. Suppose that you were a competitor—small, precariously financed, without a large support organization, and without a big reputation in the field—but with a good product. How would you feel if the big IBM Company took the action which you propose to take? Would you regard the IBM Company as taking an unfair advantage of you? Would you consider that the IBM Company was using a sales tactic that IBM possessed solely because of its size and reputation, and which, therefore, was unavailable to you?... We simply cannot shoulder people around or give the appearance of doing so."[9]

Table 2

Number of First-Generation Computer Systems Installed with
Customers by Type, 1955–59

		Computer System Type						
	701	702	704	705	709	305	Total	605
Date Announced	1952	1953	1954	1954	1957	1956		1953
Year								
1955	18	11	—	—	—	—	29	145
1956	14	13	28	31	—	1	87	437
1957	9	11	66	67	—	3	153	748
1958	6	8	85	95	3	155	352	955
1959	4	8	88	112	35	491	738	1134

entific 709, in 1959. By 1955, a total of twenty-nine model 701 and 702 systems had been installed, each one losing money but holding the market for IBM; the total number of IBM computers installed almost tripled to eighty-seven by 1957.

IBM also came out with the model 650, an electronic unit record accounting machine that used punch cards, in 1953. Its initial status as a true digital computer is open to debate, but its rapid installation rate shows that unit record accounting machines remained important for IBM even as computers grew in importance. In fact, by its own measure, in 1959 computers still accounted for only 5 percent of the total number of IBM machines then installed.

Computers may not have been initially profitable, but by the end of the decade they were generating more than their share of revenues for IBM. The typical computer system rented for much more than the typical unit record installation and therefore appealed only to IBM's very largest customers. In 1960, when computers still accounted for less than 10 percent of the company's installed machinery, they contributed fully 35 percent of its total revenues.[10] More important, by that time the growth in revenues from computers had far outpaced growth in unit record equipment: computers accounted for almost two-thirds of IBM's total revenues by 1964.

As might be expected, though, IBM took its time in coming to depend on computers for the bulk of its profits. It had every incentive to rely on profits from unit record customers for as long as possible while marketing computers at prices low enough to squeeze the profit margins of competitors. As exotic as it may have seemed at the time, the computer business was actually easier to enter than the punch card machinery business. Between 1951 and 1954, some thirty-six different engineering groups worldwide were engaged in the construction of large-scale computers, some of which were prototypes for quantity production. By the 1960s, there were as many as fifty major suppliers of computers of all sorts, and more than 700 organizations employed some 30,000 persons in one part of the computer field or another.[11] The expensive computer systems were installed primarily by scientists and a few large commercial customers; there remained in the 1960s a tremendous number of small unit record customers who just couldn't afford to install a computer at all. Those trapped customers continued to provide the profits IBM needed to switch its largest data processing customers from one horse, as it were, to another.

IBM's first two computers had negative profit rates, but even eight years later, in 1960, IBM computers as a group still showed only a relatively narrow profit margin of 11 percent. The profitability of the soon-to-be-obsolete punch card machines was 356 percent higher, a typical (for IBM) 39.2 percent, and still rising, to 42.4 percent four years later. But IBM's future was in computers. As it consolidated its power in computers, it would raise their prices and increase their profits. From 11 percent in 1960, the profit rate on IBM computers would almost triple to 30.2 percent in 1964.[12] The commercial data processing monopoly that Watson, Sr., had devoted the last half of his life to building was maintained. As his son would later remark, no other company in the world had been better situated to exploit the computer's potential as a commercial data processing tool.

To which he might have added, no other company had the necessary cash flow and monopoly position from which to effectively price-discriminate during a period of profound technological change and tremendous overall growth. Having begun the decade as a company of just over $300 million in annual revenues whose arch-rival was ahead by two years, IBM finished the 1950s on a roll with total sales at over $1.8 billion and a commanding 70 percent-plus share of the market for computers.

4. The Five-Year Generation

We're a highly ethical company, with a clear set of guidelines for employees to follow, and a determination to honor those guidelines at every level of the company.

—John Akers, President and Chief
Executive Officer of IBM[1]

The invention that rendered IBM's and its competitors' first-generation computer systems obsolete was the transistor, a tiny sliver of germanium crystal whose potential as an electronic component vastly exceeded what was possible with vacuum tubes. Invented in 1948 but commercialized only a decade later, the transistor promised to replace one of the most troublesome components of first-generation computer systems, the breakdown-prone vacuum tubes.

Much smaller than the tube, the transistor used far less power and ran much cooler. Where the tube worked by boiling electrons off a red-hot wire mounted in a carefully blown and evacuated glass case, the transistor was a solid-state device requiring perhaps a hundredth of the electrical power of a tube. Theoretically, it would last forever, for it had no glowing filament to fail. The failure rate of this previous technology had limited the potential size of computers. Given enough tubes in one machine and the high probability that one would fail, larger systems would not be able to function long enough to be viable. The transistor solved this reliability problem while at the same time making the building of logic circuits far less costly than before. In fact, the lower cost of the transistor changed the economics of constructing computers, and it opened the door not only for IBM but also for new competitors.

The industry has since marked this major change in technology as the beginning of the computer's "second generation": from about 1958 on, computers ceased to rely on vacuum tubes. As the transistor became viable, several of its producers—including the Radio Corporation of America (RCA), Philco, and General Electric—saw an opportunity to use their expertise to enter the burgeoning computer market.

But it was Remington Rand, once again, that was the first to market, delivering its Solid-State 80 in 1958. In 1959, the company tried to regain the momentum that it had lost to IBM by enhancing the system to handle eighty-column IBM cards and to execute instructions originally written for the large base of IBM 650 systems. This was one of the first attempts by a computer maker to offer systems that were compatible with a popular IBM system, and it wouldn't be the last. IBM responded just four months later with a transistorized machine of its own, the famous 1401. With this machine, IBM would dominate the second-generation commercial computer business.

During the five years it most actively marketed the 1401, from 1960 through 1965, IBM delivered *four-fifths* of the value of all installed computer systems. At the same time, the profitability of its computers nearly tripled. The company emerged from the second-generation era as a full-fledged computer company, having shed its primary dependence on unit record equipment. To bring about these substantial accomplishments, IBM exploited its still-sizable unit record base as it built transistor-based computer systems. Just as important, IBM enjoyed a rapid expansion in the demand for data processing by its largest customers. From 1960 to 1965, IBM doubled its total annual revenues to $3.57 billion and boosted overall corporate profitability from 11.3 to 13.4 percent—a rise of almost 20 percent. What was it that fueled such dramatic growth in the data processing market, even as the cost of computing fell? And how did IBM manage during this period of rapid expansion to boost its already high corporate profit rate by an additional 20 percent? Surely what IBM was selling must have appealed to some extraordinary demand by customers.

TAPPING THE ENDLESS CYCLE

As IBM and others found out, the demand for commercial data processing is highly price-elastic. That is, even over several decades, every drop in price has increased demand. Although the markets for other goods have seen temporary periods during which price-cutting stimulated a more-than-proportionate increase in demand, the computer market is unique in that demand for it shows no sign of abating. The demand for candy, designer jeans, and vacation travel, for instance, may have increased in response to falling prices at certain times, but these and most other markets quickly get saturated. At some point, customers figure they've had enough and will not acquire more of a commodity, no matter how far its price drops.

Why hasn't saturation set in with the computer? The answer is simple: There is no ultimate level of efficiency for commercial organizations, no matter how many computers, lathes, robots, or other kinds of capital equipment they install. The best a corporation can hope for are temporary periods when it is more efficient than its rivals. As producers of goods and services jockey for the lead in their respective marketplaces, their efficiency can be measured only relative to those of their competitors—never absolutely.

A commercial firm is motivated to install a computer by a desire to maximize the value of some task while reducing the cost of performing it. If the value of processed data is greater than the cost of processing it, then the decision to automate can be justified; the move to install a computer advances the firm's competitive position in relation to its rivals or to its own bottom line. As one competitor automates a particular task that is common to all competitors in a particular marketplace, rivals are compelled to follow suit or fall behind. The only limit to this virtually endless process is the number of tasks for which automation promises an economic advantage.

As computers have fallen in price and risen in performance, the number of manual and mechanical tasks worth automating has increased. Thanks to the nature of computer technology, which delivers more performance at less cost each year, the use of computers continues to grow at unprecedented rates. Along with each improvement in technology have come better prices, better performance, and a ballooning of demand.

Despite falling costs for the machinery itself, the total cost of running a large computer was—and still is—quite high. The customer has to set aside a specially equipped room for the machine; it needs air-conditioning, a raised floor to accommodate masses of cables, and special electrical circuits. The customer also has to provide a large amount of space for the machine's operators, programmers, keypunchers, and maintenance crew. Even more space is needed to store reams of punch cards, paper, and tape reels. The staff itself is costly, too, requiring specially skilled operators, programmers, systems analysts, and the usual administrative staff.

Once the computer is installed, the cost of preparing a particular program depends heavily on its complexity and the capabilities of the program and the computer itself. The faster the computer, in general, the more efficiently program developers could work—they could test their programs more often.

At any particular moment in the evolution of computers, certain tasks have been easier to program than others. Some—instantaneous access to all corporate data, for instance—remain difficult or impossible even to this day. Some large, particularly complex applications—nationwide airline reservation systems, for example—were at first economically unfeasible with second-generation computers. Such ambitious applications had to wait until later models that offered more performance at less cost became available and the art of programming had advanced sufficiently. Each decrease in cost broadened the applicability of the computer.

IBM subtly exploited its customers' need to expand their data processing operations to keep up with their respective competitors. It rented out computer systems for use during a maximum number of hours a month—generally 176 hours, or about 9 hours a day. The customer paid a flat fee for that time and could use it as he pleased. If a particularly important application that had justified the system's initial installation was completed, any time left over was effectively free to the user. More often than not in that case, the initial application would be expanded with new functions, or new applications would be added to take up the slack.

IBM and other vendors often supplied application programs at no extra charge, and they helped users write programs—all with an eye to getting a customer to order more hardware and deepen his commitment to his computer vendor. With encouragement, a user could easily find his monthly ration of 176 hours of computer time completely used up before all his data processing work was finished. He then might run extra shifts during evenings and weekends. But that meant paying IBM an extra-shift charge. Meanwhile, the congestion of the customers' new programs waiting to be tested or used in production often led to delays, which created even more demand for capacity on the system. Data processing managers found they had to acquire more hardware, in the form of new peripherals such as tape drives or printers or a larger processor. In some cases, an entirely new system, offering even better price and performance, would be installed, and the cycle would begin all over again. As will be seen shortly, this technique of dropping costs, leading to additional applications and eventually to demand for extra system capacity, was the key to IBM's revenue and profit growth.

The fact that IBM and its rivals generally leased rather than sold their computers (usually on a thirty-day basis) meant that customers could easily upgrade their machines. A rented machine was far easier to replace than a purchased one: a customer simply asked his vendor to remove the old machine and bring in a larger one of his choice. A purchased system, by contrast, was a financial burden that had to be written off if no buyer could be found. That was often the case as technology changed quickly and with it the price of computing. Leasing systems, as IBM referred to its rental of computers, took much of the financial risk off the customer's books and placed it squarely on IBM's (which could well afford it) and those of the competition (which couldn't).

In cutting costs and improving performance, all the major computer manufacturers moved in roughly the same technological directions and at the same pace. An innovation by one supplier would often be mimicked quickly by the others if it seemed valuable and in demand. IBM was by no means always the technological leader in this process, as Remington's lead in transistor machines attests. The most necessary improvement for a computer system was enabling its circuits to switch on and off more rapidly, thus speeding up the central processor. Higher processor speeds meant faster execution of arithmetic and logical instructions and therefore more data processing jobs completed each hour. Manufacturers made out well because their cost for improving a computer's performance was substantially less than the added performance's value to the customer—functional pricing could be highly profitable.

Computer manufacturing techniques improved, as well, causing the cost of a unit of computing to drop dramatically. These economies were generally applied to delivering more computing power at a constant price rather than to dropping the computer's price. Building computers was at first particularly labor-intensive, and substantial cost improvements came from automating the manufacturing process. For example, in the case of magnetic core memory, manufacturing costs dropped from $64 per thousand cores in 1955, when the job was done by hand, to only $1.07 per thousand in 1972, by which time the process was highly automated. Such steeply falling cost curves, which continue to this day for many basic computer technologies, allow computer makers to install more memory at less cost and thereby increase their systems' capabilities—and profits.

There were also improvements in software. An infinitely malleable commodity, software has virtually no manufacturing cost, only development cost. The rather skimpy set of basic programs delivered with early computers grew to include tools that helped customers write programs. One of the most important tools was the compiler, which enabled programs to be written in such high-level languages as COBOL and FORTRAN rather than in the machine's obscure language of ones and zeros. Other programs boosted an entire system's reliability. Early computers had a tendency to crash to a halt frequently due to the smallest mistakes in their programming or faulty circuitry. Improved software enabled systems to recover from such faults. It also let systems perform more than one task at a time. A properly programmed system could simultaneously read data in from cards for one job, print out the results of a previous job, and process a third job.

Along the same line, new software enabled the system to take care of the many housekeeping tasks previously required of human operators. The computer's speed often outpaced that of the mere mortal running it, and it would be forced to wait idly for, say, a new reel of tape to be loaded. Systems were enabled to switch their connections from one spent tape drive to another preloaded one as quickly as needed.

All this software, both the application programs and the so-called systems programs, as well as support services, were for many years provided to customers at no extra charge. The prices of the software and services were said to be "bundled" into the monthly rental charge.

These many improvements helped the computer accomplish its sorcerer's trick of getting more computing done for less money. From the installation of the first 701 computer in 1953 through the year 1965, the so-called throughput, or maximum computing capacity, of IBM's computers improved by about 50 percent each year. Half of this dramatic improvement came from advances in electronics while the rest derived from new system designs and from improved ways of combining the same basic logic elements and software for maximum efficiency. All the while, commercial customers expanded their use of computers.

SCIENTIFIC VS. COMMERCIAL

Computers were at first used primarily by scientists and engineers, as well as by the few corporations and government agencies that replaced large, punch card–based accounting operations with them. For those corporations, the computer was essentially a new type of equipment applied to a preexisting task. Later, however, as prices fell and quality improved, the computer came to be seen as a tool for accomplishing wide ranges of tasks that had never been attempted before: day-to-day tracking of corporate cash reserves, running factories automatically, and sending rockets to the moon, for example. It was the second generation of computers that convinced large customers that the machines were not just gee-whiz gizmos but practical tools that could handle the unglamorous but necessary routines of commercial data processing.

The commercial customer was fundamentally different from the scientific customer. Scientific needs had initially inspired computer designers, and it was in satisfying those needs that the machine had become known as a technological wonder. A scientist actually had much simpler problems to automate than did the average corporation, however. He generally wanted to load the machine with a single program, provide it with a small batch of numerical data to crunch through, and, after waiting perhaps a few hours, record the final answer—which might turn out to be but a single number. A scientific system required fairly simple hardware, mainly a processor of as high a computing rate as possible, minimal input/output peripheral gear, and simple system software.

In contrast, a commercial customer had many complex programs to run, each calling for masses of records to be processed one by one. A commercial system had to be able to store and move records in and out of its processor very efficiently. For that type of processing, high-capacity storage devices (tape and disk drives) for mass storage, fast printers for output, and complex systems software to manage these "resources" efficiently were indispensable.

These differences largely explain the relatively late adoption of electronic data processing by commercial customers. Not only was the low-cost transistor necessary, but higher-performance peripherals and special software were needed. The computer had to be made easier to use before the technically ignorant businessman would adopt it as a tool to rely on.

Entering the scientific computing market had been a relatively simple, inexpensive business proposition because scientists were usually familiar with computing and didn't require the extensive—and expensive—handholding insisted upon by commercial customers. A scientist could certainly do his own programming and at times even his own maintenance. But the computer, as UNIVAC pioneer J. Presper Eckert, Jr., put it, was thought of by businessmen as a "strange new beast" that had to be tamed by the vendor before it could be of much use.

The scientific market eventually lessened in economic importance relative to the commercial market, but it remained important to IBM nevertheless. IBM had no interest in permitting makers of scientific machines to establish themselves so well that they might later take a piece of the more lucrative action in commercial data processing. But because it was unwilling to offer price discounts on its equipment, even for large customers who did not want the standard measure of bundled service and support, IBM's prices for scientific machines were generally higher than those of its more specialized competitors that sold only scientific systems.

SOFTWARE LOCK-IN

The biggest competitors IBM faced during the second generation were, among others, Honeywell, a firm well established in electronics and industrial controls; Burroughs Corporation, maker of adding machines, banking machines, and other office equipment; Radio Corporation of America (RCA), a leader in transistors; Control Data Corporation (CDC), offering innovative, high-performance scientific systems; and Sperry Rand, the product of the merger in the late 1950s of Remington Rand and Sperry Corporation. There were others, including NCR and Digital Equipment, but none were able to dent IBM's commanding 70 percent-plus market share.

How was IBM able to master this ever-improving technology, capture the lion's share of the expanding business, and all the while boost its corporate profit rate? The key lies in a phenomenon of the commercial computer marketplace known as *software lock-in*, which refers to the strong ties that develop between the computer customer and his supplier as the former comes to depend on his computer to handle vital applications.

Until a customer chose and installed a particular computer, he was essentially free to pick from the variety of firms offering the type of system he needed. His decision could be based on a straight comparison of the actual value of the equipment and service he would receive for his money from each. However, once a system was chosen, by the time it was installed and programmed, his staff properly trained to program and run it, and masses of data collected and organized for processing, the customer generally found that the cost of switching to another supplier's system would be prohibitively high. To make such a switch would mean virtually starting from scratch again and throwing away most if not all of the original investment in programming and staff training. Unless a competing vendor could offer a very large savings in price or some means of salvaging the original software investment, a customer would stick with his first vendor no matter what.

Once IBM or any other system supplier had successfully won a customer to their fold, therefore, his data processing operations soon became tightly locked in to the peculiarities of the system in question, and he was limited to that vendor for any additional peripherals, maintenance services, or supplies. Under these conditions, it was possible for a computer vendor to charge locked-in customers high prices, higher than those charged to first-time, freely choosing prospects for the same equipment or the same increment of additional function or performance. An alert vendor discriminated between these two classes of customer and charged them accordingly.

Software lock-in is made possible by the fact that no two vendors' computers have identical internal characteristics. All computers use a binary code, but different machines usually interpret the same group of binary digits completely differently. As a result, it is quite difficult to share programs and data between two different brands of computer. In order to assist users in upgrading from one system to another, vendors often built their computers to be consistent with their own previous machines but not necessarily with those of any other vendor.

Intimately related to the incompatibility among processors is the fact that most programs for commercial data processing are written specifically by and for a particular customer. If they are not, they contain substantial tailoring of preexisting programs. There are few application programs that are usable by all customers, even among those limited to a particular type of business. This is because no two commercial enterprises are organized in quite the same way or collect and process quite the same types of data. By its very nature, an application program models one aspect of an organization's informational process, and because each organization's processes are unique, their application programs must also be unique, or else they will not be useful.

The upshot is that once an IBM customer had invested the thousands, or even millions, of dollars needed to make a complex commercial application program work properly, there was little chance he'd throw it away just to take advantage of the mere 10 to 15 percent savings in monthly rental that another computer vendor might offer. In fact, as IBM discovered, the lock-in often took effect before a computer had even been delivered: the training of staff and the planning for the writing of application programs were often sufficient investments for the user to stick with IBM.

IBM actually played up software lock-in when pitching systems to first-time customers. It reminded them to be careful not to get stuck with a system that they could not easily expand to meet future needs. Choosing the wrong machine now, IBM emphasized, might mean big trouble down the road. Scientific customers tended to be less vulnerable to software lock-in than their commercial counterparts, by virtue of the relative simplicity of their applications and the fact that their experiments were not repeated periodically, as commercial applications generally are.

Software lock-in and the price discrimination it supported became the key to IBM's increasing rate of profit during the second generation, when competitors were many and the growth of the overall market was rapid. Lock-in created a growing base of customers who were entirely dependent on IBM for extra equipment. The locked-in computer customers joined the traditional base of unit record customers in being exploited through prices that were higher in relation to costs than those charged to first-time customers. IBM's main competitive task, therefore, was to lure as many new customers as possible to its computer systems and thereby deny competitors the possibility of taking advantage of their own software lock-in. IBM had to construct a scheme that would discriminate between entry-level customers, who sought a competitively low price, and locked-in customers, who would pay higher prices based not on costs but on function.

As it locked in first-time customers, however, IBM had to keep a sharp eye out for the antitrust agencies. With its massive resources, IBM could easily have captured loads of new users simply by offering them equipment priced far below cost and throwing in large amounts of free support services. Once a customer was hooked, the initial costs could be recouped by exploiting software lock-in. That would have been Patterson's approach, and it would have made economic sense for IBM: new users would get lower prices for a product, while locked-in users paid through the nose. There was a problem, however, which IBM's own antitrust guidelines stated succinctly: "It is unlawful to favor new customers with special discounts or allowances. The prices to new customers and old customers must be the same. Discrimination in price may not be accomplished indirectly by any rebates, allowances, service, commission, waiver of charges, reduction of rental, free trial use or other term or condition of sale not made equally available to all customers."[2]

Something subtle was needed, some scheme that would effect the same price discrimination without provoking unwanted scrutiny by the law.

A TALE OF TWO FAMILIES

IBM's entries for the second-generation race were grouped into two families: the small 1400s, for commercial data processing, and the large 7000s, primarily for scientific work. Each family comprised several central processors that varied in raw execution speed and in the number and types of peripherals they could handle. For each model, in addition, there were a variety of optional features that improved the processor's function and speed.

The commercial 1400s were by far the most popular of IBM's second-generation computers precisely because they were designed and priced to appeal to the many thousands of commercial firms already using model 650 systems or unit record machines. There were four 1400 processors: the original 1401; the subsequent and larger 1410; and the still later but smaller 1440 and 1460. Generally, all 1400 models could share programming, so a customer could swap one processor for another more powerful one without a costly rewrite of all his software. Even larger machines, the 7010 and 7080 processors, were also designed to run 1400-type code and were offered as upgrades to customers that had outgrown either a 1400-type machine or IBM's first-generation commercial systems, the 700 series.

The scientific 7000 family consisted of eight processor models that varied similarly in price, raw performance, and function to the commercial 1400s. The most important was an upgrade for the 709, the 7090, which eventually was enhanced to become the 7094 and 7094II systems. These were high-powered processors designed for massive calculations.

As these systems became available, the computer market's center of gravity was shifting to the area of IBM's greatest strength—commercial data processing. In 1959, the number of IBM's major commercial and scientific computer installations had been roughly equal—about 120 computer systems of each kind. By 1965, however, IBM had shipped more than 10,500 commercial systems but only a little more than 600 scientific systems. The shift was reflected in IBM's financial records: during the active marketing life of these second-generation systems, computer revenues were estimated to be $5.1 billion on the commercial side but only $1.6 billion from scientific machines.[3]

Because the scientific market was saturated much earlier than the commercial sector, it offered far less opportunity for growth and profits. There were many more commercial customers and governmental agencies that could use computers than there were potential scientific customers for computers. IBM priced its commercial systems to ensure itself of large profits from locked-in commercial customers (with whom IBM traditionally had the most power), and it maintained competitive prices (meaning lower profits) in the scientific sector, where its hold was less secure against competition.

Out of the blizzard of financial figures, market projections, and other data made available during the various court actions against IBM emerges a picture of its basic pricing pattern. This pattern, which IBM would continue to use for the rest of the 1960s, is most clearly seen in the 1401, which was by far the most popular and important IBM second-generation computer. The 1401 alone brought IBM total revenues of $2.8 billion during its life, compared with the combined total of $2.35 billion generated by the other five 1400-compatible machines.[4]

The 1401 represented the vanguard of IBM's commercial data processing monopoly in the shift from tabulating machines to computers. The 1401 had been expected to scoop up as many new computer customers as possible but still contribute the profits IBM needed to compensate for the profits no longer collected from accounting machines. The small computer had to appeal to new customers, many of whom could just as easily have ordered from competing vendors, but it had to do so without such a low price as to hurt overall profit objectives or provoke antitrust problems. These goals were met.

Clearly, when offering a customer his first complete computer system—which included a central processor, peripherals, and software—IBM had to make sure that the price for the equipment and maintenance services was not greater than what its competitors charged for comparable gear. At that time, customers didn't much care whether the price of a processor was excessive and the price of peripherals low, or vice versa. What they really wanted was a complete, workable system, backed by a dependable vendor, that could handle their data processing reliably and for less cost than either other computer systems or unit record equipment. Nonetheless, IBM had to assign each component of its systems a separate published price, if for no other reason than to serve the customer who wanted to add equipment to an installed system. The 1956 Consent Decree, too, required the company to establish separate lease and purchase prices for each product.

The pricing pattern IBM created was carefully designed to segment its market according to its power. Some of its products were designed to appeal to its more dependent commercial customers, those with little or no choice beyond IBM—from these, IBM earned high profits. Other products designed particularly for less locked-in users were priced lower and therefore earned IBM lower profits. First-time customers, who were not beholden to IBM, were lured in by appropriate products with low price tags. As a user's dependence on IBM grew, however, and as he required additional capability in his system, IBM steeply increased both its prices and its profits. This was the company's basic strategy in episode after competitive episode; it ensured the continuation of the monopoly and its abnormally high profits. In time, IBM's product line broadened to include a wide variety of systems, but the basic pricing strategy remained unchanged.

MEMORABLE PROFITS

Proof that IBM discriminated between first-time and established computer users would require evidence of pricing that brought low or even negative profits from entry-level computers and excessive profits for larger ones. The profit data for

Table 3

Revenues, Profits, and Percent Profit for Major IBM
Second-Generation Computer Systems
(in $ million)[5]

	REVENUES	PROFITS	PERCENT PROFIT
Commercial Systems			
1401	2,800	1,252	44.5%
1440	649	243	37.4
1460	479	198	41.3
1410/7010	943	378	40.0
7080	281	118	42.0
Subtotal	5,152	2,189	42.5
Scientific Systems			
7040/44	292	87	29.8
7070/7074	463	104	22.5
7090/7094II	859	379	44.1
7030	NA	NA	NA
Subtotal	1,614	570	35.3

IBM's second-generation computers, however, appear to refute that contention, as Table 3 shows.

IBM earned 44.5 cents on each dollar of 1401 revenue and 37.4 to 42.5 cents on the larger 1400 models. This seems to suggest that IBM was not discriminating to any significant degree between these systems. In fact, at this level of detail, with profits for all parts of the system aggregated together, IBM seems to have met its lawyers' injunction that established customers not subsidize new ones.*

And perhaps IBM was not price discriminating. Yet a tantalizing statement from Hillary Faw invites a closer look: "The [Department of Justice] complaint specifically covers varying profit margins. An intensive investigation of this issue would reveal the extent of our price control and its supporting practices. Such a revelation would not be helpful to our monopoly defense."[6]

What were these "varying profit margins" that Faw worried might be revealed to IBM's detriment? They are certainly not apparent in the above data. Perhaps a more "intensive investigation of this issue" will uncover what Faw was hinting at.

IBM actually offered the 1401 not as a single computer system with a single price and profit rate but rather as a mix-and-match group of a dozen different

---

* Before rejecting the proposition that smaller systems earn less profit than larger systems, a more detailed examination of how overhead expenses are allocated is also required in order to see if profit differentials are hidden in the way IBM calculates profit rates for each of its products. For example, if locked-in users pay a disproportionate share of the joint overhead used by both new and locked-in users while new users receive most of the benefit, then the profit figures would hide the true disparity in profits between the two groups. Such was in fact the case, as a later chapter will show.

processor variations and many peripheral devices. When each of those components' profit rates are considered, price discrimination does become evident.

The 1401 processor actually came in four different models, lettered A through D, which varied as to their ability to use a selection of special, extra-priced peripherals and several "optional features." These latter included such items as special circuits to speed multiplication and facilities for attaching certain advanced peripherals.

Now, the A model was the simplest processor, able to use only four of the ten special features, while the C model included five of the features as standard items and could optionally use the other five if the user were willing to pay extra. (The 1401-D processor was designed not as a general-purpose commercial processor but as a printing slave yoked to large 7000 series systems; thus, it does not figure heavily in this analysis.) IBM made each lettered processor model available with one of three different memory capacities. The suffixes 1, 2, and 3 referred respectively to memory sizes of 1,400, 2,000, and 4,000 cells. Generally, the more memory was attached to a processor, the more work it could do in a given amount of time, because then there would be more "space" for applications and their data to reside fully in the processor; they would not have to be moved in piece by piece from relatively slow external peripherals. As IBM and other manufacturers discovered, customers have consistently sought more memory for their processors because for those customers needing it, extra memory boosts any system's overall performance.

As seen earlier, the aggregate profit rate for all twelve models of the 1401 system was a respectable 44.5 percent. Certainly that was not discriminatory compared with the lower profit rates on larger systems. However, the breakdown of profits by individual model in Table 4 shows the pattern that Faw hoped would stay hidden.

IBM made more profits from the model 3 processors—those with the biggest memories—than it did from small-memory, entry-level model 1 processors. The larger machines, with profit rates of 38 percent, earned money for IBM at a rate

Table 4
Profitability of the Various
Models of the 1401 CPU and
Memory Size[7]

Model	Memory Size		
1401	1	2	3
A	29.5%	34.9%	38.9%
B	31.4	37.1	39.8
C	33.1	36.0	37.8
D	14.7	20.1	24.3

that was *one-third higher* than the entry-level rate of 29 percent. The more memory and features the customer added, the more performance he got from his system, but also the higher IBM's profit rate became. Here, in the additional performance required by locked-in users, we find the first clue to a discriminatory pricing pattern.

Let's look closer at the memory pricing. Published data on the manufacturing cost for the magnetic core memory used in 1401 processors show that in 1959, 1,000 memory cells cost in total about $212. (See Appendix B for the specifics of this calculation.) We can compare this conservative cost estimate with the purchase price IBM charged its customers. Table 5 shows that a customer paid an extra $800 to add 600 cells of memory when upgrading from a 1,400-cell to a 2,000-cell processor. At that rate, the price to the customer for 1,000 cells was $1,333. In the case of moving from a 1,400 cell to a 4,000-cell, however, the price was $1,900 for 2,600 cells, or $737 per 1,000 cells.

Now, knowing IBM's total expenses were no more than $212 for these 1,000 cells of memory, we see that IBM earned quite hefty profits from memory upgrades. The move from a memory size 1 to a 2 earned it 84.1 percent profit, while the move from a memory size 1 to a 3 earned 71 percent. For every additional dollar of revenue IBM collected from upgrades, between 70 and 85 cents was pure profit. As with the earlier unit record printer, the increase in price had very little relation to IBM's actual costs: this was functional pricing. With the 1401, as with the old printer, there was little protest from the customer, for, after all, he knew nothing of IBM's profit rates or of the underlying cost of memory. There was, moreover, no other source than IBM from which to buy such compatible memory upgrades. The customer got what he wanted—increased performance.

IBM profited greatly when customers expanded their systems. Quite often, a customer would acquire his first machine for a single important data processing application, but with IBM's "free" help in supplying and tailoring application

Table 5
Purchase Prices for 1401
CPUs, by Model and
Memory Size[8]
(in $ thousands)

Model	Memory Size		
1401	1	2	3
A	70.5	71.3	72.4
B	78.0	78.8	79.9
C	105.4	106.2	107.3
D	81.8	82.6	83.6

programs at his disposal, it was not long before he envisioned new tasks for his computer and began adding them. Eventually, he either upgraded his present computer with extra memory or other features, or he installed an entirely new and larger processor. And soon that, too, would require more memory. It was a never-ending cycle that, understandably, IBM exploited to great advantage. IBM's fortune was to be the sole source of a highly valued, scarce commodity—in this case, compatible memory.

The overall success of IBM's pricing strategy is seen in the general increase in system size among 1401 users. Table 6 shows the breakdown of the number of each 1401 model IBM had installed in the United States as of mid-1962, when the machines were at the midpoint of their active marketing life:

Thus, many more large 1401 processors—C models in particular—than smaller A models were installed. The largest memories, moreover, the 4,000-cell model 3s, were more popular than the smaller ones. Customers evidently found their entry-level processors insufficient to handle all their data processing, and they quickly moved upscale to the larger machines. Each move they made boosted IBM's profits.

Memory proved to be a good mechanism by which IBM could segment the commercial computer business to its liking. New customers needed only a little memory, but locked-in users needed a great deal, and they would pay for it. Seeing the opportunity for even more memory profits, in May 1960, IBM came out with the 1406, a box that provided additional memory for the 1401 processor. The new product came in three sizes, the 1, 2, and 3, and contained 4,000, 8,000, and 12,000 additional memory cells respectively. Overall, according to IBM documents, the 1406 was expected to earn $190.2 million in revenues and net $116.4 million in profits. The profit rate? A healthy 61.2 percent.[9]

Discrimination in memory does not explain all the variations in profits between the true entry-level 1401 processor and its bigger 1401 brothers. Func-

Table 6

Number of 1401 CPUs Installed
With Customers, by Model and
Memory Size

| Model | | Memory Size | | |
1401 CPU	1	2	3	TOTAL
A	700	300	550	1550
B	250	200	950	1400
C	20	75	1935	2030
D	50	120	50	220
Total	1020	695	3485	5200

tional pricing on the ten add-on features also helped. As noted earlier, the lesser 1401 models could use far fewer features than the big C models. A new 1401 customer wouldn't have much need for these performance-enhancing features, but as he expanded from an A to the larger models, more features became available, useful, and even necessary. Not surprisingly, the features were priced to earn as much as 86 cents profit on each dollar of revenue. On average, the features earned profits of 58 cents per dollar of revenue.

When inspected closely, then, IBM's pricing during the second generation conforms exactly with price-discrimination theory. For products where competition was effective and customers could choose between alternatives—namely, scientific systems in general and entry-level commercial systems in particular—IBM's prices were relatively low. Where IBM had market power because the customers had no choice, as locked-in commercial users did not, its prices were high relative to costs. The discrimination was quiet so as to please the lawyers, but it was effective in enhancing IBM's position in the market and in assuring it of ongoing profits with which to capture increasing numbers of newcomers to the expanding computer market.

No secret was made of this pricing scheme at the higher echelons of IBM. As Faw remarked to upper management about the pricing of system upgrades for big profits, "With regard to the pricing of the System, the optional feature prices were established so as to yield *substantially higher profit margins* than the basic machines. Features were priced to yield an average of 56.0% profit as compared with an average of 36.8% for the basic machines." (Emphasis added.)[10]

Watson, Jr., stated that IBM as a matter of course had performed certain jobs for customers precisely in an attempt to get them "to use a new and bigger machine."[11] It was always in IBM's interest to encourage users to expand their data processing operations and with them the computer hardware they needed.* The initial order for a system was the hardest to win, but once that was accomplished, the customer would soon be hitched on to the IBM gravy train.

This price discrimination would not have been possible if the structure of the computer industry had been more competitive. The high memory profits should have, in theory, drawn other firms into offering compatible, lower-priced enhancements and driven prices down to closer to costs. In time, as the cost of making computers dropped, just such compatible competition would appear. In the interim, IBM got richer.

---

* This same idea was expressed in a 1969 IBM flip chart. Cryptically it stated: "Historically IBM Has Influenced Account To: Grow DP by Discovery of Needs; Specify Requirements to Fit IBM Products; Develop Long Range DP Strategy and be a Continuing Market; Permit Detection and Countering of Competitive Activity. The Result has been: An Expanding Market for Products; A Contributor to Market Share."[12] IBM was only too willing to offer free "help" to its existing users to find new applications that would expand its market and maintain its market share.

STRETCH

If there is any lingering doubt that IBM was willing to forgo profits to maintain its grip on any important market segment that was threatened by effective competition, the case of the 7030 system, better known as STRETCH, should dispel them. In 1956, Sperry Rand began building what at the time was to be the world's largest computer, the LARC (named for Los Alamos Research Computer). A competitor's bringing out a superior computer in *any* market segment would have caused some consternation at IBM headquarters, but another company's planning to deliver the world's most powerful system was just too much to take. Watson, Jr., soon ordered a crash development effort to build a machine that would compete with LARC. It was to be built at any cost.

IBM never delivered STRETCH with all the capabilities first promised, and, tellingly, it lost more than $20 million trying to get the system to work at all. The first STRETCH was delivered to Los Alamos in 1961, but an embarrassed Watson had to tell the next fifteen customers that the system would not perform as planned and that therefore its $13.5 million price tag would be cut significantly. The machine was taken off the market after only seven STRETCH systems were completed and installed.

By rushing STRETCH to market prematurely, IBM again contradicted its own interpretation of the antitrust laws, which stated, "A seller may not sell or offer to sell new products, until such products are actually in production and can reasonably be expected to be ready for delivery when promised, without risking charges of unfair trade practices."[13]

The point is not that IBM should not engage in large research projects if it chooses to. Rather, it is that when a monopolist prematurely announces a product that it has little reason to believe will actually get delivered, and it does so at a money-losing price designed to undercut competitors, the effort takes on a different caste. Yet IBM would not be deterred from repeating this tactic again later.

IBM could afford large losses only because of the high profits generated by the large base of locked-in customers. Sperry Rand, and later Control Data, lacked comparable customer bases and found the STRETCH strategy difficult to compete with.

STRETCH proved to be a great embarrassment for IBM. The company later tried to justify the expenses of its failed development effort by pointing to the technological spinoffs it prompted and the engineering talent it attracted to IBM. But these were benefits it could have gained by expanding its research and development without actually announcing a product before its time. As it turned out, the STRETCH system may go down in history as one of the more expensive knockout machines ever made. Old man Patterson would have liked that.

5. Rushing the 360s

The prevailing philosophy was to . . . hold market share. This re-sulted in prices at lower profit returns than our historic past.

—IBM describing how it marketed
certain of the System/360
computers

The 1401 was a great success. It alone accounted for about a fifth of the value of the entire U.S. computer systems market in 1963, and its sales helped push IBM's revenues over the $2 billion mark that year. It wasn't long, however, before the 1401's high profits attracted keen competition. The machine offered an alluring opportunity to intercept IBM where profits were highest—in the products it offered to locked-in commercial customers.

It was clear to its competitors, who knew as well as IBM the true cost of building computers, that IBM was forcing customers with large 1401s, as well as those with other large-memory 1400/7000 systems, to contribute more than their share to its high corporate profits. It seemed a good bet to the competitors that many of IBM's large-memory users did not particularly like IBM's milking them as cash cows and that they might be lured away to other computers if they were offered more data processing for their dollar.

Rapid improvements in technology set the stage for its competitors to launch a particularly effective attack on the commercial core of IBM's monopoly. As the 1960s progressed, transistors and related circuit packaging techniques underwent tremendous advances in performance and cost; thus, building a better, lower-cost machine than IBM's, which was based on late-1950s technology, posed little problem. Also, because customers with large 1401s already had application programs running and had their own trained staffs in place, they were more independent of IBM than most. The only problem in getting them to leave IBM was to produce a machine that could easily execute their valuable 1401 programs. Somehow, the underpinning of IBM's expanding commercial business—its software lock-in—would have to be broken. That done, established users could be offered alternative hardware to IBM's.

It was Honeywell, a relative newcomer to data processing, that most success-fully put the pieces together and attacked the lucrative 1401s. In a move that must have kept the midnight oil burning for many a night at IBM headquarters, Honeywell launched the H–200, a system that indeed ran faster than the 1401 and sold for less. It was clearly superior to the 1401, offering a maximum of 65,000 memory locations and taking only a single microsecond to execute its basic instructions; the 1401 was limited to 16,000 memory cells and a far slower instruction time of 11.5 microseconds. Most important, the Honeywell machine could run the 1401 programs with little or no modification. It came with a clever software package, appropriately dubbed "Liberator," that could translate the 1401 programs line for line into exactly the right format for the Honeywell hardware.

Honeywell was well positioned to make the Liberator ploy work. Ironically, the company's very weakness in the computer market gave it an advantage over the better established of IBM's competitors. It had relatively few pre-Liberator computer customers to service, so, when designing the H–200, it was able to make a radical change in the design of its computers without fear of losing much business. It just did not have that many established customers to worry about disappointing or even losing when it introduced a system that was incompatible with their installed machines.

The H–200/Liberator combination hit the market in December 1963 and was an immediate success. In six weeks of marketing, *Datamation* magazine re-ported, the system garnered 400 orders, most of them from 1401 users. IBM de-termined, in fact, that in the United States alone, some 2,200 1401s, which brought in about $12 million a month, were vulnerable to potential replacement by the H–200. IBM management was alarmed to see this upstart from Minneap-olis storming the 1401 base and grabbing customer after high-profit customer. But basic economics was working: when offered better hardware value for their money along with protection of their software investment, many sophisticated customers were not afraid to leave behind the comfort of the IBM security blanket. Despite IBM's heavily touted respect for its customer, its stellar mar-keting force, and its renowned service, customers' loyalty to IBM was surpris-ingly thin and their buying decisions were assuringly rational. When provided with a less expensive, compatible alternative to IBM, many were quite willing to order from a relative newcomer to the business. IBM's position in the market, it was plain to see, was the result not of its being freely chosen by customers but of an absence of competition due to software lock-in.

Honeywell succeeded so well that it pushed the industry leader into a state of panic. As well as gaining Honeywell substantial orders and boosting the firm's recognition throughout the industry as a viable computer supplier, the Liberator quickly pushed Honeywell's share of the computer market up a full percentage point in its first year. That success, as well as pressure from other competitors, caused IBM's share to fall over three points.

Now, if there was one thing IBM would not tolerate, it was losing market share. Market share was—and still is—the single most important measure of success at the company, more important even than profit. It had been that way ever since the days when Thomas J. Watson, Sr., took over the faltering C-T-R. He had learned at NCR that a commanding market share provided power to set prices and control the marketplace in innumerable ways. Now his son, Thomas, Jr., was in charge and evidently of the same mind. "I think the main aim of this company must be to protect and expand our position in the market place," he stated in a 1964 memo to a colleague.[1] In January 1966, a particularly difficult time for IBM, he elaborated on this notion:

> It has always seemed to me relatively simple to state the goal [of the company] in the following fashion—that IBM should attempt to maintain its market share in the immediate and foreseeable future with the idea that with the industry growing as rapidly as it is, other companies can grow quite rapidly under this general mandate. It would seem to me that any variance from this goal toward a goal of maximizing profit would surely see us, over the long term, reducing the total amount of our profit as our market share reduced. I have always felt that as someone in a discrete field, like data processing, decided that they would try to pick and choose the areas in which they wanted to be strong, that they were embarking on a dangerous and frivolous course, because in so doing they make it easier for their competitors and they reduced their effectiveness to compete across the board as their market share declined.[2]

The elder Watson, like his mentor Patterson, would have been pleased by his son's turn of mind: fight it out across the board, in every contested area of the market, and get as rough as need be to win. To lose market share is to risk losing future profits. If a choice has to be made, go for market share first—profits can wait because they will be much easier to earn once market share is back up.

Watson, Jr., had good reason to be explicit about what he wanted. IBM in the early 1960s faced competitors on many fronts: the H-200 in the commercial market, the Control Data 6600 in the large-scale scientific market, and a half-dozen or so other commercial and scientific competitors that were in hot pursuit of IBM's high profits. By grabbing bits and pieces of market share, the competition threatened to cut IBM off at the pass. In a single year, by its own measure, the company lost 3.6 percentage points while Honeywell almost doubled its share (Table 7).

Determining accurate percentages of market share, as the *above* figures try to do, is no simple task, but it was done often at IBM, especially when the heat

Table 7

Percent Share of Dollar
Value of Installed and
On-Order Data Processing
Equipment of IBM and
Competitors, 1964–65[3]

COMPANY	1964	1965
IBM	80.0	76.4
Burroughs	2.1	2.8
Control Data	3.0	3.3
General Electric	1.8	2.2
Honeywell	1.5	2.5
NCR	2.4	2.5
RCA	1.9	2.5
Sperry Rand	5.4	5.5
Other	1.9	2.3

from the competition rose. Even IBM's own analysts had a difficult time, faced as they were with various types of products (i.e., computers and unit record equipment, as shown in Table 7), different product lines, and different yardsticks (i.e., dollar value or units). Just months after Watson's 1966 memo was written, a group of his executives presented a comprehensive analysis of the company's share of the computer business alone. They concluded that "although the information is based upon various units of measure, i.e., purchase value, monthly points, net position, the 1965 information indicates ... the IBM share is about 70–72%." Looking ahead ten years, they foresaw IBM then as still having its "fair share" of about "70% of the total."[4]

The experts can quibble about the accuracy of different methods and about how market share should be properly measured, but what was most important at IBM at the time was not the absolute number but the change. In 1964, IBM was watching its bloated share slip. It was enough to cause panic at the very top of the corporation. "By '62 we were beginning to hurt in the field," Watson, Jr., commented later in a retrospective memo:

By the spring of '64 our hand was forced and we had to, with our eyes wide open, announce a complete line—some of the machines 24 months early, and the total line an average of 12 months early. I guess all of us who were thinking about the matter realized that we should have problems when we did this, but I don't think any of us anticipated that the problems would reach the serious proportions that they now have.... [We] were so up against the wall saleswise that had we waited another nine months to announce the line we would have lost positions that we could ill afford to lose.[5]

If he felt this strongly about IBM's losing market share, one wonders how its much smaller competitors, whose market share was at most less than a tenth that of IBM's, felt about the impact of IBM's rushed announcements. But then, IBM has a different sense of what its fair share is. In 1970, in the context of analyzing the use of computers in management science, an IBM executive stated that "it is vital that IBM adopt . . . a strategy in order to capture its fair share of a lucrative new market and maintain its current share of an existing market."[6] And what was that "fair share"? "[IBM's] management science strategy is to maintain a 70% share."

The power to "maintain market share," to stop competition from eroding its position, was clearly available to IBM. What it needed was some means of orchestrating that power, of managing it so that resources were used as effectively as possible. IBM's dominance, in fact, was carefully planned through a series of two- and five-year plans that determined goals and sales quotas for each level of the corporation. In 1966, a two-year plan's primary goal was stated as "MAINTAIN MARKET SHARE."[7] Detailed and voluminous, the plan lays out a series of strategies to be followed in each of a variety of market segments, and it concludes with a discussion of market shares measured before and those expected after the plan was executed. IBM states that its share (based on a still different measure of the value of then-installed and on-order equipment) was slipping from 78 percent in 1964 to 76 percent the next year, but once the plan had done its job, the erosion would stop and IBM's share would level off at 74 percent in both 1967 and 1968.[8]

IBM rushed its famous System/360 systems in to the breach to stop Honeywell, Control Data, and other competitors. It was the mere promise of that family of computers, as much as their actual installation, that saved the day for IBM. IBM's telling customers about the System/360 helped it corner an overwhelming share of the fast-expanding market for computer systems, even though several models of it did not make it into customers' hands until almost two years after their April 1964 introduction, IBM's share of unfilled orders, only 68 percent in January 1964, climbed to 81 percent by November 1965, just before actual deliveries began.[9] Having captured most of the orders, IBM then had to make good on delivering what it had promised, which was a great deal. Producing the 360 systems was a far larger task than IBM had planned for, but not even their technical flaws prevented the machines from doing their job: winning the lion's share of the expanding computer market for IBM.

IBM's immediate concern, as it prematurely announced the System/360 was protecting its share of the commercial market in general and, in particular, in neutralizing the Honeywell H-200 as quickly as possible. If Honeywell were too successful, IBM knew, other manufacturers might catch on and begin building similar IBM-compatible machines. IBM could not stop the Liberator, however, simply by dropping 1401 prices across the board. To be effective, a price cut would have to be quite drastic, and, worse, it would have to be deepest at the high-price, high-profit end of the 1401 product line. A broad price cut would also discourage users from moving on to the 1401's successor, the System/360. If prices were cut solely on the most threatened, large 1401 models, the effect would be similar: low-end users would rush up the 1401 scale to take advantage of the price cuts instead of moving to one of the 360s waiting in the wings. Suddenly, the requirements of IBM's functional pricing, the source of its profits, were a great burden and were being used against it. Yet discarding that pricing scheme in favor of cost-based pricing would simply be too high a price to pay in lost profits just to stop the still-small Honeywell.

HIT AND MYTH

Ready or not, IBM unveiled the System/360. It solemnly promised customers a broad line of computers —six models to begin with, with several others to follow—that were to "revolutionize" data processing for years to come. The 360s were described as providing an unheard-of range of function and raw computing performance.

Despite a long list of initial problems in technical design, development, and manufacturing, the 360 family generated revenues and profits that far outperformed initial projections. Although they were expected at their April 1964 introduction to bring in revenues of $7 billion, the 360s actually gave IBM close to $16 billion in revenues and more than $6 billion in profits. Within six years of their introduction, more than 18,000 of the systems had been installed in the United States. As a result of that enormous success, the 360 line radically reshaped the burgeoning computer industry. The line quickly became the central core of IBM's business, and its descendants, the System/370s, function even today as the main source of IBM's dominance in the computer market. The machines' popularity created de facto technical standards that became the basis of federal laws and of the business plans of dozens of new companies. More important, the System/360 helped IBM push several competing suppliers of complete systems right out of the market.

So damaging to other systems makers were the 360s that in 1969 the Justice Department's Antitrust Division filed a wide-ranging case against IBM that was to last thirteen years. In the course of that trial and the twenty-odd private antitrust actions it prompted, many thousands of IBM financial documents and strategy papers were put on the public record. From them can be drawn a picture of how IBM exploited market power that was wholly unavailable to Burroughs, Sperry Rand, Honeywell, NCR, General Electric, RCA, or any other company.

Because of its unquestionable success in the marketplace and the sentimentality of the many people for whom it was a first computer, the System/360 has attained mythical status within the industry. Popularly accepted history has it that in the early 1960s a group of prescient engineers and marketing men at IBM came up with the idea of building a family of computers that would use identical programming and peripheral devices and whose range of performance would be broad enough to satisfy the needs of all sizes and types of customers in both commercial and noncommercial markets. In their now famous SPREAD report to upper management, these IBM planners formulated the 360 family concept as a means of providing users with a smooth growth path through successively larger computers while also giving IBM manufacturing economies of scale. The family was called the 360 to reflect its all-encompassing breadth of function and performance.[10]

IBM, the thought was, would no longer need to design, build, and maintain different sets of disk and tape drives, printers, and other hardware attachments for a variety of families of processors, as it had for the second-generation machines. For the 360s, all peripherals would work with all processors. More important, IBM's costs—and those of users—for writing and supporting (through constant debugging and enhancement) programs for these systems would be greatly reduced because now a single set of programs would work on any machine. Customers would benefit from not having to rewrite their applications or suffer other common disruptions each time they moved to a larger system.

The popular myth of the 360s thus centers on the systems' supposed technical superiority over their competition and on the making of several crucial decisions by IBM's managerial elite. These two factors, it is claimed, helped the company overcome the 360s' admittedly awkward beginnings and win what *Fortune* described in an oft-quoted story as a $5 billion-dollar we-bet-the-company "gamble."[11] To this day, IBM is only too willing to encourage acceptance of this view, for it draws attention away from the true reasons for the machines' commercial success. Paeans to technological and managerial "excellence" support IBM's later argument in court that the 360 family was "one of this country's greatest industrial innovations."[12] But IBM documents from the time show that exactly the opposite view was held, that IBM concluded that its vaunted 360s were actually "mediocre."

IBM was hardly pushing the state of the art when, in April 1964, at several dozen press conferences across the country, it unveiled the first six models of the 360 family. Not long after that, in November of that year, C.R. Bashe, group director of technical planning at IBM, told Watson, Jr., and other top IBM managers that in seven out of ten major technical areas (e.g., processor performance, disk and tape drives, communications, and programming) the 360s were only equal or inferior to competition.[13] Calling Bashe "the technical conscience of the

IBM company," Watson expressed shock, dismay, and disappointment at the wrongness of the decisions that produced the 360s.[14]

Was this "excellence" in management? Was this the best IBM could do against its tiny competitors with the enormous resources at its disposal? If so, why was B.O. Evans, the man with worldwide responsibility for developing the 360 family and other mainstream products, transferred out of that job in late 1964 to the backwater of the Federal Systems Division? Evans himself described his demotion as a "punishment" and a "spanking" for having neglected time sharing and other technical aspects of the initial 360 models. A December 1964 memo from Watson to his brother Arthur reads, "I think B.O. Evans is one of the most dangerous men who has ever been employed in the IBM company. He is dedicated, loyal, able. However, his judgement of what the competition can do against him led the company and his team to follow blindly toward mediocre results."[15]

But Watson knew better than anyone that IBM's success was not the result of technical prowess: "Because we've been operating in a fortunate position all through our technological history compared with our competition, we have been able to generally take safe, conservative steps, and our percentage of wins has been exceedingly high. All you have to do is recall Bo Evans' presentation of the last week to understand that we rarely lose."[16]

The 360s' technical failings were further underscored by the experience of Dr. Fred Brooks, Jr., a principal designer of the machine from 1961 to 1965. By February 1967, he had left IBM to become director of the Research Triangle Computation Center in Raleigh, North Carolina, which served three local universities. That month, he told IBM that he was disappointed over the late delivery and poor performance of its large 360 model 75 system. "I have had some inputs over the last week that indicate we are still having some difficulties with Dr. Brooks' installation . . . ," wrote an IBM manager of the complaint. "I understand there is a question of an acceptance test for his equipment and this is in some way related to what he considers to be poor performance on his equipment and difficulties with the programming system.

"I believe this is an almost untenable position," the IBM manager continued, "in that the father of the System/360 hardware and OS/360 is taking that kind of position about the equipment and the programming he helped bring into the world."[17] Evidently, the company couldn't accept that a former IBM man such as Brooks would actually demand that IBM prove its system's worth by submitting it to a performance test. But "the father of the System/360" (an inflated description—Brooks initially opposed the 360 and later was responsible primarily for the machine's software) was probably one of the firm's toughest customers at that time.

Among the major problems IBM identified with its new machines was their lack of competitiveness against non-IBM scientific machines of all sizes, its lack of time sharing, its inability to operate with more than one processor in a system, its reliance on an outdated logic circuitry, and its ungraceful hulk of an operating system, OS/360. IBM had to spend considerable time to remedy these flaws, some of which still linger in its product line.

Consider just one of these, the operating system. IBM had promised a great deal when first describing OS/360, but it was for a long time unable to deliver much of that ambitious program's planned functions. "With programming," commented T. Vincent Learson, IBM president, in 1966, "we did what the late Charles Kettering, an engineering genius and President of General Motors Research Division, always advised against: we put a delivery date on something not yet invented."[18]

The operating system would make the 360 machines far easier to operate and program than any previous machines, IBM claimed. It would incorporate many of the tedious and detail-oriented housekeeping tasks that otherwise had to be performed by costly technicians. But the program was riddled with bugs when it was first delivered and, despite some 2,000 programmers who were thrown at the problem, it was more than two years before the mess was even partially straightened out. What was finally delivered as OS/360 was far less robust than what had been promised by IBM in 1964; IBM simply "decommitted" certain of the functions it had originally promised, leaving them out because they were too difficult to program properly. Never before had such a large programming effort been attempted, and IBM had vastly underestimated the time it would take to complete it. Although OS/360 had originally been slated to serve on any and all 360 processors, it soon grew so large and inefficient that only the biggest 360s could make good use of it; smaller machines received a stripped-down version called DOS/360, for disk operating system, and thus a major incompatibility was introduced into the 360 line: programs written for small DOS systems would not run under the control of OS/360, or vice versa.

"The blow-up [in program complexity and/or program development efforts] of OS/360 comes as no real surprise to Product Test,"[19] stated that group at IBM, which had direct responsibility for inspecting products early in their development cycle and advising management of their commercial feasibility. The Product Test Department had identified OS/360's problems early on, but its warnings had gone unheeded in the corporation's higher echelons. A month before the 360s were unveiled, Product Test advised top management that proper testing of OS/360 could not possibly begin until five months *after* the product's public introduction. A few months later, the director of programming wrote, "I have been saying for a year that there is considerable functional and schedule performance exposure in proceeding with announcement prior to Alpha test . . . the purpose [of which] is to establish feasibility"—meaning that in their rush to block Honeywell and the others, IBM management had simply skipped the main step in its formal product testing procedure.

The inevitable result of IBM's haste was late deliveries and dissatisfied customers. After stating in October 1965 that deliveries of 360 systems would be delayed by two to four months, IBM officials told the board of directors that 11 percent of the outstanding orders would miss even that schedule by a month, and a similar portion would miss it by even more. Some 360 deliveries would be as much as eight months late.[20]

"Henceforth, we will instruct our people to avoid like sin ... any announcement before its time," wrote John R. Opel, then a marketing official, on June 6, 1966.[21] Perhaps Opel's people did not receive his message or they just liked to sin, for in fact they would preannounce products many times again.

BETTER EARLY THAN NEVER

Is there anything wrong with introducing a product before it is ready for market? All companies do it, so is IBM any worse for doing it, too? From one perspective, IBM's 360 promises helped users by spurring the competition into greater action—one can argue that they developed even better machinery than might otherwise have been the case. But when a company with as much power as IBM preannounces a product merely to counter the success of a much smaller firm, it is troublesome. After all, Watson, Jr., had warned his workers to avoid tactics "which IBM possessed solely because of its size and reputation, and which, therefore, [were] unavailable" to competitors.[22]

In fact, in terms of that admonishment, IBM was being quite unfair. Its very size and reputation in the marketplace gave its promises much more weight than sketchy details of some future product waved at customers by a smaller firm would have. The latter would likely find that its promises of a product line as all-encompassing as the 360 would meet with a good deal of skepticism, at least until some tangible evidence of the line was produced for customers to touch and inspect. In IBM's case, however, customers believed what they heard precisely because of the company's dominance. Despite the recent failure of STRETCH, IBM seemed to have the cash and technical knowhow necessary to successfully complete any project it undertook.

Yet it might be asked, what happened when customers later discovered that IBM was unable to deliver as promised? Didn't IBM suffer? Not particularly. In some cases, IBM's competition had superior products that were deliverable before the 360s, but IBM's promises dried up their market, and by the time IBM was finally able to deliver, the competition had simply packed its bags and left. A group of IBM customers went so far as to draft a resolution accusing IBM of originally promising many features on its 360/67 time-sharing system when competition existed but of withdrawing those features once the competition was no longer a threat.[23]

In other cases, customers seemed to be aware of the technical difficulties that IBM confronted in building the ambitious 360s, and they simply forgave the company when it was unable to deliver all that it had originally said it would. And finally, IBM was able to take advantage of a certain momentum it had generated: some of its most sophisticated customers were more than glad to help IBM work out the difficulties in its new machines.

How does a company determine when it is legitimate to publicly introduce an as yet unfinished product? IBM had established formal procedures for introducing products, but in the end it violated those rules in its rush to shore up sagging market share. "A seller may not sell or offer to sell products," the company's *Business Conduct Policies* stated, "until such products are actually in production and can reasonably be expected to be ready for delivery when promised, without risking charges of unfair trade practices."[24] To which Watson, Jr., added in a separate memo, "It is clear that the most fundamental requirement in releasing products is the assurance that performance of the product will be satisfactory both to the customer and IBM. Therefore, all new products must be thoroughly and unbiasedly [*sic*] tested."[25]

To perform such tests "unbiasedly," IBM had set up the Product Test Department as separate from the marketing organization. It established three levels of testing, the most important of which was the so-called A test, which was designed to "show whether the principles of the project design will indeed work"[26] and to check out "the soundness of the approach, the validity of the material produced so far, and the likelihood that ... [the] product will perform as its specifications say that it will."[27]

At a time when Honeywell was "Liberating" 1401 customers by the dozen, however, and Control Data was delivering the 6600, the fastest computer that scientific customers had ever seen, IBM simply overruled Product Test when it refused to sign off on premature 360 products.

Now, it was certainly management's prerogative to take this kind of business risk. There is nothing blatantly illegal about doing so. But if major problems arise later in the preannounced products, as happened with the 360s, management is foreclosed from claiming surprise. If it had waited until the product passed the A test, management would have been more aware of the problems before introducing the products instead of after. If management refuses to see the risks, it cannot easily be excused when it stumbles. IBM's refusal to act more prudently is all the more surprising because of the recent STRETCH episode. There, IBM had learned the hard way the dangers of prematurely announcing a system using new technology. That it would do so again so soon after STRETCH is just more evidence that the company did not merely make a mistake with the 360s but was following a conscious strategy of propping up its monopoly by stopping even the limited success of its much smaller rivals. IBM's promises were primarily designed to buy time.

To meet the demands of upper management that market share be maintained, IBM's marketing force had several options open to it. An effective but occasionally risky option was to discreetly disclose sketchy information about upcoming products to selected customers, especially to those that were leaning to another vendor. The message IBM's salesmen wanted these wayward customers to receive, even if it wasn't stated in so many words, was, don't buy theirs, wait for ours—it's still on the drawing boards, but it will be bigger, faster, cheaper, and better. Although effective, whispering to customers like that violated IBM's *Business Conduct Policies*; the guidelines threatened dismissal for any employee who made a "proposal or mention to a prospect of a commercial product before it has been officially announced when done to thwart a specific competitor." Nonetheless, this tactic was used and worked particularly well against Control Data, which saw orders completely dry up for eighteen months after IBM began talking prematurely of a specially designed line of scientific 360s, the model 90s.

Customers with pressing demands for extra computing capacity, however, were unlikely to wait long unless given some concrete details of IBM's upcoming product. If too many of that type of customer were vulnerable to competition, IBM would be forced to "put up or shup up," to either disclose a product, detailing its features, performance characteristics, and price, or lose the business to competitors. Believing such announcements, customers assumed the products were real, fully thought out, and planned, perhaps even soon to be delivered. Based on that seemingly solid information, customers placed orders—orders that might otherwise have gone to a legitimate competitor. In the end, however, IBM had trouble delivering what it promised, but by that time many of the order-starved competitors had been severely damaged.

Finally, IBM could price its phantom and real products with aggressively low prices. So low, in fact, that rivals with shallow resources could find themselves unable to compete and throw in the towel.

The most honorable action for IBM would have been to fund a more extensive research and development program to perfect its ambitious product line. But that would have meant delaying the public announcement of the products and permitting competitors to erode the fringes and perhaps even part of the very core of its monopoly. "We would have lost positions that we could ill afford to lose," said Watson, meaning that it would be hard to win back customers who left for other suppliers.[28]

THE 360s GO TO BATTLE

The 360 line consisted of a spectrum of processors, the first six of which were labeled models 30, 40, 50, 60, 62, and 70. Each was more powerful than the one before. The first four models were designed for commercial processing, while the last two were to handle scientific work. As competitive threats and manufacturing problems dictated, further models—the 20, 25, and 65 for commercial processing and the 44, 67, 85, and several models in the 90 series—were brought out; the 60, 62, and 70 were withdrawn without ever being shipped.

The 360/30, or model 30, was aimed directly at Honeywell, but it didn't exactly stop the Liberator dead in its tracks. In fact, Honeywell's assault may have even gained momentum when 1401 customers found out that the new IBM machine would not run their valuable application software without costly rewriting. In many cases, it was easier to move a 1401 program to the Liberator than to a 360/30. It seems that when beginning to design the 360s in 1961, IBM had purposely decided to make them incompatible with the 1400/7000 series. IBM had planned for those earlier machines to remain installed with customers through 1968, figuring that by then there would be little trouble getting customers to make the switch to a 360—thanks to new technology, the price and performance advantages would be just too much to resist. Ironically, IBM's attempt to reduce incompatibility in its product line, the 360 family, was itself incompatible with previous systems.

The pre-Liberator plans had called for the 360s' incompatibility with the 1401 in order to delay many 1401 customers from moving to the new systems too soon. They would thus be forced to lease their installed 1401s for longer than usual. Extended leases meant bigger profits, which were to be used to help pay off the substantial costs of bringing out the 360s. But purposely overlapping the two product lines, a common strategy in the computer industry, backfired when Honeywell's Liberator arrived unexpectedly and took advantage of the glaring vulnerability in IBM's pricing.

Despite the model 30's incompatibility (eventually ameliorated through an emulation facility that enabled the machine to use 1401 programs just about as is) and despite the problems making certain 360 components work, the problems writing OS/360, and all the late deliveries, IBM's panicked introduction of the 360s eventually led to success. Evidently, customers at first believed IBM's new 360 machines would do just what the company claimed they would, and by the time they found out different—that deliveries would be many months late and that peformance would fall short—it was too late for them to change their minds. But IBM was taking no chances. Its pricing of the 360s would push the memory-based pricing scheme of the 1401 to such extremes that much of what little competition was left was doomed.

6. Divide and Conquer

Avoid as a strategy objective maintaining or increasing market share or competitive position at least where the market share is currently in excess of 50%. Use the term market leadership which is sufficient to get the point across. Similarly, avoid such phrasing as "containment of competitive threats" and substitute instead "maintain position of leadership."

—IBM's lawyers' advice to its executives[1]

Seeming to support IBM's innocuous explanation of the System/360's success—that the machines were technically superior and IBM's managers were smarter than those of the competition—is the fact that, on the average, IBM's prices were higher than competitors', and that the average profitability of the 360s was at traditional levels, if not higher. As usual when confronting IBM products, competitors priced their systems between 10 and 15 percent under the 360s' "price umbrella."[2] As a rule of thumb, competitors have always had to undercut IBM's prices by at least that much on comparable or even superior gear just to catch the attention of the cautious customer for whom IBM's reputation as the most reliable and "safe" supplier weighs heavily. Nobody ever lost their job buying from IBM, the old saw goes. Had IBM priced the 360s well below competitive systems, their overwhelming success might easily be explained. But on average, according to company documents, each of the major commercial 360s was priced to earn IBM's traditional profit rate of 30 percent or so: there is no outstanding reason to suspect the company of having simply priced these machines at cutthroat, unprofitable levels.

A closer look at IBM's own analysis of its famous product line, however, reveals major flaws in this argument, some of which were shown in the previous chapter. In fact, to drive the technically troubled 360s to success, IBM once again exploited monopoly power that was wholly unavailable to competitors. It was price discrimination—setting prices high, relative to cost, on equipment that faced no competition, and setting prices low where competition was effective—

that made the 360s so successful and so profitable. Indeed, it will be argued here that, in effect, IBM gave away entire 360 systems to win those few strategically important customers that were otherwise free to take their business elsewhere at any particular point in time.

It is fairly well known that IBM's scientific and noncommercial 360 systems were priced to lose money. That issue will be examined in the next chapter. Less well known is that IBM used this same tactic in the much larger and more important commercial computer market. There, too, IBM offered systems at prices that were below its own cost.

SEGMENTS OF POWER

The data processing industry underwent rapid growth and change during the 1960s. As industry revenues skyrocketed, computers quickly became indispensable to corporations and governments throughout the world. Computing became more methodical—writing application programs, for instance, shed its alchemical nature and was seen as able to benefit from traditional engineering techniques—which greatly helped electronic data processing systems weave their way into daily commercial activities as never before. Machines that could store and process information were recognized as strategic weapons in virtually every industry. Meanwhile, innovations in computer design brought astounding calculating power to scientists and engineers. Every new computer that was installed stimulated more creative minds to dream up new applications for them. That enhanced the computer's mystique, but, more important, it also fueled the demand by customers for more computers. As the 360s came to market, computers were no longer perceived simply as replacements for punch card machines. They were quickly proving to be an entirely new species of industrial tool whose range of application seemed boundless.

As the 1960s progressed, IBM found itself operating in a market quite different from that of a decade before. As IBM raised the overall profit rates of its commercial computers and completed the shift of its monopoly away from punch card machines, its competitors also shifted the focus of their computer efforts to the rapidly expanding commercial business. Many had previously done best in noncommercial, scientific markets where the cost of entry was far lower. With new technology making never-before-seen types of computers possible, however, several neighboring market sectors emerged as areas where competitors might establish footholds and from which they might later expand into the commercial arena. General Electric, for instance, was specializing in time-sharing computers, and Control Data was coming on particularly strong in high-performance scientific computing. Because the 360 line was initially almost totally incompatible with previous IBM computers, competitors figured they had a good chance of cutting IBM off at the pass and capturing its customers before they got hooked on a 360.

IBM was quite aware of its weaknesses and the threats it had left itself open to. IBM's plans from that time read:

> Individual competitors, by developing expertise in a particular industry, market and product areas have collectively, *significantly raised the total capabilities of our competition.* We therefore can plan that competition, when viewed in the aggregate, will have a more effective position in the marketplace.
>
> In the *traditional administrative and accounting areas* competition will continue to be active with IBM customers. However, *their success or failure will primarily depend on trading share among themselves.*
>
> In other areas in which IBM is broadening its base we will face mature, *experienced competitors firmly entrenched with customers, as well as new competitors* which will have specific areas of competence that can be marketed with considerable effectiveness. (Emphasis added.)[3]

A later IBM document stated:

> IBM must *vigorously contest* competitive price/performance threats in our traditional area. IBM must also be on *guard against the intentional or unintentional abdication of any significant growth segment* of the marketplace to competition. Competition can be expected to concentrate their thrust on the new growth areas where IBM is not entrenched. . . . Here they can get in on the ground floor of rapid growth areas without meeting the severe contention of our main line strengths. (Emphasis added.)[4]

To defend its "traditional area" of strength—commercial systems—and to protect its newly exposed flanks, IBM had to divide the overall computer market into several isolated segments and offer a tailored 360 system for each one. In areas where it was relatively weak, where it was "not entrenched" and competitors were effective, prices would be set low to stop competition and capture a major share of an emerging market. These segments included entry-level commercial computers, large 1401 users where the Liberator and other potential copies lurked, and in the entire noncommercial market, where it now faced some distinguished competitors selling truly innovative systems. Quite simply, IBM had to discriminate between customers who were free to choose and those in whom the software hook had already been set. The latter, of course, could be used to subsidize competition-stopping systems. The best vehicles for isolating market segments from each other, it turned out, were the processors and their memory—though IBM did continue to functionally price its peripherals, also.

"In this way," the document explained, "specific application areas can be optimized and installed position [i.e., the number of specialized machines built] . . . limited to a reasonable quantity, thus *meeting competition in their own field and minimizing IBM . . . exposure.* No other alternative strategy [can] be visualized which accomplish[es] these objectives to this extent." (Emphasis added.)[5]

A price-discrimination scheme similar to that used on the 1401 would still work, IBM knew. But because of the real threat posed by Honeywell's highly successful Liberator strategy, IBM evidently decided it had to drop entry-level 360 prices to the absolute limit. This would ensure that those 1401 users contemplating a move would seriously consider an entry-level 360 before jumping ship to Honeywell. In the long run, Honeywell's economic viability—and therefore the long-term threat it posed to IBM—depended on building a large enough base of customers to be profitable. Very-low-priced entry-level 360 systems would frustrate that mission and ensure IBM's dominance.

This quiet knockout plan required cash to subsidize the low-priced and money-losing machines. IBM, in fact, had unmatched cash resources at this time. Its pockets were being fed by three high-profit areas of its data processing monopoly. There remained a tapering but still sizable revenue stream from the aging punch card machines, weighty rental payments from the many large 1400/7000 series systems still in place, and, once shipments of the 360s got under way, recurring lease payments from a swiftly expanding base of 360 users who would become irrevocably locked in to the high-performance, high-profit reaches of that product line. Between 1960 and 1971, IBM's total fund of cash and marketable securities grew from $400 million to $1,800 million, all of it available to finance any money-losing activities it might require.

No other vendor had as big a bankroll as that. In fact, all but a few major computer makers operated without profit while competing with the 1400/7000 and 360 ststems. As IBM's history has repeatedly proven, it doesn't much matter what great technology or clever marketing ideas some rival might have to offer. They can't compete long against an IBM product priced below cost. As with the 701, the 702, and the STRETCH before, the 360 floated its way to success on a river of cash. Even Honeywell, as successful as it was with the Liberator, had trouble making ends meet. IBM, evidently, was quite confident that most of its competitors could not afford to match the breadth of its whole product line and would have to settle for attacking narrow slices of the fast-expanding data processing pie: "It would appear that only a few companies will be able to sustain an 'across-the-board' marketing program. . . . It is highly unlikely that there will be a 'late entry' that will attempt to compete 'across the board' due to the huge financial outlays required."[6]

The prediction was correct. Not only would there be no more new "across the board" competitors, but one by one over the next decade, several of those that had competed broadly against IBM would find it impossible to continue at all as their losses painfully mounted. Denied sufficient bases of locked-in customers from which to earn the profits necessary to successfully match IBM's price discrimination, General Electric, RCA, Xerox, and Singer simply gave up and left the marketplace. Honeywell, Sperry Rand, Burroughs, Control Data, and NCR saw little expansion in their base of commercial customers after that, except when they bought the computer business of one of the failed companies. More than a few of their ledgers were bloodied by the 360s.

EQUAL BUT RARELY BETTER

A major contradiction to the myth of the 360 is shown in the company's own rating of the individual system models. Surprisingly, the enormously successful 360s were ranked by IBM as technically merely equal to those of competitors. Rarely did any of the major 360 models rate as superior, and in several cases they were found to be plainly inferior to the competition. It was for this reason that according to IBM's records its 360 systems only won about one-third of the procurement situations where they faced competition. (See Appendix C for specific IBM data.)

During the 360s' active marketing years, IBM drew up Quarterly Product Line Assessments, or QPLAs, which provided comprehensive evaluations of each 360 system model for the Data Processing Group, which actually marketed the machines. Each was rated in comparison to competitive systems of similar performance and price. In only a single case out of twenty-four ratings (the six commercial models rated at year end for four years) was an IBM machine rated superior to its competition—that was the model 50 in 1967. Nine of the ratings showed IBM as "deficient"; in the rest, the machines were only equal. By 1970, all models but the model 65 (rated equal) were deemed deficient. Clearly, according to its own assessment, IBM's products held no great technological edge over the competition.

How then did IBM win so much of the business? In part, it was because most of the business was not contested. IBM measured each machine's "competitiveness": each was given a number that reflected the portion of sales situations in which the machine was actually confronted by a competitor. It found that during the 360s' peak years, the various systems faced competition an average of only about a third of the time (36 percent). The main reason for such a low percentage of systems being contested was software lock-in: few rival vendors could spend thousands of dollars to prepare a bid for a customer who they knew was already using IBM gear and had become heavily committed to it. There was little chance the rival could win, no matter what price it put on its machine or how superior that machine might have been, because in many cases the customer was moving from one 360 model to another and was already locked in by his application programs. In other cases, the customer was being directed by a corporate data processing policy to buy from IBM only: large, multidivisional companies often sought to have each of their individual data processing centers standardize on systems from a single vendor to facilitate easy communication of data and application programs between several systems and to avoid the redundant training of personnel. As the biggest supplier of data processing equipment, IBM enjoyed the benefits of such factors more than its rivals—evidently about two-thirds of the time.

IBM collected further evidence of the strength of software lock-in. During each of the years 1967 through 1970, IBM saw only a fraction of one percent of its installed machines replaced by those of competitors. This was particularly ironic in 1970, when the vast majority of its commercial systems were rated deficient. IBM had little to worry about by then, however, because its customers had been made aware of a new set of IBM promises in the form of the System/370 successor product.

Software lock-in had other ways of holding customers tight to the IBM fold. Even the initial failure of OS/360 seemed to do IBM little harm. Most customers ordered 360s based largely on what the company had promised to deliver, and they waited patiently for it to remedy the operating system's initial problems. Faced with the Honeywell Liberator onslaught, in 1966 IBM reckoned it would lose about 200 orders for the 360/30 over that system's active life as a result of continuing delays and problems with OS/360. Later, however, it concluded that "this loss of 200 systems is no longer expected, with one reason being customers' already expended effort in planning for System 360." In other words, the time, effort, and money users had invested to prepare for the installation of a 360— investments in staff training and perhaps beginning to convert their application programs from 1401 format—was a further aspect of software lock-in that limited users' choice. Just for IBM to win an order was enough to adversely affect its competition—even when IBM failed to deliver as promised, competition still could not win.

COMMERCIAL VS. NONCOMMERCIAL SYSTEMS

IBM financial data (see Appendix D for a description of IBM's Greybooks—the source for the following financial data) show that it expected commercial 360s to bring in far greater revenues and profits than noncommercial systems. Looking forward seven years from December 1966, a year and a half after the 360s were unveiled, the company forecast total commercial 360 revenues to hit $9.3 billion; noncommercial revenues were to reach only $1.3 billion. Profits in the two markets were expected to be $2.9 billion and $158 million, respectively. In contrast, when it had been forecasting the 1400/7000 series' income a few years earlier, IBM had expected noncommercial revenues of $1.6 billion—higher than for the comparable 360 revenues—and commercial revenues of only about half ($5.2

Table 8
Projected and Actual Revenues and Profits for 360
Systems, 1966 and 1970[7]
(in $ millions)

| | 1966 Study | | 1970 Study | |
	REVENUES	PROFITS	REVENUES	PROFITS
Commercial	$9,288	$2,931	$14,170	$5,827
Noncommercial	1,253	158	1,810	292
Total	10,541	3,089	15,980	6,119

billion) those of the 360s. The greatest growth, therefore, would be found in IBM's home court, commercial data processing.

In 1970, near the end of the 360s' economic life, a study of its financial performance showed that the market for all 360 systems was even larger than had originally been projected.

The 360 product line was more successful than had been planned largely because customers ordered more hardware and kept it installed longer than had been originally expected. The overall profitability of commercial 360s as a percentage of revenues was projected to be 31.6 percent in 1966, but by 1970 the figure was measured to be about a third higher, a whopping 41.1 cents profit on every dollar of revenue. At the same time, noncommercial 360s showed a lower overall profit rate, projected to be only 12.6 percent in 1966 and actually measured at 16.1 percent in 1970. The difference in profitability certainly conforms to the notion that IBM was weakest in noncommercial markets—there, as the next chapter will show, it would have to fight hard, if unfairly, to win.

Where the 1401 had once been IBM's most popular system, among the 360s, the small model 30 would earn the most profits:

Table 9
Expected Total Revenues
and Profits for Major IBM
Commercial Systems
(1966 study—in $ millions)[8]

SYSTEM	TOTAL REVENUES	TOTAL PROFITS
360/20	$1,644	$ 492
360/30	3,914	1,241
360/40	2,027	709
360/50	926	307
360/65	776	185
Total	9,288	2,934

Together, the commercial models 20, 30, and 40 were projected to earn 82 percent of the total commercial system revenues. That made these machines particularly important to IBM's 360 strategy. In order to understand more about their pricing, consider the average monthly rental that IBM expected in 1966 from its major commercial 360s for the years 1967 through 1971:

Table 10
Average Monthly Rental Price for IBM's
Commercial Systems, 1967–71
(in $ thousands)[9]

SYSTEM	1967	1968	1969	1970	1971
360/20	2.5	2.8	3.0	3.2	3.3
360/25	—	—	6.5	6.9	7.1
360/30	9.8	10.0	10.2	10.3	10.3
360/40	18.7	18.7	20.9	20.7	20.4
360/50	31.1	32.8	33.6	34.3	35.2
360/65	53.3	60.3	61.9	63.7	65.3

In general, each model's average monthly lease price was about double that of the next smallest system. However, these numbers are averages, and each user's system contained a different mix of peripherals and memory; so a customer moving from, say, a model 30 to a model 40 would probably move from a larger-than-average 30 to a smaller-than-average 40 system. The change in monthly rental that he would see would actually be less than the doubling in price that these data indicate. Note also that over time the average rent was expected to increase as the systems were enlarged with more memory and extra peripherals.

THE STRATEGIC GIVEAWAY

The core of IBM's business has always been commercial data processing—preparing payrolls, balancing accounting books, tracking inventories and incoming orders, and so forth. As noted earlier, this type of processing is quite different from that sought by scientists and engineers, for whom the computer remained a comparatively simple, albeit extremely powerful, calculator. Commercially oriented computer systems required not sophisticated arithmetical capabilities but rather the ability to move and sort long lists of data stored on punch cards, magnetic tape drives, and, with increasing importance during the 360 era, magnetic disk drives. The arithmetic needed to prepare a payroll was trivial compared to the complex task of sorting employee names and preparing perfectly ordered tax forms. As these data show, commercial data processing was the biggest target for IBM and its competitors.

This is not to say that noncommercial computing was unimportant to IBM— far from it. IBM perceived any and all computer makers as potential threats to its commercial business. Its tactics against noncommercial competitors were particularly aggressive, but they wouldn't have been as easily employed had IBM not had so solidly profitable a footing in the lucrative commercial market. Hence, the commercial 360 business will be described first.

The main tasks confronting IBM as it brought the commercial 360s to market were two: it had to beat competitors such as Honeywell, RCA, NCR, Burroughs, and Sperry Rand to as many orders from newcomers as possible and hang on to its traditional share of the commercial market, while at the same time achieving rather ambitious goals for profits and the corporation's growth as a whole. Accomplishing those goals required that IBM price its machines to appeal to first-time computer users, get them locked in to a 360 to prevent them from leaving to the competition, and begin moving them to more sophisticated systems where IBM could earn high profits. These were essentially the same methods as those used during the second computer generation, but they were applied more severely. Evidently, the company had panicked over Honeywell's success and was determined not to lose any more business, even if it meant pushing its price discrimination to the limit.

As with the 1401, the three major, separately priced components of a 360 system were its processor, its memory, and its peripherals. (Software remained bundled into the hardware price until late in the 360s' active life.) Each component came in a variety of models that varied as to performance, function, and price. (There was also similarly ample opportunity for IBM to discriminate between new and locked-in 360 users when pricing peripherals.)

Let's consider the processors first, for they were the one component that was unique to each system model and that largely determined its overall performance and target market segment. IBM's five main commercial 360 processors were the models 20, 30, 40, 50, and 65, each of which could be equipped with varying amounts of memory and, respectively, larger sets of peripheral devices such as disk and tape drives, printers, and remote communications gear. Except for the model 20, these commercial processors were software-compatible with each other to a degree—they could share data and application programs among themselves.

As with the 1401, adding memory to a processor helped improve a system's performance, often dramatically. IBM labeled the various sizes of its 360 memories alphabetically, beginning with the 4,096-byte B size, the 8,192-byte C, and so forth, up to the 1,048,576-byte J memory. Following industry convention, however, we can round these numbers off to kilobyte (1,000-byte) notations that follow the powers of 2: thus the B is a 4K memory, the C an 8K, and so on up to the 1000K, or 1-megabyte, model J. Not all 360 processors used all sizes of memory, but the faster the processor, the bigger the maximum memory it could use.

Table 11
Memory Configurations for Commercial 360 Processors[10]

| | Memory Sizes Available | | | | | | | |
Processor Model	4	8	16	32	64	128	256K	512K	1 Meg.
360/20	B	C	D						
360/30		C	D	E	F				
360/40			D	E	F	G	H		
360/50					F	G	H		
360/65						G	H	I	J

Again, the smallest memories were designed to appeal to first-time computer users, particularly in the models 20, 30, and 40 range, which was where IBM expected most customers leaving punch card machines or 1400-series computers would enter the 360 spectrum. If IBM was in fact discriminating in favor of these first-time customers, we would expect those processors to show low profits. By the same token, processors with large memories, used by customers that were locked in to IBM through their having valuable application programs to run, would be expected to have high profit margins. Indeed, a close examination of IBM's Greybooks reveal just that—and more.

Evidently, IBM was taking no chances—only hostages. These prices indicate that it was more worried than ever about capturing new customers, for in all but one 360 processor, the 50, the entry-level version was priced to lose money in December 1966. And since there were no major differences between processors of the same model using different-size memories, it seems clear that it was again with memory that IBM segmented its market, controlled its customers, and earned profits. The basic processor itself, stripped of all but the minimum amount of memory, lost money, but with each additional increment of memory the profit level of the overall processor/memory combination increased.

IBM gained from this memory-based discrimination in several ways. The lowest-memory processors were very competitive in luring first-time computer customers and those replacing a previous IBM system. But once one of those customers had installed his first 360, it wasn't long before he discovered he needed extra memory to boost his system's performance, most importantly to make room for additional application code. The only supplier of 360 memory was, for several years anyway, IBM, so the customer was forced to pay whatever price IBM charged. Meanwhile, a customer moving from one 360 processor to a larger one in order wasn't likely to install the new machine with its smallest possible memory. Instead, because his application programs often required a minimum memory size to function, he would equip his next processor with at least that much memory. In other words, the customer running a model 30-F would move up to a model 40, say, with at least an F-size memory.

Table 12
Total Revenues, Profits, and Percent
Profit for IBM Commercial CPUs, by
Memory Size
(1966 estimate in $ millions)[11]

	TOTAL REVENUES	TOTAL PROFITS	PERCENT PROFIT
360/20-1 (card system)			
B	$ 15.6	$ −5.8	−37.2%
C	133.2	9.0	6.8
BC	11.8	.9	7.5
D	8.1	1.0	11.9
360/20-2 (tape system)			
B	6.4	−.8	−12.3
C	74.5	15.2	20.4
BC	154.5	32.4	21.0
D	230.8	94.6	41.1
360/30			
C	44.9	−5.2	−11.6
D	279.0	33.6	12.0
E	555.5	160.1	28.8
F	417.7	134.7	32.2
360/40			
D	.6	−.6	−96.8
E	30.8	7.0	22.7
F	167.3	53.9	28.8
G	441.0	153.2	34.7
H	194.6	75.9	39.0
360/50			
F	4.9	.4	8.4
G	98.5	28.9	28.9
H	288.0	88.9	30.9
I	68.0	28.2	41.5
360/65			
G	2.9	−1.7	−59.3
H	79.8	−12.0	−15.1
I	94.1	4.3	4.6
J	8.4	1.2	13.9

IBM was naturally pleased to find 360 customers moving up its memory scale as fast as they did. Ironically, IBM's failure with the OS/360 operating system only helped. As that master control program grew like Topsy, it required much more memory (double, in some cases) than initially planned to run efficiently. When finally delivered, OS/360 turned out to be massive—most of its code had to "reside" in memory, not on disk. The code continued to grow, too, as additional functions were added to it; the result each time was less memory space left for customer programs. All customers could do was expand their systems' memories to make room for the IBM software and their own—all to IBM's profit. Only a monopolist can gain when it loses as well as when it wins.

Another factor fueling memory expansion was the unexpectedly strong appetite customers showed for additional tape and, particularly, disk drives. Each extra peripheral called for additional control programming in the processor. IBM documents of the time make repeated mention of customers' expanding their 360 memories: "The shift to larger models (an average increase [in monthly rent of $600] per [processor]) has occurred for two basic reasons," IBM found for its typical model 30 customer. "The [memory] requirements for programming systems has increased. . . . More files, tapes and card equipment is being sold with each system which in turn requires more [memory]."[12]

The pressure on the customer to expand his processor and memory was inexorable. IBM estimated in December 1966 that customers would rent their entry-level 360/40-D processors for an average of only fifteen and one-half months, while larger E, F, G, and H models would remain in place for sixty-six, fifty-five, fifty, and forty-seven months, respectively.[13]

What were IBM's actual profits from this extra memory? Repeating the calculation performed earlier, we can conservatively estimate that IBM's cost for memory was about $1,000 per kilobyte in 1965 (the 1401 comparison was for 1,000 bits, or only an eighth as much memory capacity), which fell, thanks mostly to automated manufacturing, to only $100 in 1970. Its prices, however, remained constant during that period and ranged from $1,220 to $2,880, depending on which processor the memory was packaged for. At those costs and prices, profits were initially healthy, to say the least. And they became even more so with time, so that one can safely say that IBM effectively gave away entry-level processors in order to attach high-profit memory on to them. By the end of the decade, IBM's memory prices were so far above cost that several independent firms smelled a highly profitable opportunity and attempted to enter the market with 360-compatible memory at prices much lower than IBM's.

The alert reader may be wondering if IBM might not have compensated for the low or negative profits on entry-level processors and memory with high profits on peripherals. This is a legitimate question, for, after all, IBM was traditionally strong in disk and tape drives and it faced no direct competition in those products as the 360s first came to market. What's more, of the $10.5 billion in revenues expected in 1966 from the 360 system line as a whole, more than half, $5.8 billion, was to come from peripherals. Mass storage devices, the disk and tape products so necessary to commercial computing, alone were to bring in $3.5 billion.

In fact, IBM financial data show quite the opposite: the most popular entry-level mass storage device, the magnetic tape drive, was priced to break even at best. Profits from 360 peripherals were indeed high, but only from those higher-performance products that appealed to locked-in customers. IBM's prices once again discriminated greatly in favor of the free-choosing entry-level customer. The strategy was to close orders from first-time customers with simple if only marginally useful systems that carried highly competitive price tags. Later, with little disruption to daily operations, extra memory and peripherals would be installed to boost significantly the 360s' overall productivity.

Consider the tape drive, the successor to the punch card and the standard means of storing and entering large amounts of data to entry-level 360 systems. The key characteristic of this device, as far as system performance is concerned, is the rate at which it moves data to and from the processor, the so-called data transfer rate. The higher that transfer rate, the better the processor is served with data and the more work the system as a whole can perform. The data transfer rate is determined by the density at which data are stored on the tape and by the speed at which the drive moves those data past the read/write head, or sensor.

IBM's tape drives for the 360s were known as the 2400 series and consisted of various packaged combinations of the basic tape transport, the 2401, and supporting electronics. The performance of these different packages—the 2401 alone, and the 2402, 2403, and 2404, each of which combined several transports with electronics—was dependent essentially on the transfer rate of the 2401, which came in three submodels, the 1, 2, and 3. Each transferred data at progressively higher speeds: 30,000, 45,000, and 90,000 8-bit characters per second, respectively. IBM later came out with even higher-performance models of the 2401, the models 4, 5, and 6, which respectively doubled those rates. Facing no competition whatsoever in 360-compatible tape drives, IBM characteristically priced the various 2400 packages functionally, as Table 13 shows.

Most popular with entry-level customers were the tape drives with the lowest performance, those based on the slow-transfer-rate model 1 transport. Those, of course, were priced to earn zero profit. Such prices only helped make IBM's entry-level systems that much more competitive and alluring to the many new customers IBM wanted to get its hook into. Certainly these model 1 tape drive prices did nothing to make up for profits dropped out of entry-level processors and memories.

A low-performance tape drive was introduced in April 1965 just for the small 360/20 and 30 processors. This model 2415 transferred data at only 15,000 characters a second, and at first it came in three models—the 1, 2, and 3. Again, the entry-level model 1's profit rate was a mere 0.7 percent.

Disk drives, discussed in later chapters, offered far greater mass storage per-

Table 13

Expected Revenues, Profits, and Percent Profit for Various Models of IBM 2400 Series Tape Drives (announcement study—in $ million)[14]

	TRANSFER RATE (Kbps)	REVENUES	PROFITS	PERCENT PROFIT
2401				
1	30	$ 6.1	$ −.0	−.0%
2	60	8.2	1.3	18.8
3	90	2.1	.8	37.4
4	60	43.7	6.5	14.9
5	120	51.3	15.3	29.8
6	180	29.6	13.2	44.4
2402				
1	30	8.0	−.3	−.0
2	60	25.2	4.6	18.2
3	90	7.7	2.9	37.9
4	60	63.8	7.7	12.1
5	120	132.3	32.8	24.8
6	180	78.5	32.7	41.7
2403				
1	30	8.3	−.2	−.0
2	60	8.3	.7	8.2
3	90	2.0	.4	21.4
4	60	43.9	7.6	17.4
5	120	61.2	13.9	22.7
6	180	26.2	8.4	32.0

formance than tape drives, but they were generally too expensive and technically sophisticated for first-time computer users to consider.

FIRST-TIME VS. ESTABLISHED USERS

We have seen so far that, in general, for the simplest configuration of each of the major commercial 360 systems—a system including minimum memory and the 2401 model 1 tape drive—prices resulted in losses. The customer would have to move to a more complex configuration, one including more memory, higher-performance tape drives, and IBM's higher-priced disk drives, before he began earning IBM any profits. In fact, the pricing described so far actually understates the price discrimination IBM engaged in to capture uncommitted new users.

IBM was willing—and uniquely able—to offer money-losing products just to win first-time computer customers. That was part of its basic strategy. But its own corporate antitrust guidelines plainly forbid such practices: "It is unlawful to favor new customers with special discounts or allowances; the prices to new customers and old customers must be the same."[15] In other words, IBM could not just give away equipment without running afoul of the law. Its pricing had to be able to withstand scrutiny should the antitrust agencies be aroused and begin an investigation.

IBM's clever memory-based pricing carefully camouflaged the favors it bestowed on first-time users. If pushed, IBM could produce the aggregate system profit rates for small, medium, and large systems; such profit-rate averages would be roughly equal and remarkably unsuspicious. But IBM's quiet favoring of entry-level customers actually went further. It had a powerful means of effectively cutting the prices of selected systems and increasing their value to the customer without changing a single number on its published price list or risking antitrust liability.

This subtle tactic entailed providing, at no extra charge, valuable assistance to customers that were either installing their first system or, more rarely, thinking of moving away from the IBM fold to another vendor's equipment. The amount of assistance that IBM was capable of delivering—to help a customer analyze his data processing needs, plan his application software, and even write his software for him—was essentially limitless. The early technical problems with OS made IBM's support services that much more valuable to customers. IBM supplied such support services at no charge—their price was said to be bundled into the standard price the customer paid for his system. The hardware price included an unspecified amount of support and software at no additional charge, an amount that IBM could and did vary for its own purposes.

Data showing the economics of bundling and its effect on customers' choices must be looked at in a way that is different from the previous discussion of price discrimination. Instead of focusing on specific models of equipment, we must consider the size of IBM's accounts—that is, the amount of money each customer was billed every month. This amount varies, of course, according to how many systems a customer had installed, their size, and the number of peripherals attached to them, among other factors. Table 14 shows the number of accounts by size, measured in terms of equivalent monthly rental dollars for 360 systems in 1967. Table 14 shows that the majority of IBM's accounts were small; the top two categories, large-medium and large, together accounted for less than 1,000 accounts. Table 15 shows the typical system and monthly rent an account in each group might have installed.

Table 14
Distribution of IBM Accounts,
by Size Category, 1967[16]

SIZE OF ACCOUNT	NUMBER OF ACCOUNTS
Small (under $2.5K)	20,279
Small-Medium ($2.5–10.0K)	5,206
Medium ($10–50K)	2,374
Large-Medium ($50–100K)	430
Large ($100K and above)	430

Table 15
Account Size and Average System Size, 1967
(lease systems data)[17]

SIZE OF ACCOUNT	TYPICAL SYSTEM IN SIZE CATEGORY	AVERAGE RENT (IN $ THOUSANDS)
Small (under $2.5K)	360/20	$ 2.5
Small-Medium ($2.5–10.0K)	360/30	9.8
Medium ($10–50K)	360/40	18.7
	360/50	31.1
Large-Medium ($50–100K)	360/65	53.3
Large ($100K and above)*		

* Accounts of this size would have more than one system installed.

When the distribution of IBM's installed equipment is broken down into similar groups, however, a quite different pattern emerges. Here are the percentage of monthly rental dollars that IBM collected from each machine-size category.

By 1967, more than half of the value of all 360 equipment had been installed in IBM's largest 430 accounts. Indeed, the top two groups together comprised less than 1,000 customer accounts but represented 63 percent of the installed base. (This major concentration of system value in a small collection of customers has persisted: in 1974, IBM estimated that 75 percent of its business came from only 1,350 of its customers. Moreover, it expected that over 90 percent of the growth in the years 1974 through 1978 would come from its largest 1,200 customers.)[19]

To understand how these relatively few customers were discriminated against in favor of the many thousands of smaller users—including those strategically important new users—it is necessary to understand how IBM calculated and apportioned overhead costs when preparing its accounting records for the 360. Overhead costs are those associated with building and marketing products but

Table 16

Distribution of IBM Accounts
by Lease Value[18]

SIZE OF ACCOUNT	SHARE OF LEASE VALUE
Small (Under $2.5K)	5.4%
Small-Medium ($2.5–10.0)	9.5
Medium ($10–50K)	23.0
Large-Medium ($50–100K)	12.0
Large ($100K and above)	51.0

that are not directly related to any particular product. Overhead costs must often be covered by a disparate group of products, and some method, very often an arbitrary one, is needed to allocate those costs to each individual product so that its individual profit or loss may be estimated. The statistics used in this analysis are IBM's, calculated to allocate overhead costs directly to various products. Here we will examine the discriminatory impact of these procedures.

Now, there is a legitimate question as to how overhead costs should be allocated to individual products so as to arrive at a total average cost for each unit of production. IBM itself used a variety of such allocations, each based on different criteria, to prepare the 360s' books: product cost, engineering cost, and revenue. Of these, the largest is revenue, which was used to cover costs incurred by the field force, those men hired to provide these highly discretionary services to customers.

In the 1966 study, this revenue apportionment varied from 27 percent for the 360/20, 30, and 40, to 23 percent for the 360/50 and 21 percent for the 360/65. This would seem to indicate that the smaller systems, whose users generally needed the most support services, were charged a higher overhead rate. However, the study clearly states that the differences in overhead rates among processor models are in fact due to the substantial number of large 360s used by IBM itself for internal accounting, administration, and testing of products before delivery to customers.* Because those IBM-operated systems required no support at all by the external IBM field force, the revenue apportionment for all large systems was less than that for the many small systems installed at customer sites. With this exception, IBM's prices covered a fixed overhead charge for all equipment expected to be installed with customers. Each user, large or small,

*According to the IBM Greybooks each of the commercial systems 360/20, 30, 40, and 50 was charged a "normal" 28.69% of lease revenue for this apportionment. However, this apportionment was reduced "Due to Internals": 0% for the 360/20s, 1.09% for the 360/30s, 3.13% for the 360/40s, and 10.69% for the 360/50s.[20]

paid a constant portion to support IBM's field force, according to the company's accounting method.

How, in fact, did IBM use its highly trained and highly valued field force? In 1967, the company had 10,970 such personnel throughout the country. These workers were categorized by IBM as performing three broad functions: 4,003 helped to sell systems, 5,547 installed systems, and 1,421 were charged with providing so-called field engineering, which included tailoring IBM software, developing specific applications for customers, and performing similar services. The field engineers were used essentially to protect installed equipment from competition.

Based on how the expenses associated with these personnel were covered, we might expect that the amount of attention, measured in man-years, given to each account would be roughly proportional to the amount of rent it paid each month. Large accounts paying the most would receive most of the field force's time. However, as Table 17 reveals, this was not the case at all.

Rather than receiving 63 percent of the man-years from IBM's field force, as their combined rental share might indicate, the top two account categories received only 45 percent. The very largest group, running 51 percent of the equipment, received only 35 percent of the field force's time. These were sophisticated users who had substantial support resources of their own—namely, well-trained staff that often had been hired from IBM itself—and they were less dependent on IBM's bundled services. They received less "free" help from IBM.

The smaller accounts, on the other hand, constituted only 5.4 percent of the revenue but received over 17 percent of the skilled time of the IBM field force—more than three times what they paid for. Intermediate accounts got just about exactly what they paid for.*

Table 17
Percent Distribution of Revenue vs. IBM Field Personnel for 1967[21]

SIZE OF ACCOUNT	INSTALLED VALUE	MAN-YEARS	DIFFERENCE
Small (under $2.5K)	5.4%	17.5%	+12.1%
Small-Medium ($2.5–10.0)	9.5	14.7	+5.2
Medium ($10–50K)	23.0	22.9	−0.1
Large-Medium ($50–100K)	12.0	9.7	−2.3
Large ($100K and above)	51.0	35.2	−15.8

*This seemingly insignificant 12% difference between what the small accounts paid and what they actually received amounted to a substantial amount of money. For the 360/20 expected revenues were $1,644 million (Table 9). Twelve percent of that is just $200 million—or almost half of the total profit that the 360/20 was expected to earn.

Although it was hidden in IBM's flexible bundled price, this concentration on small accounts enabled IBM to offer effectively lower prices for small, entry-level accounts than would have been possible if the charges associated with providing the services had been allocated on a more proportional basis. But making the allocations that way would have driven the profit levels on the larger systems up and, more troublesome, driven the profits on those systems used by the smallest users to suspiciously low levels. Alternatively, if the company had priced its services separately, the cost to the customer of installing a first computer system would have soared, and the door would have been opened wide to competitors.

Small accounts got a better deal, and their true profitability was even less than IBM's study indicates due to the distortions introduced by the allocation method for overhead. When the user moved to a larger system after outgrowing his entry-level machine, IBM's profits actually increased, contrary to the profit data for the average system shown in Table 9.

IBM's bundled prices were conveniently flexible. Given the high profit level that its systems earned—generally in the 25 to 35 percent range—the company had the option of adding twice the average value of support services covered by the 25 percent revenue apportionment and still breaking even. And not only could it throw in extra services to accounts where competitors were knocking at the door, it had every incentive to do so. Since other companies supplying computers faced competition on a much higher portion of their bidding situations than IBM did, their ability to match IBM's largesse and still be compensated by other, less price-sensitive accounts was limited. Once IBM captured a user, there would be ample opportunity to make up for any initially lost profits. Once the system was installed and operating, moreover, the customer would need less support, and the IBM field staff would be freer to assist some other new customer. Because services were not separately charged for, this anticompetitive price discrimination was totally hidden within IBM's bundled price. IBM's books looked clean.

The combination of money-losing processor and peripheral prices and additional services not reflected in the profit estimates leads to the conclusion that IBM was in fact losing money on many of the simplest entry-level systems it installed for first-time users of 360 computers. It was in fact buying new 360 users—something its less well-endowed competitors such as Honeywell, even with technically superior and less expensive systems, were in no position to do. And this was all accomplished without arousing antitrust scrutiny.

Footing the bill by paying high prices on additional memory and more sophisticated equipment and receiving less than their share of support services were IBM's 1,000 or so largest customers. At the time, they had no recourse, for there was no other supplier offering IBM-compatible gear.

7. Different Strokes

*Last week CDC [Control Data Corporation] had a press confer-
ence during which they officially announced their 6600 system. I
understand that in the laboratory developing this system there are
only 34 people "including the janitor." Of these, 14 are engineers
and 4 are programmers, and only one person has a Ph.D. . . .
Contrasting this modest effort with our own vast development activities, I fail to understand why we have lost our industry leadership position by letting someone else offer the world's most
powerful computer.*

> —Thomas J. Watson, Jr., August
> 1963[1]

When it came to noncommercial computers, those high-powered, exotically
programmed systems used by scientists and engineers, IBM was fast becoming a
has-been, even as it rushed the System/360 to market. While concentrating on
the more lucrative commercial systems market, IBM had largely neglected the
noncommercial business ever since pulling the plug on STRETCH. Because no
competitor had sufficient financial resources to successfully attack IBM at all
levels of the business at once, each focused its efforts on less contested segments,
or niches, in the hope of gaining entry into the market as a whole. CDC with its
powerful 6600 was pursuing just such a strategy. To foreclose such niche firms,
IBM announced comparable products designed to take the profit potential out
of each neighboring business and thereby prevent entry into its main commercial data processing business.

In the noncommercial part of the business, IBM was hard pressed to defend
its flanks against some of the most innovative systems it had yet faced. Though
the threat was limited, IBM's reaction showed its compulsion to dominate the
entire computer market at whatever cost and violation of its own business practices that required.

Watson, Jr., didn't know it as he wrote the above memo, but he was about to
give the go-ahead to a highly successful scheme that almost destroyed CDC and

wound up costing IBM some $200 million. The scheme relied on a series of specially designed knockout 360s, the model 90s, which for eighteen months stopped CDC and its janitor dead in their tracks. But both the way model 90s were marketed and the prices they carried were so egregiously unfair that they provoked a private antitrust suit by CDC which, when settled out of court, cost IBM dearly.

Meanwhile, in the emerging time-sharing market, where it was equally lacking in workable products, IBM spent over $78 million to hold the line against innovative competition. There, too, it prevailed, but not without breaking its own rules.

A PYRAMID OF POWER

Although it had previously installed many large 7090 and 7094 scientific computers, which gave it a virtual monopoly position in large-scale noncommercial computing, IBM's public killing of its STRETCH system had caused its biggest scientific customers to openly question IBM's commitment to their special needs. The lack of any clear replacement for the 7090s in the initial 360 introductions only confirmed their belief that IBM was more interested in commercial data processing than in advancing the state of the art for scientific users. With its million-instruction-per-second model 6600 system, designed specifically for scientific computing, Control Data Corporation (CDC) reaped order after order from the largest and most important scientific laboratories everywhere.

Meanwhile, small and medium-size scientific users were being wooed by several vendors with systems that were designed to provide just a high-performance engine, as it were, not an entire car, as IBM was offering. IBM's mainline 360 commercial processors had too high a price tag, too little horsepower, and too much excess baggage for cost-effective scientific computing. Moreover, an entirely new mode of computing was becoming viable and opening a promising new market segment. This was time sharing, which broke from traditional batch processing and enabled many users concurrently to interact directly with a large computer through individual terminals. Time sharing offered exciting market possibilities, but here again, IBM was behind—the initial 360 systems had missed this boat entirely.

IBM's Dr. Harwood Kolsky, a senior scientist, explained IBM's predicament thus:

> The computing market has often been described as a pyramid in which a few extremely large users, including the [Atomic Energy Commission] laboratories, are at the top of the pyramid. The market broadens down to include aerospace industries and other government supported groups next,

then the large commercial users and finally, layers of smaller and smaller commercial users. The number of installations increases rapidly as one goes down in size.

If one optimizes a computer design on the basis of income, it always turns out that a design aimed for the middle of the pyramid or the lower-middle of the pyramid will result in far greater total income than one tailored either for the top, 'Gold Chip' customers, or for the bottom myriad of small potential users where the competition is quite fierce.

The [360] market philosophy has taken exactly this point of view and seems to have optimized their whole compatible structure around total profit, which means they have been optimizing around the middle of the market pyramid.[2]

Those few, large "Gold Chip" scientific customers, Kolsky emphasized, "may not represent a particularly *profitable* market but they represent an extremely *influential* market. As they go, so go a great many of the less sophisticated but more profitable customers." (Emphasis in original.) If IBM didn't make a strong showing with the largest scientific customers, the many smaller ones would not be inclined to buy from IBM, either, he argued.

As noncommercial order backlogs at Control Data, Sperry Rand, General Electric, and Scientific Data Systems grew each day, the mood at IBM became something less than copasetic: "Give DeCarlo full, immediate, and direct command responsibility and authority for the marketing steps necessary not to lose any more of these prestige accounts," read an IBM executive memo of September 18, 1964. "Tell DeCarlo we do not want him to lose one of them ... that we want him to blast anything and anybody out of his road who gets in the way of his accomplishing his mission."[3]

IBM's objective was the usual one: Hold the market. Characteristically, it rushed quickly designed machines to market at cut-rate prices. This of course meant settling for relatively low profit rates for the noncommercial 360 processors—the models 44, 75, and infamous 90s for scientific processing, and the model 67 for time sharing. But for reasons described in the last chapter, IBM was confident that it could earn high enough profits from commercial systems to cover its knockout tactics in neighboring arenas.

IBM had serious pricing problems in trying to meet noncommercial competition this way. Its noncommercial 360 systems had to offer a great deal more computing power per dollar in order to attract performance-hungry customers that its commercial 360 models did. But the 360 family was touted as a group of compatible computer systems. If IBM were not careful, its commercial users might choose the better deal and install a noncommercial 360 instead of a lesser-performing but higher-profit commercial machine. IBM's solution to this problem was to make the noncommercial machines incompatible with the others—the two types of machines would not use the exact same programs.

Although selling noncommercial systems was critical to the competition's viability, it represented but a tiny fraction of IBM's total 360 business. In the years 1966 through 1970, the company installed only 214 noncommercial 360s, compared with 18,127 of the commercial varieties. Noncommercial 360s were forecast to bring in substantially less revenues and much lower profits than their more popular commercial counterparts.

For both groups of systems, the most revenue came from the peripherals. Moreover, the profit rates on the major peripherals were consistently in the mid-30 percent range, leading to the conclusion that IBM did not discriminate between commercial and noncommercial customers in peripherals. Its pricing of peripherals was constrained first by their design to be universally usable with all models of the 360 processor. In this case, IBM's technical choice—for an inter-compatible range of peripherals—got in the way of its desire to segment the computer market to its liking. As seen earlier, there was definitely scope within each model of disk and tape drive to functionally price, but there could be no difference in price for the exact same peripheral product being rented to a commercial as opposed to a scientific user.

A second problem was that not only did the noncommercial systems use the same peripherals, but they were introduced after the commercial systems. As a result, IBM had to stick with its established peripheral prices when offering those same peripherals for noncommercial systems.

The central processing unit (CPU) was another matter, however, for each was designed with a particular set of applications in mind: commercial or noncommercial, entry-level user or established user, batch processing or time-shared processing. To a great extent, the processor itself defined a 360 system's identity, the market segment for which it was aimed. As a result, when discriminating in favor of noncommercial users by offering them low-priced systems, IBM was forced to use the processor as the main vehicle for its price discrimination. To win an order for a complete noncommercial system meant that high peripheral prices had to be counterbalanced by extraordinarily low prices on the processor.

In fact, IBM was quite willing and able to price noncommercial processors substantially below cost. For simplicity's sake, suppose that to meet a competitor's prices IBM had to cut the price of a complete 360 system that normally went for $100 by 15 percent, to $85. The 1966 study shows that, on average, peripherals contributed 64 percent of a 360 system's total price and the processor contributed the remaining 36 percent. The hypothetical $100 system's processor, therefore, would carry a price of $36, but when IBM cut the full $15 from the processor's price, as it would have to for reasons just seen, the resulting discount would be a whopping 42 percent. That would surely be enough to wipe out even the 30 percent or so average profit IBM usually earned on commercial processors.

However, because IBM's noncommercial systems were in fact more often than not technically inferior to its competitors' and its position in that market was far less secure than in the commercial arena, it had to set prices there at differentials even greater than 15 percent. IBM was prepared to—and did—take extreme losses in order to keep its market share, as when it rushed untested, underpriced, and overpromised 360/90s to market just to stop the immediately successful CDC 6600.

If IBM's intent was to disrupt competition and prevent an attack on its central commercial monopoly, the lower the price, the greater the disruption. Given the small role that noncommercial systems played in IBM's overall business, it is hardly surprising to find that the company priced the machines for only marginal, if not negative, profitability. Table 18 shows the average profits and losses IBM expected in 1966 from various 360 processors:

Table 18
Profit Rate for IBM Commercial and Noncommercial 360 Processors (1966 study)[4]

Commercial CPUs	
360/20	23%
360/30	25
360/40	35
360/50	32
360/65	7

Noncommercial CPUs *	
360/44	6%
360/67	−20
360/75	−35
360/90s	neg.

* As with the 360/65, memory was packaged externally on the models 67 and 75 processors, so the data here refer to the processor alone, with no memory. The model 44 is the only model of these three that had memory installed within the processor cabinet itself, which helps explain that machine's higher average profit rate. (Also note in Table 19 that the model 67 came in two configurations, the model 1 having a single processor while the 2 had two.)

Each noncommercial processor, moreover, showed IBM's characteristic pattern of price discrimination between small and large memory sizes. But for these processors, all the entry-level models were projected to lose money at a higher rate than was the case for commercial entry-level processors:

Table 19

Percent Profit for IBM Noncommercial CPUs, by Memory Size (1966 estimate)[5]

CPU:	TOTAL REVENUE	TOTAL PROFIT	PERCENT PROFIT
360/44			
E	$ 5.63	−1.53	−27.1%
F	19.63	.58	2.8
G	28.51	.67	2.3
H	25.89	5.39	20.8
360/67			
1	29.56	−46.71	−158.0
2	75.96	−35.76	47.1
360/75			
H	6.28	−6.61	−105.2
I	32.35	−20.44	−63.2
J	14.22	−8.79	−61.8

In general, IBM's noncommercial systems were highly suspect. They were rushed into production, promised before IBM had fully designed or tested them, and built at the expense of more profitable products while IBM was short of production capacity. Although the record of IBM's intent is clear for each of these systems, nowhere was it more pronounced than in the case of the model 67 time-sharing system and the model 90s.

NO SHARING OF TIME SHARING

Time sharing was the first example of what is now called personal computing: the scientist or engineer or even the commercial statistician engages in an interactive dialogue with the computer, entering or requesting data, submitting programs for execution, and reading their output form a typewriterlike printer or video display terminal. Time sharing on a computer meant using few if any punch cards—a notion that must not have appealed at all to IBM.

IBM wanted its users, moreover, to install more systems rather than share any idle capacity they might have on an already-installed machine. Nevertheless, it felt pressured to enter the time-sharing market if for no other reason than to stop General Electric. That large manufacturer, a maker of transistors and other electronic components, had concentrated its development efforts on this new mode of computing and was winning prestigious customers from IBM.

Time sharing in the early 1960s was exotic. It appealed to tinkering computer scientists who needed immediate access to their data and programs, to other scientists needing experimental data analyzed quickly, and to commercial organizations where certain large applications required users to interact directly with the computer. Time sharing was made commercially feasible by the advent of disk drives and new programming techniques that enabled a single processor's time to be divided among many users at once. The idea was that a properly programmed system of sufficient power could react so quickly to each usually idle user that he would never have a clue that any other users were sharing it with him.

As the most radical departure yet from the notion of computers as sequential unit record machines dependent on stacks of old-fashioned punch cards, time sharing was a market segment IBM could not safely ignore, even though its original 360 models offered no time sharing at all.

The face-off between General Electric and IBM over time sharing is recounted in IBM memos about a large order from the Massachusetts Institute of Technology. Much advanced computer science research had come out of MIT over the years, funded by General Electric and IBM. General Electric's great advantage was that it had a computer designed specifically for time sharing. Against it, IBM promised the model 67, a standard 360/65 batch processor "patched" up with extra hardware and software to supposedly create a time-sharing system.

Despite personal visits by top IBM brass, GE won the big MIT order. IBM management was not at all pleased, and it decided it had to take its gloves off. "Blast anything and anybody," the order from headquarters read.

IBM hurriedly unveiled the model 67, tagged with a purported break-even price, but rising costs on some of the machine's features and software soon made the system show a growing loss. Proposals to raise the system's price to get an additional $9 million in revenue for further development were rejected because, as a memo of July 28, 1965, from IBM's W. A. Hartigan put it, "we should not go back to customers already contracted with another price increase, particularly after the earlier substitution of the 67 for the 64 and 66."[6] He was referring to two 360 processor models that IBM had withdrawn from the market after finding them unmarketable.

IBM's initial projections of a meager 6.2 percent profit on the model 67 were based on the assumption that its development costs would be shared with those of two other machines, the models 57 and 87. But neither of those ever made it out the factory door. When the 67 was charged for the whole of these costs, the losses were expected just two weeks prior to announcement to be about $3.9 million. In January 1967, IBM projected the 67 to lose $79 million on $138 million in revenues.[7] In addition, each model 67 processor that IBM produced required it to forgo delivery of one-and-a-half much more profitable 360/65s.[8]

In its haste to avoid losing market share, IBM's rush to market with the machine made it bring out a product that was "completely unserviceable in any manner that will result in customer satisfaction," wrote IBM's W. M. Wittenburg in a memo dated October 19, 1965.[9] Nevertheless, IBM's sales force had some sixty-nine orders for the model 67 on their books by April 1966 and 150 orders by the following November. That month, the company suspended all order taking for the 67 after considering its inoperability, and in the following January it "decommitted" several functions. Still the machine ran into operational difficulty, due primarily to the unwieldy Time Sharing System (TSS) software it required to deliver true time-sharing services.

IBM considered withdrawing the machine from the market for legal reasons, if nothing else. "We really have no guarantee that the model 67 can ever be used as a time sharing system in a productive environment," noted a January 24, 1967, memo from E. C. Smith to J. Fahey.[10]

By April 1969, losses for the stripped-down model 67 were projected at $49 million.[11] The next year, 1970, saw General Electric pull out of the mainframe computer business. In later years, the 67 and the TSS would haunt IBM. IBM paid damages to important customers that pressed their claims. It admitted in writing, moreover, to a "creditability gap" on the model 67 to General Motors, which as late as 1974 told IBM that neither the model 67 nor the follow-on 370 products had satisfied IBM's initial model 67 commitments.[12] Its other 360s did not offer time sharing, and the 67 looked to customers like a dead end. The competition would offer time sharing as a basic feature of its machines, making them fulfill more of the 360 degrees than the misnamed IBM 360.

Although they were expensive, however, IBM's promises worked. They held the market, deprived a competitor of orders, and helped insulate its core monopoly in commercial batch processing. Evidently, unlike the NCR of old, IBM had no Gloom Room in which to display the moldy carcasses of the mainframes that fell victim to its expensive knockout tactics.

STRETCH REVISITED

As weak as it was in time sharing, IBM was even further behind its rivals in high-performance number-crunching systems for the largest scientific customers. The STRETCH fiasco had caused many scientific customers to look for alternatives to IBM's machines, and IBM had had very little else to offer since. IBM management was aghast, therefore, to see the tiny upstart from Minneapolis, Control Data Corporation, bring to market what was at that time the most powerful generally available computer system, the CDC 6600.

It wasn't long after Watson, Jr., expressed his ire over that machine in the famous memo at the top of this chapter that IBM's Dr. Harwood Kolsky proposed a plan to win back the hearts and minds of prestigious scientific customers. "Only a bold stroke will save the day," Kolsky insisted. IBM needed to offer a "super-STRETCH" with "at least five times" the performance of that failed machine, Kolsky said, encouraging his superiors to pull no punches against CDC. This machine "should deliberately be done as a competition-stopper ... [and] it should deliberately be done as a money-loser (or more tactfully, a shared-cost development for the benefit of the Government)."[13]

So began the 360/90 episode, an exercise of monopoly power that, when the final bill came in, put IBM back more than $100 million for designing and occasionally building a handful of knockout 360s, and another $100 million-plus in lost assets when it essentially gave CDC an entire division, the Service Bureau Corporation, to get that company to withdraw its antitrust suit. IBM's "bold stroke" against the CDC 6600 followed a script that, except for the technology involved, could easily have been written by the rapacious Patterson.

Of particular concern to IBM was the Atomic Energy Commission (AEC), one of the largest and most important customers for advanced computers and an organization whose needs Kolsky had gotten to know well during a consulting job there. The AEC (like today's Department of Energy) had a truly insatiable appetite for computing, for much of its work involved simulating nuclear explosions. These simulations took many hours, if not days, to complete on even the fastest computers. Each time a faster system became available, AEC scientists pushed it to its limits, too, expanding their simulation programs to use as much number-crunching horsepower as they could get. The AEC was a "pace-setter," a highly visible customer whose choice of scientific computers influenced the choices of other important customers. It was distressing, therefore, for IBM to find that, as Kolsky reminded Watson, "almost all of the AEC Laboratories presently have competitive equipment installed or on order, much of it earmarked to replace IBM equipment."

Worse, Kolsky noted, these labs were strongly considering a policy of standardizing on CDC 6600s, which they deemed as "more modern and more nearly [fitting] the standard scientific problems of the AEC than does the IBM product line which they feel is now becoming too expensive and obsolete technologically." The labs, he added, "have always, at least until recently, shown a preference for IBM equipment." IBM now had only 10 percent of the outstanding orders for AEC machines, "instead of the 70 percent which one would expect from our percent of the total market.

"IBM, by not having a STRETCH-like pace setter in the market, has lost a great deal of this psychological advantage in the computing industry," Kolsky went on. "This has largely been taken over by the CDC 6600 . . . which gives [CDC] the prestige of being the pace setter in the computer industry."

Kolsky pointed out that IBM's standard marketing approaches—"apply[ing] the proper marketing posture" and talking to the "right people"—wouldn't get too far with brainy AEC scientists or with their peers in the three dozen or so other "Gold Chip" scientific accounts he had identified. "They are much more apt to be influenced by a straightforward scientific discussion of the technical problems and solutions."

But talking scientifically about the products it could deliver was not something IBM was particularly well prepared to do. Instead, it resorted to telling the AEC and other "Gold Chip" customers about a souped-up 360 designed to outperform the competition hands down. As numerous technical problems continued to plague the model 90's development efforts, IBM announced further variations of it, also with problems, and it ran up a loss of over $100 million. It sold only thirteen of the model 90s, instead of the twenty-four earlier planned.

Months before it was shipped, the machine was priced so low in comparison to cost and to the CDC machine that several levels of the IBM bureaucracy declined to sign off on it and questioned outright the advisability of introducing it. Chief Counsel H. W. Trimble voted against the machines because "the announcement of the Model 90 is motivated primarily for competitive reasons."[14] The Product Test Department also tried to dissuade Watson and his coterie of top managers from introducing it, claiming that there had been no "approved product performance or functional specifications." The machine might or might not work as promised. Financial analyst Hillary Faw argued against unleashing the machine on the grounds that IBM could never justify it to the government as a profitable program, especially "in light of its possible effect on CDC." This concern was apparently taken care of. Just prior to announcing one of the variations of the 90, an IBM executive wrote, "All parties agreed . . . that the price is a legal department price without consideration to the forecast, market assessment, market requirement, competitive pricing, performance or delivery, etc."[15] Watson himself later scribbled in the margin of his copy of the broad complaint eventually filed by the damaged CDC against IBM that CDC's charges were "probably not true except [in the case of the] 91."[16]

Nevertheless, IBM went ahead with the 360/90 plan, and CDC soon suffered. It was unable to book a single order for the 6600 for eighteen months once IBM began telling the small community of potential supercomputer customers that a super 360 was on the drawing boards. Granted, the machine was still being engineered, IBM told the scientific users, but the price and performance could not be beat. Additional 90-series machines were preannounced, each one at a price and performance capability that CDC found most difficult to match.

"Our major competitor in the very large computer part of the market," CDC's annual report for 1965 stated, "is making a highly concentrated effort to hinder our progress by frequent announcements of changing characteristics and new models, at reduced prices, of large computers reported to be under development."[17]

The IBM Management Review Committee agreed with that assessment, as a memo from H. B. Farr recalled: the CDC annual report "blames CDC's declining earnings on IBM and its frequent model and price changes. There was some sentiment that the charges were true.... I expressed the view that CDC's emphasis on our paper machines were not as unfortunate as some other emphasis available."[18]

As expensive as these aggressive tactics were for IBM, there can be no doubt they were successful. The 360/90s swept the field. In IBM's "traditional administrative and accounting areas," competition had been successfully limited to "trading share among themselves." The only opening, those users free from software lock-in, were foreclosed to competition by IBM's low-priced or money-losing entry-level systems. In the areas outside this commercial core, IBM's money-losing products succeeded in "meeting competition in their own field" and thereby precluded any hope of their expanding to threaten its monopoly. Thus did its "mediocre" 360s triumph—not by virtue of their excellence, but through a continuing exercise of power, something IBM had done since before the computer business ever existed.*

---

* For those tempted by IBM's laudatory press to believe that its success comes from an overwhelming emphasis on sales ("At IBM everybody sells!" says "supersalesman" Buck Rodgers in his book, *The IBM Way*), be warned. Relying on a group of gung-ho salesmen, all of whose standard of living depends on meeting the next sales quota or maintaining market share, can get a company into much trouble. The following "morning after" comment is contained in IBM's Management Review Committee minutes from the fall of 1965, when the difficulties of trying to deliver all that its salesmen had promised were becoming soberly clear:

"It was emphasized by Mr. Williams [then president of IBM and the only one to reach that position without serving in sales first] that, while it was proper to encourage the DP [sales] Division to be a voice crying in the wilderness, this should not be the attitude of the senior DP management. Mr. Williams felt that the company had overreacted to DP's pessimism [over competitors' early but relatively tiny success] and that IBM had on occasion reduced profit to such a point that it left no room for competition to breathe.

"Mr. Watson, Jr., made the point that when our products were inferior, we should be particularly cautious about attempting to cure that defect by price cutting."[19]

It appears that at times there is a problem taming salesmen when they reach the corporate suite and have to be concerned about more than just who is going to get the next order.

8. And the Winner Is . . .

From the very beginning, IBM has relied on one thing above all to sell its products: Excellence. It always has been IBM's policy to provide the best possible products and services to customers. . . .

—Buck Rodgers,
The IBM Way[1]

IBM's tactics enabled it to earn great profits and ensured it a continuing majority share of the fast-growing data processing market. More than that, IBM in the 1960s vanquished several rivals' computer divisions altogether and permanently damaged all others' chances of ever establishing comparable strength in the increasingly important computer industry. The fruits of the System/360's great success continue to benefit IBM today.

Long-term, pervasive price discrimination is generally recognized by economists both as a sign of monopoly power and as the single most effective means for maintaining that power. Economists, including several prominent ones who worked on IBM's defense against government charges that it monopolized the computer market in the 1960s, agree that price discrimination can be used by a monopolist to exclude from its market equally efficient or more efficient suppliers and maintain its power. Price discrimination by a monopolist significantly distorts the normal market process by suppressing those competitors. The competitive game is no longer the supplier with the best product, the lowest costs, or the most "excellent" management, but rather the one with the most money.

THE EFFECT ON COMPETITORS

It has been argued so far that IBM's commercial success—its abnormally high profits and market share—derived from its market power rather than from it superior products or management. That power was exercised mainly through price discrimination—spending profits earned in a secure market sector to subsidize

Table 20
IBM System Share and System Profit[2]

	PERCENT OF DECISIONS WON BY IBM	SYSTEM PROFIT
Commercial Systems		
360/50	92%	33.1%
360/20	85	29.9
360/30	82	31.7
360/65	80	23.9
360/40	74	35.0
Noncommercial Systems		
360/75, 85	65%	−17.1%
360/44	43	17.5
360/67	(incl. w/360/65)	4.4

low prices elsewhere. The argument depends on the presence of areas where the competition was insufficiently powerful to put pressure on the high profits IBM was earning there. The simplest measure of competitors' effectiveness is the share of orders they won. IBM's own data (Table 20) show that for commercial 360 systems, where profits were highest, it won a higher proportion of procurement decisions than in noncommercial markets, where its competition was more effective.

Though not a perfect fit, these data do support the argument that IBM's profits were highest where competition was least effective—where IBM won the largest share of procurements. These were the commercial situations where customer loyalty was greatest. But these data also imply something else, namely that if IBM's business had been split among several competing companies rather than monopolized by a single one, profit rates would have been lower. Increased competitive pressure would have given customers not only more computer systems to choose from but lower prices as well.

IBM's competitors had little chance of succeeding in commercial computing against IBM's power. The combination of software lock-in and low-ball prices on IBM products that faced competition successfully contained rivals' efforts. Superior products and lower prices notwithstanding, rival systems makers were unsuccessful in eroding more than a small fraction of IBM's dominant position.

How well did the competition actually fare against the 360? Poorly, whether the measure is by profits or by market share. In 1966 and 1967, IBM studied its competitors carefully and made the following determinations of their profitability:

98

Table 21
IBM Assessment of IBM's and Competitors' Data Processing Profitability[3]

COMPANY	1966	1967
Burroughs	No	No
Control Data	Yes	Yes
General Electric	No	No
Honeywell	No	No
NCR	No	No
RCA	No	No
Scientific Data Systems	Yes	Yes
Sperry Rand	Yes	Yes
IBM	Yes	Yes

Only a few companies were making any money from data processing, and they had generally concentrated not on the commercial systems business but on selected niches of the noncommercial market. Control Data sold scientific processors, Scientific Data Systems and General Electric devoted themselves to that and to the time-sharing market, and Digital Equipment concentrated on the minicomputer market. In general, the companies trying to compete directly against IBM for the commercial data processing business—Honeywell, Burroughs, NCR, and RCA—lost money.

During the government's 1969 antitrust trial, an attempt was made to determine the cumulative before-tax profits and losses of the U.S. data processing business—IBM and its competitors—for the years 1960 through 1972. The numbers show that while IBM earned more than $7 billion, the other ten systems companies lost almost a combined $1 billion. (See Appendix E for specifics.) If any of these companies was making a profit, it was more than compensated for by the larger losses suffered by the others. The rivals were trading profit with each other and having no impact on IBM.

The double whammy of the software lock-in tying most customers to IBM gear and the low prices IBM used to grab first-time customers left competitors in the commercial sector with little prospect of increasing their base of customers to a profitable level. Competing with IBM across the board forced them to spread their limited resources thin, too thin to be supported by market shares only a tenth the size of IBM's or less. They decided to look elsewhere for profitable investments. RCA left the business, selling its computer operations to Sperry Rand; Scientific Data Systems sold out to Xerox; General Electric's computer business went to Honeywell, which several years later bought out Xerox/SDS; and Singer sold its computer business to International Computers Ltd. (ICL) of Britain.

None of these companies was blind to IBM's power to eventually override their best efforts. A story is told of Max Palevsky, the entrepreneur who sold SDS to Xerox for $900 million, as commenting on the deal, "We sold them a dead horse before it hit the ground." For those willing to take notice, the handwriting was on the wall by 1969, when that sale was made: IBM and its 360 would prevail.

Just how great were IBM's profits compared to those of other U.S. companies? Measuring the relative profitablity of a group of companies is not easy. It is not sufficient to look at the absolute amounts of profits shown on each bottom line, for by that measure small companies would rank inordinately low compared to large ones. Rather, the rate of profit must be calculated and compared to some base figure. But what is an appropriate base? We must first look at the role profits play in our economy.

High profits in a particular market are a signal that more investments should be made there. Assuming that capital is mobile, it can be expected to seek investment in ventures that promise high rates of return. In theory, additional investment in a profitable market should lead to an expansion of production, which in turn should increase the competition between products there. Over time, competitive pressure should in theory squeeze the profit rates on products earning high profits and bring them down to the level of the overall market. When excessive profits have finally been eliminated, additional investments will be discouraged from entering the market.

Theoretically, then, profits should be measured in comparison to the investment that earns those profits. In accounting terms, this means relating them to the stockholders' equity in the company being examined. It is the return on stockholders' investment that attracts the additional investment that expands production. Assuming the mobility of capital, this model implies that over the long term there will be a rough relationship between the profitability of all investments throughout all sectors of the economy. If the general equalization of profit rates does not occur over a long period of time, we can presume that there is some obstacle to the free flow of investment into a particular segment of the economy. Something, some force, some barrier, must be preventing capital from entering that market segment and eroding the profit rate there.

Which precisely describes the data processing market. IBM's profit rate on computer operations—its net earnings divided by stockholders' equity—has come close to being twice that earned by U.S. manufacturers as a whole (Table 22). IBM's profit rate is consistently higher than that of all U.S. manufacturers as a group, as well as that of the top forty-seven manufacturers alone. Although the top forty-seven averaged only 12 percent during the years 1960 to 1975, and all manufacturers averaged just over 11 percent, IBM pulled in an average of

Table 22

Profit Rate* of IBM, the Top 47
U.S. Manufacturers, and All U.S.
Manufacturers, 1960–75[4]
(in percent)

YEAR	IBM	TOP 47 MANU- FACTURERS	ALL MANU- FACTURERS
1960	17.3%	—	9.2%
1961	17.5	—	8.9
1962	17.5	12.1%	9.8
1963	18.2	12.3	10.3
1964	19.1	13.5	11.6
1965	18.5	14.3	13.0
1966	15.8	14.1	13.4
1967	17.0	12.6	11.7
1968	19.1	12.3	12.1
1969	17.7	10.3	11.5
1970	17.1	7.8	9.3
1971	16.2	8.6	9.7
1972	16.9	11.0	10.6
1973	17.9	13.4	12.8
1974	18.2	15.5	14.9
1975	17.4	12.7	11.6

* Calculated as net earnings divided by stockholders' equity.

over 17 percent. IBM earns money at a 40 percent greater rate than the rest of U.S. industry.

It should be noted that for a variety of reasons, the large disparity evident here actually understates the real situation. Within this group are other companies that have areas of significant market power of their own. During this period, moreover, IBM possessed large amounts of cash and marketable securities that none of its competitors, and few other manufacturers, could match. This fund, which ranged from $400 million in 1960 to over $6 billion in 1976, tends to decrease the company's reported profitability because it earned money only at market interest rates. These rates are substantially less than the rates at which IBM's computer products earned profits. So if we deduct this money from stockholders' equity and subtract its earnings from IBM's profits, the company will actually show an increased overall profitability.

Another distortion in the profitability comparison arises from accounting conventions in the area of depreciation. An accelerated depreciation rate causes a company's reported profit rate to seem smaller in the early years of a capital investment than if the depreciation is spread over a longer period of time. By examining a company's cash flow rather than its reported profit, we can achieve a truer indication of its profits on operations. This process tends to remove some of the ambiguity in the treatment of depreciation by adding the depreciation charge back to profits. Recall the younger Watson's comment that IBM "had a cash flow that others didn't have to support a very expanded research and development program."[5]

IBM's staff studied the company's cash flow in 1964 and 1965 and compared it with that of General Electric, one of its biggest competitors. Their study found that although in 1965 GE's revenues were $6.2 billion, or 74 percent greater than IBM's $3.6 billion, and its operating assets were 15 percent greater, IBM's cash flow was $1.1 billion, or 86 percent greater than GE's. The year before, IBM's cash flow had been a whopping 152 percent larger, at $1 billion, compared to GE's $419 million. (Operating assets were defined by IBM as assets used in operations less depreciation.) The moral of the story is, as Watson, Jr., stated, IBM had far more cash on hand to fund research and development and other necessary investments, including expensive knockout tactics.

In the years 1960 through 1976, IBM's estimated adjusted cash flow, calculated as a percentage of revenues, ranged from a low of 35.7 percent in 1966 to a high of 62.2 percent in 1976. This is far higher than its profit rate. Moreover, the cash flow rate at IBM was increasing with time and was more than twice that of its competition.

There is no doubt, then, that during the crucial 360 era, IBM's profits and cash flow were substantially and consistently higher than those of its competition and of other comparably sized companies. What do these excess profits signify? First, that the return on additional investments made by IBM were substantially higher than those needed to induce a comparable level of investment in other markets. But then, maybe the risks faced by investing in IBM were greater than in other markets. Yet an examination of the variability of its profits over time showed them to be much more stable than was the case for firms earning a much lower level of profit. If IBM faced greater risks, they did not show up on its bottom line. Thus, a further irony: extraordinarily high profits that were not earned as compensation for extraordinary risk.

That IBM's profits are both greater than needed to induce investment and unrelated to risk raises the question of what societally useful purpose they may fulfill besides enriching IBM's stockholders. Are the profits actually the fruits of its monopoly? As long as they continue at such excessive levels they cast a pall over all competition that attempts to compete directly with IBM.

Was IBM's unusually high profit rate earned at the expense of an eroding market share? Precise measurements of market share are difficult in the data processing industry. Economists attempting rigorous measurements there often consider myriad factors, arguing that some are more relevant than others, but we can safely skip that debate here. Our goal is merely to establish some indication of the relative size of IBM and the companies it competed with in its commercial computer systems business, as well as any trends.

What is to be measured? The discussion has focused on the computer *systems* business so far. IBM and its competitors made and marketed computer systems, and it is within the system context that IBM constructed its elaborate scheme of balancing prices among various products. That was clearly the domain of IBM's power. But what systems should be included in an analysis? Since the precise boundaries between commercial and noncommercial usage were not always distinct—some scientists performed at least some accounting applications on their machines, for instance—most observers have included all comparably sized computer systems in their measurements. Therefore, we shall include IBM's 360 systems, commercial and scientific, and the comparably sized machines offered by other companies.

Although IBM's and its competitors' systems were made up of separate components that could be mixed and matched in numerous configurations, two points can be made: first, there was always some minimum combination of processor and peripherals under which a customer could not perform useful data processing; and, second, the swapping in and out of components always took place between systems all included in the overall survey sample used to measure market share. (After the 360 era, competition changed from a systems basis to a mixture of systems and boxes, and we shall likewise expand our measurements when the analysis requires it.)

Since IBM, like most industry analysts, traditionally measured its own performance by looking at its share of the value of installed equipment, we shall emphasize the total installed base of systems as opposed to the value or number of shipments. (Again, when the market shifted to selling systems and away from leasing them, other measures based on annual revenues will be considered.)

Within these general guidelines, a multitude of market share data were presented at the government's trial against IBM. Sources included such respected companies as Arthur D. Little and International Data Corporation, IBM's own records, estimates made by the government based on responses to subpoenas, and testimony by IBM's competitors. From all these sources of market share data, each of which was calculated by slightly different methods and based on slightly different assumptions, a range of values can be determined: the highest and lowest estimates of IBM's market share for each year between 1964 and 1972. All other estimates fell between these two numbers each year.

Several conclusions can be drawn from these data. The most obvious and important one is that IBM had the dominant share of the systems market during this entire period. The ten or so systems companies active in the market then were left to fight with each other over 36 percent of the business at the most—

Table 23
IBM Minimum and
Maximum Market
Share, 1964–72[6]

YEAR	MAXIMUM	MINIMUM
1964	82.7%	72.3%
1965	81.8	70.0
1966	76.8	71.2
1967	77.2	69.6
1968	76.1	66.7
1969	76.7	66.6
1970	75.4	67.0
1971	74.6	65.3
1972	74.3	64.1

and more likely they were constrained to only 20 percent or so. There is also a noticeable fall in IBM's average market share, about 8 percent over nine years. This happened during a time when the market was growing extremely rapidly. But this apparent trend may be deceiving, however, because in each of the underlying sets of statistics, IBM's market share was higher when data were limited to only its core monopoly—large systems used primarily for commercial data processing. So we should understand the figures above as the minimum, not average, values of IBM's core business.

Two other factors support the conclusion that IBM's share of the commercial systems business was substantially larger than even these figures indicate. The federal government's share of the total computer market, which is included in these measures, decreased during this period (for reasons described shortly). Also, IBM's competitors often discounted their machines to win contracts, while IBM rarely did so. Because market share calculations generally relied on list prices—not the less easily obtained prices specific to each bidding situation, which were often below list—the market share value numbers for IBM's competitors are likely to be overstated; conversely, IBM's share is actually understated.

Taking those qualifications into account, it is clear that despite a small drop in market share during the ten years following the 360s' introduction, IBM was quite successful in achieving its primary goal of maintaining market share. During ten years of rapid market growth and technological change and in the face of concerted assaults on its stronghold, IBM stemmed an initial loss and kept the vast majority of the data processing business for itself.

IBM's success contradicts basic economic theory. Its unusually high profit rate should have attracted new competitors to its central commercial monopoly. And yet each of the systems competitors that could easily exit the business did so and invested their resources elsewhere. At every turn where they might otherwise have made inroads and expanded their customer bases enough to become profitable, IBM's pricing and marketing strategies neatly blocked their advance. The resulting lack of effective competition—a lack enforced primarily by the wall of software lock-in—left IBM free to price its gear functionally instead of competitively according to cost.

9. Facts and Theory

Our thesis is that during the first three generations of electronic computers, IBM's success derived mainly from its unique position of power and from its exploitation of that power through discriminatory pricing. This success hung on two conditions: first, that throughout much of its wide product line, IBM had great discretion in setting prices, and second, that IBM could successfully partition its business into those sectors where competitors were active and those where IBM was quite secure. After briefly considering additional evidence that IBM did indeed enjoy such pricing discretion and that its market share dropped precipitously in the one major market sector that it was powerless to segment, we can step back and take a broader look at the implications of price discrimination as a way for a monopolist to do business.

SALES VS. LEASING

IBM's discretion in setting prices is seen most clearly by comparing its sale and lease prices for the 360s. The company priced those machines in favor of customers who leased rather than purchased their systems. Had IBM been indifferent to these two classes of customer, it would have earned roughly the same profits from each, but IBM was anything but indifferent. The company wanted very much to discourage customers from purchasing equipment and to encourage leasing. Leasing was a competitive tool that IBM could use to hamper the activities of rivals. They found it quite expensive to match IBM by building up their own large bases of leased machines, for leasing requires clever financing and lots of up-front cash. By emphasizing leasing, IBM forced competitors to divert scarce funds that they might otherwise use for research and development or marketing.

IBM had only agreed to offer its machines for purchase at all at the dogged insistence of the Justice Department's Antitrust Division in 1956. Feeling pressured to resolve the second government antitrust case, IBM had committed itself to abide by all the conditions of the consent decree, including offering its machines for sale as well as lease. (See Appendix A for a relevant section of the 1956 Consent Decree.) But given its power, IBM was hardly constrained by competitive pressure when setting purchase prices. IBM used its freedom in pricing to make purchases less attractive than would have been the case if its prices had been based on IBM's costs. Table 24 shows the expected profit rate these two different prices were expected to earn for IBM:

Table 24

Estimated Relative Profitability of Lease vs. Purchase for IBM Commercial Systems, 1966 and 1970
(in percent profit)[1]

| | Year in Which Estimate Was Made | | | |
| | 1966 | | 1970 | |
SYSTEM	LEASE	PURCHASE	LEASE	PURCHASE
360/20	29	44	27	29
360/30	30	44	28	46
360/40	34	48	35	46
360/50	31	48	35	45
360/65	20	37	32	46
Average	30	44	32	45

In at least two ways, these numbers understate the true extent of the lease-vs.-purchase discrimination. First, IBM's profit projections did not consider the interest it could earn by investing the full amount of cash it collected at the time of installing a purchased system. In contrast, it collected money from a lease in relatively small amounts at regular intervals throughout the lease's term.

The second distortion comes from the fact that these projections were made after IBM had changed the 360s' announced prices: it dropped purchase prices by 3 percent and raised lease charges in September 1966 by 3 percent to alleviate the cash problems that had resulted from the great expense of bringing out the 360s. This was later referred to as the "3-by-3" price change.

The manner in which IBM collected revenues from installed systems actually had little or no effect on its costs. If the average profitability of leased systems shown above is cut by 3 percent and the average purchase profit numbers are raised by 3 percent, we can estimate roughly the differences in profitability at the time of the 360s' introduction. The original leasing profit rate was closer to 27 percent and purchase profits about 47 percent—in other words, purchases appear originally to have been on the order of 74 percent more profitable to IBM than leases.

If IBM's customers insisted on purchasing when it so clearly did not want them to, its prices would "make them pay." Such wide differentials are possible only when a company has great discretion in establishing prices. A company in a highly competitive market in which prices are by definition based on costs would sell nothing if its purchase prices were so much higher than its lease prices. Customers would merely turn to other suppliers offering cost-based purchase prices. But IBM did not operate in a competitive market, for even with these inflated purchase prices, there was substantial demand from customers to purchase its systems. (As will be seen in a later chapter, so many were the purchased 360s that their owners, mostly independent leasing companies, eventually threatened to buy all IBM's equipment leased by customers.)

Recognizing IBM's freedom in setting purchase prices, the Department of Justice attempted to use the 1956 Consent Decree itself to prevent this strategy. The agreement itself contained the explicit provision that purchase prices not "be substantially more advantageous to IBM than the lease charges . . . for such machines."

In fact, however, the Table 24 data from IBM's pricing studies show that 360 purchase prices were at least half again as profitable as lease prices. The moral seems to be that judgments limiting a monopolist's ability to price discriminate, must be diligently monitored and enforced, or they will be ineffective. Based on this evidence the company evidently failed to comply with the Court's Decree, a decree it had accepted in order to stop the Department of Justice's then pending case.

SELLING TO THE FEDS: IBM LOSES ONE

The second condition necessary for IBM's successful price discrimination is that it be able to segment its market to prevent customers of its high-profit products from moving over to its competition-stopping, low-profit products. Evidence that that condition was critical can be seen in the one instance where such partitioning was not possible: in selling to the federal government. Unable to segment the market, IBM lost substantial market share there.

Like all suppliers of data processing equipment, IBM sought the federal government's business, for it was, and still is, the world's biggest customer for computer systems and services. However, the government's size has given it the power to dictate certain terms and conditions in the marketplace in which it buys such gear.

The government's use of computers breaks down into two main categories: military and standard data processing systems. The military market is unto itself, requiring specialized computers of no direct immediate use in the commercial market. But the government's procurement of commercial systems has also diverged from the commercial market because the legislative process has intervened and altered the relationship between supplier and customer.

According to law, all bids for installing such computer systems for the federal government, once the manufacturer had qualified as adequate to the task at hand, were to be evaluated solely on the basis of price and performance. Efforts were made to ensure that each computer procurement was open and available to all vendors. In other words, the government wanted to avoid software lock-in—it wanted to give all vendors a chance at its substantial business and thereby provide itself with the widest range of alternatives at the lowest prices.

One way this was accomplished was by the government's insisting that vendors offer certain government-defined programming languages with their computers. The idea was that the government could then write applications in a common language and run them on any of a variety of machines. The fact that the government's purchases of computers are so large has meant that vendors, often reluctantly, have supported these languages just to gain government business. The language COBOL is a prime example of such a language, as is the currently controversial ADA language.

Efforts by the government to institute such product standards posed a fundamental threat to IBM. Its pricing structure had been built on extracting large profits from locked-in users, but here was the biggest customer of all declaring that all procurements must be open and competitive. To stay in the game, IBM was forced either to drop prices on its high-priced equipment or see its share of the sizable government market drop. However, if it were to cut prices for the government, large private commercial customers would surely demand the same concession, which would lead to the collapse of its carefully contrived pricing scheme. IBM was unable to segment government usage of commercial computers from the private usage of the exact same computers. Since it couldn't segment, it couldn't discriminate, and it lost market share.

So it was that IBM walked away from much of the market—a bitter pill to swallow, no doubt—rather than suffer the loss of profits that would result from a price decrease throughout its product line. Its share of the number of installed systems in the federal government, for example, fell from 54 percent in 1964 to 34.9 percent just two years later. This was less than half the share IBM enjoyed in the private sector and approximately equal to the level at which it won those nonfederal bidding contests in which it faced competition.

When a rigorous comparison of price and performance was made without the protection of software lock-in, government agencies for the most part chose other suppliers. As a result, government business became the major area in which these competing computer companies could establish themselves. The intense competition for government business, however, made it less profitable than many firms would have liked; it didn't provide the resources they needed to fund direct assaults on IBM's commercial monopoly.

SO WHAT?

Even if it is accepted that IBM's pervasive use of price discrimination was the basis for its success, there are those that will ask, So what? What difference does it really make? To see the full implications of strategic price discrimination requires stepping back from the computer industry and considering the strategy in general.

Price discrimination occurs when, over an extended period of time, a supplier can charge different prices to different groups of customers for what are essentially the same goods. As has been seen repeatedly, different prices mean different profit rates. The discrimination is in favor of those paying the low price and against those paying the high price. The reader may ask, Is it not common practice for suppliers to charge whatever the market will bear for their products? Certainly there is no law that says all of a firm's products earn exactly the same profit rate. Price wars, loss leaders, special discounts, fire sales, and the like are fixtures of our economic system and are generally to be encouraged rather than condemned. It is only smart for a firm to charge prices that are high relative to costs, is it not?

Should anyone care if Pepsi, for instance, when engaged with Coca-Cola in a price battle over the soda pop market, charges different prices for the same product in different geographic areas? Gillette's famous success formula was not so different from IBM's: it gave away razors in order to sell blades. Some customers, after all, benefit from these low prices. Lower prices are an incentive for companies to become more efficient, drop prices even further, and make their products affordable to a larger group of customers. Is IBM to be held to a different standard?

The answer is yes, but the reasons why may not be obvious.

IBM and the market it dominates are unique in several important ways. Not only is it the most powerful company in the world and growing rapidly, but IBM dominates the computer industry, which is the single most important industry for the future of the United States and the rest of the world. Computers are not soda pop, and to have the bulk of this critical industry monopolized by one company is of great concern to us all—at least, it should be of concern.

IBM's size and the importance of its markets for the security and economic vitality of our nation, if not the western world in general, demand that it be scrutinized from a different perspective than soda pop and razors are. That perspective should be informed by a concern for what is best for society as a whole rather than by a concern for what is good for IBM. The United States has traditionally valued diversity, freedom of choice in open markets, and personal freedom. Regardless of what public esteem it may draw, IBM's growing accumulation of economic power has ominous implications.

IBM's price discrimination demands attention because it has continued unabated for decades; variations of it continue even today. Unlike other instances of differing profit rates caused by unanticipated changes in demand, IBM's ability to discriminate through pricing over long periods of time indicates that there is something wrong with the organization of the computer industry. We have seen that for three generations of computer systems, the market has not responded as the competitive economic model would predict. IBM's abnormally high profits have not attracted the added competition one would expect. The company has consistently been able to enjoy the best of two worlds—high profits and high market share.

Again, so what? the reader may ask. Perhaps a look at a similar situation in another, more familiar market will shed light on the computer industry's predicament. Traditionally, the U.S. automobile industry has had one dominant company, General Motors. It, too, was able to succeed in highly profitable price discrimination for many years, a former top executive wrote in 1979. GM's "forte historically has been selling big cars."

> Its large profits have come from bigger, more expensive cars. . . . American car customers, historically, have been willing to pay hundreds of dollars more for a few extra pounds and inches in their cars. The returns to the company were obvious. When I was with GM [in the 1960s and 1970s], a $300 to $400 difference between the building costs of a Chevrolet Caprice and a Cadillac DeVille, a bigger car, was compared to a $4,800 difference in the sticker price. The difference in profit to General on the two cars is over $2,000.[2]

Depending on its target customer, the same car, fundamentally, carried widely different prices, one being much closer to cost than the other. GM was able to succeed in this discrimination because consumers are at some level economically irrational: they seek comfort and status more than inexpensive means of transportation. But again, was there anything wrong with GM's selling high-profit Cadillacs when Chevrolets would get Mr. Six-Pack to the shopping mall just as well? The customer, after all, was free to choose. What's the harm?

Let it be said first that this form of price discrimination could never have prevailed as long as it did if the U.S. auto industry had been truly competitive, with a multitude of economically viable manufacturers of comparable size actively competing between themselves. In that case, one of GM's competitors would surely have instigated price cutting by them all by taking advantage of GM's high prices on the Cadillac. In time, even luxury car prices would have fallen under competitive pressure to come more in line with costs. In reality, the industry's structure was quite lopsided: the enormous GM occupied a major share of the business and only a few competitors of any size (Ford, Chrysler, and American Motors) shared the rest. The result of that lopsidedness was that the U.S. auto industry's prices strayed far from true costs.

Long-term price discrimination, practiced by all four major car manufacturers, compelled them to concentrate their efforts on high-profit luxury cars—at the expense of small cars, of course. Had those small autos been enhanced with features that cost less than the extra $400 it took to turn a Chevy into a Cadillac—bucket seats, better suspensions, and fancy interiors, for example—customers would have felt less incentive to buy the high-profit machines. GM's pricing structure, however, forced it to leave its small cars impoverished.

With all the major U.S. automakers playing by the rules imposed by the dominant GM, it was not at all surprising to see foreign competition initiate its attack on the U.S. market at the low end, against the U.S.-manufactured small cars. If GM and Ford did not find it in their self-interest to add a few dollars to the low-priced cars, Nissan, Honda, and Toyota were only too willing to do so. Because they were not active in the luxury car market, they were spared concern about the impact on their product lines.

Worse for U.S. companies and the workers they laid off once things got rough was that the very pricing scheme that had left their low-priced flanks vulnerable to attack severely hampered their ability to respond to the well-targeted foreign competition. As long as the foreign threat remained small, any change by U.S. firms in their pricing would cost more than any gain to be had from denying competition the few points of market share it first captured. Had they enhanced their own small cars, the U.S. companies would have seen many of their customers forgo the Cadillacs and other high-profit models. Their changing to counter the foreign competition was delayed until the threat became sufficiently strong to break these long-held pricing patterns by U.S. suppliers. GM and fellow U.S. companies had been caught in and restricted by a web of their own making, a web that never would have formed around them had they not been so complacent and lacking in real competition for so long.

A more competitive U.S. auto industry—one structured with, say, a half dozen large firms all competing vigorously among themselves; that is to say, an industry more resembling the Japanese market—would not have tolerated such rampant price discrimination. Natural market forces would have eliminated discrepancies such as high-profit Cadillacs. As it was, the lopsided, four-company structure encouraged inefficiency; costs of both management and labor increased far more than the productivity they offered and further reduced the U.S. firms' ability to respond once the foreign invasion began in earnest. Only free competition-defying price discrimination could have funded the inflated salaries enjoyed at all levels of GM and its U.S. "competitors."

The U.S. automakers' response to the waves of Toyotas and Hondas landing on California shores was to pressure Washington into putting a ceiling on imports, but dealers and customers of the foreign cars had enough political clout of their own to ensure a continuing, if reduced, flow of imports. During the many difficult years of defeat suffered by U.S. automakers at the hands of efficient Japanese manufacturers, few have been the voices calling for a restructuring of General Motors. In fact, public opinion seems to have accepted as fact that only a giant firm such as GM can successfully oppose the foreign threat. That GM's dominance and unchallenged price discrimination provoked the Japanese success in the first place is almost completely overlooked.

The lesson to be learned here for the computer industry of today is that long-term price discrimination, which can happen only in a market lacking true competition, affects profoundly how suppliers in that market can and will operate. To the extent that a noncompetitively structured domestic market encourages inefficiency, it also invites attack and erosion by more competitive foreign interests. Efficiency is not fostered in markets with such a lopsided collection of competitors. IBM's enormous resources have not resulted in clearly superior products and lower prices—because, of course, its success did not in fact depend on those factors. Were competitive products and low prices important to its success, IBM would have greater incentive to seek maximum efficiency. But IBM, as was GM earlier, is a prisoner of its own power.

The most disruptive aspect of price discrimination is not that it extracts high profits from customers with few choices but that under the right conditions it is the single most effective method for a monopolist to shape a market to its desires. In the U.S. auto market, GM by its very size was able to dictate price structures that all other domestic car makers found it in their interest to adopt. There was no competitor large enough to stand up to GM and successfully price differently. By the same token, the entire U.S. computer industry—and, as will be seen, that of the rest of the world—is dependent on IBM's tolerance for its survival. By pricing for low or even negative profits with the intent of bleeding smaller, relatively poorly funded competitors dry and protecting its monopoly, IBM has effectively frozen the commercial structure of the technologically dynamic computer market. The outcome of the competitive process is determined not by efficiencies of new competition, superior management, or technical innovation, but only by the amount of cash IBM is willing to spend to maintain control.

THE EXPERTS SPEAK

Although it has not been previously specifically identified in the computer industry or with IBM's success therein, price discrimination has long been generally recognized as a surefire means of successful monopolization. One of John Patterson's peers was John D. Rockefeller, whose Standard Oil monopolized the U.S. petroleum business. "He applied underselling for destroying his rival markets with the same deliberation and persistency that characterized all his efforts,"[3] according to Ida Tarbell, a historian that studied Rockefeller, "and in the long run he always won." Rather than segmenting his market with incompatible processors and memory sizes like IBM, Rockefeller divided his market geographically. Where a small, localized competitor refused to sell out to Standard Oil, Rockefeller simply cut his own prices in that neighborhood until the competitor was run into the ground.

Such brutally effective tactics against vulnerable but otherwise viable suppliers led to the political consensus that adopted the antitrust laws of the early years of this century. The body politic decided it did not want to live in a one-company country, and it wrote laws to limit the ability of powerful companies to preempt the competitive process. It was Watson, Sr.'s, recognition of this very consensus that led IBM to become cautious in publicizing its pricing methods. It was better that people believe its success flowed from its adherence to basic principles like respect for the individual, superior customer service, and excellence in all things.

Much has been written about the theories and methods of monopolies over the years, but ultimately there are two points about price discrimination upon which all economists can agree—even those that worked so vigorously to defend IBM against the wave of antitrust accusations it has faced in the last fifteen years. One point is that such anticompetitive pricing can be engaged in for long periods of time only by a firm with significant monopoly power. The other is that successful, long-term price discrimination gives that firm the power to drive equally efficient but less endowed companies out of the market.

Drs. Frank Fisher, Richard B. Mancke, and James W. McKie, distinguished economists, all worked for IBM's defense, and, not surprisingly, all rejected the notions that IBM monopolizes the computer business. However, even they seem to have no theoretical problem with the idea that price discrimination is an important source of power to the supplier able to successfully employ it. After applying themselves to an intensive study of the computer industry, these three economists concluded that IBM is not a monopolist and that the computer business is indeed competitive. In trial testimony, Fisher, Mancke, and McKie stated this expert opinion, as did Fisher again, with the assistance of John J. McGovan and Joen E. Greenwood, in a posttrial book, *Folded, Spindled, and Mutilated: Economic Analysis and U.S. v. IBM.*

In his foreword to that book, Dr. Carl Kaysen states that he shares Fisher's conclusion that the government "had no case." He writes, "The government's argument was based on erroneous conceptions of competition and a grossly inadequate understanding of the facts. . . . Assistant Attorney General [William] Baxter, who withdrew the government's case as 'without merit' after making his own review, was not alone with Fisher and me in that conclusion."[4] Kaysen has astutely recognized throughout his written work the importance of price discrimination to monopoly power. Obviously, when he reached his conclusion about IBM, he was unaware of the rampant price discrimination IBM was practicing.* If he had been aware of that tactic at IBM, he most likely would not have agreed with Fisher, who claims that "correct analysis shows the computer industry to be highly competitive."[5]

Now, considering only the theoretical aspects of price discrimination—its role as an indication that monopoly power exists and as a tool for exploiting that power—consider what Kaysen had to say in 1956 about a noted antitrust case against the United Shoe Machinery Company. (Kaysen, by the way, states in his foreword to *Folded, Spindled, Mutilated* that any analogy between the United Shoe and IBM cases is "totally inappropriate.") As related by Kaysen in his analysis of the government's case against United Shoe, that company commanded most of the business of producing machines for making shoes, and the existence of price discrimination was taken as an important indication of its market power: "United's behavior in the past shows results which could flow only from great market power, namely continuing wide variations in the relations between prices and costs of different machines."[6]

In fact, Kaysen reports, United Shoe's management freely admitted that its prices were not based on the costs of making the machines, as would be the case in a competitive market, but rather on their value to the customer: "Our terms are really based primarily, and, in fact, on the important machines entirely upon the benefit of the machine to the shoe manufacturer."[7]

Not surprisingly, at 91 percent, United Shoe's share of the market for those "important" machines was higher than its 74 percent share of the minor machines. Where market share was lower, prices had to take into consideration the costs of manufacturing and marketing the machine, although they were still based mainly on user benefit. The same is true at IBM, according to the testimony of Mr. Northrop, the person at the time responsible for its pricing methods. He stated that all its products are functionally priced; that is, according to the value of the product to the user and not the costs to IBM of producing the product.[8] In both IBM and United Shoe, the existence of more effective competition drove prices from an artificial measure of user value down closer to

---

* Because IBM listed Kaysen as a potential witness for its defense, the government took his disposition. At that time, he stated that he had not studied the computer industry, and possibly for that reason did not actually appear to give testimony at the trial itself. His credentials in the area of antitrust and economics, however, were substantial. For instance, he is coauthor with Donald F. Turner of the leading work on predatory pricing.

the actual costs of the machine. Monopoly power, and with it the power to set prices above costs, depends on an absence of effective competition. In the final analysis, this means sufficient power either to deter entry of new companies or to drive active companies out if they become effective. Kaysen himself says as much:

> Monopoly power (market power) has been defined [in a previous antitrust case] . . . as the power to exclude. This is indeed the essence of the matter, for without the ability to prevent competitors from entering the field a firm with a large share of the market must either behave in such a way as not to attract competitors—which means that its actions are hedged about by the threat of potential competition or indeed suffer the entry of competitors who will diminish its market share.[9]

Patterson and Watson, Sr., would have understood Kaysen well, for they were as concerned as United Shoe about actual and potential suppliers of competitive equipment. But how does price discrimination enable the monopolist to exclude both existing and potential competition? Kaysen describes United Shoe as supplying a full, broad line of equipment, while its competitors concentrated on various narrow lines of machines—a situation remarkably similar to that which IBM has enjoyed since the beginning of the computer industry: "The major effect of the full line is the opportunity it gives United to compete against single-line or short-line sellers through price discrimination," he writes.

> An opportunity which exists as long as there are important machines in United's own line which face no competition. By pricing machines facing no competition at high markups over cost, United makes the achievement of success by short-lined competitors much more difficult than it would be if United could not discriminate in price. The potentiality of this kind of competition may be as strong a deterrent to the would-be competitor as its existence is a limitation on the ability of actual competitors to thrive and grow.[10]

Price discrimination, Kaysen asserts, is an effective strategy for the monopolist. Its power "may exist without being used to the full: checking a competitor's growth may, taking all factors into consideration, be a wiser business policy than attempting to exploit to the full every potential weapon in order to drive him out of the market. . . . Price discrimination may enable United to drive out a single-line competitor if the two are equally efficient in producing and marketing the machine in which they compete."[11]

The parallels to IBM and its relatively poor competitors is striking. Even if the monopolist declines to exploit price discrimination as fully as it is capable of doing, the mere potential of the exploitation can be enough to drive off vulnerable competition. When considering IBM's apparent toleration of small, specialized, technically innovative competitors, the question to be asked is not whether IBM *will* exclude them, but rather, is IBM *capable* of excluding them if it should so desire? With so much power at its disposal, it is only a matter of time before IBM decides to "contain" its rivals or even drive them completely out of business. All competitors, regardless of size, technical savvy, or clever marketing tactics, exist entirely at IBM's sufferance.

At the simplest level, IBM's inflated profit levels could allow it to substantially cut all its prices and just break even. Forced to meet those prices, its less-profitable competitors would be driven to losses. IBM's high profits, therefore, are in and of themselves sufficient to give it great power over all its competitors. But rather than such a blunderbuss approach, IBM's strategy has been to segment the market and limit its price cuts to those products that "[meet] competition in their own field and [minimize] IBM . . . exposure."

One wonders why, if Kaysen insists on the theoretical importance of price discrimination to monopoly power, he and his fellow economists who chose to defend IBM did not notice IBM's rampant use of that strategy. If they did notice, it seems to have had little bearing on their conclusion, presented both in court and in the later book, that IBM is not a monopolist.

As seen earlier, IBM's overall profit rate during the years 1962 through 1975 was 17.6 percent, compared with the 12 percent average seen for the top 47 U.S. industrial companies during that period. That 5.6 percent difference works out to excess profits of greater than $4 billion during that time[12] (or about $785,000 per day during this period), profits that IBM would not have earned had it faced effective competition and been limited to a normal rate of return on its investment.

The 17.6 percent rate may well be, as recent defenders of the company insist, the product of managerial "excellence," but the evidence suggests that it is due just as much to the systematic exploitation of the power that IBM held over all its competitors and that it used to shape the market to its needs.* No matter how "excellent" the competition's managers might have proven themselves to be, there was simply no way they could have won without the help of a comparable monopoly.

---

* Even Fisher et al., as convinced as they purport to be that the government had no business charging IBM with monopolizing the computer business, concede that the computer industry may not be structured as efficiently as it might. "Economists may speculate," they admit in a short footnote toward the end of their book attacking the government case, "as to whether it is . . . true that the organization of the industry is in some sense optimal." But they avoid looking any further and conclude that "in view of the unparalleled history of progressive performance [shown by computers] . . . it seems to us dangerous to hope to do better by tinkering with the structure of the industry."[13] It was precisely that structure that the government's antitrust case, albeit imperfect, was attempting to remedy.

CONCLUSION

The importance of IBM's pricing and profits on entry-level systems is in a way comparable to the contours of a well-made knife blade. Just as the part of the blade that starts the cut must be sharpened to as thin and as narrow an edge as possible, IBM's entry-level prices and profits were similarly honed down to get a wedge into the customer's data processing room. Behind the sharp edge of the deeply cutting knife follows the broader and stronger body of the blade. Similarly, IBM's follow-on prices—and profits—for larger systems were greater. Though the overwhelming bulk of its product line was priced to earn high profits, at any given time there was a small group of entry-level products whose profits were thin. As with the knife, what followed was already determined.

There can be pits, rust, or a faulty handle on a knife, but those flaws are ultimately less important in explaining its cutting action than where and how that finely ground edge of the blade is brought to bear. By the same token, knowledgeable chefs will shun a well-advertised knife that bears a fancy handle, gleaming finish, and attractive shape if its cutting edge is no good. The knife—IBM—depends for its success almost entirely on its edge—its ability to capture new customers before the competition does so.

Once caught, these customers become locked in to IBM through their mounting software investment, and IBM can easily charge them higher prices. Of course, high profits eventually prove to be irresistible to competition. Having been stopped by IBM's disruptive, money-losing tactics in the various systems markets, its competition searched out new alternatives to avoid IBM's system-to-system defenses. As Honeywell's Liberator had done during the second generation, this new competition would aim directly for IBM's largest, most tightly bound, and most profitable customers. IBM responded by changing the aim of the cutting edge, moving it away from new, uncommitted customers and toward the newly fought-over large users. IBM also fashioned for its defense a new, smaller knife whose blade, however, was as deadly as ever.

Part 2

The Game Changes

10. The Market Splinters

Avoid loose, inaccurate or unnecessary documents which talk about IBM's market share, either as a whole or in any segment of the market. . . . Avoid references to large customer investments in programming or any other factors which might point towards a "lock in" of IBM's installed customers. . . . Avoid references to the inexperience or naivete of IBM's customers or to their dependence on IBM.

> —IBM legal memo on laundering
> internal documents of
> incriminating material in light
> of Department of Justice
> investigation, July 9, 1968[1]

Charlie Chaplin notwithstanding, IBM's business is based primarily on its overwhelming share of the market for large computers. It is these million-dollar large machines, not thousand-dollar personal computers, that, built on the foundations laid during the punch card era, continue to serve as the solidly anchored base from which the corporation extends its powerful reach.

However successful the System/360 may have been in controlling the dozen or so companies selling complete computer systems in the 1960s, its very success also provoked a whole new form of competitive threat to IBM. There came a time late in that decade and early in the next when IBM's entire mainframe base threatened to be washed away under the combined force of many waves of change.

IBM's customers increasingly were demanding interactive as opposed to batch systems. Moreover, users were combining the work of several small computers onto single large ones, a centralization that created strong demand for access to computers from geographically distant locations. These changes in the very mode of data processing exposed glaring weaknesses in the 360s' basic design as well as serious gaps in the company's overall product line.

As IBM's hitherto most important largest competitors—the Seven Dwarfs, they were appropriately dubbed—scrapped among themselves for the 20 to 30 percent share of the systems market not captured by IBM, a new horde of smaller, mostly young companies also eroded the 360s' profits from several directions at once. These companies did not sell entire systems but rather offered replacements for those components of the 360 that were priced high and that were technically vulnerable.

By 1968, IBM had installed some 14,000 System/360s with customers in the United States. Most of the systems were by then far larger than entry-level size and therefore incorporated large processor memories and many peripherals such as disk and tape drives.

The small, rival manufacturers were allied with still another group of companies that were competing for 360 profits—computer leasing firms. These firms purchased IBM systems and leased them to users at prices below IBM's. Not only did they take away profits and market control from IBM, but they were potential nuclei around which more threatening and more broad-based computer systems companies might form. A flood of talent and knowledge about the making of computer hardware, its marketing and maintenance, and its application to business organizations was leaving IBM in the form of engineers, salesmen, and managers who started their own companies or joined established ones. Many left IBM with vital documents under their arms, further diluting IBM's control of computing knowhow.

Finally, as if changing user needs and attacks from nimble competitors weren't enough, the shadow of the antitrust laws again fell on IBM, forcing it to step carefully. Control Data Corporation filed suit against IBM for its knockout marketing of the 360/90 series, and in January 1969, during its final days, the Johnson administration filed a wide-ranging suit charging IBM with monopolizing the general-purpose computer systems market. The government action and subsequent battles encouraged many private antitrust suits, several of which would be brought by the very same new companies that were skimming the profit from IBM's 360 line.

IBM reacted to all the legal action in part by unbundling the prices of much of its software and service offerings.* Previously, users had been able to choose from a wide range of "free" application software packages and had received "free" help from IBM in writing their own programs. Now each new package and service had a price. That change lured a flock of software companies and consultants to descend on 360 users, further reducing IBM's control of the marketplace. No longer was it quite so easy for IBM to selectively increase the

---

* IBM documents stated that it wished "to be the most bundled unbundled vendor possible within legal constraints." In order to be able still to control customer migration from one system to the next, the operating system was kept bundled with the hardware, a source of control it would use with great effectiveness later.[2]

value of an IBM system by throwing in lots of extras at no charge. Some users were delighted: "I couldn't [consider independent suppliers in the past]," one customer was reported as saying. "My IBM salesman wouldn't let me. Since unbundling my salesman can't tell me what to do anymore."[3] Not surprisingly, outside consultants often steered customers away from IBM's overpriced gear and its often inefficient software. They led users to any of the large number of independent software and service companies that sprang up once there was a published IBM price list against which to compete.

Fueling much of the growth of all this independent activity was the wealth of capital on Wall Street available to practically any company claiming to be in the computer market. These were the "Go-Go Years," and it didn't take much more than a clever name and promises of advanced technology to raise money. Literally hundreds of new firms, most of them trying to sell to IBM's 360 base, jumped into the market. Many brought true innovations with them.

For IBM, therefore, the 360 base, as large as it was, seemed to create as many problems as it solved. The very pricing scheme that had made the 360s such a success now drew the sights of many competitors who, taken together, might cost IBM a great deal of business. The pricing scheme, along with antitrust considerations, initially restrained IBM from reacting too forcefully, but eventually, as the damage mounted, the company reacted strongly. In this observer's opinion, the very survival of its sixty-year-old monopoly was at stake.

To a degree that only a monopolist could have achieved, IBM demonstrated its awesome power over the marketplace by completely reversing its hold, shifting the price discrimination 180 degrees, and dictating where profits were to be made—and lost—by those who had dared to enter the arena against it. Where it had long relied on the memory and peripherals used by its largest, most locked-in customers to earn high profits, the company now found it necessary to slash those products' prices, to manipulate the packaging of new products, and to make up for those lost profits by boosting the prices of products where competition was less effective. It introduced new leasing plans and generally made it difficult, if not impossible, for all new competitors to operate successfully.

IBM rebuilt the marketplace around itself, leaving little space for the newcomers. They complained bitterly in the antitrust courts, competed as best they could by advancing technology and cutting costs, but in the end, a decade later, all but a few had passed from the scene, leaving IBM triumphant and its all-important market share largely intact.

GOING ON LINE

The 1960s saw the very notion of commercial data processing change radically with the rise of interactive computing, which enabled users to communicate directly with the computer through a terminal rather than indirectly through punch cards.

Traditionally, commercial computers had been installed to replace punch card tabulating equipment. As a result, a computer was programmed merely to read data records, to sort and process them, and to print out results. The computer was fed large batches of records, either punched on cards or recorded on magnetic tape, along with a program—the program and its data together were called a *job*. Jobs were entered into the computer one at a time—a sometimes tedious process that kept users waiting hours or even days to see their results. The delay was largely a result of the early computer's not being able to perform more than one task at a time. It could either read cards or process them, for instance, but not both at the same time. However, because many early applications were of a batch nature—a bank updating accounts each night, for example—the inevitable delays weren't a bother. Later, the need for shorter "turnaround time" grew urgent.

The solution to the delay was to build a special computer program, known as the operating system, that managed several jobs in the computer at once. The operating system was the host in the machine, calling in programs, activating them, serving them data collected from punch cards and tape, and moving their results to a printer. The operating system stayed in the computer at all times, keeping the computer busy between applications and, increasingly as operating systems matured, keeping track of the myriad details required to manage the system's extraordinarily complex operations. The operating system evolved to incorporate all sorts of functions that previously had had to be handled by slow, nonelectronic humans.

One of the first improvements made in the operating system was the addition of multitasking, a type of computing in which several batch jobs could be active concurrently. While one program was being read in, another could be processing data, and the results of a third could be printed. The advantages were obvious: the computer system was kept busy more of the time and could therefore handle more jobs per hour.

IBM's biggest probem was with its operating system. OS had been originally designed, as was most of the 360 line, for batch processing. Although it was certainly capable of organizing and managing multitasking batch computing with several concurrent jobs, it was inefficient at handling the two new types of computing that customers wanted most. These were, as will be discussed in more detail in later chapters, time sharing and transaction processing.

IBM enhanced OS to make it more useful in time sharing and transaction processing, to be more reliable and secure against crashing to a halt (as computers were wont to do), and to enable it to serve users more efficiently and flexibly. But all these boosts in capability created a new problem. Each new function made the software larger and more needy of the limited memory on the 360 processors. Like any other program, the more memory it had access to, the better OS could perform, but it soon obtained such a size that there was little room left for users' application programs. Tight memory space was a major cause of intolerably slow responses in interactive computing—another strike against IBM. On the other hand, IBM did not mind selling users as much memory as they'd take—it was a high-profit item.

CENTRALIZATION

In step with the development of time sharing and transaction processing was the centralization of data processing within customer organizations. Increasing numbers of IBM users moved up the 360 range to install single large computers instead of many smaller ones for reasons of price and because of their desire for central control of the corporate enterprise. IBM's functional price curve made this move attractive, even though users of large machines were unknowingly contributing more than their share to IBM's profits.

The consolidation to large computers created a new need, that of enabling remote locations, branch offices, and other outlying parts of the corporation that in the past might have had their own system to gain access to the new larger, centralized computer. The solution was data communications—transmitting data across telephone lines—which saw a tremendous boom beginning in the 1970s. Methods were developed by which users could submit batch jobs remotely, interact with time-sharing systems via remote teletypewriters, and use transaction processing systems via an array of visual display terminals. However, as exciting and powerful as data communications was, it was yet another area where IBM's knowhow and products were severely deficient. As a result, users increasingly turned to other vendors, including AT&T, to solve their problems. IBM saw its franchise with users slipping away. The data communications market will be discussed in Part III of this book.

It has been argued up to this point that large users—those with the most IBM products installed and using its biggest processors—brought the company the most profits. A typical customer, however, had a much different perception of data processing economics: the larger the computer, the better the deal one received from IBM (or any other vendor). The evidence on which that perception was based was the comparison of the prices IBM charged for its range of 360 processors and the performance they delivered. There was no denying that IBM's biggest machines delivered more raw performance for the money than its smaller machines did. In order to contain the many competitive attacks against the large user, IBM would totally reverse its traditional price discrimination to be in favor of and not against these now-vulnerable large customers. Before the next decade would be out, the public perception would in fact become the reality.

IBM, during the first three generations of systems, had been able to charge less per unit of computing and still earn large profits from big machines because, in fact, the cost of building computers does not rise in proportion to their performance. The common wisdom among users said that a doubling of price brought a quadrupling of performance. In fact, economies of scale work to a computer manufacturer's advantage, for each increase in capability is relatively less expensive than the last; this enables manufacturers to apply functional pricing with ease.

Consider the following example, based on IBM's August 1968 Quarterly Product Line Assessment (QPLA) for the 360 line. Recall that each QPLA contained a comparison of IBM's systems with competing systems in terms of price, performance, features, and the like. The idea was to take some measure of how competitive IBM's products were with those they faced in the marketplace. IBM determined the performance of its own machines by running a standard set of programs on each one and measuring the time it took to complete their execution. A typical mix of programs was used, attempting to reflect the kinds of jobs—sorting, processing, time sharing, and so on—that users actually performed on each type of machine. Table 25 shows the price, performance, and the price per unit of performance for optimum configurations of four popular models of the 360.

The pattern is as to be expected. The larger the system, the better its price performance. The price per unit of performance falls considerably between the model 30 and model 65. If a user's data processing workload could justify, say, four model 30s, he would actually do better by ordering a single model 65,

Table 25
Price and Performance Measures of IBM Commercial 360 Systems[4]

SYSTEM	MONTHLY RENT ($ K)	PERFOR-MANCE	PRICE PER UNIT OF PERFOR-MANCE ($ K)
360/30	$12.3	.8	$15.6
360/40	14.4	1.1	12.8
360/50	20.0	1.7	11.8
360/65*	32.0	3.2	9.8

* Because the data for the 360/65 systems were based on a different programming mix than the rest of the systems, they have been normalized.

which would deliver the same total performance but at only slightly more than two and a half times the price of a single model 30. That kind of savings was significant—over $200,000 a year, in this case.

The story of centralization does not end here, however, for it must be pointed out that despite the user's getting more bang for his buck in the large IBM processors, the large systems offered even more performance than seen above, but it was not available to the user to perform productive work. Deficiencies in OS and a major imbalance in IBM's systems wasted much of this extra processor power. Measuring the overall output, or throughput, of a computer system is not easy. The system's overall performance hinges not only on the raw speed of its circuitry and on the capacity of its various components but also on their logical and physical interrelationships. To complicate the equation even more, software's internal logic and system dynamics mediate the relationship between hardware components in ways that are sometimes surprising. For this reason, a great deal of effort goes into "tuning" computer systems—working to smooth out bottlenecks that occur when one process in the machine waits intolerably long for the execution of another process to finish. The system as a whole is only as fast as its slowest necessary component.

The performance figures above took into account the throughput of a complete system, configured with processor, peripherals, and a typical mix of software. However, when each is considered alone, the 360 processors differed much more dramatically in raw speed and in the amount of their processing power available to the user than they did taken together. For example, the model 65 system was seen to be just four times as powerful as the model 30. However, the two processors differed in raw speed by much more. The model 65 could add two simple numbers in 3.5 millionths of a second while the model 30 loped along at 78 millionths, making the 65 some twenty-two times faster at adding. Why this disparity between system performance and raw processor performance? Was there a bottleneck of some sort in IBM's systems?

There was, and IBM's numbers explain it. IBM measured the proportion of time each of its processors was busy in typical user systems. The idea was to see how much of the time the processor was actually executing code—either the operating system's housekeeping routines or a user application program—and how often it was waiting idly. This measurement was known as the central processing unit, or CPU, *utilization rate*. In fact, the model 65 processor, when engaged in typical commercial applications, was found to be busy only 22 percent of the time; evidently it was so fast that the rest of the system could not keep up with it. Much of the raw speed that users were paying for was wasted by the rest of the IBM system; they were buying performance that was actually unavailable to them for useful work.

One of the main reasons for the low utilization rate was the inability of IBM's disk drives to feed the processor data and programming code fast enough. The processor's electronics outperformed the disk's ability to move information in and out of memory. But before long, as we shall see, the IBM mainframe system's components would change radically. The operating system would be enhanced to more effectively perform interactive processing. In addition, the disks would become more capable with the 3330 and subsequent disks offered by IBM and its compatible competition. The result would be a complete reversal: the largest processor, rather than being used less than a quarter of the time, would be used to full capacity. Customers would demand larger processors, and when they could not get them, they would search out alternatives to help carry the increasing load of their applications.

NEW COMPETITORS EMERGE

The most important initial threat to IBM, however, came not from the processor but from the peripherals that attached to it. In 1968, the customer renting a typical 360/30 system paid IBM $10,126 a month, of which more than $7,000 went for peripherals: a card reader/punch, printer, tape drives, and disk drives.[5] Peripherals, as we have seen, were where IBM made much of its money in the 360 line. IBM had priced the 360s' peripherals to earn big profits, and, not surprisingly, it was now in that arena where its next serious challenge emerged. As in other products where IBM was to face competition, small companies could deliver comparable peripherals for less than IBM charged.

Customers were not wholly unaware of this. Those who were most discriminated against, the users of the largest commercial 360s, began to bridle at paying such high prices for their IBM gear. They received no discounts for installing large volumes of equipment or for waiving the generous support and services IBM offered to lesser accounts at no extra charge (though this would change after these were separately priced), nor any break in the extra-shift charges that IBM collected when computers were used more than 176 hours a month. These were IBM's best customers. Many of them had patiently waited while the company struggled to get the 360 working properly and had then helped IBM broaden its market by pioneering sophisticated applications. Yet they were supplying a disproportionate share of IBM's profits. These large accounts were more than ready to hear from an independent supplier of peripherals who could save them money.

One such disgruntled customer was Du Pont, the Delaware chemical manufacturer, a large IBM account that actively encouraged several independent peripherals suppliers to build tape drives to directly replace IBM's products. Du Pont was joined by other large IBM customers, and before long several dozen companies had jumped into the marketplace with equipment that was claimed to be "plug compatible" with IBM's.

The idea was that there should be as little change as possible in a customer's routine: there needed to be no modifications in his application software or operating system, no retraining of his staff, no changes in the way the system would perform. Plug compatibility meant that an independently supplied tape drive would literally be able to plug in to the same socket in the processor as IBM's tape drives did and to use the same electrical and logical signals to communicate. Although they were certainly attracted by the potential savings they saw, users were initially cautious about installing non-IBM gear—in one ear they heard about the plug-compatible machine's cost benefits while in the other they heard IBM's cautions to avoid risks and stay with the proven supplier. (See Appendix F for an example of IBM's overblown statement of the risks.)

Initially, IBM had little more than cautions to offer. It had fallen severely behind in mass storage peripherals. While it had been busy shipping 360s, other companies had been improving disk and tape drives for rival systems vendors. Those vendors had encouraged developments in tape and disk drives to make their systems technically more competitive with IBM's. Now the small manufacturers saw a market opportunity to sell advanced peripherals to the huge base of 360 accounts—and the world would never again be the same. In fact, the rival systems vendors had begun to make many of their own peripherals, rather than continue to rely on these independents, as a way to cut costs and boost profits. It was only natural that the small, peripherals-only manufacturers turned their attention to IBM's market. A huge number of disk and tape drives and much processor memory were being installed at very high prices, particularly on large 360 systems.

By focusing on large users such as Du Pont, these small suppliers could avoid the complex problems associated with installing a first system with a new customer. In addition, the volume of equipment moved in one sales call could be very large, helping them overcome their lack of large sales forces. Finally, maintenance in these large accounts was simplified because they could justify their own full-time repair staff and an inventory of spares. These advantages, along with new technology, enabled the new competitors to offer hefty discounts off IBM's bloated prices. All that was needed was to modify the electrical connections so that their drives could attach to IBM control units and thereby replace IBM drives. The potential profits were irresistibly high.

TAPE DRIVES

From the beginning, IBM had been aware of weaknesses in the tape drives offered for the 360 computers. "Competitors will attempt to market I/O devices with particular emphasis on tape drives," the 1964 study of the 360s' market had concluded.[6] The IBM 2400 family of tape drives was vulnerable to competition because it had "stretched old technology too far, too long."[7] The Model 2401 tape drives that IBM introduced with the System/360 were a "rehash" of the twelve-year-old model 729.[8] As a result, IBM concluded that it "was not presently in a position to compete tape drive for tape drive with competition ..."[9] As IBM had predicted, independent suppliers had developed tape drives that ran faster, that used a better method of sensing the tape's movement, and that used a simpler, more delicate mechanism to pull the tape from reel to reel.

That mechanism was the single-capstan drive, a clever solution to the long-standing problem of moving tape in such a way that the magnetic particles—and the data they contained—weren't rubbed off by mechanical friction. Both IBM and its competitors used electric motors to move the tape, but they used different means of actually pulling the tape past the read/write heads. IBM relied on a rubber roller to press the tape against the motor's shaft as it turned. Both sides of the tape were touched in this process, and as a result the IBM drive wore tapes out more quickly than users would have liked. The independents improved on this design with a drive that relied on a vacuum to gently hold the back side of the tape against the motor shaft. The magnetic surface of the tape never touched the transport mechanism, and thus wear and tear were greatly reduced. It was a simple, cost-effective solution that delivered better performance for less price.

The rush of users to these superior drives is reflected in the rising estimates IBM made of its losses to independent suppliers. In late 1967, it figured on losing about 1,000 tape drives at most.[10] That was an underestimation, however, for only a few months later, it estimated its potential loss at $27.6 million in annual revenues.[11] By the end of 1968, the estimate increased to 8,500 tape drive installations to be lost through the end of 1971.[12] In early July 1969, the estimate was up to 4,000 drives for that year alone and 16,000 by the end of 1970.[13] Later that month, the estimate doubled.[14]

DISK DRIVES

As noted earlier, IBM had traditionally led the industry in disk drives, so it was none too happy to see itself get beaten in that sector as well as in tape drives. Disk drives were fast becoming the preferred storage device for on-line, interactive systems, and they were vital to IBM's profitability.

By April 1969, upstart plug-compatible suppliers had introduced disk drives that not only were superior to IBM's current disk products but also were better than anything IBM had on its drawing board. Their competitive advantages stemmed not only from their lower price but also from their ability to operate faster, thanks to an advanced mechanism to move the read/write heads from data track to data track over the spinning magnetic surfaces of the drive.

IBM's disk drives were constructed, as most others were, as a stack of thin metal platters attached to a vertical shaft, or spindle, that was driven by a powerful electric motor. Data were recorded in concentric tracks on the top and bottom surfaces of each platter by a series of read/write heads—tiny magnetic coils that all but touched the smooth disk surface and were attached to a long-toothed, comblike assembly. This assembly moved all the heads in and out along the platters' radii, situating them over particular tracks as dictated by the drive's electronic controller. Moving this assembly quickly and precisely was crucial. The data tracks were but a few thousandths of an inch apart, but each fraction of a second spent moving the heads was time wasted.

The competition had replaced IBM's bulky and at times messy hydraulic head-positioning mechanism with a more elegant and faster-moving electric motor. Called a *voice-coil actuator,* it used the same physics as a loudspeaker. With sensitive control circuitry, it was possible to make the actuator move precisely and quickly. The trick had been to give it enough power to do the job without its magnetic fields spilling onto the platter and erasing data stored there. Excessive magnetic shielding would have increased the weight of the head assembly and slowed the actuator. IBM's competition was the first to market workable voice-coil actuators, and customers took to them rapidly. With the non-IBM disk drives, they could gain access to data about twice as fast as they could even with the drive IBM was planning to introduce as a replacement for its standard 360 disk. Moreover, the non-IBM drives were less expensive than IBM's. As with the tape drives, when users were offered an attractive, compatible package that gave them more performance for less price, they grabbed it.

Also as with tapes, IBM drastically underestimated the amount of business it would lose to the compatible disk drive makers. In early 1969, it predicted they would replace only some 4,000 of its drives. By August of that year, the competition was working on its second thousand drives, and IBM boosted its estimated loss to 7,000 drives by the end of the first year of production. Its highly important and profitable disk drive business was clearly in trouble.

MEMORY

Another group of manufacturers soon after took aim at the very center of the IBM business—the large profits IBM earned from the memory attached to the 360 processors. The 360s' functional pricing once again created strong incentives for independent suppliers. By the late 1960s, magnetic core memory had become a commodity product available from several sources, and it was packaged by various systems vendors to work with their respective machines. Some suppliers offered memory that both outperformed and undersold IBM's.

Firms such as Ampex and Cambridge Memories reckoned that users of large

360s, who required lots of memory, would switch to an independent supplier if the price were right and the transition easy. Users knew that if they swapped out IBM's memory but kept the processor itself, they could still enjoy IBM's bundled services and access to its software, but their monthly bills would be substantially lower. They seemed unconcerned that IBM would be able to collect rent only for its low-profit, or even money-losing, minimum-memory processors once its peripherals and memory had been replaced by compatible products.

By 1968, Ampex and several other companies had introduced 360-compatible memory at prices and performance that beat IBM's. In 1969, their success was enough to cause IBM to consider cutting its memory prices in retaliation. It rejected that plan due to the potentially "large financial loss involved." By December of that year, four companies were selling 360-type memory, and by September 1971, they had installed 259 large memories with 360 users.

As with disks, IBM's initial concern with the memory was for units for its next systems, the 370s, for they required a long lease life in order to be profitable. The 370 was planned then to use semiconductor memory instead of core. There were companies that already had a larger and more efficient semiconductor manufacturing capacity than IBM, and IBM feared they would muscle in early on the lease life of its future machines. It promised to be a lucrative business; IBM at first figured it could make more than $8 billion in revenues on memory alone during 1970 through 1975.

Together these three types of 360-compatible hardware threatened to skim the profit from IBM's systems and leave it with only the low-profit processors. As these compatible-product firms succeeded, IBM's market share eroded and profits were threatening to sag. The picture got bleaker for IBM in February 1970 when, after the plug-compatible manufacturers had been around long enough to prove themselves viable, the U.S. government decided to save money by replacing all the memory, disk drives, and tape drives it leased from IBM with independent gear. That move, IBM figured, would cost it almost $200 million in revenue a year.[15]

The threat to IBM was serious. It stemmed directly from its pricing scheme, which bore little relationship to its manufacturing costs. The new plug-compatible manufacturer rivals were merely doing what any supplier in a competitive market would do—coupling prices to cost rather than to some artificially fostered scale of performance and function. IBM's prices were very high in relation to the cost of providing its equipment, especially to IBM's largest customers. This left great room for other vendors to enter the market with lower prices and even higher-performance equipment.

It was a nightmare for IBM: now a customer could use IBM to get his first computer installed, take advantage of the many extras it threw in at no charge to win his order, and, once the system was running smoothly, replace all the IBM memory, disks, and tapes with independents' gear. IBM would have only the minimal rent earned on the processor to recoup its expenses. And with the emergence of still another competitor to IBM, the leasing company, IBM might lose even that.

LEASING FOR DOLLARS

Computer leasing was a game IBM thought it knew how to play well. After all, it had been leasing accounting machines and computers for years. Only government action had forced it to sell machines in the first place. The first few years after the 1956 Consent Decree saw only a few companies get into the business of buying IBM gear and leasing it to customers, but when the 360s finally began rolling out of IBM's factories, a pack of fast-talking, cash-laden lessors appeared and almost bought IBM out. They supplied the financial solvent, as it were, that threatened to dissolve IBM's lock on the mainframe market.

In fact, leasing companies had initially been favorably viewed by IBM, for they paid cash and helped it install more 360s. IBM had cleverly used these early leasing companies to price discriminate. A particularly price-sensitive customer who was considering another vendor for his system could in effect be offered a lower price if the IBM salesman suggested he finance his IBM system through a leasing company.[16] IBM could keep its prices high while selectively remaining competitive for the business of the price-conscious user. The independent leasing companies exhausted IBM's tolerance, however, when they began to grow rapidly following a shortsighted IBM price change that made purchasing more attractive. (The already-mentioned "three by three"—a 3 percent decrease in purchase price and a 3 percent increase in lease prices.)

The smart, independent lessors bought IBM processors, added non-IBM peripherals and memory, and then leased complete systems for less money than IBM charged for comparable configurations. These companies were successful largely as a result of two factors: independent suppliers had created a source of very low-cost IBM-compatible peripherals, and IBM's hold on many large customers was becoming tenuous. Because these hybrid systems were completely compatible—the processors, after all, had not changed—users had no problems installing them. Software lock-in was broken, and they could freely choose suppliers. Since most of the 360 equipment leased by IBM was returnable to the company on thirty days' notice, the customer was quite free to have it removed as he pleased.

IBM preferred to lease equipment for a variety of reasons. It provided a predictable revenue stream, which made planning future growth much simpler. Purchase income tends to be cyclical, coming in strongly when a product is first introduced and during general economic expansion but slowing down when products became obsolete and during times of recession. If nothing else, leasing smoothed IBM's growth and helped it to avoid laying off high-skilled labor during economic downturns.

Leasing also helped IBM control its competition. Financing a lease required a good deal of cash, a resource most of the competition was perennially short of.[17] Leasing also helped IBM maintain good relations with its customers. They enjoyed the freedom of simply returning to IBM any equipment they didn't need or want. Since they did not own the machines they leased, users could move to larger systems as they wished. Finally, leasing meant IBM kept control over its equipment. When it was no longer needed, all leased gear was returned to IBM. Since much of IBM's power came from how it chose to package new technology, purchased systems could easily get outside its control and frustrate its plans. Purchased equipment could be enhanced to compete with its current product line, thereby disrupting its ability to move or to migrate its users as it wished.

Although leasing's advantages to IBM were obvious, users needed to make some financial calculations to determine its value to them. The monthly lease price of a particular machine had to be multiplied by the number of months it was to be installed, giving a lifetime cost. That number was then compared to the purchase price; other costs such as interest charges, fees collected by IBM for servicing purchased hardware, the residual value of a purchased machine once released into the used equipment market, and tax considerations also came into play. For the 360 systems, the relationship between IBM's purchase price and its lease charges, a number referred to as the multiplier, was generally in the range of forty-five to fifty months. After leasing a machine for that length of time, about four years, a user would have paid IBM the full purchase price—any extra months of rent would be clear profit for the computer company. On the other hand, purchasing a computer let the user avoid paying IBM's extra-shift charges for using the machine more than 176 hours a month—a fee that often accounted for as much as 15 percent of the total bill paid by large customers—and allowed the user to sell it for cash whenever he liked. All things considered, however—including investments in training a staff, writing software, and coordinating the data processing operation with the rest of the user organization—a four- to five-year commitment does not seem overly long for the typical businessman to make.

Why, then, the preference of customers for leasing over purchase? One reason was that a customer was never exactly sure of how large a computer he would need in the future. Leasing enabled him to enlarge his system with little hassle, for IBM would deliver and take back extra hardware no questions asked. Furthermore, a user who installed a processor, say, as it approached the end of its active marketing life, when a replacement was just about to be introduced, would rather lease it than purchase a machine that would be considered a white elephant after the announcement. It was clear that IBM itself needed to earn profits on its machines before obsoleting them. Finally, the fact that IBM encouraged leasing was sufficient advice for more than a few customers; what IBM said, they did.

In sum, IBM offered users flexibility through its leases, but for a price. A user who was certain about future needs could more easily justify purchasing a system, especially if it were fairly new on the market, than one who was not. And the bigger the customer, the easier it would be to find a new home elsewhere in the corporation for a purchased machine once it was replaced in its initial application. But ideally, IBM liked to keep its users as unsure as possible of their future needs and of its product plans. Then the user would tend to value highly the flexibility of his lease contract. Once leasing, the longer the delay in replacing the product, the greater IBM's profits. IBM benefited from keeping its customers in the dark—until, of course, compatible vendors appeared and the free user choice could be used against it.

Many of the new leasing companies played a simple game against IBM. They offered users discounts on their lease charges in exchange for an increase in the length of time of the lease. Where most IBM customers used a thirty-day cancelable lease, the leasing companies specialized in writing longer-term, custom lease plans for each customer, varying monthly charges according to the commitment the user wanted to make.

There were two types of lease offered by independent lessors: the full payout lease (or financial lease) and the risk lease. The former was a conventional time purchase plan under which the customer agreed to pay a monthly fee for a long enough period to cover a machine's purchase price and financing charges. This kind of lease essentially spread out the period over which the asset had to be paid off. If the period were longer than four years, depending on prevailing rates, the monthly payments would be lower than IBM's corresponding lease rate.

More interesting was the risk lease. Here the user didn't have to make a long-term commitment; he could return his machine to the leasing company at any time for any reason. The only way the leasing companies were able to risk early returns was by knowing the computer market well enough to be able to quickly find a new customer for a prematurely returned machine. As with IBM and its thirty-day lease, the burden was on them to find a new customer, and perhaps still another, until a system's purchase price, expenses, and profits had been earned. During the heady days of the late 1960s, it could safely be assumed that new lessees could be found for returned machines because there was a strong demand for computers.

The independent lessors were able to undercut IBM's lease charges through clever accounting that enabled them to depreciate their assets. They depreciated

IBM computers for up to ten years instead of the four years IBM used. This meant that to show a profit, these companies had to generate less money per month but for many more months. Lessors based their depreciation life on the fact that electronic equipment generally didn't wear out as quickly as strictly mechanical gear. Furthermore, they reasoned that it was in IBM's interest to maintain the market value of its equipment. They weren't too far off, for IBM's own analysis came to the same conclusion: a ten-year life wasn't unrealistic.[18]

Nevertheless, the industry leader actually depreciated its equipment in its own books over only four years. That rapid pace decreased its reported profits during the initial years of the 360 over what they might have been had it used the more realistic, longer term. But IBM, of course, didn't need to raise new capital in the same fashion the independents did, and its reported profits were high enough already.

IBM's shorter depreciation period meant that any time after four years, it could replace the equipment. At this point, the risk-leasing companies would really be at risk for the remaining six years they still had to depreciate their equipment. The risk lessors, therefore, involved themselves more in the computer business than did the companies, mostly banks, that offered strictly full pay-out leases. The risk lessors found it necessary to keep track of the market's development so as not to be caught by a surprise move by IBM and to formulate strategies to keep up the value of their assets if IBM did move. Thus, of all purchase customers, the risk-leasing firms had the greatest interest in enhancing their systems—and thereby frustrating IBM's careful migration plans for its customers.

It was clear that computer technology was advancing rapidly and the resulting risk just as clear: IBM would almost certainly introduce new computers during the next ten years, and these leasing companies would have to continually find ways to increase the value of their machines so as to keep them competitive, installed, and collecting rent. They would try to keep the 360s alive and profitable, even as IBM came out with new machines, the System/370s, to kill the 360s and with it these "parasites."

Yet the conditions that had enabled IBM to offer risk leases were actually highly particular. It required a good deal of market power for IBM to place overpriced equipment on an easily cancelable lease and still make a profit. This power was threatened by companies such as the plug-compatible manufacturers and the risk-leasing companies that were causing IBM leased equipment to be returned prematurely.

In 1965, after the 360 had been on the market for only a year, leasing firms had purchased only $1.9 million worth of the IBM systems. The number shot up to $90 million the next year and on up to $297 million in 1967. By the end of 1968, leasing companies owned $1.5 billion worth of IBM systems, a value that far exceeded the $192 million worth of unit record equipment that they had owned since 1956 and the $247 million worth of 1400/7000 series second-generation IBM machines.[19]

IBM discovered in 1968 that 59 percent, almost two-thirds, of all purchased IBM machinery was owned by leasing companies, up from only 27 percent a year earlier. That same year, 21 percent of the IBM computers on lease were owned by independent lessors, up from 7 percent in 1967.

Although the most popular 360 system among the independents was the model 30, leasing companies held a bigger share of the large systems market. Like the compatible equipment suppliers, the lessors did best with IBM's largest and most sophisticated customers, for those customers had the most to gain by leaving IBM's lease plan and were most able to do without IBM's usual attention.

The biggest threat IBM saw in the leasing companies was their potential as the center around which other suppliers, namely compatible hardware firms, might gravitate and form a broad-based challenge to the IBM empire. Such a conglomeration might, once it had established itself by installing enough peripherals, enter the processor business as well.

"A combination of factors may well lead to the evolvement of the leasing company into the sales arm of the peripheral manufacturer, ..." noted an IBM document of July 1968.[20] "Leasing companies have focused on this [large] customer group and it is with these customers that they have their equipment. Additionally, it is this type of user who has the confidence to experiment."

Perhaps because of IBM's actions against the leasing firms, no long-term, viable combination of large leasing companies and peripherals firms was successfully able to enter the computer systems business. Nevertheless, the leasing

Table 26

Number of IBM-Leased Systems and Leasing Company Purchases, for 360 Systems

SYSTEM	NUMBER LEASED BY IBM	NUMBER PURCHASED BY LEASING COMPANY	PERCENT LEASED OUT OF TOTAL PURCHASED
360/20	5,253	244	4%
360/30	3,303	1,498	31
360/40	824	485	37
360/50	330	273	45
360/65	88	127	59
Total	9,798	2,607	27

companies became broad-based suppliers for a time and even established their own maintenance forces to service the gear they installed.

THE LIMITS OF POWER

The root of many of IBM's problems during this time was the System/360 itself. Each of the system's components—its processors, its disk and tape drives, its printers and terminals—were designed to work in almost any combination with each other. This easy mix-and-match compatibility, along with the ability of users to move their application software from processor to processor, made the machinery an attractive target for independent manufacturers.

IBM was well aware of this, for even at the time of the 360s' introduction in 1964, it noted in an internal memo:

> With the introduction of the System 360, featuring compatibility across the complete line and constituting a major commitment by the IBM corporations, the possibility of competitive manufacturers developing IBM compatible equipment takes on a new dimension. . . . Competitors will attempt to market I/O devices.[21]

Attempt they did. IBM had foreseen these so-called plug-compatible manufacturers who would seek profits by selling equipment at prices under IBM's high and stable price tags. Remember that even as the cost of building the 360 systems fell, IBM's prices mostly remained constant. It brought out new models of the 360 and its operating system, offering more performance or different capabilities, but the 360 family as a whole remained a sitting duck just waiting to be exploited by outsiders. The compatibility and the simple and stable characteristics of the interfaces that it required among the various 360 components made life that much easier for independent suppliers. Once they had designed a disk drive, say, they knew it would work with most, if not all, 360 processors.

IBM had made a choice in the early 1960s between maintaining or even increasing the segmentation of its computer offerings into a series of incompatible families, each aimed at a narrow group of users, or obtaining the economies of scale available from bringing out a homogeneous family of machines, among which customers could move as they pleased. The former route, of course, would have raised barriers to competitors, who would have been less likely to produce machines marketable to such small segments, and it would have raised IBM's costs as well. Taking the route it did, the second route, IBM was able to enhance the marketability of its systems, cut its internal costs, and appeal to the needs of a larger market. Moreover, the wide-ranging 360 systems attracted users by enabling them to start small and relatively inexpensively and move easily to larger and more sophisticated equipment. IBM concluded that it could make the most profits by offering the widest possible range of compatibility in the 360 product line, but it paid a price by making it possible for new competitors to offer compatible equipment to replace parts of the IBM system. In the next decade, when it faced more intense competition, IBM would reverse this basic decision and introduce a series of incompatible and more narrowly focused product lines. It would choose the higher costs that this strategy entailed in order to frustrate its competition.

Not only was the rivals' potential profitability high, but when they first surfaced as viable suppliers of 360-type machinery, it was not in IBM's commercial interest to stop them. IBM earned the most profits from keeping its leased equipment base as stable as possible, seeking to collect those last few months' clear profit. Therefore, cutting prices deeply enough to thwart competitors would have cut into IBM's bottom line as well. In a normal, purchase-only market, the worst that could happen to IBM would be that its sales of certain products would slow down or even stop. It then could have either closed down certain operations or shifted to making products facing less competition. But in this rental market, there was a more serious problem: If the competitive pressure were sufficiently intense, the net demand for a given product might turn negative, and then users would return their IBM gear and the company would have to take write-offs and losses.

As long as it was leasing most of its equipment, any price cut would decrease its lease revenues from that whole base and thus its profits. In order to successfully maintain its dominance, IBM's only option was to create a moving target—not an easy task in the lease-oriented market it had fostered. It had to drop prices and boost the capability of its own peripherals in order to remain competitive, but without upsetting its lease calculations. IBM faced a dilemma. Any attempts to create the needed moving target, whether through price cuts or changing product capabilities, would impact its ability to continue profitable leasing of its systems. As Watson, Jr., put it in a pair of 1964 memos, "The most important question before us is do we meet competitors' pricing methods, maintaining a modest umbrella, step for step, thereby preserving our strength in the marketplace but not our profit . . . or do we hold our line and allow ourselves to be etched away market-wise,"[22] and, "We will always have a great problem of having any price reduction on new equipment prejudice or disrupt our pricing of current products of the same type. Nevertheless, I think the main aim of this company must be to protect and expand our position in the market place and this must be a consideration well above that of profit."[23]

From the perspective of the upstart companies, there was still another major factor above and beyond its commercial self-interest that limited IBM and that was the antitrust laws. For IBM to take action against these new competitors who were nibbling at its profitable monopoly could cost it more in revenues and profits than it would gain. The antitrust laws called for a tripling of damages incurred by the hurt party; if IBM were convicted of a violation, it would have to pay the antitrust plaintiff three times the revenues it had lost from IBM's unlawful action. In effect, this meant that a party suing IBM couldn't lose. Either it won in the marketplace or it won in the courts, after having first lost in the market. IBM was therefore neutralized, and the initial success of the peripherals competitors and memory suppliers was assured. They entered the market in droves, all well aware of the bind IBM was in.

Of course, IBM finally did act. It took its short-term losses in revenues and profits and even opened itself to a series of lawsuits. Watson, Jr., stated that IBM should "swallow whatever financial pills required now and get ready for the future."[24] Swallow it did, and the vast majority of the new entrants, most of whom were offering only a single product line and were thus highly vulnerable, suffered. Once having thrived, they one by one turned into dying companies. IBM's eventual success, after its competition was destroyed, gave it the profits it needed to pay for high-priced lawyers who would successfully defend its actions during protracted antitrust litigation.

Many of these new competitors were actually less robust than they had first seemed, having sprung, at least in part, from the unnatural marketplace that IBM had created for itself. They were highly dependent on IBM's not changing its marketing practices or prices; when it finally did, they failed. Their vulnerability came in large part from their ambiguous position. In one respect, they were clearly competitors with IBM: they offered equipment that replaced IBM's products. But in another respect, they weren't competitors. IBM sold complete computer systems and a wide range of products and services to support those systems. The new manufacturers limited their action to those areas where IBM appeared to be most vulnerable, but they were not competitive at all with the wide range of IBM offerings.

No matter what these companies did in the way of offering advanced technology or lower prices, IBM retained important sources of power. It was a situation similar to that of twenty years earlier when the transition from unit record machinery to electronic computers began. IBM alone still had a broad base of power, while many of the competing computer vendors sold only that: computers. IBM's hold on the largest share of the market, as slippery as it might have seemed at this time, gave it a base from which to use price discrimination once again. Just as it had previously earned little profit from its first computers, making up for it with big profits from punch card machines, now it would move the profits from peripherals to processors, from large users to smaller ones.

"We have reached a point where every piece of I/O gear must be able to hold its own, in terms of price/performance, in a highly competitive market," noted IBM's August 1968 QPLA statement.[25] However, no such requirement had to be met for the non-input/output equipment—the processor.

HOW IBM SAW THE WORLD

Lest it be thought that the present analysis of IBM's dilemma is merely a figment of an overactive imagination, there is the testament of Hillary Faw, financial executive at IBM during these years when the plug-compatible and leasing threats arose. Evidently, Faw was a quiet man. His naive intellectuality and innocent honesty permitted him to commit to paper such thoughts as might have put the company in great trouble, and they reputedly cost him any advancement through the ranks at Armonk headquarters. Faw, whose expertise in financial matters was renowned in the company's upper echelons, was called upon by Frank Cary, heir apparent to T. Vincent Learson's throne and then chief marketeer for 360 systems, to put the company's situation into some perspective and to offer suggestions for a remedy. One of his memos, in November 1969, in particular, provides an illuminating view of how IBM viewed the changing marketplace.

He wrote, "IBM's risk lease is dependent on price leadership and price control. By means of price leadership, IBM has established the value of data processing usage. IBM then maintains or controls that value by various means: timing of new technological insertion; functional pricing, . . . refusal to market surplus used equipment; refusal to discount for age or for quantity; strategic location of function in boxes; 'solution selling' rather than hardware selling."

Nowhere else, perhaps, has such a clear, frank description of IBM's power been written by such a knowledgeable observer. In fact, as his memo to Cary went on to point out, Faw was one of the few in the company who, because he had access to the pricing numbers that counted above all, knew where IBM's power truly lay: "The key underpinnings to our control of price are interrelated and interdependent. . . . These interrelationships are not well understood by IBM Management. Our price control has been sufficiently absolute to render unnecessary direct management involvement in the means," he concluded.[26] IBM managers, in other words, could operate the company and had operated the company without quite knowing where its power resided.

Two years later, when the company's problems were even worse—the compatible hardware companies were doing better than ever, and the Justice Department had filed its antitrust suit—Faw expanded his analysis in a longer memo. Here he sketched out a history of IBM's pricing scheme in particularly frank language, concluding that IBM had created and shaped the data processing market to its own needs only to find that that market structure itself was the source of many problems.

He distinguished between the "systems" business—supplying hardware, software, and services together—and the "box" business, which dealt in individual components. As Faw described so well, IBM's preferred market had long been one in which leasing complete, bundled systems had been the norm, for that enabled IBM to create its artificial pricing structure for individual parts of the system. The new competitors had been able to exploit that structure by marketing individual boxes whose price was tied more to low manufacturing costs than to the system "value" that IBM marketed. Faw wrote:

> During the punched card period boxes were priced and marketed on the concept of displaceable cost: discrete measurable value—determinable by cost of customers' current administrative methods. (This made possible functional pricing—i.e., price to dollar displaced rather than to cost of the machine-service package being offered.)
>
> Incidentally that offering was much more than mere provision of a machine and its maintenance. Then as now, it included methods analysis of existing administrative procedures, conversion, education systems service and a continuing stream of advice and counsel for extensions and an implied guarantee the system would work as promised.
>
> These services could all have been priced separately. We chose to use the box as our billing vehicle for the total package, thus establishing the box price as our sole means of recovering all our investment and return on that investment. This was convenient and rational, in that a rough correlation existed between the quantity of boxes and the utility value gained.

He neglected to state it, but certainly Faw was aware that the functional price structure that IBM had constructed gave it other advantages as well. Offering complete systems made it more difficult for specialized competitors to enter the computer systems business while it enabled IBM to undercut the competition where it was active and still earn high profits on the rest of the product line. Faw continued:

> At the dawn of the electronic data processing era, pioneer users of EDP (insurance companies, large banks, Federal Government, airframe and defense industries), in the main, were not motivated by displaceable cost considerations. Sheer transaction volume (or complexity of computational requirements) were such that punched card technology was inadequate regardless of quantity utilized.
>
> We priced our 701 arbitrarily at $15,000 per system (a known loss price—$30,000 was required) because we thought there would be no takers at the required price; this was simply too far outside the range of displaceable cost considerations.

Faw may be slightly ingenuous here, for, as we have seen, IBM's model 701 system lagged behind Remington Rand's UNIVAC computer, and IBM was weakest in the scientific area. In the case of the 702, designed for the commercial user,

We priced the 702 in error at $30,000 (some costs were not provided for) expecting only 6 takers. We obtained 60 orders. This unplanned price (or value) test was useful, if embarrassing. It demonstrated that large users were willing to experiment with a potential escape from the unit record bind without assurance of cost displacement.

We then withdrew the 702 and substituted the (only slightly modified) 705 at $45,000 and retained most of our original takers. This apparent absence of price elasticity led us to high functional pricing of improvements (such as expanded memories and faster tapes). Perhaps there is a lesson to be learned from the fact that the memory price slope of our present M-9's on 360's was first established on the 704 in 1955 at a very high price in relation to cost. (With the expectation we would reduce the price over time as required.)

Success of initial installations of 701-702-704-705 naturally broadened the market among large concerns. The advent of the 650, its ease of operation, reliability and high speed (compared to the 604-607) brought the stored program concept to many medium sized companies, who became easy converts to tape processing when it was made available on the 650. Many of these installations were sold on a displaceable cost basis. However, many users relegated cost-of-the-old-way vs cost-of-the-new to a minor consideration when the flexibility and functions of EDPM became better understood and appreciated by managements beset by growth problems and new complexities being introduced in their businesses.

By 1959, utilizing a computer had become a prestige factor in large and medium sized concerns, which caused a further depressing influence on displaceable cost as a criterion for placing an order.

The overwhelming success of the 1401-1410 family in replacing the 650 in medium sized concerns marked the beginning of the end of reliance on unit record machines as the core D.P. installation. The functional output of the various sized EDP systems was simply not comparable to what had been available before. The idea grew that one simply could not afford to rely only on unit record equipment and remain competitive.

This historical perspective is necessary in order to gain an insight into the erosion of the displaceable cost motive for obtaining data processing equipment. A new value (price) system had become established arbitrarily and artfully by IBM (the gross profits of that value system supported heavy investment in market growth and the 360 investment).

During the early '60s, demand for data processing systems continued to outpace the supply. These systems, simple and limited as compared to today, came to be regarded as necessities, not capital asset acquisitions to be painstakingly evaluated for their potential return on investment. (Still more erosion of "displaceable cost.")

The advent of the 360, with its increased speed, compatibility, improved function and nearly equivalent price rendered totally unnecessary a comprehensive cost analysis as a criterion for placing an order. The reason for this was that a series of eminently successful forerunners were in place. These had a perceived value which was now unquestioned, although rarely, if ever, quantified. (The economic expansion which prevailed during the '60s was hardly conducive to prompting comprehensive value analyses of such a minor portion of a typical user's general and administrative expense.)

The explosive growth of EDP after 360 is a known fact. What is important to this discussion is that users ordered this equipment on a value system related to the perceived and unquantified value of the predecessor systems. (Not to displaceable cost in the traditional punched card connotation.)

What is equally important to us to understand is that IBM, as price leader in the industry, established unilaterally the dollar standard of that value system. In furtherance of our own corporate profit objectives we established our prices in relationship to the previous (unquantified) standard and, in addition, maximized functional pricing for enhanced profits. Through the market acceptance of our maximized "functional pricing," displaceable cost in the traditional sense disappeared. We now sold price-performance and improved function by comparison with a previously established value system, which had been created by ourselves (without analytic reference to true value as it would relate to some alternative approach to doing the job, and without a specific relationship to the manufacturing cost of the boxes involved—i.e., memory prices set in 1955 were unchanged although costs had dropped precipitously since 1955).

This argument is ignoring for reasons of emphasis the new account area, where displaceable cost had and will remain a key criterion for a sale.

So not only were new customers still concerned about displaceable cost, but IBM had established with the 360 family a pricing system specifically structured to keep the machines competitive for these yet-to-be-locked-in customers and in addition (as will be seen later) would bring out a series of new and incompatible systems, such as the System/3, in order to remain competitive for them.

Only in 1970, which marked the end of a decade of almost uninterrupted economic expansion, did users begin to question the issue of true economic value. The unbundling decision sharpened this questioning and provided a few (but not many) answers. Because we had no alternative, our pricing structure after unbundling continued to rely on the "box" price to recover our systems marketing, control programming and theft-vulnerable product development expenses.

In other words, IBM was a prisoner—it "had no alternative"—of the very pricing system it had created. From the beginning, it had established prices for the entire computer industry, prices that were "without specific relationship to the manufacturing cost of the box involved."

During the first three generations of computers, its competitors played the IBM game, for it was the "price leader in the industry." This meant that they merely matched or exceeded IBM computers' performance while offering their machinery for lower prices. With the advent of these new forms of competition, however, firms were playing a different game: they were pricing their boxes based on manufacturing costs, not on a system value basis. IBM's many peculiar costs were too high for it to win such a game. Wrote Faw:

> We have a whole series of things we do that don't fit. . . . For example, all work associated with improving function in SCP's [System Control Programs, or operating systems] and all E.C. [Engineering Change] work that is released to make boxes work together as a system at a required engineering level. In addition, our marketing effort (which produces systems solutions, is given to users independent of whether the user is purchase or lease) creates demand for boxes. It is worth noting that this system marketing services provided to users, opens up box markets for box suppliers. It also opens up markets for suppliers of other system elements, e.g., independent software houses.

The prior pricing structure had become burdensome, for it opened the door to narrowly focused competitors who could take advantage of the many bundled services IBM provided.

> Whatever its nature there now should be no question remaining that the existing value system no longer related to a box price and that box billing no longer offers a rational and viable recovery medium for the investment and risk of the D.P. systems vendor. This is true for both purchase and lease but particularly important as it relates to risk leasing. This anomaly is at the root of many of our recent problems.
>
> • It contributed to leasing company ability to undercut our box price.
> • Emergence of PCM's whom we subsidize by doing their marketing, systems control programming, systems support and in many cases their engineering so that they need recover in essence only manufacturing cost.
> • The oversupply of boxes being created by PCM's to displace our market—rather than to fill a new need—thus expanding our discontinuances and write-offs.
> • The inability of the price-performance oriented 370 to attain growth (unless it is purchased). We cannot win a box price-performance

game if our box price must continue to cover the marketing, software
support and box design costs for all IBM CPU users.

The dilemma posed by enhancing SCP for a large purchase inventory—
from which we can expect no return—and which provides additional
motivation for PCM incursion and a longer leasing company inventory
life.

The market IBM had created had changed profoundly. The giant would react
with fundamental changes to protect its favored position. The specific strategies
needed to deal with this complex and interrelated series of threats would take
time to develop and work. They would be implemented in myriad specific product introductions, in marketing changes, and in a basic change in pricing that
would take years to complete.

11. IBM Responds

We built the ship in which we are sailing, we have a hundred foreign smaller ships in tow who are relaxing in the wake of our weakening sails, and we cannot simply lower our sails or anchor, because we are in mid-ocean. We have no alternative but to patch our sails, establish a true course and proceed to our port of destiny.

—Hillary Faw, memo to
Frank Cary, December 10,
1971[1]

"Due to increased amount of competition," wrote Hillary Faw on June 15, 1970, "it is our belief that the concept of functional pricing is no longer the most suitable way to price in the magnetic tape area. Apparently manufacturing costs of high and low performance [tape] drives do not differ substantially and competition has concentrated in the higher performance area and priced their drives very competitively.... a continuation of this policy would contribute to future losses."

IBM would either have to change or see its market share decline dramatically. Although Faw was concerned that day about only one piece of the System/360, magnetic tape drives, the perceptive IBM financial executive could easily have been discussing any of IBM's 360 peripherals. Lean, efficient manufacturers of 360-compatible tape and disk drives and add-on memory were disrupting the functional pricing scheme to which IBM had adhered for so long. As Faw had put it earlier, what had long been a business in which complete systems were the focus of competition was fast becoming one in which individual boxes mattered most. Customers now had a choice of vendors and were no longer forced to pay IBM's high, functionally set prices. The rapidly expanding 360 system market, Faw explained to his superiors, was threatening to become an "appliance" market that was being wrested out of IBM's control.

Faw's metaphor was apt, for it sheds light on how IBM responded, and how it still responds, to the many narrowly aimed attacks on its 360s and on its later commercial data processing systems. Consider: Just about everywhere, electrical power is supplied by a legal monopoly—Consolidated Edison in the New York City area, Pacific Gas & Electric in parts of California, and so on. Within a given area, there is but one legally approved source of electricity. In exchange for having all this business to itself, each electrical utility submits its major business decisions to government regulators, who in theory represent the utility's customers.

Consider for a moment, though, what would happen if such an electrical utility were not regulated, either because it was not generally perceived to be a monopolist or because it was viewed as being a "good" monopolist that could be trusted not to abuse its position. Assume, too, that the utility supplied not only electrical power but also a range of electrical appliances that used that power. Under these circumstances, a number of opportunities would be open to the utility. By adroitly exploiting its unique market position, the company could earn a high rate of profit while commanding the vast part of the appliance market. The monopoly could forbid customers from plugging any but the appliances it made into the power grid, the justification being that one customer's unapproved toaster, say, might damage the network and interfere with service for other, rule-abiding customers. Another option would be to price discriminate by charging high prices for electricity but low or even money-losing prices for appliances—that would keep other appliance makers out of the market.

But there's a third alternative. Since all appliance makers would depend totally on their products' being able to be plugged into the utility's power lines, they would always run the risk that the monopoly would manipulate its electrical supply in such a way that only its own appliances could use that current. For instance, the utility might arbitrarily change the line voltage from 110 to 185 volts or alter its frequency from the normal 60 to 100 cycles per second. Or the use of a three-pronged plug and wall socket might be made mandatory. Creative engineers at the utility could easily conjure up some technical justification for the change—more efficient transmission of power, greater safety, or maybe just a simplistic but seductive appeal to the merits of "advanced technology." Frequent advertisements and other publicity measures would ensure that the utility's rationale for the change would be widely known among customers.

As it made the change in the electricity, of course, the utility would also change its own line of appliances accordingly. But the other appliance makers, kept uninformed of the specifics of the change until the last minute, would be caught off guard and left behind, at least for a time. Thus, the unregulated power company would be able to drive all appliance-making competitors out of business, even if their toasters and refrigerators were superior in price and performance compared with the utility's appliances. By virtue of its running the only generators and power network in town, the utility would have the unique advantage of knowing in advance the changed characteristic of that network. Being in the dark, competitors would be unable to design products to work with a new voltage, frequency, or plug until they knew exactly what the new electricity's characteristic would be. And by that time, of course, the utility would be in the market alone with large numbers of self-compatible appliances. Unless rival appliance manufacturers, too, could provide each customer with power for their appliances, which would be highly unlikely, they would be quickly driven out. After only one such episode, customers would forever be wary of buying a non-utility appliance, which might not work in the future when the utility changed the electricity supply again.

Luckily, we do not live in such a world—power companies do not make toasters, and their freedom to arbitrarily change their electrical currents and network plugs is limited by government regulators. But this has not been the case in the computer business ever since the late 1960s. Then as now, IBM, whose computer systems dominate the industry, is like the imaginary utility, and at the same time it makes "appliances"—the peripherals that attached to its systems. As we have seen, the computer industry began to concede the high-performance sector of the commercial systems market to the hugely successful 360s, and entrepreneurial attention shifted to building numerous devices that attached to the widely installed 360s: it was disk and tape peripherals at first, but soon entire computer networks loaded with terminals, personal computers, and even factory robots, would be attached to the 360s. By 1970, IBM 360 systems were coming to be viewed as holding the main set of "sockets" into which all other computer devices had to be plugged—even entire systems installed by other vendors. Because it controlled the mainframe processor that was central to all these systems, IBM was in a sense free to change the nature of those "sockets," as well as to add some new ones and take others away, just about any way it pleased. To complete the utility analogy, it soon seemed as if IBM were changing the shape of all its customers' kitchen wall plugs to make sure that only IBM toasters could be plugged in there.

The point at which two components of a system, any system, connect to pass signals or energy between them is known as an *interface*. There is, for example, an interface between a stereo receiver and its loudspeakers and another, more complex one between a computer's processor and its peripherals. Typically, a computer interface is quite complicated, meaning that in order to be compatible, the two devices must match each other precisely across a long list of parameters. A computer interface is defined not only by parameters such as specific voltage levels and the physical dimensions of a plug and socket, as in the utility analogy, but also by a precisely structured, logical script shared by the two devices that dictates the sequence and timing of the signals they exchange. Of course, because their definitions are so complicated and because the parameters are determined largely by modifiable software in each device, computer interfaces are more malleable than the simple electrical interface in our analogy. That inherent malleability works to the advantage of the systems monopolist's growth plans, for it facilitates the job of modifying the processor side of the interface, say, just enough that previous disk drives that used to fit perfectly can no longer be plugged in. A slight change in an interface by IBM, as we shall see, is as good as slamming the door in the face of competitors.

Not only does control over interfaces enable IBM to shut out unwelcome visitors, but that control can also be used to force customers to buy inferior IBM products. In order to function properly, the device on one side of an interface (a disk drive, for instance) may rely heavily on the logical function of the box on the other side (the central processor). That puts great power in the hands of the vendor who controls the device (processor) upon which the others depend so much. As we will discover, IBM has gone—and still goes—to great lengths to make sure that *all* devices that attach to its systems remain functionally dependent on a central IBM computer system, ignoring even its largest, most important customers' pleas to do otherwise and ignoring as well technological trends that other vendors may at first profitably exploit. Within the IBM system's mainframe, of course, lies the unique OS operating system, a bulging collection of basic system functions upon which virtually every other program in the processor and every piece of hardware in the rest of the system rely. To a degree that demonstrates fully its continuing, overwhelming power, IBM has bucked competitive trends, gone against strong technical tides, and still hung on to most of the expanding computer market, all by using its unique, unregulated control over interfaces. In doing so, it has forced customers to buy IBM products even when better-performing, lower-priced goods were available from other vendors.

In some cases, it may be necessary for IBM to unveil a new interface as part of a new product that offers better performance or price than earlier products, and IBM will make much of that product's superior performance. But many of IBM's improvements in products do not require new interfaces that are incompatible with what went before. Rather, in most such cases, IBM is simply trying to shake competitors off its central mainframes by changing an interface they had counted on (wrongly, as it always turns out) to remain stable and therefore usable by them over the long term. Rarely do purely technological considerations dictate new IBM interfaces; rather, they are part of the corporation's fundamental drive for isolated, competition-free market segments—and the high profits such segmentation yields.

When IBM changes an interface on competitors, as it does as a matter of strategic policy, their options for response are as limited and ultimately ineffective as those of our fictional appliance makers were. Just as the toaster makers could not enter the electrical utility business, peripheral makers and others trying to cash in on high 360 peripherals and memory prices could not enter the IBM-dominated systems business and fight IBM on a broader front. Their only choice was to follow IBM, to decode its changing interfaces as best they could, and to build compatible products as quickly as possible. Of course, because IBM denied them critical information about upcoming interfaces until its own products embodying those interfaces had actually been shipped to customers, competitors have always been late to market with newly compatible gear, often by a year or more. Over time, customers lose interest in the always-late, non-IBM vendors. Not only are they always to market months or even years after IBM, but the independent manufacturers leave doubts in the customer's mind as to whether they will be able to keep up with IBM over the long run or even remain in business. Needless to say, IBM relies heavily on such doubts, which, due to IBM's unchecked power, are well justified.

With the electric utility analogy in mind, let's see how IBM responded to the plug-compatible peripherals companies that were taking advantage of its price discrimination, uncompetitive peripherals, and well-understood interfaces. IBM could not, as it had in the past, simply refuse to let its customers connect non-IBM peripherals to the processors they leased. The United States Supreme Court had many years before stopped IBM from requiring its customers to use only IBM punch cards. So a similar ban on non-IBM disk drives, for instance, would not play well with the Justice Department. Besides, many 360s had been purchased by leasing companies and some large users, and IBM could hardly tell them what to do with the machines they owned. Straight price competition would not work, either. IBM's costs were relatively high, and it could not let investors down by cutting into its above-average profits. And with technology steadily improving, the competition would have a good chance of bringing superior products to market and replacing IBM's leased gear before IBM had a chance to make a profit. Leasing gave customers the freedom to bring in competitive equipment, but to discourage leasing in favor of selling would be to see even more equipment escape IBM's control. Something more subtle was needed to steer customers away from the competition's often-superior peripherals and memory.

Over time, a clever strategy emerged that has been the basis of IBM's success ever since. At first, it called for making new products use new interfaces. The improved price and performance of a new product, which would retain software compatibility with established application programs despite its new hardware interface, would be enough to lead customers to wherever IBM wanted them to go. But the changing interface would cause ongoing difficulties for competitors. With each new disk or tape drive, network communications box, or other peripheral it brought out, IBM was effectively free to offer customers not just a new appliance but, if commercial interests so dictated, a new wall outlet that supplied a new type of electrical current.

Naturally, the changing-interface strategy moved IBM away from the stability of interfaces that it had initially tried to establish with the flexible 360 family. Originally, there had been clear breaks between the 360 processors and their peripherals: the interface between them had been purposely kept stable to stimulate customers' orders for more peripherals. But even as they made the 360 systems easier to configure, stable interfaces also created easy targets for competitors; their whole plug-compatible business was based on the premise that IBM's interfaces would remain open and well understood. So as IBM began shifting the functions of the 360 systems between different boxes in an effort to create new interfaces, in some cases dividing one box's function between two other boxes, the 360s lost much of their original mix-and-match flexibility. IBM certainly had to spend more to repackage these functions and build new interfaces, but it would be well worth it if the market could be segmented into newly incompatible sectors and if prices increased substantially over costs.

Meanwhile, as IBM's new strategy evolved, the pricing would change. Profits would be shifted away from product areas that drew heavy competitive fire—peripherals and memory—and toward the one product that, at first, was untouched by competition, the central processor. Where once the processor had been a low-priced, even money-losing component of the 360 systems, it would now become the major source of systems profits. At the same time, once-costly memory would come down in price. The new formula tied prices not so much to IBM's own costs as to the even lower prices of its compatible-product rivals. Also, the broad midrange of the commercial market, populated by thousands of relatively cautious customers, would now become IBM's base of power. By paying higher prices, they would supply the profits needed to subsidize the low, competition-stopping prices on products aimed at the small but terribly important group of large, adventurous users of high-end 360 systems. Finally, products that in the past had been separately priced would be bundled together under a single price, and certain others would receive prices for the first time. These changes, some of them profound, took years to complete—IBM, after all, had been using the same functional pricing scheme for decades: the higher the performance, the higher the price and profit—but as the company's enormity today attests, they were a success.

With much internal pain, IBM stood its long tradition on its head to stop competition and prevent its systems-oriented market from splintering into a box-for-box "appliance" market. In each case where a new pricing relationship or interface was required, IBM was motivated first by commercial gain, often to the exclusion of its customers' interests or of even the efficient use of computer technology.

This two-pronged change in strategy—the massive reversal of price discrimination combined with the changing of interfaces to resegment various markets and functionally bind separate products together—affected the entire range of IBM's computer products and, arguably, the entire computer market. There was much interrelated action in a very short space of time. First, we will examine the leasing companies, who were compelled to enhance their systems with new technology in order to keep them rented. Next, we will look at IBM's actions in the most important peripherals market, that of the disk drives. This was the site of one of IBM's crudest but ultimately most resounding successes with the new strategy in the hard battles it fought against highly effective peripherals makers. Then we will turn to a further examination of the 360s' central processor, which along with its memory underwent some significant changes. The history of these two classes of equipment—disks and processors—is important because today they account for more than one-half of IBM's revenues and even more of its profits. The analysis of how IBM defended each of these two major components of the besieged 360 fortress will lead directly into an examination of how right now IBM is leveraging off its now-secure monopoly into the widening array of businesses collectively known as information technology.

BLOWING AWAY THE LEASING COMPANIES

The first to feel the heat of IBM's new anticompetitive strategy were the risk-leasing companies. They had purchased the most 360 equipment, and they were therefore the most likely to disrupt IBM's plans to begin changing interfaces. In a quick series of carefully timed blows, IBM eliminated many of the financial and marketing advantages that these companies had initially relied on for success. It quickly deflated the market value of the thousands of 360 processors that lessors had purchased. Dropping the prices on 360s gave the risk-leasing companies trouble in maintaining profits, in raising working capital, and even in staying in business at all. The best way to devalue the 360s, IBM decided, was to replace them with software-compatible processors that packaged better performance and improved functionality for less price. To ensure that risk-leasing companies would not threaten it in future years, IBM made the purchase price of the new equipment even higher than that of the 360.

Crucial to the leasing companies' initial success was the 1956 Consent Decree, for it defined the terms under which IBM had to sell its equipment. Yet Consent Decree or no, by 1968 IBM was clearly gunning for the leasing companies. The IBM purchase task force concluded: "Every possible action should be taken to promote rental. . . . In the future, unless actions are taken to prevent it, we will be forced to market in a new and different environment we do not control. . . . These actions must be total company changes (i.e., policy, pricing, technology, technical strategies and SE manpower)"[2]

IBM, being the only source of supply for any new equipment, certainly could make the necessary "total company changes." The only problem was that each change arguably violated, if not the letter of the Consent Decree, then certainly its spirit; each was an action taken with the clear intention of discriminating against those that purchased the new equipment. Consider: if indeed the initial purchase prices for the 360 had been established at a level not "more advantageous to IBM than the lease charges," as the decree required, then when those prices were altered with the Three-by-Three price change, it would appear that purchase prices would have lost that initial balance with lease prices. (Naturally the leasing companies did not complain about this change, for lowering purchase prices relative to lease prices made their life easier.) Thus the challenge for IBM was to stop the leasing companies without running afoul of the 1956 Consent Decree and provoking the Department of Justice.

IBM first struck in January 1968, when it launched a new 360 processor model, the 360/25. IBM described it as one whose "performance approaches that of the Model 30 but at a price below the Model 30." Immediately, the market value of the many thousands of model 30s owned by leasing companies dropped. Blow number one.

Next, IBM changed the model 25's price in order to discourage the leasing companies from simply adding that model to their offerings. Instead of having a purchase price equal to forty-six monthly lease payments, as the model 30 had, the 25's multiplier was fifty-two months. That meant that in order to stay competitive with IBM's risk-lease prices and still break even, lessors had to keep the model 25 installed at full rent for six months more than if it were a model 30. And to make sure its sales force got the point, IBM restructured their quotas and commissions to favor leasing instead of purchasing. Blow number two.

In January 1969, IBM found itself being scrutinized by the Justice Department, which was preparing to file its antitrust suit. In part to enhance its antitrust posture, the company unbundled the prices of many of the field services and much of the software that it had previously provided the customer at no charge. It was untying a previous tie-in sale. To compensate for the newly unbundled charges that users were now expected to pay, IBM cut the price of its entire computer line by 3 percent. The effects of 1966's three-by-three price changes, which had invited leasing companies to enter the market in the first place, were reversed.

The problems of the leasing companies were threefold. First, IBM's hardware price cuts were not retroactive to earlier acquisitions; they affected only those purchases and leases that took effect after the unbundling. This meant that the leasing companies would have to pay, just like every other customer, for the IBM software and technical support they had counted on receiving at no charge throughout the life of their IBM equipment. The second problem was that to remain competitive, they had to cut prices on every one of their machines that was either waiting for placement with a customer or already installed under a risk lease. IBM, on the other hand, suffered no such loss; it actually forecast revenues would rise 6.9 percent from the new fees it would collect. Finally, the largest users, those who had received the least support when prices were bundled, actually saw their prices drop now. Much of the increase in revenues that IBM saw after unbundling actually came from midsize customers. Blow number three.

KILLING THE 360s

There were many more punches to come, but some were more deadly than others. Blow number four called for obsoleting large 360 processors as quickly as possible, but killing the highly successful models 50 and 65 turned out to be easier said than done. IBM's most effective way to devalue them was to limit strictly their ability to use any new peripherals or other add-on products that, because they were based on improved technology, provided customers with more performance or function for their monthly dollar. If only the post-360 processor were able to use the high-performance, relatively low-price disk and tape drives and faster memory that IBM now had cooking in its development labs, then the value of that processor would soar relative to that of the increasingly obsolete 360s. Large, performance-hungry customers, IBM reckoned, would shun 360s altogether.

Again, IBM planned to segment its market and price discriminate among different segments. To be successful, the plan required the selective relocation of certain functions, a move of logic and other crucial circuitry from one system box to another. Different plugs, so to speak, that would be incompatible with the 360s' plugs had to be created for the new peripherals and processors to connect with each other.

IBM brought huge resources to this effort. Its competitors had small product lines, were relatively tiny, and always poor. IBM's abundant cash flow funded the development of a broad range of 360 and follow-on products: processors, disk drives, tape drives, printers, terminals, and more. Far less than its competition was IBM in danger of depending too heavily on one product for profits. IBM still had a few areas of monopoly power upon which to rely. One was the OS/360 operating system (and its later derivatives), which by the end of the 1960s had become enormously complex. Because IBM still provided OS/360 at no extra charge to customers, no competitor was likely to invest the millions that would be needed to build a replacement for OS that was compatible with customers' application programs. Modifications to OS, often undertaken in the name of increased efficiency and function, provided IBM with one means of frustrating competitors who tried to attach gear to the 360 system.

IBM also maintained power in the market for processors themselves. Prices for 360 processors (considered alone, without any memory) had been set very low right from the start, and no competitor had yet seen any profits to be made from duplicating that relatively complex piece of hardware.

IBM also kept its strength in the international market, where its competition's activities generally lagged by a year or two. Although IBM had to fight compatible vendors in the United States during the early 1970s, it could rely on its strong standing in foreign markets where, initially, there were fewer and less-robust competitors to deal with.

Not surprisingly, risk-leasing companies raised the strongest resistance to IBM's attempts to kill the 360s. They had millions invested in 360 hardware, much of which was returnable by customers on thirty days' notice. The leasing companies had planned to depreciate their 360s over ten years, and that meant keeping their machines installed at full rent for at least that long if any profits were to be made. If those 360s were suddenly to become obsolete and lose value, few if any would make it to the ten-year mark, profits would become harder—if not impossible—to obtain, and working capital would be harder to raise: lessors would begin to collapse.

Despite IBM's efforts to force march customers to the System/370, the leasing companies added non-IBM peripherals and memory to their 360s to keep them competitive. Much of that non-IBM equipment was superior even to certain new hardware that IBM was promising exclusively for the System/370. Some lessors even went so far as to modify their 360 processors' internal circuitry and unleash capabilities there that IBM had, for functional pricing reasons, kept locked away and unavailable to users.

IBM determined that the 370 processors' pricing would be the "key factor" in determining the "long-range viability" of independent lessors. To meet IBM's needs, the 370s had to be priced to discourage purchases or else lessors might profitably buy them for re-leasing as they had the 360s. IBM determined that a multiplier of fifty-two would deny the lessors any profits, but just to make sure, when the first two 370s were introduced in June 1970, their multipliers were up a notch more, to fifty-three.

The first two 370 processors, the models 155 and 165, were designed to replace the highest-performance commercial 360 processors, the models 50 and 65, respectively. To make the 370s faster and less costly to manufacture, IBM built them from a new type of electronic building block, the integrated circuit, and gave them new internal features. The model 155 was claimed to be three and a half to four times more powerful than the 360/50 that it replaced, while the model 165 boasted two to five times the speed of a 360/65, depending on the application being run.

These 370 processors used exactly the same software as the 360s—thus saving users' still-growing investment in application software—and, for the most part, the same peripherals. But to achieve their full potential, the new processors were best used with a new disk drive, the Merlin, or model 3330. That drive, which offered a sizable gain in storage capacity and better price but was unusable on any 360 processor, was one of the major incentives for customers to discard the 360s. Not only did it store more data, but its speed helped increase the processor utilization rate, leading to further economies for the entire system. Another draw for customers was the 370s' ability to use more memory—up to two mega-bytes on the 155 and three megabytes on the 165—than the biggest commercial 360s. Also, the memory on the 370s was priced much lower than on the 360s—after three system generations during which costs had plunged, IBM was finally beginning to cut profits out of memory.

The leasing companies were not totally daunted, however, for the technology was very malleable. There remained myriad ways of enhancing the still-vital 360 processors. The companies' success in disrupting IBM's customer migration plans was evident well after the large-scale 370/155 and 165 (introduced in June 1970) and the medium-scale 370/145 (September 1970) and 370/135 (March 1971) were in the market. The May 1973 QPLA, for example, discusses the fight these "third-party" (i.e., owned by leasing companies) 360s were giving mid-range 370s in particular:

- The competitive position of the System/370 Model 135 relative to third party System/360s has been weakened by developments which tend to improve the pricing and throughput capability of System/360:
- Packaged third-party offering which includes [plug-compatible] peripherals, maintenance, system software and system engineering services.
- Proposal of two third-party System/360 Model 30s and 40s in place of a single System/370 Model 135.
- Announcement of a hardware accelerator for the System/360 Model 30.
- Expanded CPU storage on System/360 Model 30 to 256K; on Model 40 to 512K.

  These developments are particularly significant because System/360 Model 30s and 40s compete with the Model 135 more effectively than all other competitive offerings combined.[3]

Not a surprising conclusion, given that the 360s' software was closer to that of the 370s—and identical in most cases—than any other machine on the market.

The leasing company 360s were still very much alive, even in 1973, proving that it was quite possible technically to extend the 360s' life. In light of that fact, it is interesting that the one company owning the most 360s was IBM itself. It received stacks of them back from earlier rentals. These 360s could have been enhanced, had IBM wished, and their rental life could have been extended for many years. That was not done not because any overwhelming technical obstacles stood in IBM's way, but rather because its commercial interests led it elsewhere. Had IBM avoided selling its machines in the first place and only rented them, its migration plans would not have been so vulnerable to disruption by competitors. The episode is reminiscent of Patterson and his lieutenant Watson wiping out the used cash register business: it was better for the monopolist to own all its equipment than to let others purchase it and compete with higher-profit replacements.

In the end, however, the leasing companies' threat to IBM was limited by the fact that they owned a fixed supply of 360s and their customers needed extra computing capability that even souped-up 360s could not deliver as cost-effectively as standard 370s. This was particularly true at the high end of the 360 and 370 spectrum, where IBM was encouraging its customers to push their systems to the operational limit.

SEALING OFF THE LOW END

IBM's desire to reverse the price discrimination in its mainstream computers raised a serious problem. The initial 360 pricing had been designed to win new customers by low prices on small machines. If the price discrimination were now reversed to benefit large users, IBM might easily find its entry-level system prices uncompetitively high. That would never do. Advances in computer technology had not only made better 360 and 370 peripherals possible, but they had dropped the cost of entry-level systems to new low levels. With each drop in cost, computers became available to a broader range of potential customers, including small businesses and branch locations of large corporations. As it battled to save the 360 monopoly, IBM worried about losing orders to competitors who were selling complete systems priced below the smallest 360s. Every order lost there meant one less customer for the future.* Once lost, software lock-in would make it difficult ever to win that customer's business again. It was vital,

---

* IBM's competition would remain very active at the low end of its product line. IBM was well aware of the attractiveness of this part of the market. Its Market Evaluation Department wrote, "Most of the major systems vendors are showing intense interest in this new account business, evidently realizing the advantages IBM has enjoyed in growing a customer up through unit record into substantial systems."[4] Moreover, there was always the threat that a competitor would establish a profitable base of these users and try to expand upward into the heart of IBM's monopoly. The Market Evaluation Department concluded, however, that the announcement of the System/3 would insure that "the attention of NCR will be directed towards the low end, away from the medium and large scale area towards which their publicity indicated they were driving."[5]

therefore, that IBM have some kind of low-priced system with which to capture new customers.

IBM had emphasized smooth upward migration and common peripherals in its 360 line, but extending that compatibility down to smaller systems would limit its ability to discriminate against the midsize system customer. The latter would simply move to these less-expensive smaller systems, and IBM's revenues and profits would drop. IBM's answer was to segment its market further, creating a new line of computers that were incompatible with the 360s but priced to win new customers.

The vehicle for this effort was the System/3, unveiled in July 1969 by the General Systems Division, a unit set up just to "obtain new accounts." In order to limit its impact on 360s, IBM had the System/3 use a different programming language, RPG, which was crude compared to the 360s' COBOL and FORTRAN. Also, the new, small machine used a different binary data code and a different size and shape of punch card. IBM hoped to isolate the System/3 and 360 markets from each other as much as possible so that each could be priced according to the competition it faced.

Overall, the System/3 was expected to show much lower profits than the 360, for it was competing in a much more competitive arena. IBM's July 1969 profit statement showed a negative profitability for the domestic System/3 market balanced by positive profits outside the United States: the total was only just positive, despite the assumption of an extraordinarily long life—more than five years—for the machine.[6] Just one year after its introduction, as customers began acquiring more sophisticated systems, domestic System/3 profits were projected to be only 7 percent. The model 10, introduced in 1971, was slated to earn only 9.1 percent profit.[7]

After a sluggish start, during which the System/3s sold better to established 360 customers than to the first-time customers it was designed to entice, IBM revamped the machine with new peripherals and better processors. Installations picked up, and IBM was again able to take advantage of software lock-in and earn profits from expanded systems. Some of those profits derived from returned 360 disk drives that had been reworked and repackaged for the System/3. In effect, the disk's rental life was extended well beyond its point of full depreciation as it was cascaded down from the 360 market to the System/3 base.

Like the 360s, the System/3 family comprised several processor models of varying performance, each of which came with a variety of memory sizes and peripherals such as disk and tape drives, punch card machinery, and printers. As in the 360, the different processor models generally used the same software, making it fairly easy for customers to upgrade from one level of performance to the next.

The pricing pattern was the by-now-familiar one: functional pricing in mem-

ory and other add-on items that appealed to locked-in users. There was no
pesky plug-compatible competition to worry about. The model 6 processor, for
example, came in three memory sizes: 8,000, 12,000, and 16,000 bytes. The profit
rate IBM recorded for these three sizes ranged from almost zero to respectable:
0.8, 11, and 19 percent, respectively. As for extra features, to attach the machine's CRT display screens, a special facility was required: its profit rate was 53
percent. Special command keys that made interactive programming more con-
venient earned IBM fifty-two cents on every dollar of revenue. A low-end model
of the machine's printer had a profit rate of only 2 percent, while the more powerful model earned 21 percent. The more powerful a machine the customer
needed, the more profit he contributed to IBM's coffers.

IBM eventually came out with a total of seven different System/3 processors.
They ranged from rudimentary punch card–based systems to those that used
disk and tape. It later extended the line with the Systems 32, 34, 38, and 36, in
that order, which were small computers designed to operate interactively with
varying degrees of sophistication. The model 34 was particularly successful—it
was claimed by IBM to have been installed in over 60,000 locations. Its successor, the model 36, has also been highly successful.

IBM offered other small systems during the 1960s to make sure it didn't lose
out on emerging markets that neighbored strict commercial data processing.
Two of these were the 1800 and 1130, respectively aimed at the narrow factory
and process control and the small scientific processing markets. These separate
and incompatible product lines, aimed at markets where IBM's power was less
than in commercial data processing, once again showed IBM's traditional pricing: low profits overall and functional pricing for add-on memory and special
features.[8]

The System/3, the 1800, and the 1130 were important to IBM not only as
means to hold the low end of the commercial market but also as remote exten-
sions of large 360s. As will be examined in detail later, connecting computers together over long distances over telephone lines was rapidly getting easier. Small
computers served well to collect and distribute information for and to 360
mainframes. By the time IBM was extending the reach of its data processing
systems from the central computer room to regular office spaces, branch offices,
factories, and other remote locations, it had already seeded those locations with
competition-stopping gear.

12. The Disk Drive Market

IBM certainly does not make arbitrary *changes in the way it connects its products. . . . Telling engineers to introduce gimmicks into our products would be totally inconsistent with our own business conduct ethic and our own commercial best interests. Our customers would not let us get away with it. (Emphasis in original.)*

—John R. Opel, IBM
chairman, 1984[1]

IBM's price discrimination and its manipulation of interfaces were most forceful in combating compatible disk drive makers. IBM had much to lose to them, for disk drives were key to the performance of the interactive and transaction processing systems that were becoming the norm in commercial computing. For IBM to lose control of the disk drive market would have severely threatened its future as a monopoly.

It was in the disk drive arena, too, that IBM faced some of its cleverest and most effective competition. Two rivals in particular, Telex and Memorex, were so successful at selling 360-compatible disk drives in the early 1960s that they soon branched into additional peripherals markets—printers, communications gear, and the like—in an effort to encompass as much of the 360 peripherals spectrum as possible. Memorex, in fact, went so far as to bring out its own 360-compatible processor, thereby being able replace IBM systems completely. Telex and Memorex were each the darlings of both Wall Street and users alike until IBM deliberately hobbled them.

The story of how IBM defended its disk drive business is richly documented and demonstrates several aspects of the company's power. A wealth of hard data—shipment, revenue, cost, and profit information as well as descriptive IBM memoranda—is available to illustrate IBM's planning process, the anticompetitive tactics it used, and the thinking and even the emotions of its managers. The company's inner workings were revealed during the many antitrust suits filed against IBM in the 1970s by hurt disk drive competitors and others who suffered from those tactics.

Because rival disk drive manufacturers posed the largest and most immediate threat to IBM's monopoly over the systems market, their duels with the company offer an important case study that also helps to explain later competitive episodes. If ever IBM was caught off balance, with its pricing actually encouraging competitors rather than protecting the company, with only inferior products to sell, and with fears of antitrust litigation and other factors constraining its responses, it was in the disk drive arena beginning in the late 1960s. The wonder is that IBM got away with all that it did and still avoided all penalties, either legal or financial.

Like so many other computer products, independently manufactured disk drives relied totally on their capability of being attached to IBM systems for their value to customers. To be at all functional and useful, the disks had to interact intimately, on several interrelated levels, with the IBM processor. As IBM's present 85 percent-plus share of the large-disk-drive market attests, its unique ability to define where and how outsiders' products connect to and communicate with its systems gives it an unassailable advantage over all competitors.

Virtually all computer and data communications products of any consequence depend on being able to connect to, or communicate with, IBM's ubiquitous mainframe computers. IBM's monopoly over the central hub of all corporate data processing—the mainframe computer and its complex operating system software—gives it extraordinary power in every neighboring market. It therefore behooves us to look carefully at how IBM exploits its control over the system interface to the detriment of competition.

DISK DRIVE TECHNOLOGY IMPROVES

Disk drive technology improved a great deal during the 1960s as the industry developed techniques for packing more bits of data into a smaller area of the disk's magnetic platter and for retrieving those data faster than before. Advances were made in the smoothness of the platter surfaces, the speed at which they rotated, the time required by the read/write head to move from one data track to another, and the transfer rate at which data left the disk on their way to the processor. The greater its storage capacity and the faster its access time and transfer rate, the better a disk drive's overall performance was and the better it could serve an on-line interactive computer.

Although the disk drives that IBM brought to market during the 1960s were improved in most aspects of performance and price, in this case the company did not lead the industry in bringing the latest technology to market. A number of independent disk drive manufacturers who had sold disk drives to IBM's systems competitors for many years managed to push disk drive technology sufficiently to get ahead of IBM by 1968. By settling for less profits than IBM, using the independent leasing companies for marketing and distribution, and otherwise running leanly, competitors began offering 360 users disk drives that worked better than IBM's did and sold for less.

Table 27, detailing IBM's various large capacity disk drive products for the 360 and 370 lines, helps show IBM's vulnerabilities. Notice first that the company labeled its disk drive models in ascending numerical order. Next, note that between 1965 and 1970, when the 360 was fast taking over the market, IBM did not announce a new disk drive. It was precisely during this period that the compatible vendors entered the market and achieved their greatest initial success. Curiously, in 1970, when IBM finally did react to them with a new product, the model 2319 disk drive, there was barely any improvement in performance over the preceding product. This anomaly in the otherwise steady improvement of IBM disk drive performance, especially after a heated five years of intense market action, begs for scrutiny. Was IBM unable to match its competitors' technology? Was it late in bringing products to market when it most needed to? Did it therefore rely on tactics other than straightforward product improvements to tackle competitors? Yes, yes, and yes.

The story of those five years begins with the 2314 disk drive. The 2314 offered substantial improvements over the preceding 2311, primarily a quadrupling of total capacity. However, the 2314 was offered only as an inseparable package of nine disk spindles—only eight of which were ordinarily operational; the ninth rested as a spare—and a controller. (A spindle is the basic disk drive apparatus, including a motor, a drive shaft, or spindle, on which the disk platters are mounted, the read/write heads, and a certain amount of electronics.) IBM re-

Table 27
Characteristics of Major IBM Disk Drives[2]

MODEL	DATE	CAPACITY	ACC-TIME	TRACKS	DENSITY	RPM	TRANS*
1311	1962	3.0MB	150ms	50	1100bpi	1500	77
2311	1964	7.5	75	100	1100	2400	156
2314	1965	233.6**	75	100	2200	2400	312
2319	1970	29.2	60	100	2200	2400	312
3330/1	1970	100.0	30	200	4040	3600	806
3330/11	1973	200.0	25	400	4040	3600	806
3340	1973	35 or 70	15	300	5636	3999	885

* The headings for each column are: the date of the announcement, the amount of information it could store, the speed at which the heads can access a particular location, the number of tracks and the density at which data is stored per inch, the rotational speed that the disk spins, and the transfer rate at which data moves between the disk and the CPU (KB/sec.).
** 8 drives each with 29.2 megs.

ferred to this nine-spindle combination as the 2314 direct access storage device, or DASF. IBM put a single price on the DASF, but internally it considered the product to be three separate pieces of equipment. In fact, it manufactured the three main subcomponents—controller, four-spindle drive unit, and one-spindle spare—separately and even shipped them separately. Only at the customer's premises were they bolted together to form the complete 2314 DASF product.

IBM was pursuing several broad objectives by bundling 2314 disk drives as the DASF. It wanted to encourage large users to expand their disk drive usage, as opposed to that of tape drives. The DASF forced customers to install substantially more storage capacity than they might actually need. Once it was installed, however, the nine-drive package begged them to use its full capacity. Second, to protect its profits, IBM needed to limit the use of the 2314's advanced technology to only certain users. The company was making hefty profits on the older 2311s, in the 40 to 52 percent range,[3] and it did not want orders for that disk drive to dry up once the improved disk drive became available. In finance executive Faw's words, the company was carefully controlling "new technological insertion" into its lease base.[4] By making the 2314's performance available only in a high-priced, extra-high-capacity package of nine spindles, IBM discouraged small and medium-size customers from replacing 2311s with disk drives that earned profits of only 32.5 percent, or about a third less. In sum, the DASF tie-in sale segmented the market, limited the availability of new technology, and maximized profits.[5]

Finally, and most important, IBM combined the controller and the disk drives into a single product—indeed, a single box—to create a major barrier to potential compatible vendors. Electronically, the controller fit between the mainframe processor and the disk drives themselves; as its name implies, it interpreted commands from the processor and directed each of its disk's actions and the flow of data back and forth between them and the processor. IBM foresaw in 1965, when it unveiled the DASF, that other vendors would seek to attach their disk drives to the same controllers that IBM's disk drives used throughout the 360 line. But by physically combining the controller with the disk drives themselves, IBM removed an otherwise attractive port of entry into the 360 system.

In fact, as IBM knew well, this point of attachment, or interface, between system components was, thanks to the extreme plasticity of computer circuitry, almost totally arbitrary. There was no technically compelling reason for IBM to separate its controller from the processor, or the controller from the disk drive. All three could have been (and are, in today's personal computer) packaged in a single box, selling for a single price. However, for sales and financial reasons, IBM chose to package the vast majority of the 360 peripherals in separately priced boxes that the customer could mix and match with great ease. The pattern—to which the 2314 DASF was a clear exception—enabled the company to enhance different functions of its system at different rates, to charge different prices for each, depending on the competition it faced, and, most important, to ease the customer's migration to ever-larger and more profitable systems. (It has been said that the main factor limiting IBM's packaging of different components into a single box was the size of its customers' freight elevators: too large a box would have been undeliverable. The 2314 DASF avoided that limitation by arriving at the customer's site in several manageable pieces.)

So firm was IBM's control over the crucial interfaces between processor, controller, and disk drives, and so dependent were outside manufacturers on being able to duplicate those interfaces, that altering and moving the interface soon became a major weapon in the company's anticompetitive arsenal. IBM alone defined how and where everything attached to its systems. It dictated the interfaces' physical, electrical, and logical characteristics: the shape and size of the plugs on the connecting cables, the voltage levels of the signals those cables carried, and the information those signals needed to convey. Each of those three layers of the interface was independent of the others and therefore could be manipulated as competitive pressure demanded. In fact, as it did with the DASF, IBM could enclose several separate components into a single box, completely eliminating an interface that competitors might use. Like a conjurer unexpectedly moving a pea among nutshells, IBM could relocate functions in the different boxes of its system. By doing so, it could control the value—and therefore the price and profit—of each box. If a rival were to aim a product at some high-profit IBM box, IBM could move a particularly valuable function—and profit—from that box to another, cut prices on the vulnerable box, and still retain an overall profit. It generally took a rival twelve to eighteen months to catch up with an IBM move, by which time IBM would be shipping its new products in volume and be well ahead of the game.

There had been two major peripherals interfaces in the 360 line, both of which outside vendors initially counted on to remain stable. The most stable, in their eyes, was that between the processor and the various peripheral controllers. Each broad peripheral category—printer, disk drive, and tape drive, to name a few—had its own type of controller, which was essentially a small, specialized computer. Since IBM had intended it to be easy for users to upgrade their 360 systems by changing processors and adding whatever peripherals they needed to accommodate growing application loads, it had kept the interface between the processor and the various peripherals controllers unchanged. Over 256 separate IBM devices connected through various types of controller to the 360 processor, and the company was not about to do anything that might make those controllers, and thus all the peripherals that attached to them, unusable. At least, that's what independent vendors thought as they prepared to add their disk drives to the growing list of 360-compatible peripherals.

The other major peripherals interface in the 360 line was located where the controller connected to its respective peripheral devices. Each type of controller used a peculiar interface there, one that was tailored to the characteristics of the information that passed across that interface. But because this controller-to-device interface was simpler to duplicate than the other, and because the early disk drive competitors were better at building disk drive mechanisms than at building controller electronics, they designed their first disk drives to attach to IBM's standard disk drive controller through its well-established, well-understood interface. With the 2314 DASF, IBM served notice that it could make that strategy difficult—it could bundle the controller with the disk drives themselves and leave no socket, as it were, for outsiders to plug their disks in to. However, those same competitors knew that IBM still had to be careful not to affect the ability of its own widely installed disk drives to connect.

In pricing the 2314 DASF, which came to market a couple of years before the compatible vendors were active, IBM offered no discount below a comparably configured collection of 2311 disk drives. The users enjoyed the decrease in the cost of storing a given amount of data, but they actually paid slightly more for the nine-spindle box than they would have for eight 2311s: on rental, $5,250 a month for the DASF, compared to $5,125 a month for eight 2311 spindles and controller. The DASF sold for $252,000, while the 2311s and controller went for $237,000. Storing as much as 233 million characters, compared to the 60 million for the eight spindles of the 2311 disk drive, the DASF did well for IBM, as Table 28 shows:

Table 28
Number of Major IBM
Disk Drives Installed in the
U.S., 1963–70[6]

YEAR	1311	2311	2314
1963	788		
1964	5,169		
1965	8,314	258	
1966	9,209	5,537	
1967	7,342	15,566	370
1968	5,464	21,171	1,792
1969	3,716	23,690	3,844
1970	2,542	18,635	6,359

But note in Table 28 that the installed base of older 2311 disk drives continued to grow from 1967 through 1969, even though the 2314 DASF provided superior performance. Had IBM offered the 2314 disk drives individually, unbundled from the DASF package, that highly profitable growth in 2311 installations would certainly not have taken place. However, the very large base of older-technology 2311s—18,635 of them installed by 1970, earning high profits, plugging into a separately priced controller, and installed predominantly on thirty-day risk leases—offered a broad target for compatible disk drive suppliers with their superior technology. They could provide 360 users with 2314-level performance—or even better—in single-drive, not bulky nine-drive, increments.

During 1969 and 1970, as 2311 installations peaked and then started to decline, the 2314's installation rate rose sharply. That happened because in January 1969, when the competitive pressure from outside vendors was particularly intense and IBM management was worried that the impending Department of Justice antitrust suit might charge the company with illegal tie-in sales, IBM actually unbundled the DASF disk drive package, as it also unbundled software and services. Users could then buy IBM 2314 controllers and disk drives separately, taking advantage of their better performance (which was now better than ever, for IBM also improved the individual spindle's access time by 20 percent) in smaller steps. Many users began to return their 2311s and install single 2314s.

Plug-compatible vendors were locked out, however, because IBM's 2314 disk drive attached to a different controller from the 2311 controller they had been using. Any outsider not offering its own controller—and almost all did not—now had to decipher the newly available 2314 controller interface and redesign its equipment accordingly to remain competitive. This they did.

IBM was not yet ready to engage in a full price war, however. A look at the prices of the 2311, the original 2314 DASF, and the newly unbundled 2314 shows no real decrease. In fact, customers actually paid $210 per month *more* for the increased flexibility of unbundled 2314 equipment than they did for renting a nine-drive DASF.

In 1969, at the time of the 2314 unbundling, there were five compatible vendors selling comparable disk drives that attached to 2311 controllers. They had penetrated the market only moderately. According to IBM, the unbundling "took much of the glamour out of [compatible disks] as an IBM growth device [the unbundled 2314] is put in sight of most 2311 users."[7] In July of that year, F. G. Rodgers, president of IBM's Data Processing Division, wrote to company President Learson that the unbundling would be "a major deterrent" to competitive losses in the 2311 arena; he added that the 2314's "pricing and physical drive attachment should minimize exposure" to competition.[8] IBM could have unbundled the 2314 DASF right from the beginning, but the main reason it was doing so now was to hit back at compatible vendors—they offered 2314 technology to the overpaying 2311 customer at a price that was hard to refuse.

APRICOTS AND DUCKS

Unbundling the 2314s helped slow competitors' success with users of large 360s, but IBM continued to face major problems. The independent vendors were now turning their sights to the many small and medium-size 360 sites that still used outmoded 2311 disks. They were also pushing ahead with new disk technology that outpaced IBM's. West Coast–based Information Storage Systems (ISS), formed by ex-IBM employees, disclosed in early 1969 that it planned to ship a drive that topped not only the 2314 but IBM's next generation drive as well. "I am concerned that our large inventory of [disk] files is exposed," Learson wrote Frank Cary in May 1969.[9]

Worst of all for IBM was that it seemed likely to face a repeat of the 360 disk situation with its upcoming line of System/370 processors. Those new machines were designed to run the same applications as the 360s, but were expected to handle even greater interactive processing loads and would therefore depend even more heavily on disk drives. IBM was working on two new disk products, the Merlin/3330 for large 370s and the Winchester/3340 for smaller machines, but those products would not be shipped for as much as three years. At first, the 370s would just have to make do with the same 2314 drives aready under attack by superior competition in the 360 market. Technically, there was no problem attaching 2314s to the 370s, for the same interfaces were involved, but that left IBM as vulnerable to competition as ever.

"We have no complete answers on how to eliminate this exposure," Cary responded to Learson in 1969. "We are attempting to get as many 2314s out this year as possible. The Merlin file will give us a significant advantage at the high end of the [370] line and SDD [an IBM division] is working on technology to support a new [disk] development effort to replace to 2314 at the bottom and middle of the line. . . . While waiting . . . [a] repackaged 2314 is [the] best alternative."[10]

Repackaged, repriced, and reinterfaced, to be exact. IBM embarked on an audacious scheme of reintroducing the 2314 as a new disk drive that would sell to 370 users for much less than it had in its original incarnation but that would use an interface unknown to competitors. The door was to be shut in their collective face.[11] IBM's scheme for metamorphosing the 2314, a plan internally dubbed Apricot, called for wiping out the processor-to-controller interface, which outsiders had long assumed was immutable. That required physically mounting the controller circuitry in the processor. A so-called integrated file adaptor would be built into upcoming small and medium-size 370 processors that would enable individual disk drives to attach there directly. This was a radical change from the old 360 approach, which had relied on a separately boxed disk controller, but IBM planned to justify the inboard file adaptor as offering a significant advantage: it would save costs by applying the central processor's great power to certain functions formerly handled by the separate controller. (For the user whose processor had capacity to spare, this scheme could in fact be cost-effective; for other users, stand-alone controllers would still be available.)

Apricot was intended to meet several objectives. It would show competitors that IBM was not beyond changing an interface that they had assumed was fixed. Moreover, by design the built-in file adaptor would cut in half the number of sockets where disk drives could attach to the processor, thereby limiting rival vendors' potential market. Finally, with controller and processor mounted in the same box, rival vendors would be placed at a cost disadvantage. Their free-standing controllers would be more expensive to build than IBM's functionally equivalent file adaptor because IBM's could share a power supply and chassis with the processor. A clever vendor might come out with its own file adaptor, but to install it would mean physically entering the IBM processor box and risking IBM's refusal to maintain the processor any further. No customer was willing to take that risk just to save a few dollars a month on disk drives. Since the independent vendors could not service IBM processors, particularly those that were leased from IBM, they would be forced to price their more costly controllers equal to or less than what IBM charged for the integrated controller—no simple trick.

But IBM had yet another goal in mind. To help induce large 360 users to move up to the new 370 processors, the company wanted to offer them better disk drive performance on the latter systems. The Merlin/3330 disk drive was to be a main part of this inducement. IBM needed to make it clear to customers that they could enjoy the benefits of better disk drive performance on large systems *only* if they moved to a 370. Users of small and medium 360s—the models 20, 25, 30, and 40, of which over ten thousand were installed—would be reluctant, however, to discard 360s and move to a 370 unless they, too, were offered superior disk drive performance. The Merlin disk drive was too expensive for their needs, but IBM figured it might lure them away from 360s if it offered a substantial price cut on the 2314 disk drives. The price change would have to be isolated so that it would not cut into profits from the many 2314s still being leased to 360 users. The disk drive market needed resegmenting.

IBM had to simultaneously create incentives for migration to the 370s, to protect current revenues and profits from 360-attached disk drives, and to still create a strong barrier against compatible vendors' goods. Therefore, new plans were drawn up to produce a specifically modified 2314 disk drive that would attach only to the in-board file adaptor of the medium-size 370/135 and 145 processors, and that would carry a particularly low price. The disk drive would not attach to any 360 processors; it would use an interface never before seen by the independent manufacturers. IBM decided to split the controller's circuitry between the 370 processor's file adaptor and the disk box itself—thus an entirely new interface and an even bigger obstacle for independent manufacturers was created. With Merlin/3330 coming to market soon, this new reinterfaced 2314 disk drive would clearly have a short product life, and outsiders would therefore be reluctant to spend precious cash on duplicating it. But it would hold the 370 market for IBM until better disk drives were available.

Apricot became Mallard, a revised plan, and the 2314 became the 2319-A, a repackaged disk drive. So began a textbook example of how changing interfaces reinforces IBM's price discrimination. IBM would favor 370 customers at the expense of 360 users, offering each group essentially the same product but at widely different prices. Where IBM charged $256,000 for eight unbundled 2314 spindles and a controller for use on the 360, a similar number of 2319 spindles along with the file adaptor on a 370/135 processor went for as little as $145,415. The comparable monthly rental prices were $5,675 for a set of 2314s, but only $3,575 for a set of 2319s attached to a 370/135.*

The 2319-A seemed to solve IBM's problems, even though privately the company knew Mallard was but a "gimmicky tactic"** and a "3-file kludge" whose sole purpose was to disguise a direct price cut on the functionally identical 2314.[12] The 2319-A was simply a repackaging of old technology, a stopgap measure designed to hold competition back until Merlin was ready. IBM's legal staff became concerned about its purely anticompetitive nature.[13]

As the 370/145 with its built-in file adaptor and the matching 2319-A disk drive were unveiled to customers, IBM turned its attention back to protecting the more than 27,000 original 2314 disk drives still attached to 360s on risk leases. Compatible manufacturers had already installed close to 1,400 of their own 2314-type disk drives there, and now, seeing how the 2319-A was locking them out of the 370 realm, they renewed their efforts in the 360 arena. IBM raised its estimate of their potential success from 2,800 to 3,400 drives installed by the end of 1970 and concluded that there were some 7,000 "doubtful situations" in which it might lose additional disk drive business.[14] By November of that year, IBM was aware that the major independent vendors were about to enhance their own 2314-type disk drives with a doubling of storage capacity. That alone was projected by IBM as potentially boosting the outsiders' share of leased 2314-type drives to 69 percent of the installed base 360 by 1974—and, worse, weakening the incentive for users to move up to the 370s.[15]

IBM had, in its own words, "underestimated the early and rapid [compatible vendor] build-up" of 2314 drives on 360 systems,[16] and it now found that it did not have "satisfactory strategy or action programs" to protect its own disk drive

---

* The full extent of the price discrimination in the 2319-A can be seen by comparing its rental and purchase prices to those of the 2314. The 2319-A disk box, to which had been added new control circuitry not used in the original 2314, rented for $1,000 a month and sold for $45,000. Yet standard 2314 spindles rented for $1,309 or sold for $59,164. Also, the controller for the unbundled 2314 rented for $1,525, while the 370s' file adaptor rented for only $475 to $550 a month. In all respects, 370 users got the better deal. (Note that IBM did not charge any more for the 2319-A1 box, which included the controller function along with three disk spindles, than it did for the less functional A2 disk box.)

** IBM vice president P.W. Knaplund wrote to president T.V. Learson in April 1971 that the 2319 used a new model number to introduce a direct price cut on the 2314 disk drive and was "one symptom of [IBM's] general and deeply rooted problem" of "avoiding facing and taking necessary risks to solve real and urgent problems" by "gimmicky tactics [that] may buy us some time, [which] so far we haven't used . . . well."

profits. Clearly, some means of cutting the original 2314's price was needed to contain the compatible firms but not at the expense of discouraging movement to the 370s or cutting too deeply into profits. Too big a disk drive price cut for 360 users would reduce the relative advantage of moving up to the 370s.

As it often did when planning to defend a threatened market segment, IBM first considered a "fire sale," a big cut in purchase price designed to induce customers into buying boxes that they now leased. The idea was that independent suppliers would have more trouble replacing gear that customers had purchased. Also considered was a change in the extra-use charge collected on all leased equipment that customers used for more than the allotted 176 hours a month. The charge was calculated as 10 percent of 1/176th of the monthly rental charge; for a 2314 DASF renting for $5,250 a month, the not insignificant hourly extra-use charge worked out to just under $3. Large customers often found that this charge made up as much as 15 percent of their monthly IBM rental bill. However, independent manufacturers did not generally charge for extra use.

Both of those two options were eventually discarded. In December 1970, IBM saw the 2319 scheme of partially bundling controller and disk drive together as "a positive program to contain" the compatible vendors, so it extended it to the 360 arena. It introduced the 2319-B, yet another repackaged 2314. The old disk drive was combined with reworked controllers that had been shipped originally with 2311 disk drives. IBM had many of these old controllers in storage, and it now gave them a new coat of paint and some new circuitry. The 360-only 2319-B also incorporated a new interface, and that helped keep the competition at bay. As with the 2319-A, designed for 370s, there was a 2319-B1 disk box with three 2314 spindles and a substantial part of the controller function, to which up to two additional three-drive units, 2319-B2s, could be attached for a maximum "string" of nine drives.

This new packaging effectively cut the price of 2314 disk drives, but by having them attach to the 360 processors in a way that was different from all the 2314s already installed and by renting them for higher prices, IBM avoided having all 2314 profits plummet. It further protected the high-profit rental base of the original 2314s by limiting production of the 2319-B and reminding customers of the imminent arrival of the 370s and their superior Merlin/3330 disk drive. Thus, although the 2319-B was priced attractively, movement to it by customers was purposely slowed. In order to maintain the incentives for 360 customers to move up to 370s, IBM kept the price of the 2319-B controller high, at $1,450 a month, while the 370 file adaptors went for only $550 a month at most. Therefore, for the 360 user to obtain the improved price of the 2319, he still had to pay a high price for the control unit. The full benefit of the 2319 would be available only when he moved to a 370 system and installed the less-expensive file adaptor.

IBM calculated that this repricing would cut the independents' potential share of the disk drive market by half, down to 30 percent from 60 percent.[17] The new disk drive product also represented still another interface to match, for IBM purposely made the 2319-B interface different from the A model, just to up the development ante. In fact, while a string of 2319-A disk drives might include the original 2314s (thereby leaving the window partially open for outsiders with their 2314-type drives), the B model used only special B-type spindles.

MEMOREX AND TELEX: TWO CASE STUDIES IN DEFEAT

The crushing effects of the 2319-B on the intruders was immediate. To remain competitive, they had to lower their prices both on disk drives and, if they offered them, on controllers. They had to design, test, and build new interface electronics to make the correct attachments. That cost money that they could ill afford, especially those that also sold compatible tape drives and were suffering from IBM's comparable pricing and interface tactics in that market.

It is clear from company documents that IBM quietly scrutinized the operations of its compatible rivals, building financial models of their businesses and watching for just the right moment to strike at them. By estimating their engineering and manufacturing costs, IBM could accurately determine their profit rates, cash flows, and the time it would take them to react to its own market moves. IBM viewed Telex and Memorex as two of the most threatening vendors, and they were treated to special "commercial analysis." IBM analysts concluded—rightly—that both companies planned to grab market share with their current disk drive products and to use their profits there to expand into additional peripherals markets by leveraging off their established sales forces. Both companies suffered enormously from the low-priced 2319s, and both eventually sued IBM for violations of the antitrust laws, seeking hundreds of millions of dollars in damages.

Telex had first found success in the computer market by selling tape and disk drives for the 360, and it was in the process of adding printers and add-on memories when IBM's Mallard shattered its plans in late 1970. Like other rivals of IBM, Telex had made use of the advantage it could offer users by becoming a broad-based supplier of 360-compatible peripherals: users wanted to deal with as few vendors as possible, for that made their operations much simpler. Telex was buying disk drives from another manufacturer, Information Storage Systems (ISS), and was planning to build some of its own peripherals.

The company was mainly self-financed, but that meant its profitability depended largely on how long it could keep equipment installed and earning full rent. First, ISS had to be paid, then Telex's own marketing, service, overhead, lease financing, and other costs got paid. Only then were any profits recorded. After studying Telex in detail, IBM estimated that a 20 percent reduction in its rival's rental revenue, instigated either by a cut in price or by reduced rental life, would cut Telex's profits by more than half.[18]

Telex reacted to the 2319 introductions by dropping the monthly charge on its competing drive to an average of $333 from $450. It also cut the price of the related control unit by half. Although functionally equivalent, if not superior, to IBM's disk drives, the Telex disk drives could no longer attach to the low-priced file adaptor offered on the 370 processors. Without a fairly large investment to match IBM's new interface, Telex was unable to compete once a 360 user installed a low-priced 2319-B or moved to a 370 machine—its functionally identical disk drive simply would not connect to those IBM products.

As a result, Telex was suddenly locked out of the market. Its financial condition was further weakened because it had to drop prices not only on the disk drives it was about to install but also on all those already in place with customers. Monthly rental revenues plummeted.[19] In contrast, the contrived incompatibility between the 2314 and the 2319-B enabled IBM to limit the effect of its slashed disk drive prices to only those disk drives the customer actually changed. The compatible manufacturers, however, were forced to drop prices on all their disk drives, whether installed or waiting to be shipped to a customer, for there was no incompatibility between their old and new products.

As basic economics would predict, lower prices boosted demand for disk drives, albeit at a much lower profit rate for Telex.[20] The squeeze on its bottom line was clearly evident to the investors, and raising cash became extremely difficult for the Tulsa company. Many financial analysts as, for example, Stephen J. Butters, a securities analyst at Putnam Mutual Fund, reported in November 1970 that the principal risks facing compatible manufacturers "are price cutting and new product introductions by IBM."[21] The day after the 2319-B introduction, Butters concluded that "the recent peripherals product introductions by IBM appear to be aimed directly at the independent peripheral manufacturers."[22] As a result, Butters recommended not purchasing any securities of those companies.[23] Putnam Mutual itself began selling its 582,900 shares of Telex stock as soon as IBM unveiled the 2319-B. Within fifteen days, it had sold all but 127,700 shares, and those were gone within three months. Overnight, Telex stock crashed, losing all its former Wall Street glamour.

Memorex adopted a strategy different from Telex's, but it eventually suffered just as badly. Where Telex purchased disk drives, Memorex built them itself. That meant that its financial condition was dependent not only on keeping rented equipment installed for as long as possible but also on maintaining high volumes of production. An idle factory did not earn its keep. Like Telex, however, Memorex sought rapid expansion into new product areas—a strategy that increased its funding needs and made it heavily dependent on outside financing.

IBM's analysis of Memorex in the spring of 1970 determined that it was a strong competitor but that through 1976 it would need to borrow $75 million externally to finance its growth. Memorex was likely to get this financing, IBM reckoned, because of the attractive profits it was earning from its disk drives and certain other goods. Ominously, IBM analysts concluded that "if IBM were to turn the screw, if you will, and reduce the amount of volume, this would be critical [in] insuring that [Memorex] did not become a viable company."[24] In fact, Memorex was more needy of money and more vulnerable than IBM knew—it wanted not $75 million but $200 million, so ambitious were its plans.

IBM had particular reason to fear Memorex. Memorex had already succeeded in breaking IBM's monopoly on two lucrative products, magnetic tape and removable disk packs. Memorex used profits from those two products to fund its disk drive manufacturing and marketing. Even worse from IBM's perspective was that Memorex was busy planning a 360-compatible processor. The Memorex processor was to be competitive in price and performance with the low end of the 360 line, and, more threatening, it would be able to run programs written for the many small 360/20s that IBM had been installing. The 360/20 had been designed to be incompatible with larger 360s, so Memorex saw an opportunity to win model 20 customers by offering them a machine with which they could grow without the hassle of converting to the 360 mainstream. Memorex was also aiming at the many users of IBM's disk operating system (DOS), which was a smaller, incompatible subset of OS/360 that many small 360 users employed with great satisfaction. Those customers would eventually face a difficult conversion to OS/360, and Memorex hoped to woo them away. Besides fewer conversion headaches, Memorex's computer system was also going to offer better disk drive and communications capabilities than IBM's comparable systems. In many ways, Memorex's plan resembled the highly successful Liberator attack that Honeywell had perpetrated almost a decade earlier.

IBM's aggressive pricing of the 2319 and its segmenting of the marketplace hurt Memorex as it did Telex. Memorex had introduced a 2314 replacement in December 1969 and was just beginning shipments a year later when the 2319-A was unveiled. Memorex had assumed that the controller-disk drive interface was the least stable, and it therefore offered a complete disk subsystem, with controller and drives, for the 360.

Rather than attempt to modify its disk drive to connect to the 370s' file adaptor, Memorex was savvy enough to offer its own external file adaptor and drop its prices on disk drives and controllers: to $260 from $285 a month and to $600 from $900 a month, respectively. After the 2319-B became available to 360 users, Memorex cut the prices on its own 360-compatible drives and control units. Since its products were still compatible with the 360 processors at the processor interface, no additional engineering was required. But, like Telex, Memorex was forced to cut prices across the board on installed as well as on nearly installed equipment. Naturally, the result was lower profits.

These two actions by IBM had a profound impact on Memorex's ability to raise the capital it so direly needed to enter the processor business. It had hoped to boost production volume by supplying disk drives for IBM systems and for its own machines. These latter, it had hoped, would be a secure base of systems whose processor-disk interfaces would be defined by Memorex and would therefore be immune to changes by IBM. That would mean more predictable rental revenues. Since predictable revenue was uppermost in the minds of banks and securities underwriters offering financing, the processor project was crucial to Memorex's grand plans.

Memorex actually did install several of its own computers, and to much acclaim—customers said they were quite pleased—but after the 2319's double whammy, Memorex's financial position began to unravel. In May 1973, the company ran out of funds and terminated its fledgling systems business. With its demise, financing became much harder, and before long Memorex was on the skids, facing liquidation by its major creditors. The glamour days were over, never to be regained.

13. Smashing the Disk Drive Players

Don't make misrepresentations to anyone you deal with. . . . Everyone you do business with is entitled to fair and evenhanded treatment.

—IBM's *Business Conduct Guidelines,* as quoted by Buck Rodgers in *The IBM Way*

Let's review what IBM had done so far in the disk drive arena and see how it determined prices and profit rates for its products there. First the company developed an innovative disk drive, the 2314, which it packaged in the nine-drive DASF to appeal primarily to users of large 360 systems. When its competition began replacing older 2311 drives with 2314-type technology, IBM unbundled the DASF and offered its disk drives separately. When competition came after the 2314 business, IBM dropped its prices and split the controller in two, relocating it to change interfaces and create a moving target. This 2319-A product, essentially a repackaged and repriced 2314, was at first merely a holding operation to encourage migration to 370s, but the tactic was extended with yet another interface change to keep the competition from replacing disk drives on the still-vulnerable 360 systems, the 2319-B.

These moves enabled IBM to cascade its leased disk drives down from large users, who needed high performance as early as possible, to small users, who took advantage of the performance later; eventually some 2314s were revamped and offered for the System/3 family. Every repackaging of the hardware extended the products' lease life and brought IBM additional profits. Meanwhile, IBM introduced new disk technology at the high end in the form of the Merlin/3330 disk drive. Also, as will be seen below, by carefully repackaging these disk drives several times and always limiting their usefulness to selected groups of customers, IBM was able to keep the vast bulk of its disk drives installed at high prices for longer than would have been possible otherwise. In the process, life became extremely difficult for the competition, which was forced to cut prices, see their profit rates slide, and forgo vital financing.

Although contributing to IBM's revenues and profits, these repackaging tactics clearly must have also added to its costs. It took significant amounts of money to repeatedly repackage the 2314 equipment and to train personnel in selling and servicing each new version. What's more, with each step IBM came closer to violating the antitrust laws, for each shift in the 2314 was arguably an exercise in price discrimination by a monopolist intent on maintaining its monopoly. IBM was marketing the same product at radically different prices to different groups of customers. In each instance, the price was determined solely by the nature of the competition IBM faced. Early 2314 users paid the most and 2319 customers the least. All received essentially the same function—storage capacity, access time, and storage density—from the disk drive hardware.

IBM was certainly not unaware of the risk inherent in its actions. As R. D. Anderson, project leader of the 2319-A, stated, "Clearly the problem [with the 2319-A] was financial." With the legal department increasingly concerned about potential antitrust charges, some way had to be found to hide the fact that the 2319-A earned lower profits than the 2314 that it was based on. It is to this hide-and-seek profit game that we turn next.

Ever since the days of Watson, Sr., IBM had tread carefully around the law. After January 1969, when the Department of Justice's antitrust suit was filed, and even more after private antitrust suits were filed in the next few years, it was unlikely that the company would want to have its files combed under a subpoena by antitrust plaintiffs looking for evidence of illegal price discrimination. But there were methods of creative accounting that could effectively limit this risk. Given the wide variety of factors that affect the calculation of profits of a leased product whose fixed overhead costs are high, the problem of reconciling the 2319-A's pricing with its profitability was not insurmountable.

Hillary Faw, the IBM financial executive, wrote in late 1969 that the "[Department of Justice] complaint specifically covers varying profit margins. An intensive investigation of this issue would reveal the extent of our price control and its supporting practices. Such a revelation would not be helpful to our monopoly defense."[1]

In other words, it was necessary to get rid of damaging evidence. The IBM legal staff advised those involved with 2319 pricing to "clean out your files."[2] IBM knew, then, that the 2319-A, a "gimmick" from the start, would be the focus of many antitrust charges from competitors.

What was it that IBM was so intent on hiding? What larger pattern might have been revealed had the files not been "cleaned out"? Might it have been that IBM was losing money on the 2319-A, that the Mallard disk drives had been priced from the start to lose money just to thwart competition, to make the Telexes and Memorexes of the world "dying companies," as IBM put it?

There are several critically important considerations in pricing a product that is primarily leased instead of sold. These include the estimated cost of building the product, its rental life, and the accounting method used to make financial projections. The interplay of these factors has already been shown in the discussion of IBM's discriminatory overhead allocations for 360 systems. There, tying the allocations of support services to revenue levels masked well the actually high profits earned by large systems compared with the low profits earned by smaller ones. The result, much to IBM's benefit, was that all 360 systems appeared to be equally profitable, when in fact if the costs had been apportioned in a more realistic manner, price discrimination would clearly have been seen.

IBM had a similar problem when pricing the 2319s. Because those products' prices were only two-thirds of that of the installed 2314, which was essentially the same hardware, and because IBM had to spend money to redesign and repackage the controller for the 2319s, one would expect the later drives to have earned significantly less profit. Furthermore, the fact that the 2319-A was designed to be marketed only until the Winchester/3340 disk drive was ready and the fact that the 2319-B was used only on the soon-to-be-obsolete 360 would imply that the disk drives' rental lives would be extraordinarily short. Short-lived products do not earn much, if any, profits on lease. Finally, the 2319-B, although orchestrated in such a way as to limit its impact on IBM's 2314, would have had some impact on those installed drives, shortening their rental lives and reducing overall disk profits still more. This negative effect was, in fact, part of the reasoning behind the introduction of the 2319-B, and it should have been included as a cost item in IBM's financial analysis of the Mallard plan.

Therefore, the 2319s could easily be taken to be money-losers for IBM, their only purpose being to stop competitors who were offering better performance at better prices and eroding IBM's market share. In addition, the 2319-A was viable only because IBM controlled the market for the 370 processor to which it attached and therefore controlled the interface between processor and disk drive. If the 2319-A and -B were both money-losers, the only way IBM could have afforded to market them was by price discriminating: it could subsidize them with profits earned elsewhere in its product line. Lacking broad product lines that included areas of virtually complete monopoly, the suppliers of compatible peripherals were doomed once IBM began to lower its prices in the narrow areas where they competed directly.

COOKING THE BOOKS

IBM solved its competitive problem: It forwent what would have been the fair response—cutting the 2314's price across the board, because that would have hurt revenues and profits from the many installed disk drives and disrupted

IBM's migration plans for its customers. Instead, it decided to segment the market again by changing interfaces and by price discriminating, all the while fixing the books to cover its tracks. Using revenues as the basis for allocating overhead not only gave the company a good deal of flexibility in shifting costs, it also helped cut prices. A drop in price reduced a product's revenues, which reduced its overhead allocation, and that, as if by magic, improved the product's financial standing.

To understand the wonderful flexibility of this accounting method, consider the following example. Assume a new product is brought out with a sales price of $100. Its directly estimated manufacturing cost is $35 and its apportioned cost is $35, resulting in a total cost of $70 and a forecast profit of $30. Now, assume that the price is cut by $40, leaving a new sales price of $60. If there are no changes in the costs of making and marketing the product, the new price should result in a decrease of $40 in profit, or a loss of $10.

Under IBM's accounting method, however, there is no loss. Because of the relatively high, revenue-indexed apportionment, the product will still show a net profit, as Table 29 shows. (Alternative A shows the initial forecast, B the price cut with no change in cost allocation, and C the results of IBM's allocation method.)

So for a product earning a 30 percent profit, IBM was able to drop its price by 40 percent and still show a profit on its books—this despite the fact that there was no change in the underlying costs associated with manufacturing and marketing the product.* In the case of the 2319s, since they were "new products," these costs would actually have to be higher, not lower, as the firm's accounting method indicated. The repackaged disk drives required, among other things,

Table 29

Example of Implication of Revenue
Apportionment on Price Cuts

	Alternatives		
	A	B	C
Revenue	100	60	60
Manufacturing costs	35	35	35
Apportioned costs	35	35	21
Profit	30	−10	7

* IBM, naturally, was well aware of what its accounting techniques meant to its freedom in setting prices. In early 1969, one of IBM's financial personnel stated, "An allocation to revenues gives us greater pricing flexibility than an allocation to total cost." In July 1971, the IBM Management Review Committee recognized that one implication of changing these techniques would be that "the leveling effect of current revenue apportionment technique is reduced" and "low profit CPU . . . would fall into a loss position."

additional manufacturing, inventory, training, marketing, and installation costs. Yet the pricing method called for overhead to be allocated to other products—those earning more total revenue—rather than to the one actually requiring the support. The accounting understated the real cost to IBM of installing 2319s after all was said and done, and therefore it overstated any expected profits. Although it was a distortion of reality, this pricing method at least had the virtue of being relatively consistent over time; IBM used it before and after the 2319s, on most of its products.

Other assumptions made in pricing the 2319s lacked even that temporal consistency. For instance, what value would be assigned to the 2314 equipment returned to IBM but not re-leased to other customers? Since IBM intended to produce 2319 disk drives from these old 2314s, this was an important question. Here again, IBM had much flexibility. It could set a high value derived from the market price that competitors received for comparable equipment. Or it could use the undepreciated asset value of the equipment, or the book value carried on its accounting records, or even the salvage value, the worth of whatever parts and precious metals it could retrieve from the returned hardware, if there were no longer any market for the product as a functioning whole. The value IBM established for the 2314 would greatly affect the profits of the 2319s, as shown in IBM's books.

The disk drives returned to IBM were technically comparable to disk drives that other vendors offered, but IBM charged more than its rivals. Now the IBM disk drives were being refused by customers because they were overpriced. Had IBM been willing to drop its prices to a competitive level, the gear would have remained installed. Nevertheless, IBM did not use the 2314s' market value in its calculation of the 2319s' profitability but rather the net book value. Since the company depreciated these 2314 disk drives rapidly, less than 10 percent of the initial book value of a new 2314 was assigned to the cost of a 2319. Moreover, IBM made this assumption even as it was building completely new 2314s. Thus, these disk drives were neither in surplus nor fully depreciated by 90 percent. IBM built new disk drives and modified them to make 2319s, but it assigned only 10 percent of the product's cost to the 2319s. The result was an unusually low initial cost—certainly far lower than any competitor could match—from which to establish a price. On the revenue side, because IBM's accountants assumed that 88 percent of the 2319-As and 93 percent of the 2319-Bs would be leased, their estimate of their respective rental lives was a major factor in estimating total future profits. In fact, they used forty-eight months for the model A and fifty months for the B, despite the fact that the forthcoming Winchester/3340 disk drive would begin shipping long before that time. Not only would the Winchester obsolete the 2319s' disk drive technology, but the 370 machines to which the new disk drives attached would soon be replacing the 360s to which 2319-Bs were connected.

By contrast, the Merlin/3330 disk drives, which contained truly new disk technology, were assumed to have a rental life of forty-eight months. (In a later analysis, IBM gave the 2319-A a more realistic rental life of twenty-six months and the B from nineteen to twenty-five months.)

Using these arbitrarily determined variables, the company was able to create a self-serving set of books that showed much higher profit rates for the repackaged 2319s than would ever have been possible using realistic assumptions. One can only assume that if the files hadn't been "cleaned out," the realistic assumptions would have been discovered by the courts when the independents finally went to trial over the matter. Experts in subsequent antitrust cases, in fact, examined IBM's financial analysis of the 2319s and concluded that the 2319s were purposely priced to lose money.

It appears that IBM first established its $1,000-a-month price for three disk drives solely for the purpose of containing the competition. That done, it then had to contrive an official price analysis to support that "conclusion." In the process, IBM considered three prices for the three-drive 2319-A: $1,000, $1,200, and $1,400 a month. It rejected the highest price, despite the fact that it could have earned greater profits, because it was estimated that competitors would undercut the $1,400 tag and gain a 23 percent share on 370/135 and 145 systems. The lowest price was finally chosen because it was projected to limit the other vendors to only a 6 percent share on those processors. IBM was willing to forgo profit in order to limit its rivals to that deathly level. As Watson, Jr., had said, "market share" was the company's primary goal.

(Similar pricing problems arose with the 2301 model 8 tape drive that came into the market about the same time as the 2319. It, too, was a product that was still in use under its former designation and was being returned by users to IBM, which repackaged and repriced it to contain the competition in another market segment. In order to show a profit on the books even while the revamped tape drive was priced low to stop competition, IBM set the value of the returned tape drives to zero so that, on the books at least, new value could be added. And as with the 2319s, the 2301 model 8 tape drive was given an unrealistically long rental life of fifty-eight months, despite the fact that it was based on old technology and limited to recording just seven tracks when customers were moving to nine. The price cut on the aging tape drive also artificially reduced the product's revenue apportionment for overhead. IBM neglected to take into consideration any impact the tape drive would have on currently installed equipment. The IBM legal staff complained, but the product was introduced nevertheless.)

QUESTIONS OF LAW

IBM's clever bookkeeping and the nature of its prices and costs pose intractable obstacles for antitrust enforcers. Ideally, when investigating charges of predatory pricing by a monopolist, one would like to know the exact assumptions used in setting a product's price: if the price is below cost, one must question the monopolist's intentions. A sophisticated monopolist will engage in artificial pricing and then rid its files of damaging evidence, leaving law enforcement agencies able to prosecute only the unsophisticated—those who fail to cover their tracks sufficiently. The alternative would be for prosecution experts to reconstruct what the allegedly guilty monopolist should have known in making its pricing decisions and then hold it accountable to that standard, but that is equally unattractive. Judges are not likely to accept such after-the-fact judgments when large damage claims hang in the balance.

Even if complete and accurate data actually are available from a monopolist, the problems for effective antitrust enforcement are not over. There remains the question of whether all such below-cost pricing engaged in by a monopolist is condemnable. In short, how low can the monopolist's price go?

Some observers have settled on viewing not the average total costs but rather the much lower marginal cost. This view is based on the observation that in some instances a company can minimize its losses by selling at any price above the costs directly associated with making the product. Such a strategy results in the firm's covering more overhead than would be the case if prices were kept high and the firm sold nothing.

Although it is an interesting theoretical question—and relevant in many other industries—it is largely irrelevant in IBM's case. This is because during the period in question, IBM was constrained by insufficient manufacturing capacity and therefore had long waiting lists for its equipment. IBM's devoting this scarce production capacity to products that did not contribute fully to the company's costs would be at the expense of other, more profitable products. Thus, IBM did without profits it could have earned on other products just to offer a product with a low price designed to stop its competitors. This in turn means that the actual marginal costs associated with the decision were very high, for the profit calculation had to include not only the product in question but also the lost profits on products never built or built late.

Secondly, the marginal cost test for predatory pricing in IBM's case leaves entirely too much room for anticompetitive action to be any meaningful restraint on a monopolist's freedom to crush competitors with low prices. The direct product costs in this industry are in the 20 to 30 percent range. In that case, IBM could have cut prices by 70 to 80 percent with impunity. Therefore, adopting such a standard, given the structure of the costs of its products, would be tantamount to granting it antitrust immunity. Yet there have been many that claim just such a standard is appropriate.

Finally, most observers are reluctant to accept marginal cost tests in evaluating prices in industries that are difficult for companies to reenter once low prices have driven them out and a monopolist is left free to increase its profit rate. In the computer industry, it is very difficult for a firm to successfully reenter if for no other reason than that one can expect IBM to again respond forcefully.

Over these issues, the debate raged as to how the antitrust laws should be enforced. Lacking a clear consensus, IBM felt free to exploit its power, knowing that the certainty the courts needed to punish it would be lacking. It turned out to be a safe bet.

MORE DISK DRIVE ACTION

The 2319s were by no means IBM's last shot at the vendors of compatible disk drives. It had given them much to think about by showing them that IBM was not beyond shedding reluctance to act out of fear of adverse self-impact and antitrust action. IBM's actions suddenly made financing much harder to come by for its smaller and relatively impoverished rivals. With its large areas of power in other parts of its product line and in other geographical markets where the peripherals companies were less active, IBM's position remained secure. In fact, it would soon pump extraordinary amounts of cash into research and development efforts as a means of erecting new long-term defenses against future attacks. It began to push disk drive technology at a pace that only it has been able to maintain. Staying in the disk drive game would get much harder during the rest of the 1970s for other vendors.

There was still a good deal of fight left in at least some of them. Demand for disk storage remained strong as customers expanded their interactive systems. IBM's year-long delay in delivering the Merlin disk drive gave its rivals a much-needed breather. Severe technical problems arose with that disk drive, which was IBM's first truly new one since the 2314 had been brought out in 1965. The delay in the Merlin also forced a delay in introducing the first two 370 processors, the models 155 and 165, which IBM hoped would lure large customers away from their 360/50s and 65s.

In February 1971, two months after announcing the 2319-B, IBM determined that it "could lose over one-half of the lease base [disk] market over the plan period without additional products."[3] In March of that year, the company projected that at current rates, by 1975 compatible vendors would have installed about 22 percent of all tape drives and 47 percent of all disk drives leased to 360/370 users. That much lost market share, IBM figured, would cost it $406 million in tape drive revenues, $243 million in add-on memory, and a colossal $1.01 billion in disk drive revenues.[4] IBM management was informed on April 23 that competitors were eroding its lease base at a rate of about 1,000 disk drives a month—the "tape drive area is also being impacted and printers and memories will be next."[5]

The 2319 repackaging strategy—to offer essentially the same products to different customers with widely different prices and changed interfaces—had damaged, but not completely stopped, the competition. Chairman Watson stated that he wanted "a clear understanding that [IBM] swallow whatever financial pills are required now and get ready for the future."[6] The binds of self-restraint were breaking fast. IBM was about to unleash on the compatible companies a punch harder than anything yet. It hit them in May with the rather innocuous-sounding Fixed Term Plan (FTP).

IBM's traditional risk lease had made it quite easy for compatible vendors to replace its equipment. IBM shouldered all the financial risk, so no penalty was incurred when a user switched to a newcomer. He simply asked IBM to remove its hardware and moved in the rival gear.

What IBM needed now, therefore, was a new form of lock-in, a method of tying customers to their IBM gear and locking out competitors for at least a few months. The cost of leaving IBM had to be shifted from IBM to the customers themselves, and an incentive had to be created to encourage them to make longer commitments to IBM. The obvious incentive was a healthy price cut.

Despite a special task force's conclusion in February 1971 that there were "serious policy, legal and cost objections to be overcome before any contractual [long-term lease] could be implemented," in May 1971 IBM unveiled the FTP, making it available only for a select group of threatened peripherals.[7] It gave users an 8 percent cut in monthly charges for leases of twelve months and 16 percent for twenty-four-month contracts on disk drives, tape drives, printers, and their respective controllers. In addition, IBM dropped all extra-use charges for products installed under the FTP. IBM also cut by 15 percent the purchase prices of all products covered by the FTP. It also let customers accrue up to two years' worth of credits toward purchasing the equipment they leased.[8]

The idea was that once they had signed a one- or two-year lease contract with IBM, especially one that offered a sizable discount, customers would be less likely to leave. In exchange for the discount, IBM imposed a stiff penalty—as much as five months' rent during the first year of a two-year deal, or about a fifth of the contract's value—for prematurely breaking the lease contract. To match IBM's offer at sites where the FTP was in force, competitors would now have to discount their prices to cover not only IBM's new low price but the penalty charge as well. It was that or wait until the FTP contract was up, but given IBM's quickening pace of new product introductions, waiting might easily turn out to be futile.

IBM gained much from the FTP. It was far more advantageous than a simple price cut—to be effective that solution would have entailed too great a loss in revenues and profits. According to a study presented to the Management Review Committee, IBM would have had to slash prices to the bone to remain competitive: 50 percent on 2314 disk drives, 55 percent on the 2311 and 2841 controllers, 20 percent on the Merlin/3330 and its controller, 50 percent on 2401 tape drives, 60 percent on 2420 tape drives, 50 percent on 2803 controllers, and 15 percent on 3420 tape drives and controllers.[9] The FTP's price cuts of 8 percent and 16 percent looked small in comparison but were highly effective.

Moreover, when finally returned, the hardware would remain under IBM's ownership and therefore would not enter the used-equipment market. It could be refurbished and cascaded down to smaller systems to earn additional profits. If competition still managed to replace some equipment by getting a customer to break an FTP contract, IBM not only got its hardware back for further marketing, it got much of the discount back from the not-inconsequential penalty.

Even better for IBM was the FTP's power to lock other vendors out for many months and force them to look elsewhere for business. IBM's S. P. Bowers, a financial analyst, studied the effects of IBM's long-term leases on peripherals competitors. He concluded that such leases would keep them out of competition with IBM for about 20 months, thereby causing each to have lower corporate revenues and no funds for engineering or manufacturing, and causing each to become a "dying company!"[10] It appears as if at least some people at IBM were actually trying to run competitors out of business.

The impact of IBM's actions on the future profitability of these firms was not missed by the financial community, which advised clients to unload the stock of these firms, thereby increasing the difficulty they faced in raising new capital. Later, in court, several of these competitors claimed that IBM went even further in affecting their ability to raise capital than just dropping prices and introducing long-term lease plans. Their claim, described in Appendix G, was that IBM directly used its influence with many of the major financial institutions to ensure that they would not invest in these firms.

The FTP's incentives had to be strong enough to prompt users to forgo the freedom of risk leasing. IBM tracked its customers' responses to the FTP and found that just one month after its unveiling, approximately a fifth of the value of all leased tape drives, disk drives, and printers was covered by the plan. By September 1971, that number was up to 55 percent of tape drives and disk drives; by December, the compatible firms were noticeably suffering, and IBM bragged internally that "FTP has had the effect of reducing PCM installation rate of tape drives from about 250 per month to about 100 per month, and installations of disk spindles from about 900 per month to 500 per month."[11]

In February 1972, the company forecast that the compatible disk drive makers would achieve significantly less penetration from 1972 to 1974 than they had in the years 1969 through 1971, largely because the price differential between them and itself would "be far smaller." FTP was finishing the job the 2319 had begun.

Still, the corporation was not entirely pleased with this radical change in business practices. Not only did the lawyers withhold complete endorsement because of the obvious antitrust implications—the FTP's primary justification was as a means of keeping competition away from IBM customers—the financial department also had reservations. IBM had to pay a price to stop its competitors. In March 1972, an "approximate sizing of . . . annual gross revenue loss resulting from the FTP program" showed $29 million for 1971, $90 million for 1972, and $109 million for 1973.[12] The FTP also had a significant impact on profits. For instance, it had been discovered in July 1971, two months after the FTP went into effect, that $102 million in profits would be lost. To counter that negative effect, an internal study recommended that "price increases . . . be instituted wherever possible, including getting some plus out of any Memory/CPU rebalancing."[13] Within the month, a 4 percent boost in 360 processor and memory prices and an 8 percent boost in 370 processor and memory prices were approved. The FTP, which did not apply to the unthreatened processor, in effect committed the customer to his present peripherals. Once he was committed, IBM could safely increase the processor price, for without that box the peripherals were worthless. Once they had signed on to FTP, customers were in effect locked in to their processor, giving IBM greater freedom in raising the price of the processor.

"The net effects of the FTP and price change will probably be a wash," the firm concluded. "The net effect of the FTP and price changes will not significantly increase [the user's] total costs."[14]

This was price discrimination, plain and simple. Profits that might be lost on the exposed peripherals were moved to the secure processor. In the process, the narrowly focused peripherals competition was kept resource-poor. Customers were lucky that the price increases were no greater than the savings they gained from the FTP. IBM had gotten the average customer to give away his freedom to choose suppliers for literally nothing in return.

Internally, IBM had subtler concerns about the long-term leases. It feared that once a user had committed to using a particular piece of equipment for so long, he would be reluctant to migrate to the larger, follow-on items. There was also the concern that by making long-term leases more the norm, compatible equipment vendors would find it easier to negotiate such leases themselves, and their cash problems with short-term leases would be ameliorated. (IBM need not have worried, for banks were unwilling to extend the independents much credit on a two-year lease beyond the penalty the customer would pay if the lease were broken.)

THE RESULTS OF THE 2319s AND FTP

To further press the competition, the Fixed Term Plan was offered on the already-low-priced 2319 disk drives. Not surprisingly, the cumulative effect of this on the average customer, who normally paid about 12 percent extra each month in IBM's "additional use" charges, was substantial: in some cases a savings of almost two-fifths over the unbundled 2314 drives, as shown in Table 30. The cumulative discount is calculated for three, six, and nine-drive configurations and for twelve- and twenty-four-month contracts:

Table 30
IBM Price Reductions

UNIT PLUS	LEASE PRICE	2314-A PLUS 12% ADDITIONAL USE	12-MONTH CONTRACT	DISCOUNT	2319-B under FTP 24-MONTH CONTRACT	DISCOUNT
3 drives	$2,935	$3,287	$2,282	30.8%	$2,083	36.6%
6 drives	4,145	4,642	3,202	31.0	2,923	37.0
9 drives	5,505	6,166	4,122	33.1	3,763	39.0

The coincidence of the three discounts shown at the far right is no accident. IBM had studied its rivals carefully, particularly Memorex, which had been deemed most threatening to the monopoly, and in a program known as STRIPIM it determined that a 35 percent price cut on disk drives would be just the right "death discount" to do that company in.[15] At that level, IBM reckoned, Memorex would no longer be able to match the IBM discounts, and it would become a "dying company." In fact, all the compatible disk drive rivals of that period eventually ended up dead except Memorex. IBM won the bulk of the fast-expanding disk drive market for itself.

Long-term leases, some extending beyond the FTP's initial two-year maximum, would later turn out to be winners for IBM. In formulating the FTP, the company had been limited by the fact that the equipment into which it wanted to lock customers was already installed. With the new machinery that was just entering the market, there would be more freedom. IBM could merely increase the base price it charged to users who wanted only thirty-day cancelable leases and offer discounts off that inflated price to those customers willing to sign a one- or two-year contract. In this manner, it would cost the company nothing to lock users in and keep rivals out.

IBM did just that in March 1972, when it expanded its lease offerings with the Extended Term Plan. Here the customer had to sign a two-year contract, for which he received a 17.5 percent discount off the list price and was automatically signed up for an additional year when he finished the first two. This extended plan was available only on new peripherals. Prices after the discount were in the same relation to IBM's purchase prices as the standard thirty-day contracts had been in the past. The month-to-month leases carried a premium.

This way, IBM avoided the revenue and profit losses experienced with the FTP. Competitors were excluded without any effect on IBM's bottom line and, again, without the customer receiving any real price benefit.

Despite setbacks and fatalities, the compatible disk drive industry struggled along through the 1970s and into the early 1980s. The independents came under increasing pressure from IBM, which now used financial as well as technical tactics against them. As disk drive prices fell, demand soared, but the rivals' profits never reached the levels they had enjoyed during the 2314 era. Table 31 shows the reported profit and losses for the major firms for the critical years 1969 through 1972.

Those that did not collapse or merge into other companies hung on by trying to match IBM's successive disk drive products with their reduced financial resources and generally getting to market twelve to eighteen months after IBM began its first shipments of a new device. In spite of their constricted starts they often embellished IBM's designs, offering users an extra measure of performance or function, but they always had to sell for 15 to 20 percent less than IBM.

In August 1972, IBM came out with two computers able to use virtual memory, the 370/158 and 168. Virtual memory is a method of making computers able to handle programs and sets of data that are much larger than the processor memory's actual size. Virtual memory was vital to the success of interactive systems, for it enabled several large application programs and their attendant systems programming to be executed in the memory's limited space all at the same time. The 158 and 168 replaced the nonvirtual 370/155 and 165, which had been introduced just eighteen months earlier. The virtual systems relied heavily on disk storage for cost-effective operation and brought with them more interface changes.

Table 31
Plug Compatible Industry—Net Profit (Loss)
After Tax[16]
($ Million)

PCM FIRM	1969	1970	1971	1972
Calcomp	1.0	2.0	1.0	−10.0
Marshall	1.0	.4	−5.2	−10.0
Memorex	7.0	3.5	−14.6	1.3
Potter	2.2	2.4	2.1	2.9
Storage Technology	—	−.7	−4.1	2.9
Tracor	2.1	2.0	−.1	−27.2
Telex	4.6	7.8	3.3	.7
Total	17.7	17.5	−17.6	−42.9

The disk of choice for these virtual 370 computers was the same Merlin that had been unveiled for the nonvirtual 370s, but now a different method of attaching a disk drive to a processor was used.* Where the nonvirtual systems used a separate control unit, the 370/158 and 168 had control circuitry built into them. It was conceptually similar to what was used on the 145 processor—the 158 and 168 had an integrated storage controller (ISC). The ISC was priced significantly lower than the stand-alone, outboard controller, but, equally damaging to the competition, it worked only with a specially priced version of the Merlin, the 3333. That disk drive contained the rest of the control circuitry. IBM also came out with an alternative, stand-alone controller, the 3830-2, which also let the virtual processors control the 3333 disk drives. This new controller handled twice as many disk drives as the 3830-1 it had replaced, and it therefore provided large customers with another price break—they could halve their controller requirements. Together, the ISC and the 3830-2 formed the beginning of what IBM termed a "new attachment strategy."

This plan called for attaching interdependent strings of disk drives to the processors: first, two spindles of 3333 disk drives were attached, which included some control circuitry. Then came up to three standard Merlin/3330 disks, each containing two spindles, for a maximum of eight spindles per string. The string itself now attached either to the processor's ISC or to a stand-alone 3830-2 controller. This method, keeping a substantial part of the controller function in the first disks in a string, was to become standard for IBM, for with it customers had to install at least some IBM disk hardware no matter what. The number of strings that could attach to each control unit eventually increased, as did the ability to mix strings of different types of disk drives.

IBM priced the ISC at $2,200 a month, or $200 less than the outboard 3830-1 that it replaced. The 3830-2 went for $2,050 a month. The real savings, however, came from the increased capacity of the new control units. The 3830-2 could handle twice the number of disk drives, up to sixteen, than its predecessor, and the ISC could handle up to four times as many. The large user did not have to buy as many expensive controllers now.

The new attachment strategy implied several things for the compatible vendors. Now their Merlin-type disk drives could no longer be used as the first two drives in a string—they did not yet have 3333-type master disk drives to market. Worse, they had yet another IBM interface to match, with all the incumbent en-

---

* This was surprising, for the 3330 drive and its control unit (the 3830) had been announced but two years earlier (in June 1970 along with the first 370 systems) and initial shipments to customers had begun only in August 1971. Thus, only one year later (and just at the point that the disk competitors were beginning to ship off their own 3330-like drives), IBM was unveiling a modified and less expensive control unit and a modified drive to work with it. Not surprisingly, the announcement cut short the prior control unit's expected rental life—from 47 months at announcement to just 19 months. As a result, IBM then expected it to lose $28.7 million.

gineering effort and cost. As they worked to catch up, IBM had the market to itself for months or even years. In addition, by reducing the need for controllers, IBM now offered the best deal to large users, those that were the compatible companies' best customers. For a thirty-two-drive configuration, IBM in effect lowered the purchase price by $180,000, or 19 percent. For sixteen drives, the discount worked out to $65,000, or about 12 percent less than before.

IBM had devised a way to drop prices where it was most vulnerable while maintaining prices where competition was least effective. The smaller user, with less than nine 3330s to attach, gained only minimal savings—the several-hundred-dollar decrease in rent for the new control units from the original 3830-1 controller.

In order to encourage them to make the jump to virtual computing, IBM offered the best of the Merlin/3330 technology and the discounts only on virtual machines. A large nonvirtual user therefore had the choice of either going virtual or paying the high controller costs and remaining nonvirtual. This opened an opportunity for compatible firms to market their already lower-priced controllers and disk drives for nonvirtual systems, but in the end the nonvirtual market shrank in size and profits on it suffered due to intense competition from the rebuffed compatible vendors.

In March 1973, IBM finally unveiled the Winchester disk drive, the 3340, for small and medium-size 370s. It offered several technical innovations, the most important of which was the way in which its disk platters were contained with a set of read/write heads and access arms in an airtight plastic cartridge. In most previous disk drives, just the platters were made to be removed, but that meant exposure to contaminated room air that might contain troublesome amounts of dirt that could destroy data. As disks were made to pack more data per platter, the read/write heads were brought so close to the platter's surface that any dust particle there would make the heads "crash" and physically damage the recording surface. By sealing the heads with the platters in a clean, self-contained package known as a data module, the gap between head and platter surface was safely reduced and recording capacity boosted. Also, because the same heads and platters were kept together, their alignment was easier to maintain and further improvements in recording density could be made. The Winchester/3340 recorded at 1.5 million bits per square inch—about twice the density of the 3330 and nearly eight times that of the 2314.

IBM offered three versions of the Winchester data module, which it called the 3348. The model 35 module stored 35 million bytes of data, and the model 70 double that. As an option, the model 70 could be ordered with a set of so-called fixed read/write heads that could very quickly access 500,000 bytes. Unlike the others, these heads were always situated over specific circular tracks of data, and they could therefore read from and write to those tracks extremely quickly without the usual positioning delay.

IBM has continued up to the present to provide its largest customers with en-hancements. Mid-1973 saw it enable the integrated and stand-alone controllers to use more disks and to take strings composed of mixed types of disks. It also brought out a double-capacity version of the Merlin/3330, the 3330-11, which stored 200 million bytes of information. Its price, however, was only about 35 to 40 percent higher than that of the original 3330. The new 3330s soon became ex-tremely popular with large users, for they saved not only money but valuable floor space in computer centers. A group of thirty-two of them stored a total of 6,400 million bytes.

Capacity continued to rise, and the cost of storing a byte of data dropped. IBM came out with the model 3344 and 3350 disk drives in July 1975. The for-mer was based on the Winchester/3340, but its sealed data module was fixed to the drive box in a permanent fashion. IBM had discovered that with the in-creased storage capacity in each module, few users were removing the modules, so it might as well attach them to begin with. The 3344 stored four times the 3340's 70-megabyte capacity. The 3350 was derived from the Merlin/3330. It, too, had a fixed data module that used Winchester module technology. With 317.5 megabytes of storage, the 3350 also offered a higher transfer rate than the 3330, which made it a popular choice for interactive computing.

Users paid the equivalent of $4.57 a month per megabyte on the 3330, but only $2.37 on the 3350. Where the 3340 cost users $6.02 a month per megabyte, a megabyte cost only $2.86 on the 3344. During the five years leading up to 1970, IBM had offered no new technology or price changes in its disk drive busi-ness, but from 1970 to 1975, the price of storing large amounts of data dropped by as much as two-thirds. And IBM was again favoring its largest users, those who could take advantage of its biggest and best disk drives.

In sum, IBM greatly increased the on-line storage capacity of its systems and cut the cost of storing data. At the same time, it had erected numerous barriers to rival manufacturers. It accomplished these two goals by 1) constantly pushing the limits of disk drive technology; 2) extending the capabilities of controllers to handle more drives and mixes of different types of drives; 3) boosting the capac-ity of its 3330 and 3340 products with midlife kickers such as the 3344 and 3350; 4) complicating the interface between the disks and the processor: each string had a master drive and a set of slaves; 5) moving most customers from risk leas-ing to multiyear lease contracts and, through price cuts and selective enhance-ments, encouraging the use of increasingly capable integrated—instead of stand-alone—controllers. This latter move, by the way, increased customers' demand for processor capacity—which, as will be seen later, increasingly earned IBM high profits.

These changes took their toll on competitors. IBM's share of disk drives in-stalled on 360 and 370 systems never dipped below 80 percent during the 1970s or 1980s. In 1977, over a year and a half after the 3350's introduction, IBM faced serious disk drive competition from only four companies: Memorex, Itel, Storage Technology, and Control Data. Each offered comparable disk drives at prices 15 to 20 percent lower than IBM's, often with higher performance and special features. Tracor, Marshall Industries, Ampex, and Potter Instruments, among others, had dropped out of the race, and CalComp's disk drive operations were in their death throes. The increased pace of technological change, IBM's now-you-see-it-now-you-don't repackaging of controller functions, and its aggressive FTP financing had made the going too rough for them.

The demand for disk drives grew enormously in the late 1970s, topping a compound rate of 50 percent a year, and IBM's factories were unable to satisfy all the orders they received. As a result, Storage Technology, for one, was able to capture a significant share of the booming 3350 disk drive business by taking up some of the slack. IBM continued to push the technology and introduce new drives for 370 users. In January 1979 came the 3370, for use on a new series of 370 processors. It was quite similar to the 3350 but offered more performance per dollar. It stored a total of 571.3 megabytes—nearly twice that of the 3350—by using tiny thin-film read/write heads that recorded data along very narrow tracks. These heads, used also in a subsequent IBM disk drive, the 3380, were built using a costly and rather tricky semiconductor fabrication process that posed substantial problems for the few competitors left to try to match. Even IBM missed its original schedule for delivering the 1,200-megabyte 3380 product, but so advanced was the technology by that time, 1980, that its competition gained little from the delay—they were struggling to work out the thin-film technology themselves.

In fact, they never recovered and only slipped further as IBM plowed billions into engineering and manufacturing and closed the gap between announcing products and delivering them. By 1985, Control Data had thrown in the towel and left the IBM-compatible disk drive business altogether. Storage Technology operated under the protection of the federal bankruptcy laws, but it still claimed it would invest to keep up with IBM's latest disk drive products. Memorex, by then a struggling subsidiary of Burroughs, was the only one left of the initial domestic competition, but it evidently had trouble keeping up with IBM's technology race. From across the Pacific there is some Japanese manufacturing of 370-compatible disk drives, but it has lagged behind IBM's technology.

These were the basic products and strategies IBM used over time to reestablish its control over disk drives attached to its processors. Within this overall flow of battle, there are several that deserve a bit more attention.

LEADER OF THE PACK

The benefit of tie-in sales to a monopolist such as IBM was never so evident as in the battles it fought over disk packs in the early 1970s. IBM enjoyed almost complete discretion in choosing whether to offer two related products indepen-dently, with separate prices, or as tie-in combinations under a single, bundled price.

IBM pioneered removable disk platters, which let customers mount a number of different sets of data on a single disk drive by switching disk platters. Changes in customer habits and in IBM's competitive needs, however, eventually made fixed platters the more popular after all. The Winchester data module's greatly expanded capacity, for instance, let customers store more data than ever on a single removable pack of platters. The more data it held, the more reluctant cus-tomers were to remove the disk pack. They figured that data modules were best kept safe right where they were, on the drive box itself rather than on a shelf. Also, interactive computing demanded that data be kept instantly available to the system at all times.

Far more compelling than the technical reasons favoring these so-called fixed disk drives were the competitive advantages they offered IBM. The major focus of this book's analysis of IBM's success has been the company's fundamental reliance on price discrimination. Despite the one-third drop in the price of disk storage during the 1970s, it would be incorrect to assume IBM was not still dis-criminating in its pricing without a comparison of its actual costs and prices.

As will be seen in greater detail in the next chapter, IBM during the 1970s was beginning to face a new competitive threat, that of companies offering 370-like processors. To counter the compatible peripherals threat of the late 1960s, IBM had dropped its profits from the memory and peripherals and boosted them on its processors. Then, in the mid-1970s, once that switch in price discrimination had taken care of the disk and tape drive makers, its extraordinarily high pro-cessor prices drew competition from a new set of rivals. One could assume that IBM would then begin to increase its prices relative to its costs on its increas-ingly secure disk drives and use the profits there to compensate for the tactical lowering of prices that would become necessary in the processor sector. To test this theory in the peripherals market, we must examine IBM's prices. A good candidate is the disk drives. As more of the value of these devices moved from the drive to the increasingly complex data module, IBM gained an opportunity to recapture much of this business.

There is no doubt that IBM's competitive position was helped enormously by fixing disk platters to the disk drive because in doing so it deprived one of its main disk competitors, Memorex, of a major source of revenue. During the 1960s, Memorex had made much money selling disk packs—in fact, it practi-cally drove IBM out of leasing packs altogether.

Larry Spitters, Memorex president, was a particularly resourceful busi-nessman. His experience in commerce and as an antitrust lawyer gave him a strong background for finding and attacking the vulnerable spots of IBM's mo-nopoly. In the early 1960s, he plotted Memorex's first success in making and selling magnetic computer tape. As it had done for so many years with blank punch cards, IBM made better-than-average profits from blank computer tape. IBM purchased its tape from Minnesota Mining and Manufacturing, which had pioneered the use of plastic film instead of metal in magnetic recording and had then established a dominant position in the emerging tape industry.

It was an opportunity that Memorex, whose sales force was dedicated to selling only tape (and that a product superior to IBM's), was well positioned to exploit. As Spitters had no doubt foreseen, once Memorex's success in the tape market became evident, neither IBM nor 3M could very well stop it. Each was a monopolist locked into the other's grasp. IBM could do nothing to cut 3M's costs or to improve the quality of its tape, for it had no other supplier to turn to. 3M, on the other hand, could neither cut the marketing costs of its best customer nor lower IBM's prices to stimulate demand for tape. Neither company wanted to engage in a real price competition for fear of losing what had been a quite profitable business. Memorex, and eventually other firms, rushed into the market, undercutting IBM's high price of $50 to $70 per reel of tape. Computer users benefited greatly as prices fell and quality improved, and a paralyzed IBM watched its market share plummet. Spitters proved himself a keen judge with his foresight that IBM's self-interest would inhibit its reaction to successful competition.

IBM and Memorex next fought over the disk platter business, a neighboring market.[17] These platters, mounted in removable packs, were more expensive than tapes, so customers tended not to order them as standard supplies. The platters were usually leased rather than purchased, leaving customers quite free to replace their IBM products and acquire Memorex's higher-quality packs at a lower price.

IBM's first removable disk pack was mounted on the early 1311 disk drive that had been used on second-generation computers. Much to IBM's surprise, users acquired several packs for each disk drive they had, keeping one mounted on the drive and the others on a nearby shelf. IBM originally had not even given the pack a product number but had rather considered it part of the drive. However, when demand for extra packs increased, the pack became designated as model 1316. Demand for the later 2316 pack, used on the 2311 and 2314 disk drives, grew so quickly that IBM was unable to make them fast enough. A lucrative gray market soon developed in which distributors ordered large numbers of 2316 packs and resold them to users at inflated prices.

Spitters again recognized an attractive marketing opportunity. He sent Memorex into the market in 1967 with a replacement for the 1316 pack. Other companies entered as well, fueling competition, and users again benefited from better products, better sales terms (e.g., Memorex's five-year warranty instead of IBM's ninety-day terms), better service, shorter delivery times (Memorex delivered within thirty days while IBM often took twelve months), and prices as much as 60 percent below IBM's. It was another example of the tonic that effective competition provided in an area previously monopolized by IBM. Many customers left IBM for Memorex and other independents, and the industry giant found itself accepting carloads of returned disk packs coming off lease.

IBM improved the quality of its packs, but its prices remained relatively high until 1969, when it dropped the purchase price and boosted the amount of credit toward purchase that customers received from past rental payments. That did not stop Memorex, so IBM took the 1316 and 2316 packs off lease and made them purchase-only products. When the Merlin/3330 disk drive was introduced, IBM also refused to lease disk packs for it. That policy assured IBM of selling at least one pack with each drive, ironically regardless of whether the drive was leased or purchased. Moreover, because it would take time for the competition to engineer replacement products, they would arrive to market late and IBM could capture the initial demand. Purchased packs would be more difficult for IBM's competitors to replace than rented ones, too.

When the Winchester/3340 disk drive was unveiled, Memorex faced a new technical challenge. Packaged with the platters in this disk drive's data module were the heads as well, all sealed in an airtight, molded-plastic enclosure. Building a compatible duplicate would be no easy task. Also, more of the disk drive's value was now contained in the pack (data module) price than in the past.

Memorex had traditionally financed the start-up costs of its new peripherals and other equipment in part from profits made from disk pack sales. When IBM changed the pricing of disk drives with the 3344 (and later with the 3350), which fixed the once-removable data module to the drive box itself and carried only a single, bundled price, Memorex saw a major source of funds begin to dry up. The majority of its disk packs were installed on IBM disk drives, but now there would be only one pack per drive and that would be the one that came when the drive was first installed. IBM, moreover, refused to assign a separate price to the 3344 data module, even though it was almost identical to the earlier removable one, was almost as easily removed by a field engineer (as Memorex showed in court), and had traditionally been sold for a separate, published price. Thus, even if a user wished to get a Memorex data module for his IBM 3344, the pricing prohibited him.

Memorex's disk pack business was all but over with these later drives, and it was forced to compete with IBM for the only other disk product left—the complete drive with data module included. In that market, however, the Santa Clara, California, company's market share was contained to only about 10 percent, a long way from the commanding 70 percent share of the disk pack business it had once enjoyed. Tying the pack to the disk drive assured IBM of as major a share of the data module market as it had of the drive market.

IBM established a task force in 1971 to examine ways it might increase net revenues over the next few years. A major conclusion was the need to "RE-DUCE PCM [plug-compatible manufacturer] impact," and that called for IBM to "FIX THE PACK," according to a flip chart used during one of the task force's presentations.[18] Unsaid was that what new revenues IBM would enjoy would come at the expense of, among others, Memorex, which would be unable to compete successfully against the bundled price of disk drive and disk pack together.

Memorex cried foul and tried to extend its already-pending $3 billion antitrust suit against IBM to force IBM to offer the 3344 disk drive and data module with separate prices rather than as a bundled pair. It was not that IBM should not design its products as it did, or that the pack could not be attached to the drive by customers themselves, Memorex argued, but given the history and evolution of the disk drive business, the data module should retain a price separate from the drive's. After all, how would IBM be harmed? Continuing the traditional, unbundled approach would cost IBM only the nominal amount of printing the lines in its price lists. Compare that with the benefit to users of greater choice.

Actually, IBM was in a tight spot. If it were to price the disk drive and data module separately, it would have to choose between only selling the two products or letting customers lease or buy them. If they were offered on lease, Memorex could more easily replace them. If they were sold only, users would be encouraged to also purchase the drive box, for now the data module contained a major portion of the working drive's value—it made no sense for the customer to lease a drive box to use with data modules he owned. Better for IBM not to offer the two items separately at all and thereby maintain the ability to lease complete disk drives, as it much preferred. The court rejected Memorex's argument that it was excluded from a traditionally important part of its business because its major competitive product, the disk pack for IBM drives, no longer had a separate price. IBM was free to start raising its prices for the now-bundled data module.

PRICES VS. COSTS AT IBM

Finally, if price discrimination does in fact explain IBM's ongoing power, then it should be possible to show that after IBM had shaken off the compatible-disk threat so successfully, it had begun reinflating profits on its disk drives back to pre-threat levels. This would not only have been a natural course of action for the company, which is not known for overlooking uncontested markets, but it would also help explain how IBM has been able to afford slashing the unit price of its 370 processors by almost 1,000 percent since 1977 as it battles competition selling 370-compatible processors. IBM, we can surmise, was able to reinflate disk drive profits easily because, unobserved by its customers, who were enjoying the undeniably falling price of disk storage, the manufacturer's cost of such products was actually falling even faster. IBM's prices, it can be safely stated, have hardly ever fallen in strict relation to costs.

Unfortunately, the government trial record begins to thin after 1975, so the internal IBM documents necessary to construct a complete picture of its changing costs and pricing of disk drive hardware are not publicly available. However, using information revealed during Memorex's private antitrust suit against IBM, IBM can indeed be seen taking the opportunity to boost its profits on disk products that no longer faced competition.[19]

Consider the Winchester/3340 disk drive and its enhanced, bundled version, the 3344. The differences between the two were in fact minimal. Although the latter stored four times as much data, important performance specs such as rotational speed, data transfer rate, and recording formats were identical. The 3344 was clearly a repackaged 3340, a prime example of IBM's midlife kicker. The read/write electronics of the two products were different, and the 3340's removable module had a handle and automatic loading mechanism not found on the 3344, but otherwise the drives were the same product. In fact, after studying IBM planning documents—code-named by IBM the Phase 2 Madrid papers—Memorex concluded that IBM's cost to build the 3340 and its two modules (both products comprised two drive spindles, each with its own data modules) was $6,838, while the comparable cost of a 3344 was just 3 percent higher, or $7,040. Most of that $200 cost increase stemmed from the later product's improved platters, actuator motor, and heads.

When it came to prices, however, there was a vast difference. The 3340 was priced at $32,400 when purchased. The comparable two-spindle 3344, which Memorex found it so impossible to compete with, went for $49,500, or 53 percent more. Evidently, once IBM found that its grip on the disk drive business was strengthening, it began to raise prices there greatly in excess of the increases in its production costs.

A closer examination of these disk drives, in particular their fixed-head options, provides further evidence of continuing price discrimination. A 3344 with two fixed-head modules sold for $65,000, or 77 percent more than the $36,800 purchase tag on a comparably configured 3340. But comparing the price of a megabyte of fixed-head storage on each disk drive shows IBM reinflating prices and profits now that competition was neutralized. The only difference between standard and fixed-head 3340 data modules was the half-megabyte of fixed-head storage contained in the latter. Therefore, the price for one megabyte of fixed-head storage on the earlier disk drive amounts to twice the difference in price between the two types of 3348 data module, or $4,400. The comparable megabyte on the 3344, with its two data modules each containing a megabyte of fixed-head storage included in the drive's price, can be calculated by halving the difference between the standard and fixed-head modules' prices, or $7,750.

IBM had established the earlier Winchester/3340's $4,400-per-fixed-megabyte price in 1973, when it faced severe disk drive and platter competition. The later 3344's $7,750 price for that megabyte was determined two years later when the heat was off and the modules were protectively bundled into the price of the drive. Improving technology and dropping costs notwithstanding, IBM inflated its prices in order to help it fight off plug-compatible processors, which were just coming to market.

14. The Bigger the Better

A seller with a strong position with respect to its competition as to one of its products may not force its customers to make other purchases from it by "tying in" with the sale of the one product the sale of one or more products. . . . As one Supreme Court Justice has stated, "Tying arrangements serve hardly any purpose beyond the suppression of competition."

—From IBM's *Business Conduct
Policies: Responsibilities and
Guide*[1]

As we've seen, a great deal of the profits IBM obtained from its computer systems derived from the high prices it charged for memory attached to the central processor. The more memory a customer installed, the more profits he contributed to IBM's bottom line. Those profits naturally attracted competition, especially as new technology became widely available. Then, as IBM began slashing the prices of its threatened peripherals to defend its business there, it was forced to move even more profits into the processor/memory complex. Before long, its competitors were building complete 370-compatible processors that could replace IBM's overpriced machines completely and still enable customers to run their valuable application programs unchanged.

This chapter and the next chronicle the major battles IBM has fought over the processor and its memory ever since the 360 gained supremacy in the systems marketplace. It is a story that shows how heavily dependent IBM is on its immense market power to thwart competition and retain market share that in a truly competitive market would go to more efficient vendors. It shows how remiss IBM was in delivering advanced technology that its customers demanded and first obtained from rival manufacturers. It shows how the company tricked many of those customers into laying out millions of dollars for a pair of products that had hardly been installed before they were purposely made obsolete. And it shows that because IBM's technological prowess is far less than advertised and its success more dependent on sheer market power, the company's vaunted managers are not above stretching the truth or even speaking falsehoods when they need to.

ADD-ON MEMORY

IBM's processor-related problems began in the late 1960s when competitors caught sight of the high prices it was charging for 360 memory and the particulars of how it offered that memory to customers. The pricing, as earlier chapters have shown, was functional in nature, bore little relationship to underlying costs, and provided IBM with increasing profit rates with each extra portion of memory the customer installed. If a customer were to order a 360 processor with only the minimum possible memory from IBM and then install as much lower-priced independent memory as he needed, he could save a great deal—as much as $20,000 a year on a model 40 processor leased for four years. But pricing aside, IBM opened the door for independent vendors by setting arbitrary upper limits on the amount of memory customers could attach to each of the 360 processors. While the machines were technically capable of using a great deal more memory, IBM for marketing reasons had established artificial ceilings for each processor model; that way, when a customer reached the limit on one processor, he was forced to install the next larger processor to get the memory his growing application software demanded. What's more, despite the profits it could have earned, IBM generally refused to lease extra memory to those customers who had purchased their 360 processors. Many of those purchasers, of course, were leasing companies, and once again they were eager buyers of independently produced, 360 add-on equipment.

Memory companies felt sure of their products' advantages. They could undercut IBM's prices by pricing their memory according to cost, not function. Later, when new memory technology based on semiconductor chips became available, their costs could be lowered even further. And they knew, too, that breaking IBM's upper limits on memory size would require modifying the 360 processor only slightly. But memory profits were too important for IBM to tolerate their success. We shall see that it took IBM two tries before it finally protected its exposed memory from competition.

Memory on the largest 360s was a sitting duck for the independents due to the way IBM had packaged and priced it. In the 360/65 and larger machines, there were just too many logic and memory circuits to be mounted in a single cabinet, so memory was kept in a separate box of its own and connected to the processor by cable. But as a separate box with a separate—and relatively high—price, that memory box became a natural target for competition. IBM manufactured much of its own memory, but it also purchased substantial amounts from memory specialists such as Ampex, a West Coast manufacturer. Well aware of memory's decreasing production cost and IBM's high prices, Ampex and other companies began selling memory directly to 360 users. They aimed first for the largest 360s, for those machines tended to need the most memory and the independents had the fewest disadvantages there.

Attaching independent memory to smaller 360s was another story. In those machines, IBM had mounted all memory within the processor cabinet, even though it continued to charge separate prices for the processor and each increment of memory. The independents knew they could compete in price with these small 360 memories, but they had to contend with an entirely new problem. Shortly before the independents entered the memory market, IBM had shown the limits of that kind of competition. It had brought out two models of a particular tape drive, one offering more performance than the other, which differed in manufacturing cost by a mere $50, but whose purchase prices differed by some $20,000.[2] Recognizing that leasing companies, or clever users, might circumvent this functional pricing by themselves modifying the slow tape drive to run faster, IBM determined that its best defense would be to simply refuse to service any customer-modified gear.

Hence, Hillary Faw wrote, "I have not yet been able to discover any reason based upon maintenance costs which would support a refusal to offer [a] maintenance agreement . . . on such a machine. If there is such a reason, we should establish it now, rather than wait for what I suspect is an inevitable question."[3] In fact, because IBM controlled so much of the maintenance knowhow for its equipment, even the simple threat of withholding service on gear modified by outsiders was enough to keep customers from letting such modifications proceed.

To avoid the maintenance issue, the memory companies packaged their memory for small- and medium-scale 360s in separate boxes, too. That beset them with two disadvantages, however. If their memory was to be outboard from the processor, IBM's inboard memory would be physically closer to the processor and could therefore interact more quickly with it. The cable between memory box and processor introduced electrical delays that tended to slow the processor's operation. To compensate, competitors sought to make their memories respond to the processor faster than IBM's did. More costly, however, was that in order to be functional, their separately boxed memory would need to duplicate several components—power supply, cabinetry, chassis, and the like—that IBM's machines did not. IBM's memory boards took their power from the processor's supply, for instance, and were mounted in the same cabinet.

Nevertheless, even though the independent memory makers had to contend with extra costs, they were easily able to undercut IBM's inflated prices and earn reasonable profits. Even though the production cost of the basic memory component, magnetic cores, had fallen by an order of magnitude or more since the

1950s, IBM in 1969 was still charging essentially the same price for 360 memory as it had for that on 1401s. No wonder competitors were drawn into the market.

The competitors' market expanded once word got out that a successor to the 360 was on its way. The leasing companies, as we have seen, had invested heavily in purchased 360 machines, and they sought to boost those machines' performance to match the forthcoming 370 line. Exceeding IBM's arbitrary limits on 360 memory sizes was one of the most promising potential enhancements they could make, given that systems in general ran more efficiently when given more memory to work with. But adding that extra memory also entailed some minor, but internal, modifications to the 360 processor, so customers would thereby risk IBM's refusal to maintain the systems. Consider, for instance, the trouble IBM caused for one of the most successful pairs of competitors in 360 add-on memory, Itel Corporation, a lessor, and its memory supplier, Advanced Memory Systems (AMS). The two worked out a method for installing extra memory in midsize 360s and exceeding IBM's limits. Itel quickly booked many orders from eager customers. Aroused, IBM moved to exploit the power that it alone had, namely the almost complete control of 360 maintenance services. About 95 percent of the 360 processors installed in the United States were serviced by IBM under contract. It employed about 97 percent of all the persons sufficiently trained to service the machines, and it had similar control over the spare parts for the 360.[4] Moreover, no one but IBM's own technicians were allowed to service the 360s it leased.

Soon after Itel began taking orders for and installing the AMS memory on 360s, reports circulated among customers that IBM found it "impractical" to maintain the affected processors. Although they were more than willing to service their own memory boards, Itel and AMS were quite unable to assume maintenance responsibility for the entire 360 processor. By threatening to withhold maintenance on modified processors, IBM put a severe crimp in Itel's plans.

In order to salvage this promising business, Itel and AMS went to great lengths to help IBM maintain the processors that used their memory, but IBM bluntly refused to cooperate. For one thing, it would not tell the two competitors exactly what made servicing modified 360s so "impractical" (clearly a reference to the language in the 1956 Consent Decree—see Appendix A). Itel offered to make its memory connect in exactly the same way as IBM's, and it even offered to use a certain piece of hardware that IBM used with its own add-on memory. But IBM refused to supply that hardware, even though it made the part available to customers as a standard replacement part. AMS offered to foot the bill for training IBM repairmen to service AMS memory—all that was required was a three-hour home-study course and some updating of IBM's service manuals. IBM would have none of it.

Frustrated but undaunted, Itel took IBM to court and asked that IBM be required to make its "best effort" to fix the unaltered portions of its machines, despite any "foreign" attachments. At issue was not that IBM would not get paid for fixing altered machines—Itel was willing to pay for its share of the bill—but rather whether IBM should be permitted to use its monopoly over 360 maintenance to block competitors from entering the market with products that customers obviously wanted but that IBM chose not to offer. Could IBM's control over maintenance be used, Itel asked, to frustrate attempts to break IBM's control over its customers' choice of equipment?[5]

Despite the market disruptions that IBM's threats caused, actual instances of IBM's withholding of maintenance were few. Ironically, one case involved the U.S. Department of Justice's own IBM system. In December 1971, IBM set out to test its side of the case by threatening to withhold service on a Data Recall memory attached to the Department's machine. If that agency did not object, IBM reckoned that it was in the clear and could use the tactic unheeded. Although the Department was already preparing its antitrust case against IBM, it stayed as quiet as a mouse.

Nevertheless, Itel won concessions, first in, or rather in front of, a U.S. courtroom and then in West Germany. On the courthouse steps, on March 21, 1972, IBM agreed to Itel's demands—it would make its best efforts to work around non-IBM memory.* It was something of a Pyrrhic victory, however, because the many model 30s that Itel hoped to upgrade with extra memory were fast becoming obsolete; just a year before, IBM had introduced the 370/135 and 360/22 processors, and a few months later it came out with the 370/125. Each was priced to be unattractive to Itel and other leasing companies, and each replaced and devalued the widely installed model 30.

It was just another demonstration of the fact that because the computer industry changes so fast and because IBM has a multitude of tactics available to stop competitors, litigation is often ineffective. By the time a court decision is reached or a case is settled, often a drawn-out process, it is very often irrelevant to the current state of the market.

The Itel/AMS episode also showed all its competitors that IBM could hamper independent companies with ease simply by threatening to withhold maintenance on any of its products that were entered or modified by outsiders. From then on, the industry saw a risk in getting too creative when trying to enhance

---

* The Stipulated Final Judgment between AMS/Itel and IBM stated ". . . IBM shall not refuse to attempt to service and maintain the unaltered portions of such [360/30 processor] in a best efforts manner . . ." A similar result came from the case brought in Germany. The Judgment there stated that IBM was "prohibited . . . from refusing to provide any maintenance services which it is obligated to provide under a rental or maintenance agreement for the 360/30 . . . on the grounds that maintenance is impracticable because of . . . AMS/Itel add-on storage unit attached . . . to increase storage capacity from 64 K bytes to 96 K bytes."[6]

IBM machines. IBM showed that it could force competitors to service not only their own gear but, if they persisted, IBM's as well. That was a difficult task, given the general lack of trained personnel and the restrictions in IBM's lease contracts. Competition was forced, therefore, to offer products that mimicked IBM's boxes feature for feature rather than offer unorthodox innovations of their own.

THE 370s

IBM continued to face competition from add-on memory makers even as it began to bring out its new line of processors, the 370s. These machines were needed to block further inroads by plug-compatible equipment suppliers and leasing companies. Recall that IBM's defensive strategy against those vendors was a major reversal of its price discrimination, a shifting of profits away from exposed peripherals and into the relatively secure processor. To encourage customers to replace their 360s with the 370 machines, which used different peripherals interfaces and offered special new functions, IBM priced the 370s to be particularly attractive to its largest users. As we shall see, however, the company at first blundered by making the 370s' memory, still priced to earn high profits, vulnerable to the competition.

In May 1970, just months before the 370 processors were unveiled, IBM summed up the situation: "A new ingredient in the competitive picture is acknowledged exposure to our memory boxes, an exposure heretofore observed primarily in the I/O [peripherals] areas. [IBM] has established Goals which tend to induce such strategies as will minimize this exposure, and it is clear that [IBM's] objectives are dependent on being successful in this task. . . . The risk is potentially significant and the [company's] business volume Goals are dependent on successfully managing this risk."[7]

A comparison of the monthly rental charges for the two largest commercial 360 processors and their comparably sized 370 replacements shows the "strategies" designed to minimize IBM's exposure. The processor prices were increased while memory prices were cut. But those memory price cuts did not mean IBM was just letting profits slip away. IBM President T. Vincent Learson stated in an April 1970 memo, "Originally, I advised them to price memories and CPUs [central processing units, or processors] both at 30%. They readily agreed that CPUs cannot easily be duplicated [by competition] whereas memories can easily be duplicated on a plug-in basis. I would, therefore, conclude that we should have 25% profit on memories, higher prices on the CPU, and end up with an overall profit in the 32% range."[8] And that was exactly what IBM did, once again discriminating between areas where it faced competition and those where it was relatively secure.

IBM was still using memory to segment its market, but it was reversing the direction of the price discrimination to contain new threats. The 370s' comparatively high processor price represented the beginning of a reversal of the prior scheme under which entry-level processors, in order to attract new customers, were priced below cost and profits were made entirely from add-on memory. Now, since most 370s went to locked-in users, the price of the processor could be safely inflated. In addition, this reversal benefited customers who used the most memory—the very customers the compatible equipment vendors were so successful with—while discriminating against the medium- and small-size customers. These drew less attention from the compatible equipment suppliers.

With their low-priced memory and their ability to use the Merlin disk drive, the 155 and 165 processors should have lured all but the most reluctant large 360 customers into the 370 realm. But the independent leasing companies (and the plug-compatible vendors they relied on for low-priced add-on gear) fought back with every technical trick they could find to upgrade the 360s and keep them installed with paying customers. They would do what, for commercial reasons, IBM had decided not to, namely enhance the 360s with many of the features of the 370s.

Yet the company was not "successfully managing this risk."[9] The design and pricing of the first two 370 processors permitted compatible memory firms to compete almost equally with IBM. Its usual advantages had been lost as a result of its packaging and pricing what was essentially the same old-fashioned core memory on the 370/155 and 165.

IBM's top executives were not pleased when they realized their strategic blunder of offering the 155 and 165 processors with the option of no IBM memory. A presentation about it to T. Vincent Learson in December 1970, six months after the first two 370s were unveiled and only eight months after his price balancing instructions, was apparently received by him with displeasure. A memo to the files by an underling who had faced the chief reports, "Although [Learson] was outwardly calm and did not eat us up, I don't believe the pitch went over well. His last few comments were 'You guys are giving away a one billion dollar business to them' and 'thanks a lot.' "[10]

Two years earlier, marketing man Frank Cary had proposed bundling memory with the 370 processors in such a way "that there is no question but that it is tied,"[11] in other words, so that there was no choice for the customer but to buy high-profit IBM memory with a 370. Just build it in from the start, Cary had proposed, and charge a single price. But that advice had been ignored; the tradition that had worked so well for years, encouraging customers to add increments to high-profit memory, died hard. It now looked like IBM might have to compete on price alone.

Or would it? What if Cary's plan were carried out after all, and 370 processors were offered with at least some built-in memory, thus guaranteeing IBM at least some memory profits? That way the independent memory firms would be locked out of a good portion of the market. There were risks, of course: "Restricting [compatible firms] from 60%–70% of their market without price competition would almost certainly provoke legal consequences and I wonder what contingency I can provide against a civil triple damage suit," wrote one IBM manager considering such bundling.[12]

Possibly, this employee's concern came in part from his being asked to violate one of the rules in the *IBM Business Conduct Policies: Responsibilities and Guide.* (See quote at beginning of chapter prohibiting tie-in sales.)

But bundling, in spite of its legal risks, offered advantages to IBM all the same. In August 1972, less than two years after bringing out the 155 and 165 processors, IBM embarked on the abtly dubbed SMASH plan. Trying a second time, IBM would solve the add-on memory problem with the same—previously detailed—blows that it had delivered to compatible-disk makers and leasing companies. Among other changes, SMASH entailed totally replacing those first two large 370s with the revamped models 158 and 168; and lo and behold, those two machines came with bundled memory. Where the previous 155 had no memory included in its base price, the 158's price included a half-megabyte valued at $2,600 a month. Similarly, the 168 included a full megabyte worth $5,200 a month. With no separate prices, there could be no competition. It was as if an electrical utility were supplying with its current the first toaster at no separate charge. Additional memory for these new processors, made from semiconductor chips, was priced at $5,200 a month per megabyte, or less than half the $12,000 per megabyte charged for core memory on the original 155 and 165 processors.

The only remaining problem was for IBM to move customers to these new systems, where it would be difficult for the competition to follow. Besides offering them a 50 percent cut in memory prices, IBM also equipped the 158 and 168 both with special hardware to create a virtual memory and with the integrated disk controller that, along with the Merlin/3330 disk drive, was the basis for the "new attachment strategy" described in the previous chapter. Customers and competitors were quite shocked to see the 158 and 168 obsolete the 155 and 165 so soon, just eighteen months after their unveiling, but, as Learson had stated, a $1 billion business was at stake and IBM had no intention of losing it. IBM kept up the pressure on customers to go virtual by limiting many of its later hardware and software products to work only with virtual systems. The message was clear: If customers wanted the best of IBM's offerings, they had better make the switch to virtual computing.

MEMORY TRENDS

It is instructive to review the historical pricing of IBM's three successive pairs of large-scale commercial processors, the original 360/50 and 65, the nonvirtual

370/155 and 165, and the virtual 370/158 and 168. IBM had from the beginning discriminated against large customers by charging them relatively high prices for peripherals and memory. Once those high prices attracted competition, IBM had to change prices to cut rivals off and maintain market share, but only in such a way as to maintain overall growth and profitability.

Consider the large-scale processors alone, without memory. Although IBM did not offer stripped-down 158 or 168 processors, the implicit price for each processor alone can be calculated by subtracting out the memory (valued at the price for additional separately priced memory) included in the entry-level processor. Thus implicitly, the 158 and 168 had respective processor-only prices of $30,700 and $48,600 a month. Table 32 compares those prices to the entry-level (i.e., without memory) prices of the previous two pairs of large processors. (A comparable calculation has to be performed for the 360/50, which contained one-eighth of a megabyte of memory in its minimum configuration.)

In less than two years, IBM substantially raised the price of its large processors as their performance increased. That may seem surprising, for the processor was made mostly from the same semiconductor components used in controllers, parts of the input/output gear, and memory, all of whose manufacturing costs and prices were falling. As semiconductor costs fell, it became less expensive each year to manufacture a computer—even one with increased performance. While the boxes of IBM's systems that faced competition were dropped in price as their performance increased, the processor was on a price curve of an altogether different slope. Table 32 also shows that the biggest proportional increase in price was with the smaller of the two machines. The 370/168 was only three and a half times more expensive than the 360/65, while the 370/158 was almost five times as expensive as the 360/50. The largest users saw the greatest incentives to move to this new processor, even though it had bundled memory and new peripherals interfaces.

Large users were important to IBM and were also the most likely to use independent peripherals and memory, as an independent market study commented:

Table 32

Rental Price of Minimum-Level Processor When Offered Without Memory and Implicit Price of Processor When Offered With Memory[13]

CPU	MONTHLY RENT	CPU	MONTHLY RENT
360/50 G	$ 6,390	360/65 H	$14,030
370/155 H	19,980	370/165 I	35,640
370/158 I	30,700	370/168 J	48,600

"Current users of [disk] drives from independents have more computer equipment at their installation—an estimated $31,000 monthly rental, versus $15,000 for those who 'would consider' [installing compatible drives] and $9,500 for the 'not interested' category." The study showed, too, that of the 3 percent of all the sites surveyed that spent more than $100,000 a month to rent computer systems, 63 percent used non-IBM peripherals. The comparable figures for the $50,000-to-$100,000-a-month category (accounting for 4 percent of the total population) was 53 percent.[14] IBM's best customers were the independents' best, too. In general, smaller users did not see sufficient incentive to come out from under the IBM security blanket and install "foreign" gear. IBM's prices, therefore, had to be most competitive at the upper end of the market where competition was most effective; this explains why IBM found it safe to raise prices for the 155 or 158 user more than for the 165 or 168 user.

IBM's traditional pricing pattern was changing. While raising the price of the unchallenged basic large processor by 350 to 500 percent, IBM dropped the price of memory (at least the price of that portion that was still priced separately) to about one-sixth its original price. High processor prices maintained overall system profits while low memory prices impoverished independent suppliers and enabled IBM to maintain market share.

The full brunt of this change was of course felt by the customers with smaller machines. Whereas in the past they had been favored by IBM's pricing, this was no longer the case. Their processors' memories were smaller, and therefore they enjoyed less savings to make up for the rise in processor price. Not surprisingly, this made them attractive prospects for IBM's competition. These small and medium-size customers found the greatly enhanced large 360s owned by leasing companies attractive compared to the smaller 370 systems. Concluded IBM in 1974, "It appears that a major factor in the intermediate Systems marketplace is the congestion caused by the purchased System/360 inventory. This inventory has decreased over time in price, and moved down the S/370 system hierarchy. This inventory now competes with System/370 in the model 115 through 145 area."[15] In addition, other competitors such as minicomputer firms like Digital Equipment would be drawn increasingly into commercial data processing by IBM's inflated midsystem prices. Thus over time, IBM would pay a price in this sector of the market. Its market share, particularly in the midrange, would fall. For the moment, however, those prices would help support IBM's high overall profit rate.

Interestingly, IBM's repricing of memory and high-end processors shows IBM's clear intent—that the overall processor/memory for the average customer stay reasonably the same while it restructured the pattern of pricing to stop competition. A simple calculation shows how much memory a user needed to enjoy a decrease in his monthly bill for processor and memory. For the 50–155–158 and 65–165–168 migration paths, that bill included the basic processor price plus the total price of memory (number of megabytes multiplied by price per megabyte). The following equations result, one for each large 360/370 processor:

Table 33
360 and 370 Customer
Processor Price
Calculation
(in $ thousands; X =
Memory in Megabytes)

System		
360/50	$ 6.4 +	$37(X)
370/155	20.0 +	12(X)
370/158	30.7 +	5.2(X)
360/65	14.0 +	37(X)
370/165	36.6 +	12(X)
370/168	48.6 +	5.2(X)

By setting any two of these price equations equal (say, a move from a 360/65 to a 370/165), we can solve for X the memory size (measured in megabytes) at which the two selected processor-memory combinations were equal in price. A customer with more than that amount of memory on the earlier machine would find his bill go *down* when upgrading to the next processor with the same size memory. For example, according to this calculation, a 360/50 user with more than a half-megabyte of memory would find his bill drop when he moved to a similarly sized 370/155.

Now in 1974, International Data Corporation (IDC), the market research company, published a set of data showing the average memory actually installed with users of each of these six processors.[16] (See Table 34.)

Here can be seen the wash in revenues that was so critical to IBM in its massive reversal of price discrimination. Note that the empirically measured average memory size is roughly equal at each performance level to the theoretical break-even point calculated above. This means that IBM's average customer saw his monthly bill stay roughly the same as he moved from one machine to another—in general, he saved enough money on low-priced memory to make up for the increase in processor price. It was this average customer that IBM had in mind as a pivot point around which to reverse its pricing structure while doing minimal harm to overall revenues. For the user having a larger-than-average memory, the incentive would be the greatest to move up and save money. Eventually even the smaller customer would need more memory, at which point he would be glad for IBM's low memory prices.

This price reversal had many implications. The drop in memory prices en-

Table 34

Average Memory Attached to Largest 360 and
to Virtual and Nonvirtual 370 Processors at
Year End 1973 and the Break-Even Memory
Size for the Price to Remain Constant with a
Change
(in megabytes)

	AVERAGE MEMORY	BREAK-EVEN SIZE		AVERAGE MEMORY	BREAK-EVEN SIZE
360/50	.5	.5	360/65	.9	.9
370/155	1.1	1.6	370/165	1.9	1.9
370/158	1.4		370/168	3.1	

ticed customers to install more memory, which allowed them to develop more extensive application programs. Those applications, many of which were inter-active, in turn fueled demand for extra peripherals, particularly disk drives. Those were supplied largely by IBM, which was fast regaining control of that market. The lower memory prices also hurt risk-leasing companies, which, though still dependent on IBM for their CPUs, had long depended on using low-cost, independent memory for much of the discount they offered users on complete systems.

Most hurt, of course, were the add-on memory companies, whose profits shrank as they cut prices to stay competitive with IBM. And as if lower prices were not enough, they now had to compete for a smaller potential market be-cause IBM was tying in a significant amount of memory to its large processors. Previously, they had connected their memory to 360 and nonvirtual 370 ma-chines that contained little or no IBM memory at all. Also, the users most at-tractive to the independents—large data processing shops that needed all the memory they could install—were the most likely to migrate to virtual, memory-bundled 370s.

Richard Andreini of Advanced Memory Systems, the independent memory supplier on the West Coast described in Chapter 14, stated at the government antitrust trial that the bundling of memory on the 370/158 and 168 had limited AMS's market to only a third or a fourth of what it would have been otherwise.* His comments are supported by figures from IDC, which in 1977 collected data on IBM's market share of memory installed with its largest systems. IBM's share of the virtual processors with tied-in memory in fact was much higher than it had been for earlier systems where none was bundled:

---

* This more limited market share was in spite of IBM's own assessment at the time of the decision to bundle much of the memory to the processor, that its costs would be "inordinately higher" than those of outside vendors once their shipments of semiconductor memories built up.[17]

Table 35
IBM Share of Value of Installed Memory on Largest IBM Systems (1977)

SYSTEM	IBM'S SHARE, BY VALUE OF MEMORY
370/155	28.4%
370/158 (with bundled memory)	81.6
370/165	41.5
370/168 (with bundled memory)	91.0

IMPLICATIONS

The commercial implications of IBM's rising market share should be familiar by now. Where there had been some nineteen IBM-compatible memory suppliers once selling memory for IBM mainframes, there were only three left by the late 1970s: AMS, National Semiconductor, and Intel. This was in spite of the fact that during this entire period IBM was usually at least a generation behind the competitors in using semiconductor memory technology.

IBM's new pricing pattern favoring large processors and cheap memory in turn drove the customers to these products. Those customers who could move up, did, with IBM encouraging them all the way: "We pressed for major centralization activities," recalled IBM's Allen J. Krowe a few years later. "We launched the DB/DC (data base/data communications) marketing concept. Applications growth was pressed for on-line terminal applications with high potential for customer savings. From every indication this thrust . . . is proving to be even more successful than we had hoped. . . . Based on the demand levels for [the 158 and 168 processors and 3270 terminals] we are likely to exceed the program forecast revenues by over $1.0 billion."

The shift to the largest 370 processors and their being loaded with interactive applications is shown clearly in IDC survey data in Table 36. IDC classifies mainframe computers in a series of sizes ranked 2 through 7: Class 2 includes the System/3; Class 3 the 360/20, 25, and 370/115; Class 4 the 370/125 and 135; Class 5 the 360/50 and 370/145; Class 6 the 360/65 and 370/155 and 158; and Class 7 the 370/165 and 168. As will be discussed below, practically all the growth in the computer business took place in the two largest classes of computer. They increased by a total of $21 billion in five years, while the smaller categories either shrank or remained about constant.

A major implication of the shift to large, centralized systems was the need on IBM's part for higher-performance systems that could deliver the quite different functions needed for effective interactive, data base–oriented applications and

211

Table 36
Installed Value of Computer Systems by IDC Class, 1974–79
(in $ millions)[18]

IDC CLASS	1974	1975	1976	1977	1978	1979	CHANGE, 1974–79	PERCENT (1979/ 1974)
7	$ 3,183	$ 5,146	$ 7,157	$ 9,018	$11,610	$14,380	$11,197	452%
6	7,024	9,270	10,994	12,614	14,819	17,188	10,164	248
5	5,683	5,709	5,966	7,115	7,795	7,453	1,770	131
4	8,427	7,957	7,950	8,318	8,319	7,660	−767	91
3	2,865	2,976	3,388	3,794	4,079	4,288	1,423	150
2	3,017	2,768	2,466	2,088	1,941	1,590	−1,427	53
7 Total	$30,199	$33,826	$37,921	$42,947	$48,563	$52,559	$22,360	

data communications. Also, by moving profits from exposed memory into the processor, IBM made the processor that much more attractive to compatible equipment vendors. IBM was quite aware of the threat they posed but at the time had little choice.

NONVIRTUAL CUL-DE-SAC

Why were the 370/155 and 165 so quickly obsoleted? If these two machines were not ready for the market, why were they announced only to be then killed? Why, moreover, did IBM abandon its initial plan to upgrade them to full virtual memory capability instead of only making the new functions fully available on the 370/158 and 168?

We should not expect to find any IBM documents that explain the early introduction of these first two 370s explicitly. If such documents ever existed, they have likely been purged from IBM's files, for the company's chief lawyer candidly advised management in September 1968, "If the [370/155 and 165] announcement is in any way accelerated, it is vitally important that no anticompetitive motive be spread in the files."[19]

The customers who purchased these two machines thinking that they could get in early on an expected long product cycle and save money by not leasing were most hurt by the hardware's short life. The day the virtual 158 and 168 were unveiled, the value of 155s and 165s plummeted; more than a few data processing managers who had recommended purchasing these systems had some explaining to do to their management. Some reportedly lost their jobs. In fact, these nonvirtual 370s look much like a trap set by IBM to capture purchase customers—the biggest and most threatening of which were not users but the leasing companies—and teach them a lesson they'd not quickly forget.

Lessors had rightly concluded that the best time to purchase IBM gear was as early as possible, for that guaranteed the longest and most profitable lease life. They also favored buying the largest possible IBM machines, knowing that when that machinery finally came off its first lease, there would be smaller users looking for just that level of performance as an upgrade. The larger the system, in other words, the longer its potential lease life. In the eyes of some leasing companies and some large customers, therefore, the 155 and 165 were financially quite alluring.

One of the biggest reasons users chose to install these first two 370s was the hardware's performance. It was greater than anything available in the 360 line. IBM compiled the performance factors shown in Table 37 for various large processors, measured in relation to the 65's performance set at 1.0. (Notice also the effects of adding processor memory—a three-megabyte machine delivered half again as much throughput as a half-megabyte model.)

So as customers outgrew their 65, they could move to a 165 and get as much as three times more processing capacity; with IBM pushing the centralized, interactive processing modes so heavily, many indeed needed that capacity.

Moreover, IBM initially intended the 155 and 165 to have a normal, long life. As late as 1970, when the machines were introduced, IBM was planning to upgrade them with semiconductor memory as a "follow-on."[21] And the extra hardware needed for virtual memory was slated for introduction in September 1971. Had IBM stuck by those initial plans, the life of the two processors would have been extended considerably. The company abandoned its plans, however, when it brought out the 158 and 168 as separate products. Never again would purchase customers assume that IBM would not make equipment obsolete early after its shipment.

Not only leasing companies were hurt by this maneuver. Many large, important customers had also purchased and installed 155s and 165s. They had in effect wasted millions of dollars on equipment that was being replaced so soon by

Table 37
Performance Improvements, by
Memory Size[20]

SYSTEM	I	J	JI	K	KJ
360/65	1.0	1.2	*	*	*
370/155	1.2	1.4	1.5	1.5	*
370/165	2.0	2.7	3.0	3.1	3.2

* Not a part of IBM standard product line.

machines that offered more function (primarily virtual memory and future, related enhancements) but only marginal—20 to 40 percent—increases in performance. So angered were some that they began to seriously consider installing plug-compatible processors.

Although IBM may have wanted to soften the blow for some of these customers, it was limited in its ability to segment one group of purchase customers from the others. Any generous trade-in allowance it made available to them would have had to include leasing companies also, which would have defeated one of the purposes of SMASH. IBM did try to placate irate customers with the so-called DAT box (for dynamic address translation), which made virtual memory possible on the 155 and 165. The DAT box was priced high, however, and did not guarantee total compatibility with the 158 and 168 systems, whose future seemed brighter. The box cost IBM less than $9,000 to build, but it sold for as much as $400,000 (no leases were available). Worse, there was only a limited promise from IBM that the DAT-equipped processors would be useful with future operating systems, which would be tailored to the 158 and 168 hardware. But no matter what IBM said, everyone could see that the 155 and 165 were going nowhere fast.

The 370/158 and 168 announcement, therefore, looks suspiciously as if it were designed primarily to "SMASH" the competition instead of as an honest attempt to offer customers superior technology that would better meet their growing needs. These processors clearly denied their customers a number of choices they would have continued to enjoy had IBM enhanced its 155 and 165 processors and not replaced them so soon. But then, IBM does not maximize its commercial profits by giving customers choices of suppliers.

There were at least two additional reasons for IBM's actions with the 155 and 165. One was that revenues took a dive in the early 1970s as a result of an overall economic slowdown. By encouraging purchases of these two machines, IBM got its money quickly and could compensate for lower revenues elsewhere in its product line. Also, it was probably impossible for IBM to sufficiently reprice its processors relative to memory in a single step; doing it in two steps (i.e., 50–155–158) made the change less suspicious.

MORE MIPS, PLEASE

Responding to IBM's many incentives, customers in the early 1970s were using their 370 systems increasingly for interactive time sharing and transaction processing. These two modes of computing required tremendous computing resources. The software needed to manage time sharing was not only extremely large in size, thus requiring as much processor memory as possible, but it used up large amounts of even the fastest processor's time. The yawning need for more MIPS (a measure of processor performance, standing for millions of instructions per second) was becoming insatiable.

So insatiable, in fact, that IBM's largest processors were insufficient to handle many customers' applications. The company surveyed some of those customers in the mid-1970s to determine how much more computing horsepower they would need by the end of the decade. The survey found that already 60 percent of the largest users were pushing their 370/168-3 processors, IBM's most powerful unit, to the limit. On average, these processor-bound users needed a machine twice as powerful to be delivered by mid-1976. A quarter of the constrained users looked forward to getting a machine three times as powerful less than two years after that. Yet IBM never delivered that level of processing power during the 1970s. Its next product after the 370/168-3, the 3033 processor, had only 1.7 times more capacity. In 1980, finally, a 370 with three times the power of a 168-3 was introduced—it was delivered a year or so later.

To give customers the capacity they needed, IBM had been counting on its grand FS—Future System—product line, which was to be a totally new family of systems designed specifically for large-scale time sharing and transaction processing. The aging batch-oriented 360 and 370 families, now showing fatal weaknesses, were to be abandoned for FS. A memo that IBM handed to the Department of Justice behind closed doors on October 14, 1974, described FS, and IBM's hopes for it, in intriguing detail. The memo reminded Justice of the supposed great risks IBM faced in bringing such a complex and costly system as FS to market.[22] IBM did its best to convince Department officials that as a settlement to the antitrust case filed in 1969, a breakup of IBM would not be in the best interest of computer users—who, IBM emphasized, were truly reaching the limits of their installed 370s. "This [new FS] system family will require a totally new and different system architecture from System/360/370," IBM told Justice.

> To bring out a totally new system family involves a huge development effort (in excess of $5 billion, more than $4 billion of which will be spent before the first machine is sold and little of which is salvageable if the project fails). That effort is far greater than System 360/370, and involves technical and market risks at least equal to any past development.
>
> Why does IBM risk this enormous investment? The short answer is, because it has to. The 360/370 architecture is old; the technology is available to and being used by competitors who have, comparatively, little development expense. The lead time gained by introducing the S/370 technology is eroding, and unless IBM can find ways to exploit the technology potential in innovative new ways which further expand function and use of its products, its revenues and profits will suffer.[23]

IBM added that in three hardware areas—main processor memory, logic circuitry, and disk drive technology—there was great potential to "drive costs down" if significant manufacturing volumes could be achieved, and that a "vastly improved software operating system" could boost the productivity of customers' programmers. However, the company argued to the Justice Department, "Unfortunately very little of the hardware or software technology potential can be utilized in the existing [370] architecture." Instead, a new and enormously costly family of systems was needed. It was so expensive as to strain "IBM's resources both financially and technically."

Thus, argued IBM, it should not be split:

> A predictable and dramatic consequence of such a split is that both companies would find it impossible to architect, develop, produce and support a new compatible system family of the magnitude of FS (and its successor). This consequence is virtually certain to follow in view of the size of the risk FS represents and the required "front-end" investment of most of the greater than $5 billion total. The simple fact (which would be known to both surviving companies) that *IBM's resources today are already strained by the effort to bring out this new system* demonstrates the reasonableness of that conclusion.
>
> Beyond the fact that the FS investment would have to be scrapped, both companies would be burdened with supporting the existing full compatible system family with half the resource. This will require that each duplicate certain functions and activities of the predecessor company at the same level and expense as the predecessor company incurred—despite the 50% reduction in revenues. (Emphasis added.)[24]

FS, IBM argued, was needed to provide a new type of processing that customers wanted and could not obtain with IBM's current product line. Although IBM's analysis of its problems was correct, the remedy it proposed turned out to be no better. FS was in fact a failure. None of its systems ever saw the light of day, its development teams were disbanded, and its ambitious plans were scrapped.

The first FS machine was planned for introduction in 1975 or 1976. In March 1975, just five months after pleading with Justice to be kept intact so it could successfully complete the FS project, IBM disclosed FS's demise. It would, after all, have to continue competing—now against aggressively priced 370-compatible processors based on superior technology—with its "old" 370s.

GIVE OR TAKE A BILLION DOLLARS

But how much did the failed FS project actually cost IBM? Was it in fact $4 billion or more down the drain? Was that much money really needed to succeed in the computer market, as the memo argued? Despite those claims to government lawyers (which were inadmissible to the trial's record), IBM's expert economic witnesses later claimed exactly the opposite when testifying under oath. Repeatedly, IBM sought to convince Judge David Edelstein that it faced many effective competitors and that only a small amount of capital was required to successfully enter the computer market. One of its economic witnesses, Professor Richard B. Mancke of Tufts University, claimed, for instance, that "there never have been, nor are there now, any significant barriers to entry into the EDP [electronic data processing] market or into any part of the market." He added:

> ... when an appropriate view of entry into the market is employed, the capital requirements drop, from perhaps the hundreds of millions ... to several million or even thousand dollars. Many companies can, and have, entered the EDP market with such relatively small amounts of capital.

So while claiming privately that only an intact IBM with massive resources could build the systems customers demanded, and that two half-size IBMs would have insufficient resources, IBM argued publicly that virtually anyone could enter the market successfully. One needed only a few thousand dollars, Mancke claimed. IBM's dominant market position gave it no insurmountable advantages.

In the trial, Richard Case, one of IBM's most experienced computer designers and a man deeply involved in FS, was asked about the cost of abandoning the project:

> Q. Can you estimate what FS cost IBM from 1972 to 1975?
> A. ... the best answer I can give is that FS from 1971 to 1975 cost IBM more than $100 million.[25]

Which was it? "In excess of $5 billion, more than $4 billion of which will be spent before the first machine is sold and little of which is salvageable if the project fails"? Or only "more than $100 million," as Case claimed? Or several thousand dollars, as put forth by Mancke? If the first, FS must rank as the most expensive industrial failure ever. If $100 million, then the cost of fixing IBM's misdirected 370 system line was well within the reach of several large, split-up IBMs. But if Mancke is correct, IBM could safely be split into thousands of pieces with no loss.

But IBM was still contradicting itself. If, as the company claimed in the back room, much of the large FS investment was in fact lost, its reputation for excellent management was brought into question. On the other hand, if, as Case implied on the witness stand, relatively little investment was lost, IBM could use much of FS's technical advances in other products and avoid a complete write-off. Even this conclusion has its price, however, for it brings into question the generally accepted reason for the 360s' great commercial success.

During the 1960s, IBM had portrayed itself as risking huge amounts of money on the System/360. That was IBM's $5 billion "We bet the company" investment. But had the 360 failed like FS, would not IBM certainly have recovered some of its investment by using 360 technology to enhance and extend the life of its 1400/7000 second-generation systems? When the 360s' success became obvious to all, the image of IBM risking its very survival and being rewarded by great profits appeared only fair.* It was certainly better than the alternative— IBM winning solely because of monopoly power. But when a similarly ambitious system design, the FS, failed, the costs of the failure magically dropped to insignificance as the technology was applied in a less grandiose manner. Maybe less was at risk with the 360s than IBM would have us believe.

Unsaid to Justice was that FS would have solved a number of troublesome competitive problems for IBM. It would, like the 370/158 and 168 before it, have dealt IBM a new hand to play in a high-stakes technological game. New hardware technology would finally have killed the 360 systems. It would have brought better performance at lower prices and helped IBM induce customers to migrate to new machines that would leave behind all vestiges of 360 and 370 compatibility. An entirely new set of FS interfaces could be instituted, prices rebundled, and compatible vendors kept at bay once more. Most important, a new operating system, incompatible with the severely limited OS/360 but of a fundamentally new design, would keep competitors' hands off the central point of IBM's power, the processor. None of it came to be, however, so IBM had to stick it out with the increasingly uncompetitive 370 processors and make do as best it could. From now on it would cut processor prices drastically and reinflate prices elsewhere in the propped-up 370 system complex. A new strategy would be required to counter the new threats.

---

* IBM's economists in their narrative statement imply just that: the 360 was a "fantastic undertaking" involving "fantastic risks" such that ". . . the success of the company was in many ways to be determined by the success of that one product." If it had failed, IBM would, according to these observers, be a "radically different company, if even in the computer business."[26]

15. The FUD Factor

It is IBM practice not to disclose, discuss or sell IBM products before their announcement. . . . Nondisclosure . . . means that an IBM representative may not attempt to delay a customer decision to order competitive equipment by hinting that a new IBM product is under development.

—IBM's *Business Conduct Guidelines,* as quoted in *The IBM Way*[1]

In 1975, with FS a failure and the 370 now having to hold the large-systems fort for IBM, the stage was set for a new class of competitors to go after the highest-profit piece of the IBM systems monopoly, the processor. There were several aspects of the marketplace that worked against IBM and in favor of these rival companies:

- In driving away add-on memory makers, IBM had loaded great profit into the 370 processor, which made that component an attractive target for replacement.
- IBM, through its own shortsightedness, did not have the right product—namely a 370 processor larger than the already overloaded 168—to satisfy users' performance needs. They were pushing even multiple 168s to their limit as they added application after interactive application.
- More than a few of IBM's most important customers had felt badly burned by the company when they purchased the quickly obsoleted 155 and 165 processors, and they still held a grudge. They were willing to take their business away from IBM if they were offered a 370-compatible processor that would run their applications code unchanged.
- The OS operating system was still available at no charge, saving any company that decided to make 370-compatible processors a great deal of development costs.
- Most of all, new technology was available that made it possible to build a processor that duplicated the 370s' essential functions—and even enhanced them—at far less cost than IBM spent on building the 370s.

The first and the most successful strike at the processor heart of IBM's 370 monopoly was perpetrated by one of the company's own, the gifted Dr. Gene Amdahl, who had led the design of the 360 family and knew as well as anyone the chinks in IBM's armor and the self-imposed pricing strictures that limited its ability to respond effectively. His story shows how well customers would take to alternative equipment if it saved them money and still ran their trusted application programs.

ENTER DR. AMDAHL

Gene Amdahl was IBM's most highly honored computer designer during the 1960s. He was introduced by Watson, Jr., at the IBM shareholders' meeting in 1964 as "the father of the System/360." Trained in theoretical physics, he joined IBM in the early 1950s and became chief designer of the 704 computer and then head of preliminary design of the 709 and 7030 processors. In 1960, after almost five years of designing computers at Philco-Ford, Amdahl returned to IBM and soon took over planning responsibilities for the upcoming 360 processor family.

The soft-spoken Amdahl was rewarded for his contributions to the 360s with IBM's greatest honor in 1965: he was named IBM Fellow. That freed him to pursue research interests as he pleased. He devoted his efforts to establishing a new laboratory for developing large computer systems but soon became involved in a major debate at IBM. Amdahl, alone at first, argued that the computers that were to follow the 360 family should be made compatible with it, that they should be able to run essentially the same software and use the same peripherals, even though they would employ advanced technology. Opposing him was a group arguing that compatibility could be achieved only at the expense of performance and that therefore only incompatible designs, such as FS, should be pursued.

Unconvinced, Amdahl forged ahead with his idea of large 360-compatible processors, and eventually, by May 1968, he proved them to be economically as well as technically feasible. He was put in charge of developing IBM's largest future computers and recommended on economic grounds that three large processors be brought to market. Top management decided it wanted only one such machine—thereby dooming his plans. Amdahl's lab was shut down in May 1969, but he immediately went to IBM's top three officers and argued that they were making a big mistake, that it was only the corporation's marketing and pricing policies, not technical limitations, that prevented it from developing the high-performance computers he had in mind.

As Amdahl tells the story, IBM was too concerned with protecting its present price and cost structure to bring out products that could provide users with better performance for lower prices. New technology was available to build such machines, but the company was locked in to its skewed pricing scheme to such a degree that it could not act without adversely affecting revenues and profits. IBM President Learson and Senior Vice Presidents Frank Cary and John Opel listened patiently, Amdahl recalls, but in the end they informed him that they had no intention of changing the company's marketing policies.

Thus was born Amdahl Corporation in 1970, headed by a man with a dream and a reputation but no money. His dream was to build not just the most powerful general-purpose computer ever but one that would be totally compatible with IBM's 360s—totally, from its peripherals to its operating system to the billions of dollars' worth of 360 applications software that users had developed over the years. His would be a better processor than any of IBM's because it would use technology IBM declined to pursue and it would deliver better performance at a substantially lower price.

Amdahl's reputation as the 360s' chief architect aided him greatly as he traveled the world, seeking help from semiconductor manufacturers who could build him advanced semiconductor chips. While IBM then was still only studying, not building, medium-density integrated chips, Amdahl's machine would use special high-density chips of his design. Each chip would pack many more logic gates into each square inch than the chips used by other vendors and far more than any IBM was about to use. The result would be a major reduction in production cost and physical size combined with big boosts in speed and reliability. Amdahl's costs for entering the 370 market would be lessened, too, by his leaving virtually all software development to IBM, which still kept its operating system in the public domain. Amdahl and its customers would be able to use OS free of charge.

Amdahl's main problem was money. Just as he began seeking the millions of dollars that he needed to develop his ambitious machine, the fate of the crushed plug-compatible peripherals makers was attesting to IBM's ability to deal roughly with competitors who threatened any part of its systems business. So uninterested in his business plan were U.S. financiers that Amdahl eventually sought substantial backing, and help with his special air-cooled chips (IBM's largest processor used the more expensive water-cooled chips), from the Japanese computer company Fujitsu Corporation. It saw an investment in Amdahl's venture as a prime vehicle for entering the lucrative U.S. market and tapping into Amdahl's innovative ideas.

Amdahl Corporation's business plan was a clever and convincing one, written as it was by a man who understood the economics of computer manufacturing, both past and future, both within IBM and without. From firsthand experience, too, Amdahl knew of IBM's heavy reliance on price discrimination. The Amdahl plan called for designing, building, and marketing a high-performance processor to sell at such a low price that the pent-up demand for its performance would ensure enough sales to cover the immense cost of entering the market. He would effectively give away processing power that IBM could not and would not deliver except at exorbitant prices. The plan emphasized that because Amdahl Corporation would enter the market without any installed base, it would be free to set prices much closer to production costs than IBM was, with its thousands of 360s—and soon 370s—still being leased. Any attempt by IBM to further lower prices on its 158 and 168 processors, where prices were now bloated, would compel more users of high-priced medium-size IBM processors to discard that hardware and rush up the 370 range. IBM was therefore unable, as General Motors had been in responding to the Japanese, to drastically change the area of its interrelated product line under attack without restructuring all its prices.

This bind would restrict IBM's options in responding to Amdahl's low-priced, high-performance processor. Amdahl Corporation delivered its first computer, called the V/6, in 1975. It worked within hours of delivery and was hailed as a great success for the company. Following a string of similarly successful installations, for which certain adventurous 370 users were willing to pay cash up front, Gene Amdahl was elevated to folk-hero status among IBM mainframe users. He had broken IBM's lock on the heart of the 370. It was not long before the company had installed many more processors with prestigious customers, had entered the public securities market, and had gained the attention of IBM users worldwide. Amdahl was injecting competition into a market that had been IBM's domain for decades, and users were rushing to take advantage of it.

Amdahl Corporation, in its first year of shipping V/6s, installed $100 million worth of computers, and before the second year was up, revenues reached $200 million. By early 1977, forty machines had been installed, three of them in Europe. The V/6 offered 40 percent more performance than IBM's 168, but it was priced at 20 percent less. Before long, V/6 shipments were limited only by the company's capacity to produce them.

To say the least, IBM was not amused to see so many of its large accounts jumping ship to join Amdahl. As the former IBM computer architect had predicted, however, IBM's choice of responses was limited. It was stuck with a pair of overpriced, underpowered processors, the 370/168 and 158, that acted as pillars in a contrived price-discrimination scheme. IBM had little technology at its disposal with which to improve the two processors. In fact, on the technological front, Amdahl was the clear winner for the rest of the decade and even later. Early 1976 saw noted industry analyst Frederic G. Withington of Arthur D. Little comment, "IBM's large computers still employ the basic architecture of the original 360 computers, and their electronic components are now well behind the current state of the art."[2] Three years later, IBM itself found that it lacked product leadership in processors, disk drives, and software for large systems, even though it was enjoying spectacular growth in those areas. The company also concluded that a long-standing major weakness was its "lack of innovation and aggressiveness"—its competition was ahead in several important areas of technology.[3]

After more than a year of V/6 shipments and rave customer reviews of the Amdahl machine, IBM finally fired back a three-shot volley late one Friday afternoon, March 25, 1977. IBM unveiled a new processor, the 3033, which, it was claimed, offered 60 to 80 percent more performance than the most powerful 168 box at less than half the price. It also cut purchase prices on the 158 and 168 processors by 30 percent and slashed purchase and lease prices on memory for almost all other models of the 370 line.

Gene Amdahl claims responsibility for this fundamental reversal by IBM. Up to this point, we have seen several examples of IBM upping processor prices—even as new technology made them less costly to build—to compensate for cuts in prices of peripherals, but now it had to drop processor prices or see its market share plummet. Beginning with Amdahl's first shipments in 1975, competitive pressure from it and other plug-compatible processor vendors caused the price of IBM 370 processor performance to drop by a factor of about ten. That is, the price per standard unit of performance, one million instructions per second (MIPS), on IBM's largest 370 processors fell from about $1,745,000 in 1975 to $186,000 in 1985. The price of a MIPS had gone up in 1975 from $1,689,000 on the original 370/158 to $1,745,000 on an enhanced 370/158-3 processor. In 1977, in response to Amdahl, came the three 303X series of processors (averaging $782,000 per MIPS), followed in 1979 and 1980 by enhanced 3033s and the 3081 ($447,000 per MIPS), in 1982 by the 3082/3 and 4 processors ($345,000), and in 1985 by the 3089/Sierra ($186,000). IBM may claim these dramatic price improvements were spurred solely by continual advancements in technology, but it seems highly unlikely that the company's prices would have declined so rapidly, after rising in the prior years (years when technological improvements were also driving costs down), had competition not been so effective.

All during this time, IBM's processors remained technically inferior to Amdahl's and other companies' 370-compatible products. Amdahl's original V/6 of 1976 was nearly three times as fast as the IBM 168 it replaced and 50 percent faster than the 3033, first delivered in 1978. It took IBM until 1982 to approximately equal the circuit speeds Amdahl shipped in 1976. What's more, to this day, IBM's large processors are cooled by water; none of its plug-compatible processor rivals has ever shipped a water-cooled machine, choosing the more efficient and economic air cooling.

All told, IBM during the 1970s and early 1980s had to struggle to get out of the rather deep hole it had dug itself into with large customers. Having first driven Gene Amdahl away with its decision to ignore the extra-large 370 processors he had proposed, the company soon began encouraging customers to build huge, centralized computer applications that relied on data base and data communications technology and that consequently overloaded the limited performance of the 168 processor. Even the 3033, which was actually a modified 168, was burdened by many centralized applications. The success of the centralization strategy, the fact that IBM's data base and data communications products were inefficient, and the fact that the new disk attachment strategy put additional load on the central processor, combined had led to a strong demand for large-scale processors and high processor profits for IBM. But those very same factors now led to an acute shortage of processing power for large 370 users, which IBM's machines simply could not satisfy. When its great leap, the Future System, failed to materialize, all IBM could do against the instantly successful Amdahl was begin slashing prices. IBM management must certainly have rued the day it said good-bye to Gene Amdahl, for he had just the product the company needed but that it seemed incapable of building in his absence. The search for IBM's vaunted "excellence" need go no further.

As we have seen many times so far, however, it takes more to achieve commercial success at IBM's expense than just superior technology and lower prices. Amdahl was ready for IBM's price cuts, but the other weapon IBM employed against his successful machine was more difficult to counter. IBM resorted to monkeying with a previously stable interface, just as it had done to upset Memorex and Telex several years before. Specifically, the 3033 differed from all other 370 processors in the nature of its interface to the OS operating system. Under the cover of providing new functions and better OS performance, IBM changed a fundamental relationship within the 360 and 370 processor architecture. Just as compatible disk drive makers had had to worry about the IBM-dictated interfaces between disk drive, controller, and processor, Amdahl's main concern in maintaining compatibility with the IBM 370s focused on the operating system and other software that users wished to run. The interface between software and processor was of a slightly different kind than that between disk and controller, but when push came to shove it served the same purpose for IBM. It could be manipulated in such a way as to segment a market and thwart a competitor's ability to compete in a timely manner on a box-for-box basis. In one sense, Amdahl had to concern himself with having the V/6 speak, as it were, the same language as IBM's processors.

Software is essentially a set of detailed procedures that is expressed as an ordered list of simple logic and arithmetic operations. A typical operation is "add," which adds two numbers; another might be "compare," which compares two numbers for equality or difference. Computer programmers construct even their largest and most complex programs from the always-small, finite set of basic instructions that their target computer provides. The instruction set can be thought of as a primitive vocabulary that is called upon by programs to instruct the machine step-by-step in its required tasks. Different models of computer have different instruction sets, and, generally speaking, programs for one model cannot be executed on another because their instruction sets are mutually incompatible.

Even though he employed different circuit technology, Amdahl of course designed the V/6 to use exactly the same instruction set as IBM's 370 processors; only in that way could users be assured that the IBM operating system and all the applications they had written themselves on 370s would run unchanged on the Amdahl hardware. The 370s, and therefore Amdahl's V/6, had a repertoire of nearly 200 basic instructions. But there was room, in the IBM hardware at least, for more.

Now, in a typical 370 system of the time, as much as 70 percent of the processor's time went to executing procedures issued by the operating system. The OS software had incredibly complex scheduling, routing, and management tasks to perform in order to manage interactive and batch jobs effectively in a single processor. With such high overhead, little processor capacity was left to customers' application programs. It was obvious that if some way could be found to reduce the time the processor spent on the operating system, 370 systems would execute more applications and respond better to interactive terminals—quite simply, the system would do more work. To that end, IBM studied the operating system carefully and determined that certain of its most commonly invoked routines—those that controlled its most fundamental activities—could be speeded enormously if several new items were added to the 370 instruction set.

In fact, the anti-Amdahl model 3033 processor—to a large degree simply a reworked and repriced 168—incorporated fourteen new instructions. To take advantage of those new instructions, special software was added to the operating system. It frequently called on—and therefore absolutely required—those instructions. IBM had profoundly changed the interface between software and hardware in the 370. Running the modified operating system—which was claimed to boost 3033 performance by 14 percent over the 168—on an Amdahl processor would not have worked at all because the V/6 did not have any of the fourteen new hardware instructions. Suddenly, there was a question in customers' minds: Could Gene Amdahl, as clever as he and his fellow designers were, match IBM's modifications—and not just this time, but each and every time IBM might add new functions to its 370 processors in the future?

Independent observers also asked that question. Wrote industry analyst Frederic Withington in 1978, "We believe that IBM is . . . likely to offer bundled software and microcode that will make it increasingly difficult for [plug-compatible mainframe vendors] to design processors that can be guaranteed to remain compatible with IBM software; IBM does not release detailed microcode specifications that [can be] legally [duplicated]. IBM may also find other ways to change its machine designs in ways that would make product duplication difficult."[4]

Amdahl actually had room left in which to maneuver. The company responded to Friday's 3033 announcement after a hectic weekend of product positioning and pricing calculations. Amdahl had been ready for IBM, and it unveiled two new machines of its own, a more powerful V/7 that topped the 3033's performance and a V/5 that competed more directly with the 158. All Amdahl machines, the company also promised, would sooner or later be completely able to work with IBM's new operating system. Although the Amdahl machine's basic architecture was not quite as flexible as that of the 3033 (IBM's instructions were implemented in programmable microcode while Amdahl's were inflexibly hardwired), the competitor was sure that once it could determine exactly what IBM's fourteen new instructions were, it could make the V/5, V/6, and V/7 simulate them with ease. Amdahl promised its V/7 for delivery in August 1978, about six months after IBM said it would ship the 3033.

Indeed, the delay in finding out the nature of those new instructions, which were far more complicated and unpredictable than a mere "add" or "compare," did Amdahl the most marketing harm. Even when asked formally through the proper channels, IBM bluntly refused to reveal their specification. Amdahl, along with the rest of the industry, had to wait a full year before IBM shipped the first 3033 and described its new microcode. Even then, of course, it would be months before Amdahl could dissect the instructions and write the necessary simulation software for its V series. The remicrocoded 3033 locked Amdahl out of the market for more than a year until it could duplicate the function of IBM's microcode and prove to skeptical customers that it had the wherewithal to play according to IBM's changing rules. IBM played on that skepticism by quietly starting rumors that more microcode changes might come at any time.

With pent-up demand for additional 370 horsepower as strong as it was, customers' immediate response to the IBM 3033 was almost overwhelming. Several thousand of the processors were ordered the first day after it was unveiled. AT&T, IBM's largest private sector customer, ordered some $150 million worth of the new equipment in one shot. So many 3033 orders were placed that day— their total value was estimated to be over $6 billion—that IBM assigned its limited deliveries through an unprecedented lottery. Especially needy customers placed more orders than they actually needed to do better in the lottery; some went so far as to pay thousands of dollars for others' early delivery positions. This despite the fact that they could get superior technology, performance, function, and price from Amdahl.

Amdahl saw its strong order rate dive for several months as customers sorted out IBM's lengthy delivery schedules and weighed Amdahl's prospects under the new regime of lower 370 processor prices and moving interfaces. As Amdahl pointed out to the Common Market's supreme court, which was investigating alleged abuses by IBM of its dominant position in the computer market in Europe for several years preceding 1984, the sudden change in OS-processor interface entailed by the 3033 "immediately created doubt of Amdahl's compatibility; that doubt was more important to users than the fact that Amdahl's products were consistently evaluated as being superior to IBM's."

The competitor's main problem in marketing products that worked with the 370s was not to match IBM's technology nor to show a working machine but rather to counter the strong skepticism among potential customers that it could maintain perfect compatibility with the 370s. The plug-compatible peripherals wars still fresh in their minds, users were not satisfied just to see the first Amdahl machine work perfectly or hear the celebrated Dr. Amdahl's assurances. They wanted to be sure Amdahl Corporation could keep up with IBM despite whatever gauntlet the giant threw down. Amdahl himself used a telling phrase to describe this IBM-instilled skepticism: the FUD Factor, referring to fear, uncertainty, and doubt. FUD was, and still is, a most effective weapon for IBM.

Amdahl Corporation lost sales due to some users' fear about future incompatibility, but it convinced many others that once IBM released specifications for the new 3033 instructions, it could quickly and successfully respond. After the year of silence from IBM, it was only three months after the specs were released before Amdahl was able to ship a software duplication of the 3033 microcode for the V/6. So well performing was that software, Amdahl later claimed, that several 158 and 168 users inquired about using it in lieu of the high-priced microcode field upgrade IBM offered for those processors.

While IBM would no doubt defend its microcode on the 3033 as a purely technical action designed to boost better system performance, Amdahl's complaint to the European court revealed evidence of IBM's plainly anticompetitive intentions. IBM's main purpose, Amdahl contended, was to avoid having to compete on the merit of its processors, which were inferior in many ways to Amdahl's, and instead create a moving target, a shifting interface between software and processor that would perpetually keep Amdahl off balance and its prospects hesitant.

IBM, Amdahl claimed, showed an early and explicit recognition of, one, its competitive advantages in the large-scale commercial systems business and, two, the importance of compatibility as a threat to its position. In January 1972, long before Amdahl had shipped its first machine, an IBM QPLA stated:

> Another common element [of non-IBM, non-compatible competitive large-scale systems] is lack of comprehensive software, which will require considerable time to develop. This leads to the conclusion that, for the present, these systems will be restricted to the scientific user willing and

able to develop or enhance software. *The exception to this could be the Amdahl entry if it were able to use System/360 or System/370 software.* [Emphasis added.][5]

IBM also told customers that it would change its interfaces without fully disclosing their specifications, Amdahl charged. It claimed that IBM often reminded users that while the 3033 and the other large 370 processors had the ability to be reprogrammed through microcoding, as had been done to add the new instructions to the 168 and make it a 3033, Amdahl's machines were hardwired and unable to be modified that way. Now, microcode certainly has some technical advantages over hardwiring (namely flexibility in designing the instruction set), but Amdahl had chosen to hardwire his machine because then it would run faster. But, as Amdahl demonstrated with his software duplication of IBM's microcode, hardwiring does not rule out ongoing compatibility.

Amdahl cited reports from the unidentified prospective customer that IBM had told him that the 370s' microcode "interfaces were not solid and could well change and could become fuzzy with time with no commitment by IBM to supply anything other than the smallest amount of information about these interfaces."

On four separate occasions, another unidentified Amdahl prospect was reported to have told Amdahl that IBM had stated that it intended to make changes beyond the 3033's microcode just to render Amdahl's gear incompatible. The prospect reported the following to Amdahl:

> The way [the new operating system modifications] have been implemented on Amdahl systems is different to the way it has been implemented on IBM systems. IBM suggested that because of this [Amdahl] are veering from the IBM "strategic" line. It was further suggested that Amdahl is likely to continue to veer from the line such that in a few years [Amdahl's] software will be significantly different.[6]

Amdahl said its prospect was then told in a separate meeting with IBM that the latter intended "to introduce over the coming years more and more microcode that will make it almost impossible for Amdahl to remain compatible." In yet another meeting with IBM, the user was told, "IBM's policy is to introduce more and more microcode both in central processors and peripheral devices. This microcode will make it almost impossible for Amdahl to remain compatible with IBM systems."

So strong was the fear among users that they might end up on an incompatible limb should they go with Amdahl, the company told the European court, that some prospects asked for contractual guarantees that Amdahl would stay compatible with future changes in the 370s' interface. Amdahl concluded, "Such extraordinary requests demonstrate the extent to which IBM's threat of creating incompatibility is a fundamental fact of existence in the IBM-controlled market. This is not an argumentative abstraction. It is the daily challenge Amdahl must confront in the marketplace." (IBM's pressure on customers mounted sufficiently to provoke *ComputerWorld* to publish a highly critical editorial in 1980 concerning its tactics. See Appendix H.)

After a time, Amdahl was no longer the only company facing such challenges, for its success—it had installed 161 machines by late 1978 and was showing annual revenues of about $500 million—paved the way for several other manufacturers to begin marketing 370-compatible processors. Soon to enter after Amdahl were the leasing company Itel Corporation, which marketed processors built to its specifications by National Semiconductor and later, Hitachi Ltd. of Japan; Magnuson Corporation and Two Pi Corporation, two small Silicon Valley companies; Cambridge Memories and the spin-out IPL Systems, which grew from an add-on memory effort; Control Data, which sold Cambridge machines under the Omega label; Nixdorf, a West German computer maker; and perhaps a half dozen lesser companies that achieved only slight market penetration. Advances in computer and semiconductor technology had made it relatively easy to build 370-compatible processors.

Not only did these companies offer hardware that was superior to IBM's, they could often deliver it more quickly than IBM could. With falling prices and the increasing use of data communications, remote minicomputers drawing on central systems, and various types of interactive computing, demand for 370 processing power far exceeded IBM's ability to deliver it. Its manufacturing plants just could not build large processors fast enough. This gave compatible vendors a chance to deliver hardware earlier and win orders that would otherwise have gone to IBM.

Amdahl and the Itel/National Semiconductor team did the best of all the compatible processor makers, together installing equipment valued at just over $1 billion in 1979. But even including the approximately $60 million in additional 370-type processor revenues reported by Magnuson, Control Data, and Cambridge that year, those revenues totaled less than 3 percent of the $37.65 billion value of IBM's total installed 370 systems base that year.

AMDAHL: IBM'S FRIEND OR FOE?

IBM's share of the large processor market was certainly diminished by plug-compatible vendors, but the company did not irretrievably lose customers to them. Because customers continued to use the same IBM operating system and, very likely, had IBM peripherals attached to their non-IBM processors, it was a relatively simple matter technically to bring them back into the fold. For that reason, IBM much preferred seeing customers who were desperate for processor capacity leave to a compatible company rather than to other systems makers because it knew they could always return easily. Many did.

Despite the entrance of technologically superior 370-compatible mainframes from a variety of sources, IBM was able to hold on to about 75 percent of the large 370 systems market. This is clearly evident in the following data collected by International Data Corporation:

Table 38

Estimated IBM Percentage of Market Share of Value of Installed Systems for Six Size Classes of System, 1974–79[7]

CLASS	1974	1975	1976	1977	1978	1979	DIFFERENCE, 1974 TO 1979
7	67.5%	68.6%	71.5%	71.5%	76.4%	76.0%	+8.5%
6	77.1	76.4	78.4	78.1	76.8	75.6	−1.5
5	65.4	66.5	66.1	68.5	67.4	61.1	−4.3
4	66.8	62.7	63.0	63.7	62.7	60.0	−6.8
3	50.3	54.8	59.7	59.9	57.5	54.1	+3.8
2	80.2	75.8	75.4	75.7	74.6	70.9	−9.3
Average	68.8	67.9	70.6	70.6	71.1	69.5	+0.7

IBM's share of the entire systems market remained relatively constant, at about 69 percent, during the six years, but in the highest growth area, large systems, its share actually increased substantially. The larger the machine, the larger was IBM's share. IBM did this by cutting prices on 370 processors again and again; that seemed to be about all it could do, given its glaring lack of advanced chip technology and the aggressive competition it faced.

In the small- and medium-size 370s, IBM was less successful in maintaining or increasing market share. Price discrimination against these smaller users made its equipment less competitive. Also, the larger leasing company-owned and enhanced systems remained competitive for these smaller customers. IBM was well aware of its problems: "Staunch efforts in marketing programs, sales incentives, management emphasis and resource allocation have failed to produce satisfactory results . . ." claimed a 1974 document.[8]

The 360 systems owned by leasing companies and customers did not affect IBM's System/3s in the same way that they affected small and intermediate-size 370-compatible systems. "The combination of ease of use, architectural differences and price have effectively insulated the System/3 from the competitive effects of the purchased S/360 inventory."[9] IBM had effectively segmented the System/3 market, thereby enabling it to show its own relationship between price and performance.

Although hard data are not available, it can be surmised that IBM's profits from large processors fell when its prices were cut to meet the competition. However, profits from software, for which prices have steadily increased, and peripherals, particularly in the disk drive arena, where IBM grew stronger each year after 1975 or so, helped make up for lost profits on the processors. IBM once again shifted profits from one product category to another as its price discrimination pattern adapted to changing market conditions. Just as economist Carl Kaysen had stated, the narrow-line competition was powerless to fight this kind of price discrimination.

IBM's combined share of the entire mainframe systems market, measured across all system size categories, went up only a few percentage points during the second half of the 1970s, but its share among the largest processors was significantly higher. Its combined share in sizes 4 through 7 (370/125 and larger) rose from 66 percent in 1974 to 69 percent five years later, according to IDC's figures, but in the very largest category alone, class 7, its share during the same period rose from 65.5 percent to 77.7 percent.

Combining IBM's share with those of its plug-compatible processor competitors provides a measure of how dominant the 370 architecture became during these years. Any gain among those machines came at the expense of IBM's traditional systems rivals. Amdahl and the other plug-compatible rivals were particularly vulnerable to IBM's interface manipulations, while the other competitors were less so. Among size classes 4 through 7 again, the 370s' combined share went from 69.5 percent in 1974 to 75.6 percent in 1979, but in class 7, machines conforming to the 370 architecture grew their share from 67.5 percent to 84.3 percent during the same time.[10] So the non-370 system makers— Sperry Rand, Burroughs, and the like—actually saw their share of the overall large-scale mainframe market drop by a total of 16.8 percent.

Of the additional share the 370 architecture won, IBM in the combined 4 through 7 classes captured 49 percent of the business; in the very largest systems, however, where it faced particularly competitive systems, IBM managed to hold on to 73 percent of the business its traditional systems rivals lost. That feat is particularly striking in light of the fact (to be elaborated on in later chapters) that IBM's products were particularly deficient in the areas so important to users of the largest 370-compatible systems—data base and data communications. Evidently, IBM's enormous power during these years more than compensated for technological and cost deficiencies that would have severely dented any other company's market share.

IBM's strategy of herding users to ever-larger, centralized interactive systems was a stunning commercial success, but it resulted in a concentration of the company's business on a rather small group of large customers. In 1974, in fact, IBM executive John Akers found that only 80 mainframe customers accounted for a quarter of the company's mainframe business that year; 380 customers provided half of the business, and 1,375 accounted for three-quarters. Akers forecast that during the four years, the company's top 1,200 customers would provide over 90 percent of the growth he expected.[11] By the time Akers presented those numbers in a speech to fellow managers, fully 86 percent of IBM's mainframe customers had committed to centralizing their operations; half of those were already running interactive data base systems. As we shall see, IBM at this point was preparing to enter the minicomputer business, which would fuel its growth even further. In 1979, IDC reported the following values of the installed computer bases of IBM and its major systems competitors:

Table 39
Values of Installed Bases for IBM and its Major Competitors
(Year-End 1979 in $ billions)

IBM	37,651.3*
Sperry Rand	3,510.3
Honeywell	3,281.2
Burroughs	3,242.5
Control Data	1,524.3
NCR	1,161.6
Amdahl	672.9
Digital Equipment	519.4
Xerox	397.1
National Advanced Systems (Itel)	358.1
Singer	150.0
Cray	73.9
Magnuson	15.2
Cambridge	1.3

* Includes IBM-compatible peripherals and memory

The top five companies after IBM were those that had been competitors since at least the 360 days, with Sperry Rand, the former Remington Rand, still dogging IBM after seventy years. Sperry Rand was the strongest competitor in the largest two system catetories (classes 6 and 7) where IBM was doing so well. Following it, Burroughs and Honeywell were strongest in medium-scale machines (classes 4 and 5), Control Data had concentrated on the scientific market, and NCR on small systems sold to retailers and banks.

Medium-size systems would continue to be a major part of the IBM system competitors' business, but in general they were used for stand-alone batch processing and were less oriented to data base and data communications–based applications than their larger cousins. Large, centralized systems equipped with communications networks were taking over from the midsize machines that had been located in remote locations of corporations and other customer organizations.[12] With relatively high prices on its smaller mainframes, and with that market beginning to dry up, IBM began to find growth hard to come by there. In 1974, it foresaw finding no more new customers for small- to medium-scale 370s (model 115 through 145), and it let the newly formed General Systems Division concentrate on small customers with the less-complicated and better-priced System/3.[13]

The larger Data Processing Division would be devoted to pushing the small but lucrative group of large-scale users to new realms of computing capacity and function. Large, capacity-strained 370 users were now beginning to use mini-computers as adjuncts to their 370 mainframes, taking advantage of those machines' unique functional modularity and low prices. Three-quarters of the company's top thousand customers were using minis by 1974, driven there largely by their need to offload processing from their 370s, which were beginning to groan under the strain of massive, interactive workloads. IBM would have to move aggressively to contain the minicomputer trend, or at least channel that trend to its own advantage, and that would call for playing tricks with interfaces once again.

Part 3

Bigger and Better

16. Ever Outward

... where we are today is just foreshadow for what will take place during the next 10 years. Not only will this industry—now best called the information industry—continue to reach out and be an integral part of many millions of people's lives, but it also has the very real potential of becoming the most important industry in the world. . . . I look at this industry as a convergence of the computer, communications, and content business.

—Peter L. Schavoir, IBM Director
of Market Research[1]

Although it was enormously expanded in terms of revenues, geography, and the cost and complexity of its products, in a fundamental respect IBM's business in 1970 had changed little since the early days when tabulator operators pushed wire pins through punch cards to tally U.S. Census data. As technologically distant as they were from the early statistical pianos, IBM's multimillion-dollar 360 systems were used for virtually the same kind of work: processing batches of data, one punch card at a time, for large, commercially oriented customers.

As early as 1960, however, profound changes had begun to take place that would eventually propel the IBM monopoly into realms that Thomas J. Watson, Sr., could never have dreamed of. Advances in electronics and computer science were making possible machines that not only processed data in large batches but engaged interactively in dialogues with their users and communicated data to them and to other computers across great distances as well. Reaching outside the air-conditioned room to which it had been confined for so long, the computer was extending long, increasingly capable tentacles into every corner of the customer organization where information was being collected, delivered, or processed. Indeed, the computer and its attendant networks, strung with a widening array of devices including video display terminals, minicomputers, personal computers, typewriters, copiers, telephone switches, modems, multiplexors, robots, and satellite dishes, were beginning to form the central nervous system, as it were, of the modern corporation. At the very heart of this corporate network, of course, was a large IBM 360 or 370 mainframe. The nature of the computer and its application to commercial activities was changing radically and in the process greatly expanding in scope. With it would come a great expansion of IBM's monopoly.

Successful against systems and peripherals competitors, IBM's price discrimination and related tactics had for the most part operated along two major dimensions: price and performance. IBM held on to the lion's share of the commercial data processing business by carefully packaging increases in strictly batch processing performance at lower prices in each of the major parts of its systems: processors got faster, disk drives were able to store more, memories got larger and faster, and the OS software got more efficient—and all the while the price per unit of batch computing work dropped. IBM had maneuvered customers into installing just the products it wanted them to and still kept the competition away. This enabled IBM to charge high prices and earn high profits while competition remained small and impoverished. Yet these increasingly powerful components continued to be applied in the main to batch processing, where the basic actions were only to read a record (from punch cards or tape), process it, and report the results (back to cards or tape, or to paper).

IBM's largest customers wanted more, however, much more. They wanted, in addition, interactive, telecommunicating capabilities of the kind that were coming to be available from other systems suppliers. Using their own and government-funded research, IBM's systems competitors—General Electric (discussed in Chapter 7), RCA, Sperry Rand, Burroughs, and Honeywell, among others— offered computer systems that easily outperformed IBM's in interactive and communications-oriented computing. As a result, even as it continued to provide customers with carefully controlled doses of better batch performance at effectively lower prices, IBM was pressured to enhance its large systems along the increasingly important dimension of function. In particular, to stay competitive, and as hinted in the story of the ill-fated FS, the heavily batch-oriented 360 had to be transformed somehow into an efficient interactive processing system.

"Function is the key to this marketplace," stated the August 1971 QPLA. "The hardware and software facilities offered most clearly provide the function necessary."[2] And IBM's equipment was seriously deficient in offering this new and desired functionality. This meant that new operating system software and new types of communications equipment were required to improve the batch-oriented 360s and 370s and prevent their fundamental weaknesses from undermining the IBM monopoly.

Yet in spite of the inadequacy of its product line, IBM still had substantial power. Just as, in the batch era, IBM had had great discretion in how incremental performance for its many locked-in customers was packaged and priced, during this interactive era it would have similar discretion in packaging additional functionability. Segmenting the market by function as well as by performance would enable IBM to maintain its firm grip on the business. The result is today's $50 billion-a-year-plus IBM.

CHANGE TO INTERACTIVE

There has been much more to the technical evolution of computers from batch machines to fully interactive systems than merely plugging in video display terminals where card readers were once attached. The functional differences between batch and interactive systems are quite profound. The change can be grasped simply by considering the different requirements for trained computer staff that each processing mode entails. With a batch system, individuals rarely touched or even saw their organization's computer. Accountants, personnel managers, sales directors, engineers, and manufacturing executives—each had to go through the lengthy, often difficult process of getting a team of analysts and programmers to understand the applications they wanted to put on the computer, write a unique program to solve it, test it, and perfect it. Writing such programs often took months of labor, but even when the program was ready to be used routinely, it might take many hours or even days for its results to become available.

By definition, interactive systems enable individuals to work directly with the computer through a terminal—at first the teletypewriter and later the ubiquitous video display terminal. Time-sharing systems enable the clever end user to prepare his own programs directly on the machine. In most cases, punch cards are eliminated altogether, and he gets to see his program's results within seconds of its execution. With a transaction processing system, a specially prepared program is kept available in the machine to handle the predetermined set of tasks—such as entering orders or supplying parts lists to workers on a factory floor. In any case, since the professional staff is not needed each and every time a program has to be run, the two types of interactive systems greatly expand the number of people able to directly use the computer.

Interactive computing did not eliminate batch processing. In fact, it increased batch usage by making the traditional programming staff more productive than ever. Time sharing aids programmers in constructing batch programs by providing them with a variety of interactive software design tools that help manage the complexity of analyzing problems and making sure programs do exactly what they are supposed to. The result is that batch programs became cheaper to write. But because interactive systems took over managing many functions formerly handled manually, they demand tremendous increases in all aspects of computing capacity: more end users at interactive terminals use more processing time, more disk storage, and more and larger programs. The result has been a continual expansion of data processing usage, which has driven IBM, along with the rest of the computer industry, swiftly to its current colossal size. There is no end in sight—with each decrease in the time and effort required to add interactive applications, their total usage increases.

But how did the computer itself, its hardware and software, change with the shift from batch to interactive? At the simplest level, in order to be useful, interactive systems had to respond rapidly—instantaneously, if possible—to users at terminals or, later, to other computers and related autonomous devices connected into a network. Within limits, a batch system could meet that requirement, but only if it were dedicated to a single user. As long as large batch computers were as expensive as they were in the 1960s and 1970s, it was economically unfeasible to dedicate a system to a single user except in the most critical of applications—a computer controlling an oil refinery, for instance, or in certain military situations. Instead, some way was needed to divide the computer's resources among several users at once, preventing each one from interfering with the others and varying the attention paid to each according to the load they placed on the system. The necessary ingredients were an operating system and central processor whose architecture was optimized to meet these new requirements.

From their earliest days, batch systems had executed programs one at a time, in sequential order, starting a program only after finishing the previous one. The most economical use of a batch system, therefore, was always to have a queue of jobs waiting to be processed. The computer was kept working constantly, but the user had to wait for his job to reach the front of the queue before it was executed. If a string of particularly lengthy jobs were ahead, the machine might be tied up for hours or even days at a time. Clearly, this kind of wait would not do for a system that was expected to service many users at once, each sitting at a terminal and wanting rapid response.

What was needed was a system that many could use at once, at irregular intervals, without suffering unreasonable response times. Instead of the user waiting for the computer, the computer would wait for the user. That called for some mechanism that could sort through the queue of jobs waiting for execution, determine each one's priority, and tend to them accordingly. Simple jobs could be given immediate attention, and their users could be sent responses quickly. But what about the more complex ones that required minutes or even hours of processor time? Surely, the execution of many other tasks would be requested before they were completed. And how could the system cope with a multitude of requests from several—perhaps hundreds—of users at the same time? Even more complex programming was required that could flexibly schedule and allocate the system's resources and dynamically balance each job's requirements against the others. The software would have to control a constantly shifting load of tasks, some simple, some complex. And to make its job even more complex, the system would have to overcome the fact that the combined size of its own code and that of all the various programs and data to be processed each second would far outstrip the total capacity of the processor's memory.

Two important new functions were called for. To prevent lengthy jobs from hogging the system and interfering with the execution of short, simple ones, a means was necessary to interrupt a program during its execution. Properly done, the interrupt function would recognize an incoming message as having priority over the one currently executing, halt the latter's execution in midstream and carefully store its intermediate results on a disk, grab the higher priority task and execute it to completion, reload the original task into memory, and, unless another interrupt came along, complete its execution. The answer to the memory problem was virtual memory, described earlier: only the active parts of a program were kept in memory while the inactive parts were kept on a disk, ready to be swapped into memory at a moment's notice. Both these major new functions added tremendous complexity to the system, for they entailed even more scheduling and juggling of resources, all on the fly—the operating system itself, which was to control these functions, had to be interruptible and use virtual memory.

There was more. Large interactive computers had to handle time sharing, transaction processing, and batch jobs all at the same time. Jobs would run in foreground or background, the former being interactive and having top priority during working hours, the latter being executed during any temporary slack periods such as late at night. To juggle these three modes of processing called for still greater complexity in software and hardware. For instance, efficient virtual memory required a complex mapping of memory locations in the processor to those in disk storage to keep track of the many segments of data and programs. That required the "relocation" circuitry be built into the processor.

So much for dynamically managing the system's workload as individual jobs came and went according to changing patterns of activity among users. What about the applications themselves? To be most cost effective, interactive applications had to be geared to a customer's general labor force rather than to specially trained technicians. The interactive system had to, among other desirable qualities, communicate with users through easily understood messages, catch typing errors, and provide helpful information when it was requested. As much as possible, the complexities of the system—in particular, the structure of its memory and disk files and the scheduling and execution of its many housekeeping tasks—had to be masked by an illusory screen image tailored specifically to the application at hand. Airline reservation clerks needed to use screen images different from clerks entering orders for auto parts, say. The faster it responded and the more lucid and immediately relevant its messages were to users, the more useful the interactive computer was. All this new function required additional software, much of which required years of development work and testing in order to work effectively.

Of course, as a computer's interactive skills were embellished, it was put to use on more types of applications, and customers came to depend on it more than ever. Their growing dependency caused them to be concerned about the system's reliability—its resistance to the inevitable hardware failures and software bugs. The fastest, most easy-to-use system was worthless if it "crashed" even once a month, taking down with it vital applications such as airlines reservations or factory automation. In the past, a batch machine's failure may have caused temporary problems, but rarely did it bring daily business activity to a halt. As the performance of large computers grew, they incorporated more circuits, the failure of any one of which might stop them dead. Knowing that Murphy's Law applies even to the most thoroughly tested and perfectly designed system, computer makers began to build redundancy into their machines: key elements such as a disk drive, memory bank, or even a central processor could be duplicated. To make such fault-tolerant systems work properly required special operating system software that could limit each fault's effects when it occurred, recover any jobs lost during the temporary halt, and, in particularly sophisticated systems such as Amdahl's V Series, phone the manufacturer and have a service technician dispatched immediately.

Adding communications capabilities to the central computer required more changes. Along with greater geographical reach in computer networks came the need for better security. A batch system could simply be kept behind locked doors, but computers attached through telephone lines to remote terminals presented a whole range of new risks. Now special facilities were needed to check user identities and prevent unauthorized individuals from doctoring software— including the security software itself—and data. The more important the applications were that a system handled, the more likely a target it would be for criminal activity.

Equally important, specialized hardware and software were required to use costly telephone circuits as efficiently as possible. By concentrating sparse message traffic from remote terminals into a single data stream, using devices known as multiplexors and concentrators, it was possible for large customers to save many thousands of dollars a month on line costs—otherwise they might have to dedicate a single telephone line to each terminal.

As noted earlier, the trend to centralize computing on a single computer system went hand in hand with interactive teleprocessing applications, for it enabled many users, often scattered graphically or organizationally, to work with the same data and programs and stay in touch with each other. A company's accounting department, for example, might share certain data files with the sales department and certain other files with the personnel department. To effectively manage the vast files accumulated in a large, centralized system, a special software package known as a data base management system was required. It acted as an automatic librarian that handled the storage, retrieval, and updating of the resulting large volumes of data.

As these and other functions were added to computers over time, many systems makers were ahead of IBM technically most of the time. For example, IBM compared the 360 line to competitors' "Large-Scale Communications-Based Systems" in the February 1969 QPLA and found its machine lacking in several key areas:

> Univac announced support in 1966 for a multiprogramming [able to process two or more jobs at a time]/multiprocessing [able to tie two or more processors together in order to boost system reliability] general purpose system for the 1108 [processor] with RJE [remote job entry, a method of using batch machines from a distance] and interactive Fortran V. BASIC is also available.
>
> Burroughs has operational interactive and RJE support on the B5500, which will reportedly run unchanged on the B6500.
>
> CDC offers RJE and interactive Fortran under general purpose operating system for the 6000 series, and provides data-based inquiry system.
>
> GE offers an integrated operating system for the 600 series with RJE, interactive Fortran and BASIC, and is stressing integrated, data-base systems.
>
> DEC's PDP-10 and the RCA Spectra 70/46 are outperformed by the IBM M[odel]65 and M75, but "two for the price of one" [referring to the greater reliability of two processors working in tandem] with far greater functional abilities is a good selling tool.
>
> IBM has no advanced ... interactive language support. High speed RJE ... is available now, but the design level is higher in price and performance has yet to be proven. ... low speed RJE is not yet available. IBM announced OS/360 capabilities in steps, thus creating the image of a system with "tacked-on" facilities. The [model 65], which appears to be a solution for data based systems, is an "only" product with no growth systems. ...
>
> Except for the [model 67 timesharing system], which does not address this batch-oriented, general purpose area, hardware features such as communications processors, relocation registers, channel controllers, virtual memory and paging are not available on the System/360.[3]

IBM had much catching up to do. Competitors such as Digital Equipment, GE, and Scientific Data Systems lacked large bases of installed batch systems and were therefore relatively free to build systems designed from the start for interactive use. IBM tried a similar tack with the Future System, or FS, project, recognizing its 360s' and 370s' inadequacies in interactive work. In the afore-mentioned 1974 memo to the Department of Justice, the company claimed that FS was needed because "the user has requirements for reliability, constant availability, networking, and so forth, which cannot technically or efficiently be realized without radical architectural changes [away from the 360]."[4] But once the plug was pulled on FS, IBM was from then on forced to continue "tacking on" interactive facilities as best it could to the 370s. Even today it still relies on the same basic 360 architecture for its computer systems that in 1974 it con-cluded could not "technically or efficiently" meet its users' interactive needs.

HOW IBM DID IT

The company's market dominance in the mid-1980s attests to IBM's success in keeping most of the all-important large-scale systems business. This success in capturing the bulk of the business generated by the converging computing and telecommunications markets is troublesome not only because of the enormous size and power it gives the company but because it has been accomplished with products that throughout the past twenty years have been rated as generally in-ferior to the competition's.

This statement may surprise the general reader who has observed the undeni-able, ongoing improvements in IBM computers and the communications net-works that tie them together. However, limiting one's comparisons solely to IBM's products provides little information about that manufacturer's position relative to its competitors'. Overlooked is the fact that IBM's much smaller sys-tems rivals, companies such as Sperry Rand, Burroughs, Honeywell, Control Data, and NCR, have comparably improved their systems over time. A com-parison at each point in time between their offerings and IBM's, in theory at least, should determine their commercial success in competitive markets. If one supplier offers clearly superior products and customers are free to choose them, then that supplier should get the business.

For IBM to have succeeded with deficient products is as telling an indication as any of the unassailable position IBM enjoys in the expanding global infor-mation processing market.

IBM had not been unaware of the fundamental changes coming to the for-merly batch-only computer market, nor of the relative deficiencies of its few in-teractive systems and related telecommunications gear. In 1964, for instance, during the preparations of the troubled 360/67 for the time-sharing market, an IBM executive wrote, "There is much more at stake than these few prestige ac-counts. What is at stake is essentially all computing business, scientific and commercial, except in accounts where tradition or the superiority of the IBM sales force can overcome the fact that we offer an obsolete product."[5]

Obsolete the product remained, for even as IBM was so concerned about the deficiencies of its own systems, it was rating others' products as superior. "There is an increasing demand in the scientific and commercial large systems area," stated the February 1969 QPLA,

> for integrated general purpose systems with terminal-oriented services and communications hardware. The complexity of today's business environment, and the centralization of computing facilities has caused a demand for large data-base systems, RJE functions and interactive problem-solving support. Predictions have been made that by 1975 over 70% of systems installed will support communications functions. *When required to compete in this total area, IBM cannot offer support comparable in function and price to Burroughs, CDC, DEC, GE, RCA, SDS or Univac systems."* (Emphasis added.)[6]

In October 1970, the company determined that "the market potential for interactive computer data base/data communications, and sensor base have remained relatively underdeveloped because of the inability of OS/360 to react to those needs in a timely manner."[7]

IBM drew similar conclusions about OS in 1974, when it privately argued in a memo to the Department of Justice that the company should be kept whole so that FS could be successfully brought to market: "The current operating system [OS/360] was designed primarily for 'batch mode' rather than the 'data base/interactive' processing and cannot efficiently perform the latter.... The potential for new function is severely constrained by [IBM's] existing [360/370] architecture." IBM, according to that revealing memo, was compelled to invest in FS precisely to overcome the 360s' and 370s' fundamental shortcomings. Ever since FS failed, of course, IBM has continued to offer the same operating system, albeit modified and functionally "enhanced," that it once insisted was so unacceptable for interactive use.

But, it might be asked, if these new capabilities were so highly valued by customers and if IBM's products were so deficient in them, why did it not lose customers to superior systems? The question is an important one, for it leads one to consider how IBM will extend its monopoly in the still-growing "information processing" industry. One way it held on to customers was through software lock-in. Although interactive and telecommunications capabilities were initially offered on systems dedicated solely to new nonbatch applications—and in many cases dedicated systems are still used—the vast majority of commercial users needed interactive capabilities added to their existing batch-oriented systems. They needed to add the new functions to their current IBM systems, not to install some separate machine, no matter how interactively efficient it was. They needed to have one computer execute both modes of processing, batch and interactive, and give applications of each kind access to a common store of data, the central corporate data base. Thus, even moving to a superior, dual-mode system from another vendor would have entailed a massive, and prohibitively costly, conversion of their 360 and 370 batch programs and data. As a result, IBM's inadequate products notwithstanding, those customers that could wait for IBM to deliver, did.

The April 1970 QPLA stated, "IBM's communications capability must again be rated deficient, . . . customers are involved in long range plans for data-based information systems to be implemented in phases starting in the early '70s. These customers do not see an IBM product line in the communications area that can grow and adapt to their changing requirements across the next five to ten years. These are the customers we are losing, at least in part, or forcing to delay their planning because of these deficiencies."[8]

For those customers who could not afford such delays because of pressing application needs, there was an alternative. Just as plug-compatible vendors were supplying peripherals that were superior to certain weak IBM products, a new set of vendors arose to fill in the interactive and communications gaps in IBM's systems. Each major deficiency in IBM's product line invited specialist suppliers to offer the products 360 and 370 customers wanted and needed. These specialized "competitors" actually enhanced the 360 and 370 systems as a whole when IBM either could not or would not do so itself. The result was that despite many of its individual products' failings, IBM's share of the overall systems business suffered no decline. It actually grew.

The aid the competitors provided IBM with functionally rich software and hardware was clearly evident in the airlines industry, which pioneered the use of large-scale, interactive computer systems. Most airlines used IBM 360 or 370 systems (along with a special Airline Control Program designed by IBM just for their use), and by April 1970, according to the IBM QPLA of that date, "almost every carrier [had] a competitive pre-processor, remote multiplexor or message switching system installed or on order."[9] Those "competitive" devices were not available from IBM, but the airlines were not about to wait; they shopped elsewhere and managed to push their systems farther down the functional path that IBM was so remiss in traversing.

In effect, one group of competitors, the specialists, helped IBM defeat another group of competitors, its rival systems makers, until IBM could upgrade its own offerings. The former provided the IBM customer with greater function while saving him the expense and difficulty of converting his batch programs to run on the machines of the latter. The systems competitors gained little commercial advantage, if any, from their technically superior systems. Rather than increasing, their market share declined even further as customers trickled away to IBM in order to take advantage of the greater choices available there. So it was that IBM's dominant market share in large-scale systems has long attracted specialist companies that add value to its machines. The compatible peripheral, software, and memory companies played similar roles. While costing IBM some lost revenue and profits, they also ironically made the total IBM system more attractive. With limited resources at their disposal, these specialists naturally aimed for the largest potential market—IBM system users. The result was that other vendors' systems lost what competitive advantage they may have held to these hybrid IBM systems. One can only speculate as to how some of IBM's strongest systems rivals—Sperry Rand, Honeywell, Burroughs, and so on—might have been faring today, given their superior interactive systems, had their size and market power been more equal to IBM's. They, too, would have attracted the specialists' attention and would have been able to offer even more functionally robust hybrid systems of their own.

The degree to which specialists helped IBM is shown clearly in the software area. With its 1969 unbundling, IBM established individual prices for many software packages. This encouraged others to build and market software products to compete with those of IBM's that were particularly weak in function or performance. Many of the first independent non-IBM packages to hit the market were designed to enhance interactive processing on 360 and 370 systems. The availability of IBM-compatible, though not IBM-supplied, software, much of which embodied truly innovative ideas, was an added inducement for users of other systems to convert to the 360 and 370 mainstream. The non-IBM systems population has never been large enough to attract as much scarce programming talent as the IBM systems base does, and it has suffered as a result.

But why, it must be asked, was IBM so remiss in providing the interactive functions its customers wanted? A partial reason was its commitment to OS and the failure of FS. More complete answers can be obtained by examining what the non-IBM telecommunications suppliers offered in its stead in one particularly important area, the communications controller. As offered by competitors, this was a relatively small, specialized computer designed to handle much of the communications-related processing needed to manage large networks of terminals. Its function was analogous to the controllers used with disk and tape devices. Though somewhat technical, the following passage from the April 1970 QPLA provides a feel for the advantages offered by these non-IBM controllers, which for the most part were programmable through software and were therefore more flexible than IBM's model 2701/2/3 controllers, which were hardwired and not programmable:

> GE, CDC, and Honeywell, soon to be followed by Burroughs, have introduced programmable pre-processors with "plugable" (program changeable) communications hardware, providing their users with both attachment flexibility and a minimum host-computer program cost. These units minimize channel interference, core requirements and program so-

phistication in the main processor, and thus justify their cost in medium and large networks on a total-system basis.

Nineteen programmable controllers were announced in 1969, specifically for System/360 attachment. They are advertised and are being ordered, to solve the following problems:

1. Overhead-Control of a large network can use 20–50% of a CPU, and requires large amounts of expensive core.

2. Attachment of any terminal to S/360.

3. Sub-system simplification by separating communications and applications programming.

4. Line costs. Increased [telephone] line efficiency can be obtained with full duplex lines and programmable remote multiplexors, which are not currently supported by IBM.[10]

The bottom line was that these innovative, non-IBM products could off-load work from the central 360 processor, freeing as much as half of that expensive component's time for doing what it did best—executing application programs. The value of that savings was sufficient in large networks to justify the cost of a specialized communications processor.

Thus the anomaly: IBM, with substantial expertise in computers, found its product line deficient because its competitors were providing specialized computers that off-loaded work from the central processor. It is inconceivable that IBM could not at least have matched what these other companies were doing, and if it could and if such products were valued by customers, then why did it not?

A major answer was that its commercial interests clashed with this technically and economically appealing approach, and those commercial interests won out. It was not until the mid-1970s that IBM would offer an even partially competitive product—the IBM 3705 communications controller and all its requisite software.

To grasp where IBM's commercial interests lay, consider that this alternative communications scheme became available from IBM's competitors just when all the other peripheral equipment attached to the 360 processor was under attack from plug-compatible vendors. IBM's primary response to those attacks was a major reversal of its price discrimination: profits were moved away from the exposed peripherals and into the still-protected processor. So IBM's profits in the early and mid-1970s came increasingly from its relatively high-priced processors. To offload function from the processor, therefore, would be to forgo substantial profits.

Just as important a constraint was that IBM lacked competitive power in the programmable communications controller business. If it offered a product there, it would be following others, and to be successful it would have had to price its product low to be competitive. The commercial impact would have been to enable the customer to trade off highly profitable 360 and 370 processor usage for far less profitable communications controller usage. By withholding the product, IBM kept the bulk of its customers waiting—to its own profit. Only the more adventurous installed non-IBM gear.

Naturally, IBM's calculations changed when Amdahl's central processor replacement arrived. Not surprisingly, just at that time—1975—IBM began offering a more useful 370 communications controller, as Chapter 17 describes.

There would have been other commercial disadvantages for IBM in offering a comparable communications controller. For instance, the other controllers attached to any terminal, from IBM or another vender. That was a function IBM intentionally refused to offer, again not for technical but for commercial reasons—it wanted customers to use its terminals and not those of its major rivals. Furthermore, the non-IBM controllers simplified telecommunications networks by separating communications and applications functions into different boxes. That also ran against IBM's commercial interests because such a clear separation might lead to a standard interface between the two that, because it could be established outside of IBM's control, would deprive the company of the power to change it as competitive pressure required. IBM's interests would be better served if the communications and applications functions were closely intertwined, for that would facilitate the extension of its power outward from the central system to include the network and all equipment attached thereto. As IBM had learned the hard way in the 1960s' peripherals battles, a fixed interface between the processor and controller only invites competitive attacks on its technologically deficient and overpriced products.

Its commercial interests outweighing other concerns, IBM could afford to wait before matching the competition's controllers. The locked-in 360 or 370 user would not leave his system for another vendor's just to get superior interactive processing, and in time IBM could recapture the small market share it was losing to the specialized "competitors" who enhanced the IBM system by adding function it declined to provide. Moreover, even when a customer attached a foreign controller to his 360 or 370 processor, that processor was kept busier, the customer installed more memory and peripherals, and IBM gained profits anyway. As customers added communications-oriented applications, IBM won even as it lost a controller order or two. The more terminals (and in later years mini- and personal, computers) attached to the central system, the larger and more powerful that system needed to be.

This is not to imply that IBM actually encouraged specialized companies to enhance the IBM product line. During the late 1960s and early 1970s, IBM considered them a real threat, for they were establishing themselves in market sectors projected to grow quite large and important—IBM wanted to be sure it captured its "fair" share. Recall its long-term competitive stance: "IBM must be on guard against the intentional or unintentional abdication of any significant growth segment of the marketplace to competition."[11]

Ultimately, of course, specialized suppliers of software, communications equipment, terminals, and the wide range of other products that attached to 360 and 370-centered networks have done no better than their counterparts in the mainframe peripherals arena—and for similar reasons. In case after case, when it finally did move, IBM recaptured the ancillary markets that others had pioneered for it. The many small companies adding function to the uncompetitive IBM systems were just as vulnerable as the compatible peripherals, memory, and processor companies discussed earlier. That is, they could offer nothing that IBM, with its deep pockets and vast pool of talent, could not, in time, do for itself. At the very least, IBM could, Patterson-style, copy their innovations. Once IBM had comparable products of its own, its interests lay in driving these hapless helpers right out of the market.

As seen previously, specialized competitors always end up dependent on IBM in ways that it is not on them, and their dependency ultimately does them in. Once aroused to act, IBM has a wide range of alternatives at its disposal for stopping them. If nothing else, IBM controls the bulk of the central system, and the competition's products are entirely dependent on maintaining full compatibility with that system to be of any value to the customer. Like the disk and tape drive makers, these communications equipment companies reckoned that IBM's self-interest would discourage it from responding to their relatively minor successes. They assumed, for instance, that IBM would be severely limited in its power to change the remote end of the standard phone line to which many of their products attached. "The rules of data transmission are in large part set by common carrier circuit offerings," stated the December 1971 QPLA.[12] "Facilities are well-defined, charges are fixed by regulatory agencies, and everyone has to 'play the game.' Performance restrictions result, and often price alone becomes a crucial factor in selection of equipment."

They also assumed that IBM's power in the emerging interactive, communications-oriented business would be weaker than usual because by definition non-IBM vendors were always involved: "Because of the need for transmission facilities which in most cases can only be supplied by common carriers (AT&T, Western Union, etc.), two vendor systems are the rule, rather than the exception. Since the carriers market terminal equipment as well as circuit facilities, a competitive exposure [for IBM] is almost inevitable," said the same QPLA. Further, different individuals at the customer organization made computer and communications-related buying decisions: "Many customers have separate data processing and communications groups. Integration of the two functions, which is often IBM's best competitive strategy, may at best antagonize some customer people and at worse prove to be politically unfeasible."

IBM had two main weapons. The first was its power to package new functionality in ways that denied the increasingly troublesome communications suppliers any possibility of maintaining full compatibility. IBM had sole discretion in the location of new functions, whether in software or hardware, in the central processor or in outboard controllers and other attached devices.

Second, by virtue of its unique knowledge of the strategic direction of its entire product line, IBM could always count on being first to market with products that contained a certain new function and, even more important, that could retain compatibility with products yet to come. As the next chapter will show, other vendors might be first with some new, desirable function—programinability in the communications controller, say—but customers could never be absolutely sure that a subsequent IBM product might not make the "foreign" device incompatible and therefore useless. IBM alone was able to define crucial interfaces between products.

To capitalize on its unique advance knowledge, IBM had to establish several important conditions. To begin with, there had to be compelling reasons for customers to move to new IBM products. Additional price and performance would not be sufficient to coerce customers down the IBM path, especially when superior compatible equipment might be available from another vendor. Instead, the most desirable functions would have to be limited only to new IBM products. Previous products would be deliberately obsoleted, as were the first two 370 processors, the 155 and 165. Of course, customers' growing desire to move from batch to interactive processing offered just the right momentum to facilitate this kind of manipulation. As it offered functional enhancements for interactive computing, IBM would take full advantage of its ability to locate new functions in such areas within its broad product line and in such a manner that it gained the most commercial advantage.

At any given stage in moving the batch 360s and 370s into the interactive age, IBM had—and still has—a wide range of alternatives as to how it could implement a particular functional enhancement. It could shift logical functions from one technology or one box to another—or from software to hardware, as when it confronted Amdahl with new microcoded instructions in the 3033 processor. There were tradeoffs between the various implementations—namely speed of execution and economic cost—but frequently there was no technically compelling reason to choose one over another. The actual costs of computer equipment may account for less than 20 percent of the selling price. This means that if one implementation of a new function entails a 10 percent higher cost than another, the increase in relation to selling price will be a mere 2 percent. Thus, if a particularly crafty solution to some technical problem enabled IBM safely to increase prices by, say, 10 percent, the additional costs were well worth it. In considering various technical solutions to its competitive problems, IBM quite naturally looked at the commercial implications of each: How easy would it be for competitors to offer a comparable product? What would the new product do to their viability? What new interfaces into the system would it provide and how useful might they be to the competition? These were essentially the same considerations IBM took into account when designing new controllers for the 2319 disk drives and splitting the controller function into two separate pieces. This "kludge" was motivated primarily by IBM's commercial interests, not by technically compelling concerns.

The single most important consideration for the competition, on the other hand, was this: Was IBM offering the new function as an enhancement to a current product, or would it be limited to some new, forthcoming product whose interfaces, prices, and operational characteristics were as yet undisclosed? As the leasing companies showed in their extension of the 360s' life, there was at least some possibility of enhancing IBM's equipment in ways that IBM, for commercial reasons, was unwilling to match. IBM's own experience enhancing the 370s following the FS failure shows just how possible this approach is. New technology, function, and performance can indeed be added to current products when that suits IBM's commercial interests. If new equipment is offered that is compatible with current products, then the value of those products, whether from IBM or a competitor, is maintained if not enhanced. If the new IBM function comes only with a new product, then the value of current equipment falls as customers drop it in favor of the new, better-functioning gear.

By limiting enhancements to new products, IBM gained an important competitive advantage: it could create new interfaces and change old ones and thereby create difficulties for rivals to attach their equipment. As customers moved to a new IBM product that offered better performance, price, and, most important, function, the competition found itself left out. Rivals were unable, at least until they could decipher IBM's new interfaces, to design competitive and compatible products and begin shipping them—to participate in the new market IBM had created. By the time they did get to that market, IBM would often have a midlife kicker to further hamper their efforts—a drop in price or a further functional enhancement. The result was that IBM had the market to itself for a long, highly profitable period.

As a strategy, limiting functional enhancements to new products has helped IBM shape customers' acquisition plans in the purchase-heavy computer market it has fostered since the late 1970s. In the previous lease-oriented market, it was in IBM's interest to enhance installed gear and keep it earning rent for as long a period as possible. In today's purchase market, IBM gets to sell not just the enhancement but also a larger package of new hardware and software that embody the enhancement. Naturally, that means more revenues. But IBM had similar motives when it introduced virtual memory to the 370s with the 158 and

168 processors, which replaced entirely the earlier 155 and 165 products. Of course, by selling, IBM gets its money while prices are high, before competition arrives; when it does arrive, IBM's freedom to cut prices is not restricted by a large base of leased machines. And to further capitalize on this crucial initial shipment period, IBM has greatly increased its manufacturing capacity to reduce the time it takes to get a newly introduced machine to customer's hands. By the time competition gets to market with comparable equipment, the market can be relatively saturated with IBM gear.

It was these practices, which differ widely from those used up until the early 1970s, that enabled IBM to recapture those parts of its business that were initially lost to specialized communications suppliers. In fact, for IBM's purposes, it is generally sufficient that customers simply believe that IBM can and might change interfaces. Whether or not the company actually does that in every case, customers will tend to shy away from the competitive gear that might suddenly become incompatible and therefore ultimately useless. Getting customers to think like that was no problem, as the Amdahl episode shows, for the IBM sales force has only to emphasize the risk of choosing another vendor for most customers to stay huddled under the seductive IBM umbrella. To win their business, competitors have to offer greater performance premiums and even deeper discounts off IBM's prices and still bend over backward to guarantee their products' future compatibility with IBM's ever-shifting interfaces.

IBM had other tricks up its sleeves to get rid of the communications competition once their help was no longer needed. It changed its financing plans to provide customers with a broader choice of options. It turned to new channels of distribution. It offered discounts on volume orders. And it rebundled certain functions as competitive pressure demanded. Finally, there was price discrimination. As IBM consolidated its position over the mainframe, memory, and disk business, it regained a strong revenue and profit base from which to price discriminate in outlying areas. It could afford to subsidize low prices for the widening array of devices that attached to the networks controlled by its 370 systems. Often in those far reaches of the network, IBM has been forced to confront vendors whose strength lies solely in a narrow segment of the market. As economist Carl Kaysen has shown, "short-line" competitors such as these have little chance against a broad-line competitor like IBM, which with price discrimination can push them out of their market segment even when they are more efficient. It is to the specifics of these battles that we turn next.

17. Reach Out and Crush Someone

Avoid implying that you might suppress technological improvements unless competition forces your hand.

—IBM's lawyers' advice to its
executives[1]

In many respects, an interactive computer is only as good as the communications network that serves it. The better its terminals and the many intervening components that help move data back and forth from the users, the more useful the system is. Beginning in the 1960s, "on-line" applications such as airline reservation systems, interactive corporate data bases, and parts-tracking systems for factories forced users to invest as much in communications gear and services as they did in central computer systems. Consequently, with its systems lacking in interactive computing and communications capability, IBM grew increasingly anxious that network requirements might begin to influence its customers' expansion of their 360 and 370 systems—or, worse, push them toward building interactive applications on superior systems from other vendors.

The threat to IBM's commercial computing business during the accelerating transition from batch to interactive systems increased with each new communications product introduced by a growing roster of competitors. IBM identified 113 computer communications products introduced in 1968, 355 in 1969, and 384 in the first nine months of 1970. No less than 251 communications companies had made their debut in the twenty-one months preceding September 1970. So promising was the emerging data communications market—and so wide were the gaps in IBM's product line.

Entrepreneurial ventures were only part of IBM's problem, however. It also faced its traditional systems rivals—Honeywell, Sperry Rand, and the rest—who were pushing into interactive markets, often with systems that took advantage of designs better suited to the new modes of computing than the batch-oriented 360 and 370 lines. These systems companies invested heavily in interactive computing, calculating that in this new arena they might win market share that had eluded them in the earlier batch-only era. They also sought to extend their control outward from the central computer and to get customers to use their terminals and related gear on growing networks. Meanwhile, established communications companies such as AT&T (by far the largest) and Western Union wanted to expand beyond their traditional role as passive "common carriers" of voice and telegraph signals and get involved in the more lucrative processing of digital data. AT&T, in fact, already had in place the vast majority of terminals in the United States: its Teletype subsidiary's keyboard teleprinters were installed throughout virtually every large corporation. It seemed to be only a matter of time before the colossal telephone company, relying on those many terminals and on its total control over the telephone wires that were so essential to all computer networks, would capture the data communications market away even from IBM. The two giant companies, many predicted, would clash head-on as they expanded into each other's area of dominance—AT&T fighting its way down the network into the computer room, and IBM fighting from within to extend its monopoly to the network's farthest reaches.

The hands-down winner in the high-stakes computer communications game, the world knows, is IBM. As it has in all other markets that neighbor its stronghold on large-scale commercial data processing, IBM has come out on top: most of the world's commercial computers are supplied by IBM, and most of the value in the networks driven by those computers is supplied by IBM.

But given the nature of the game, IBM's capture of the interactive, telecommunicating computing market over the past twenty years is in its totality an awesome demonstration of its power. With astonishing ease, IBM defied not only the tenets of our free enterprise system but common sense as well. It won in spite of severe product handicaps, many of which it imposed on itself. It vanquished a wide spectrum of competitors including, even, a comparably entrenched monopolist. It blatantly ignored firmly established industry standards that were backed by the U.S. government and most of the world's computer users. And perhaps most telling, the company won even as it ignored pressing customer needs and major technical trends for a decade or more, bluntly refusing to supply the one product that was critical to building maximally efficient and functional networks. Finally, as if overcoming these technical and marketing obstacles were not enough, IBM extended its monopoly from batch to interactive computing during a period of intense antitrust scrutiny—some two dozen suits, including that of the U.S. government, were being actively pursued against IBM during the 1970s.

IBM's success against such odds thus raises several questions. First, how, actually, did the company do so well? Superior products or prices offer no explanation, for in its own estimation IBM offered customers neither. It follows, therefore, that the company must have once again relied on its strong position in one market to limit its competition's effectiveness in another. Second, and even more important, if IBM was so readily able to win these first few rounds in the fight to control the infrastructure (computer networks and all their attendant equipment) of the emerging "information society," what does that bode for the future? Will the company rely on similar tactics to keep the world's computer networks to itself? Has IBM proven itself so powerful as to be able to extend its monopoly into whatever markets its customers' networks take it, to go wherever it pleases, and potentially into every high-profit segment of the widening "information processing" marketplace (to use IBM's term)?

The answer is, most likely, because it appears probable that the value and usefulness of a great many future information processing products will rely heavily on being able to attach into mainframe computers, and that, of course, is where IBM's expansive power is firmly anchored. To see how the company has extended its power out of the computer room into emerging but nearby markets, and to see how it will probably do the same in the future, requires a basic understanding of what it is that computer networks do. Then we can explore the specifics of how IBM exploited its strength in central computers to gain the upper hand in the network business.

BATTLE OF THE CODES

IBM was a relative upstart in the telecommunications terminal business. So how could it even have defeated the giant AT&T, which had installed tens of thousands of terminals before the much smaller computer company ever got to market? Not only did IBM come to the terminal business years late and still win, but in doing so it forced its customers against their will to adopt an IBM-only interface standard. That IBM standard openly thumbed its nose at the perfectly usable standard that had been adhered to in previous years by AT&T and all its telecommunications customers (most of whom also used IBM computers) and by corporations and government authorities all over the world. And even as it ignored that AT&T interface, which had also been accepted by the U.S. government as an official standard, IBM pretended to back its use, and in the process it managed to pervert to its benefit the standards-making process by which U.S. and world industry tries to operate. All in all, it was quite a performance.

Through its Teletype subsidiary, AT&T had over the years installed a vast number of keyboard terminals for sending telegrams and Telexes. When the time came, the teletypewriters proved to be reliable, low-cost time-sharing terminals. Clunky in operation, they resembled crude electric typewriters, but they offered just enough capability to send and receive signals conveying alphabetical and numerical characters. Each character's signal was coded as a different pattern of digital bits. This electronic alphabet, similar in function to Morse code, had been designed to enable different machines to communicate with each other. The alphabet, or transmission code, used by AT&T terminals was called ASCII (pronounced *ass-key,* and standing for American Standard Code for Information Interchange). It was accepted as a standard by the U.S. government and by telegraph authorities in many parts of the world, too.

Now, IBM designed the 360 and 370 systems and related communications gear to use a quite different code known as EBCDIC (pronounced *eb-si-dik*). Because EBCDIC was incompatible with ASCII, users found it difficult to connect their many installed AT&T terminals to IBM computers; and IBM refused in its standard product line to provide the functions needed to translate from one code to the other. So even if a customer already had a network of AT&T teletypwriters installed, he had to install an entirely different network of EBCDIC terminals for use with his interactive 360 or 370. IBM's goal, of course, was to limit AT&T's ability to participate in the fast-growing terminals business, which was being fueled by the growth of interactive computing.

This strategy might have worked had independent suppliers of communications controllers not made their products able to do what IBM's controllers would not—translate back and forth between ASCII and EBCDIC. IBM's refusal to acknowledge ASCII forced its more adventuresome customers to install competitive controllers; the rest either waited or paid the cost of maintaining two separate sets of terminals and transmission circuits. A soon-to-be-familiar pattern began to develop: devices that were for some reason incompatible with IBM's central computers and their attendant networks (in this case AT&T's and other vendors' ASCII terminals) lost value to users. Before long, computer-based electronic mail networks began to take over many of the simple message-transmission functions once relegated to AT&T teletypes. Segregation from the IBM computer network similarly affects the usefulness of most other digital or computer-based devices, as we shall see.

STANDARDS

Many years ago, the U.S. Department of Commerce set up the National Bureau of Standards to establish, with help from industry, certain standards to help U.S. companies do business with each other and ensure that customers got what they paid for. The Bureau's standards ranged from precise measures of weights and time to the physical specifications of nuts and bolts.

Now, once they are adopted by the major suppliers in a market, standards tend to change the nature of the competition among them. Because they are by definition more alike, competition among standardized products takes place less on the basis of their individual differentiating characteristics and more on the basis of price. Standards tend to make products into commodities, more interchangeable with one another than if they were not standardized. So why would a supplier willingly give up the option of differentiating his products from others by adopting a standard? Normally it is because his customers demand it of him. The biggest customer of all for most goods, of course, has been the U.S. government, and it has, through the Department of Commerce, established standards that industry usually finds it impossible to ignore. So from a supplier's perspective, if standards seem to be unavoidable, the best thing to do is come to an agreement with competitors on the most widely acceptable standard possible. Once the standard is hammered out and officially approved by the National Bureau, he and his competitors may find that their freedom to innovate is limited, but they will also enjoy a substantially larger potential market to fight over.

As an agent of the government, which is the biggest computer customer of all, the National Bureau of Standards has long been active in setting computer standards. Its efforts naturally create trouble for IBM, for they can potentially disrupt its pricing schemes. We have seen how IBM for years has set prices according to function rather than cost, but that form of pricing becomes more difficult if, for example, the major interfaces are defined by standards agreed to and enforced by others.

Although there have been many standards agreed to by IBM and other computer makers, none has limited IBM's power very much. In light of the evidence shown so far, it seems highly unlikely that this giant company, whose success has relied so heavily on its freedom to change interfaces and price goods functionally, would be so foolish as to agree to standards unless they did not really reduce its freedom.

To make it easier for government agencies, as well as private companies, to mix and match communications devices from various suppliers as they constructed their computer networks, the Standards Bureau in the 1960s set out to establish a series of standards governing computer communications interfaces. IBM was hardly enthused: "The direction of the standards effort, particularly as motivated by the Federal Government, is toward systems standards. Such a trend moves extremely close to becoming a factor in the determination of overall profits of the company," a memo reads.[2] The company's response was to "emphasize the total system concept to preserve our role as innovators of systems solutions rather than [as] component vendors."[3]

Despite its loud trumpeting of the System/360's many "standard" and "universal" interfaces, which supposedly provided customers with just the kind of flexibility that the government was now seeking, in fact the last thing IBM wanted to see were government standards for interconnecting communications and other gear—even if the standards used were its own. It saw clearly the threat posed by interface standards, as the flip chart used in the December 18, 1968, Corporate Management Committee meeting showed:

STANDARDS AND THE COMPUTER INDUSTRY

THE KEY ISSUE FOR IBM

WHICH WILL SHOW BETTER P&L [Profit & Loss]?

—STANDARDIZATION TO ACHIEVE AN OVERALL GROWTH OF THE COMPUTER INDUSTRY?

—MINIMUM STANDARDIZATION IN ORDER TO ACHIEVE COMPETITIVE ADVANTAGE?

The choice was that simple. Standards would increase the growth of the entire market because they would lower costs and give customers a greater choice of vendors and make it easier for them to configure computer systems to their own particular liking. The alternative, "minimum standardization," meant carefully contrived incompatibilities between IBM systems and all others, and between certain IBM boxes and others. We have seen how well incompatibilities between various 360 processors and peripherals, the "family's" advertised universality notwithstanding, helped IBM segment the market and price discriminate. IBM saw that, too. "I believe in looking back," commented an IBM man in a November 9, 1970, memo, "we will see that the 360 era in the 1960's was to IBM not the period of consolidation to a single product line but rather *the period where we rapidly proliferated our architecture and faced our customers with a growing multitude of incompatible products* which he has to figure out how to operationally interconnect."[4] (Emphasis added.)

The standards problem was most acute for IBM not at the peripherals interface but rather at the system-to-system communications level. Without communications standards, each computer family, although compatible within itself, would be mute to every other family. IBM knew there was already a standard for moving data between systems, whether by exchanging tape reels, disk packs, or punch cards: "The IBM 360 will become, if it hasn't already, the de facto standard of the industry. All major manufacturers recognize the need to provide some degree of compatibility to the S/360 either in I/O, data format, or source programming languages."[5]

What was needed, however, was a standard for direct electronic communications between computer equipment. The leading candidate, ASCII, existed long before the 360 ever surfaced and had been adopted by most other companies in the business. But having gone the incompatible EBCDIC route, IBM found itself all but alone, particularly when it came time to hash out a computer-communications standard with other vendors.[6] In one such meeting, IBM found itself facing Sperry Rand, SCM, Bell Labs, General Electric, NCR, Control

Data, the National Bureau of Standards, and a newspaper publisher, all of which backed ASCII. The sole company on IBM's side was RCA, which at the time was striving (vainly, as it turned out) to keep its systems as compatible with IBM's as possible. IBM was just as alone internationally in its opposition to ASCII, finding that two major international standards organizations (ISO and CCITT), the major European computer trade association (ECMA), and various national standards bodies had all adopted ASCII, too. ASCII, an IBM report concluded, "has been adopted by industry as an interchange code; it is a fact."[7]

So outwardly at least, IBM had little choice but to comply. Citing its experiences in standard-making committees, "governmental standards pressures, antitrust implications, [and] competitive marketing,"[8] the company openly endorsed a modification of the ASCII code that would make it more useful to computer, as opposed to simpler teletype, communications. But that endorsement proved to be mere lip service, for IBM evidently had little intention of actually supporting ASCII: "Maintain competitive position in [ASCII] market," the same report continued, sketching future plans.

> First analyze the market demands. Strategies then include MINIMAL PRODUCT SUPPORT FOR [ASCII]. Provide present [ASCII] requirements through Software, RPQ [non-standard, special order] Hardware and with minimal product line support. The intent of this strategy is to contain [ASCII]. (Emphasis in original.)

To honestly provide ASCII compatibility on its systems would mean opening the floodgates to all those AT&T terminals installed everywhere, and IBM had no intention of letting that happen. "IBM product line support of ASCII must be minimal," noted a January 9, 1968, position paper, insisting that less-efficient software support of the standard be favored over optimal hardware implementations. But neither should be offered unless "market requirements" demand it. "A plan based upon these policies should be developed and monitored against the marketing situation to ensure that IBM is making progress in 'containing' ASCII."[10]

Two and a half years later, in its September 30, 1970, QPLA, IBM reflected the poor results of the containment effort. Customers had not been entirely swayed. "Our current policy relative to Teletype and other [ASCII-compatible] terminal attachment creates a serious 'product deficiency' relative to competition in several areas," the document stated.[11] Teletype and similar ASCII teleprinters from other vendors had gained wide acceptance for time sharing on 360s, but IBM did not have a competitive terminal in the same price range. Also, network communications switches at many customer sites were now being designed to use the latest version of ASCII, but those switches could attach to the 360 and 370 lines only through special IBM hardware that was expensive and that created great technical difficulties for the customer. Finally, customers tended to purchase terminals and keep them installed for long periods—as much as ten years in the banking industry—and that made it difficult for ASCII terminal owners to consider moving to incompatible IBM computers.

The QPLA also found that the noticeable lack of ASCII compatibility on IBM's forthcoming 3705 communications controller would "leave a gap" in the company's "communications offering and will reduce our ability to compete." Independent software companies might add ASCII support to the 3705, but that would be a difficult undertaking, IBM concluded, because it would place "the customer and IBM at the mercy of the software house's competence." The 3705's lack of ASCII support would make the device "deficient at announcement. Improvements in the IBM terminal line [and] good Teletype support from a software house . . . could make the product equal in 1974," but that was four years hence.[12]

IBM's posture, endorsing ASCII by vote but refusing to use the standard in its mainstream commercial products, called for a major public relations effort, a disinformation campaign to assuage potential critics. On January 9, 1968, was written: "It will not be easy for IBM to disengage from ASCII. . . . these actions of containment have certain risks . . . [and] may be viewed as uncooperative by the government agencies involved in standardization. . . . Further, since IBM is presently viewed as being opposed to the ASCII standard, emphasis must be placed on building a constructive program with the governmental interests designed to accomplish standardization objectives of mutual interest."[13]

Two days later: "They were particularly sensitive," wrote IBM's G. E. Jones to colleague J. W. Birkenstock, referring to higher-ups at the Management Review Committee meeting that day, "to *using our bigness to develop de facto standards which were not necessarily of top quality for the user.* We hope that you will be able to assist Burke Marshall [chief corporate counsel] in explaining to government leaders, such as Congressman Brooks [a strong proponent of federal computer standards], the difficulties involved in setting standards in our industry and in assuring them that *our main objective is to do what is best for the user even though it may not be the most profitable for IBM.*" (Emphasis added.)[14]

But after all, IBM is a company run by salesmen, as is often emphasized in its vanity press. In fact, a customer's interest lay in having IBM offer an easy way to use ASCII terminals with the 360s and 370s. By not offering such capability, of course, IBM could sell more of its own terminals and earn greater profits.

IBM was meanwhile cooking up other mischief. "Prepare an article for release in Harvard Business Review, Datamation and similar type publications which explains the Philosophy of a leading corporation (IBM) and its role in the important industry standardization activities. Reprints, of course, would be available for further distribution."[15]

A June 1970 "Corporate Standards Strategy" document described the stance IBM would take internationally: "Continue efforts toward recognition by national industry and governments that: IBM makes beneficial contributions to national technologies. IBM is a good citizen, aware of national concerns and responsive to national programs. IBM strives for consistency among national and international standards to the extent that is desirable in light of national interests."[16] Yet public relations hype notwithstanding, its main product line would not connect to ASCII terminals.

Meanwhile, IBM figured it would look better to the world if it appeared to be more active in the official standards-setting process: "IBM must take the leadership role in guiding the development of standards."[17] And what company could better afford to "take the leadership role"? In 1965, early in the game, the company had 134 personnel devoted entirely to standards efforts in the United States.[18] That was more people than some of its competitors had on their entire payrolls. (Recall the CDC lab that designed the 6600—it had, according to Watson, only thirty-four people, including the janitor.) Roughly 400 IBM people worked internationally in similar activities. As for competitors, "There will continue to be a shortage of skilled personnel. The ability of manufacturers to participate worldwide in all the standardization activities affecting their interests will be limited."[19]

Again, IBM would meet competitors in their own arena—in this case, the various standards-making groups, which hoped to limit IBM's power through consensus—and then claim it as its own. We can be quite sure that, as the interfaces between IBM's increasingly disparate 1970s and 1980s product lines grew more complex, the standards process would not soon pose a threat to IBM's power and control over its market. Indeed, the widely hailed participation of IBM the "good citizen" in current standards activities, particularly those aimed at creating the utopian ideal of "open" networks so vigorously promoted in Europe, is no doubt guided by the same "Basic Principles" it wrote in 1968 or so:

> IBM will actively participate in industry standards programs
>
> Implementation of Industry standards is a business decision based upon market considerations.
>
> Standards are "minimums"—do not preclude added features nor product different from the standards.
>
> IBM participation or vote does not commit the company to implementation.
>
> Industry standards affect the P/L [Profit and Loss]—and therefore require management involvement.[20]

That is to say, IBM is no fool. It is not about to let standards ruin its game. And even when all other parties were lined up against IBM, as they did by backing ASCII, IBM was able to avoid conforming to their wishes.

IBM is not always so obstinate in its refusal to recognize industry standards, for in some cases they actually work to its benefit. For instance, in the early 1960s, the federal government adopted COBOL as a standard programming language for building applications. By dictating that all programs be written in a common language, the government hoped to foster competition among computer makers: their wish to win government business would be an incentive to build COBOL into their systems. IBM backed COBOL, even though as a standard language it tended to break the software lock-in so necessary to price discrimination, but only to a point. As the market developed, IBM's and other vendors' supposedly standard COBOL packages diverged little by little until they were no longer perfectly compatible with each other. Moreover, the non-COBOL applications still locked a customer to his supplier. Thus, in the end, IBM was able to enjoy continuing software lock-in but at the same time tap into the growing pool of COBOL-trained programmers needed to keep applications development moving along and fueling demand for more memory and peripherals. The differences among various vendors' COBOL implementations were not so large as to lock in programmers, but they were large enough to lock application programs in to specific makes of hardware. Thus IBM supported this effort because it was in its commercial self-interest. Providing customers free and equal choice as to suppliers was clearly not, and such a result cannot hope to be achieved through a voluntary standards process.

A TERMINAL CASE

But there were still those high profits IBM earned on its EBCDIC terminals. Competitors soon turned to compete for that business, even if it meant playing by IBM's communications rules. They planned to match its interface and undercut its prices. Not having yet seen IBM's manipulation of disk and tape drive interfaces, the new competitors followed its terminal standard and assumed that the company would not change the standard once it had installed enough terminals of its own.

One of these competitors was Sanders Associates, a New Hampshire company that had originally made its name selling military and aerospace electronics equipment. Among its products were systems designed to help battlefield commanders gather and distribute tactical data over great distances, say between a field outpost and headquarters. A crucial component in such systems was the CRT (cathode ray tube) terminal, which displayed alphabetical and numerical data on a screen similar to that of a television receiver.

As time sharing and other forms of interactive computing began to grow on IBM 360 systems, Sanders decided it could profitably adapt its terminal technology to the commercial marketplace and make a run at the IBM market. It did so with the model 620 and 720 terminals, which competed directly with IBM's model 2260 terminal, first installed in early 1966 on 360s. Like the 2260, Sanders's terminals operated under the control of IBM's 2700 line of communications controllers and those from other vendors such as Memorex.

About four years after the 2260 was first shipped, at the end of 1970, CRT terminals were still a relatively small business for IBM. This was prior to IBM's big push into large, centralized interactive systems—it had installed only 18,219 model 2260 terminals bringing revenues of just under $9 million, that year.[21] Sanders at that time was not the only independent terminal maker—others included Four-Phase, Raytheon, and Datapoint—but it was the most successful: It had 1,792 terminals attached to 360 systems, or just under a tenth of IBM's installations.[22]

As early as September 1969, according to a QPLA, IBM rated Sanders's terminal "more versatile" than the 2260.[23] In a ninety-six page evaluation of Sanders and the competitiveness of its products, IBM gave its own terminal a score of only 27 compared to its rival's score of 50. Sanders's product (along with those of other competitors) displayed data more pleasingly than IBM's, could attach to more processors than just the 360, and offered an "intelligent line concentrator." Yet the IBM 2260 rented for "more than double that of competitive devices."[24] A year later, IBM discovered in a random sampling of fifty-nine System/360 customers that fifty-three of them had chosen non-IBM terminals. More threatening, at twenty-three of those fifty-three sites the terminals had been the first non-IBM gear installed there.[25] Just at a time when interactive computing, for which CRT terminals were mandatory for the most efficient operation, was on the verge of booming, IBM's terminals were clearly inferior to competitors'.

In mid-1971, Sanders came out with a new terminal, the model 800, which was priced lower than its previous products but offered a built-in processor to handle simple editing and communications tasks. At about the same time, IBM came out with its 3270 terminal family, which included many of the features of the previous Sanders terminal but was priced lower. However, since the 3270s did not have any built-in intelligence of their own, the product was not particularly competitive with Sanders's 800, and that company confidently marched into the market thinking its product would win against IBM.

IBM began delivering 3270 products—which included CRT terminals, printers, and remote controllers—in the fall of 1972. At about the same time, it also announced its virtual 370 processors, the 370/158 and 168, which, as discussed earlier, had been priced and packaged with bundled memory as part of the SMASH announcement. All seemed well for Sanders and its 800 product until early the next year, when IBM told customers that the new 370s' virtual operating system, OS/VS, would not work with the older 2260 or equivalent terminals but only with the new 3270s. In other words, by cutting out a piece of software from the operating system, IBM had completely eliminated an interface and had locked Sanders and others out of the potentially vast virtual 370 market.

As soon as IBM pulled the plug, so to speak, on the 2260 and equivalent terminals, Sanders's terminals business began to suffer.[26] Orders were canceled and leases were terminated. As Amdahl would do a few years later in a similar situation concerning a changed IBM interface, Sanders struggled to convince its otherwise-content customers that some way, some cost-effective way, would be found to attach the 2260-compatible Sanders 800 and previous terminals to virtual 370s, despite IBM's obvious wishes to the contrary. In fact, Sanders was not at all sure how it would accomplish that reverse compatibility. Meanwhile, it took IBM to court, claiming the interface actions had violated the antitrust laws. In December 1973, Sanders got IBM to agree to reinstate the 2260 interface on virtual systems, but it was not until ten months later, in October 1974, that IBM actually made the necessary software available to customers.

The fact that IBM could later support the 2260 interface indicates that there were no insurmountable technical problems in doing so right from the start and that its initial decision to pull such support was based at least in part on commercial goals. Its actions against Sanders clearly demonstrated that, with its control over the 370 system, IBM could make competitive equipment attached to that system—even remotely over common phone lines—no longer viable by changing the relevant interfaces. In this case, it was almost three years after the 3270s' introductions, and eighteen months after the products were first shipped to customers, that Sanders could finally get to market with competitive terminals. During those many months, IBM had the market to itself, and Sanders's initial competitive advantage slipped away.

Even though Sanders stood up to IBM and sued it under antitrust law, the legality of IBM's actions and interface policies were never fully adjudicated. The two companies settled the case out of court, Sanders backing off after IBM gave it several lucrative contracts worth many millions of dollars. Once a competitor, Sanders now became a supplier to IBM.

John Akers, now president of IBM, in February 1975 would claim that IBM was doing well with its 3270 terminals. IBM by then had installed "nearly three times what we had expected in 1974. By the end of this quarter, we will have more than 100,000 of these terminals and related devices installed in the United States."[27] Chalk one up for "excellent" management and superior marketing, for in the May 1973 QPLA, IBM rated the 3270s as deficient compared to its competitors' terminals.

The IBM 3270s and a wide range of derivative products in the end turned out to have exceptionally long lives. IBM has installed many hundreds of thousands of the devices, introduced new designs, cut prices, and generally expanded the 3270s into a family of products. Nevertheless, with interactive computing fast becoming the norm during the 1970s, several dozen competitors sought pieces of the rapidly expanding 3270-compatible market. They carved a sizable niche into IBM's business, gaining a combined market share of as much as 40 percent by offering customers lower prices, faster delivery, and more functionality than IBM. As the popularity of interactive computing grew, IBM reacted in the late 1970s and 1980s with a series of price cuts on the original products, with new low-priced 3270 models, and with periodic additions of new functions. Also, the company's multibillion-dollar investment in manufacturing capacity during the previous few years helped it cut delivery times substantially.

In 1983, following the withdrawal of the government antitrust case, IBM met competitors head-on by unveiling the aggressively priced 3178, a 3270 replacement that not only boasted of improved functions and a better display screen but was made available under a volume discount plan: by ordering many terminals at once, large customers could save as much as 40 percent off the list price. In 1983, a total of 531,000 3270-type devices of various makes and models were shipped, according to IDC. IBM captured 57.4 percent of that total, followed by Telex with 8.4 percent. AT&T had a mere 3.3 percent. The following year saw Raytheon leave the market, Mohawk Data Sciences fold its tent, and several other competitors fall out of the market. In early 1985, IBM's share of the 3270 market hovered in the 65 percent range, according to a survey of over 2,900 domestic IBM users.[28]

The 3270 family is alive and well to this day, still the flagship of IBM's mainframe terminal product line. It was recently enhanced by the addition of a special version of the popular IBM personal computer, the 3270/PC. This device is viewed by many observers as the most likely IBM product to emerge as a universal work station for office workers in the future. But that is another story, to be dealt with in Chapter 18.

CONTROLLING THE CONTROLLERS

The story of adding communications to computers is one of managing increasing complexity. It has required a new type of peripheral device. The essential function of a computer network is to move messages back and forth between a number of terminals and a central computer system. The terminals are often geographically remote from the computer but are connected to it via telephone lines. Those lines usually emanate from a communications controller. Its tasks are many and grow more complex as technology improves and as networks and interactive applications gain sophistication, but its main function is to be as flexible as possible so as to adapt to and manage the extraordinary complexities of computer networks. In the competitive battles over data communications that IBM entered into, much attention centered on the controller because of its strategic role as the unavoidable bridge between the IBM-held central computer and the network. The controller provided the interface with which communications equipment suppliers needed to keep their widening array of terminals and other products compatible.

As its name implies, the controller manages the flow of messages between terminals (and, later, other communicating gear) connected to its "outer" side and the central processor attached to its "inner" side. This entails, among other tasks, switching outgoing messages to the appropriate network wire and routing incoming messages to the proper place in the processor, and preventing the inevitable noise of telephone lines from distorting the messages' informational content. By simple analogy, information within a computer moves a whole word at a time, with several digital bits moving parallel with each other to their destination; over standard, single-wire telephone lines, on the other hand, the information must move serially, each a letter, or bit, moving single file. The controller does the conversion between formats. The timing of each message's movements is complicated because different terminals respond at different speeds, depending on their distance from the central computer and their specific operating characteristics. It is not uncommon for customers to connect different types of terminals to the same computer system, some just down the hall and others in another geographic region. Finally, the controller employs sophisticated techniques to recover information from messages when they get garbled by line noise.

Performing these basic tasks, and the many others that have been added to controllers as the scope of communications networks expands, is difficult, to say the least. It becomes even more difficult as the volume of messages increases as terminals get added and as their interaction with the computer becomes more complex and frequent. As the volume increases, a customer often feels an incentive to boost the rate at which data are transmitted: the quicker the messages can be moved, the less time is needed on costly telephone lines and the lower the monthly bill. However, that increased speed further taxes the controller because, among other things, high data rates are more sensitive to line noise, and their timing must be more accurately timed and scheduled. There is no such thing as a free lunch in such data communications.

To repeat, the most sought-after quality in a communications controller is flexibility. Not only is the controller expected to adapt to changing configurations of terminals, which come and go from the network as customer needs change, but it has to accommodate a wide variety of technologies, products, and circuits. Just as IBM's largest customers were gaining momentum in their construction of regional and even national data communications networks, competition in the U.S. communications market began to be liberalized by a series of court and regulatory agency rulings that invited a proliferation of competitors in communications hardware and services. (Eventually, of course, even the AT&T monolith was broken apart by the 1982 divestiture.) As suppliers took advantage of this increasing market freedom, IBM's users were forced to choose from a wide range of options. They could, for instance, choose between standard, dial-up telephone lines and specially tuned, dedicated lines; between land lines and satellite links; between slow-speed and high-speed circuits; between highly inter-active video display terminals and simple card reading, remote job entry (RJE) stations; between cash register terminals and special devices for bank tellers; and between generic interactive terminals and a wide variety of industry-specific de-vices. At every turn, the controller's flexibility was paramount as each nook and cranny of the customer organization responded to changes in its environment—the network had to be free to adapt accordingly. Right from the beginning of so-called telecomputing, the controller was the all-important hub of the net-work, connecting its many spokes.

At the same time, the controller was the one and only communications bridge out of the central processor. Therefore, it was also expected to adapt to the growing complexity of the evolving computer system and its operating system. Customers often developed several interactive applications on a single computer system, giving each a separate network—perhaps one for engineers' time shar-ing and another to serve sales clerks. Eventually, in order to save communica-tions costs, these customers would merge their various networks into a single one and make them share certain facilities. Though economically attractive, such a merging put a greater burden on the communications controller. It now had to route outgoing messages to just the right terminal and similarly direct in-coming messages to the right application program. Going a step further, cus-tomers might authorize certain terminals on the shared network to have access to several different applications rather than to just the original one. Then the ability for terminals and applications in different, but nearby, processors to communicate with one another might be added. Soon came the need to connect processors in different cities and still give each one's terminals access to the others' applications. Ultimately, as the largest corporations have today, custom-ers built wide-ranging networks that crisscross the nation in a web of processors, terminals of all types, and perhaps dozens of interconnected communications controllers moving messages from one to another and in and out of the appro-priate processors.

This progression of increasingly complex network structures has not only called for the communications controller to provide additional function, flexi-bility, and performance but also necessitates its functions to be as separate as possible from those of the central processor. That is, the controller needs to be autonomous and able to insulate the central processor from the shifting commu-nications requirements—and insulate the network from the changing function of the central processor and its systems and applications software. As multiprocessor networks grow in complexity, they are usually most efficient if their several controllers can route message traffic among themselves as much as possible—the alternative is having messages enter and exit central processors and interrupt their execution of application programs at every move.

Let it be stated quite simply: IBM knew full well that its most valuable customers wanted radically different controller functions than those it provided them, with more flexibility, function, and performance. Yet IBM purposely designed its communications products in such a way as to protect and further extend its monopoly rather than to effectively meet these customers' requirements. By this strategy, as shall be seen later, IBM could leverage its power outward to encompass virtually every office, factory, and industrial device that is based on a computer or microprocessor. Thus it behooves us to carefully examine IBM's methods in this critical area of networking and communications.

In the battle over controllers, one of IBM's important initial competitors was Memorex, the same company that was already giving IBM such a hard time in the disk drive market. Memorex had designed into its model 1270 communications controller much of the flexibility that customers needed but that IBM had left out. The Memorex product's functions could be changed simply by plugging in new circuit cards and removing others. IBM's box, by contrast, was hardwired and relatively inflexible. As a result, Memorex outperformed IBM when it came to adapting to new types of transmission lines and other changing aspects of the communications business, and it sought a piece of the 40 percent profit rate that IBM enjoyed on the 4,000 or so communications controllers it had installed in 1970.[29]

"The [IBM] 2700 series . . . requires different hardware for each type of terminal and transmission code used," stated the company's August 1971 QPLA.[30] By November of that year, IBM found, Memorex had fifty-three controllers installed and orders for another seventy-seven in hand. "The 1270 provides up to twice the price/performance of the 2700 series. . . . As all three IBM transmission control units are outpriced by [plug-compatible] devices, all are rated deficient."[31]

Even the two controllers that IBM had on its drawing board for future introduction "still leave us exposed to Memorex where heavy extra shift rental increases our price more than 20% above the comparable Memorex configuration." Not only did Memorex's controller cost the customer less while offering more function, but it reduced the central processor's workload and eliminated charges he had to pay IBM for excess usage. Non-IBM controllers "are priced for 24-hour use, and because they do not drive the [central processor] meter, can reduce [processor] and peripherals metering in certain applications."[32] That same QPLA stated that by September 1971, IBM customers had

315 non-IBM communications controllers installed and 185 on order. Just months after Memorex introduced its 1270, IBM analysts determined that the West Coast rival had a good chance of gaining a full third of the controller market.

In 1972, IBM responded to Memorex and other communications controller makers with its 3705, a controller that supposedly surpassed the previous IBM 2700s in function but was priced 10 percent lower than even the Memorex 1270 (itself priced up to 40 percent under the 2700s) when installed under the two-year, extended-term plan. Not surprisingly, the 3705 was expected by IBM to show a profit margin of only 5 percent after its impact on previous products was taken into consideration. That extended-lease plan, introduced at the same time as the 3705, committed customers to keeping their 3705s for at least two years. This locked users in, for although the 3705 was software-controlled, the bulk of its software would not be delivered until several years after the hardware's introduction. IBM quite knowingly unveiled the 3705 long before the key programming was ready, which meant that early users could hardly get all the function they had paid for. Their early 3705 software merely emulated the slower 2700 controllers and left out all the special functions the full-blown 3705 was claimed to offer. IBM did not much care, however, because every 3705 box installed on a two-year lease was one less opportunity for Memorex to install a 1270 and one less IBM terminal network threatened to be detached from an IBM mainframe. During the six months preceding the 3705's announcement, Memorex received 101 orders for its 1270; during the following six months, orders totaled only 56.

There were several pieces of missing software.[33] The first was called NCP (for network control program). At the 3705's premature 1972 unveiling, IBM promised NCP would be in users' hands by March 1973. But it was not until November of that year—eight months late—that the software was finally shipped. Even then, however, users were still unable to take full advantage of all the 3705's capabilities, for IBM was still not able to deliver a special software package for the 370 mainframe that was equally necessary to achieving full 3705 function. That second missing software link, known as VTAM (for virtual telecommunications access method), routed messages between the application programs in the mainframe and the 3705. Without VTAM installed, many of NCP's most valuable functions remained idle and unavailable to users.

VTAM was introduced in February 1973, just after the 3705 and NCP, as a replacement for the far simpler and field-proven program, TCAM. As its name implies, VTAM was designed for use in virtual systems such as the 370/158 and 168. It was originally slated for delivery to customers in early 1974. It did not actually reach them, however, until mid-1975. Thus, it was actually three years from the time the 3705 was first shown to users to the time its many advanced functions finally became available.

Even then, customers received less than they had been promised. As IBM worked to complete the oversold VTAM software, its engineers found they had vastly underestimated the amount of memory it would require—at one point, the software used ten times as much memory as originally planned for, or three to five times that of the simpler TCAM. Worse, VTAM's actual performance was dismally slow, for it comprised three to five times the number of program instructions as TCAM. Struggling to deliver VTAM, IBM had to cut back on its function several times. As they had when waiting for the similarly troubled OS/360 operating system, however, most customers sat tight.

The financially strapped Memorex and others were unable to evolve their products. "Because of their financial circumstances," stated an independent consultant's report on the communications business, "we expect that it is improbable that [Memorex] will develop new products but will remain in the 270X replacement field."

Why did customers not simply leave IBM and install Memorex controllers, even if only to later discard them for fully functional 3705s? Memorex had shut down its 1270 production line when orders slumped after VTAM's introduction, but it actually restarted it after IBM missed its delivery schedule and users sought alternate suppliers. The answer lies in the fact that the VTAM software was introduced to replace TCAM but, as IBM emphasized to customers, applications written to use TCAM would not work with VTAM. So if they wanted to move to the more powerful virtual operating system OS/VS, which VTAM required, customers had to choose between rewriting their installed TCAM applications to work with VTAM (a fairly costly task) or running TCAM and VTAM together (which used up considerably more scarce memory than using either package alone). While waiting for VTAM to be delivered, customers were understandably reluctant to write any applications for TCAM, knowing that those programs would later have to be rewritten for VTAM. IBM's promises, therefore, held the controller market at a relative standstill and locked Memorex out, for with VTAM on the way, Memorex's TCAM-only controller appealed to few. And until it actually had a working copy of VTAM to inspect, Memorex was forced, as it had been in the disk drive market, to deal with a phantom IBM interface.

By leveraging off the mainframe side of the processor-controller interface, which it dominated, IBM could alone dictate which products could and could not attach to the 370 processor. That interface was not the only one on the communications controller, of course. The outer interface, between controller and terminal, was just as vital, and there, too, IBM's manipulations worked well against competitors.

Whenever bits of data are transmitted back and forth along a wire, certain conventions must be held to by the sending and receiving devices, say the terminal and the computer, so that the data move smoothly and do not collide.

Among these conventions are the choice of digital code used to represent the letters of the alphabet and numerals, the rate at which the data are transmitted (measured in bits, or characters, per second), and line control disciplines. These latter are a set of strict protocols that define exactly how two network devices must interact when establishing a connection and exchanging data. The two major classes of protocols are asynchronous and synchronous.

Asynchronous protocols were developed many years ago for relatively low-speed transmission over Telex and teletypewriter networks. There, the delay time between the transmission of individual characters was dictated largely by the speed and rhythm of the typist at each end of the line. Such low-speed lines were set up to handle data moving in one direction only. In order to signal the receiving terminal as to when a character began and when it ended, extra "start/stop" signals were inserted to designate each character's beginning and end. This protocol worked well for slow transmissions, keeping each device from sending when it should be receiving, but when high-speed computer devices came into use, the extra start/stop bits became an annoyance—they wasted the line's limited capacity and increased transmission time and costs.

To remedy that situation, and to provide for sophisticated methods of correcting the errors that inevitably creep into electrical transmissions, synchronous protocols were developed under which the two communicating devices periodically exchange signals that keep each from sending while the other is receiving. This synchronization makes sure each device is sending and receiving at the same data rate, obviates the need for wasteful start/stop bits, and lowers overall costs. In 1973, IBM came out with its own version of the protocol, known as synchronous data link control (SDLC), which permitted two devices to send and receive along the same line at the same time.

The rub for Memorex came when IBM declared SDLC usable only on the low-priced 3705 controller and on the even lower-priced 3704, which was introduced later to keep Memorex from selling into sites that could not yet afford the large 3705 and therefore might opt for non-IBM controllers. IBM also declared that its new video display terminals, the 3270s, would communicate only with SDLC. These intentions made users even more reluctant to install Memorex's controller for fear they might miss out on compatibility with future 3270 terminal offerings. Until it could inspect a working version of SDLC, there was no way for Memorex to convince users of its ability to maintain compatibility.

In fact, although it was introduced in mid-1973 and was slated for first delivery in late 1974, SDLC didn't make it to users' hands until early 1976. The new protocol was made available only with the 3705's NCP software. And although IBM had claimed that its new terminals would use only SDLC, it actually shipped them before NCP was available with a special switch that permitted them to connect into the pre-NCP, pre-SDLC 3705. Evidently, although IBM's interfaces may be inscrutable to outsiders, the company can easily break its own rules when it needs to ward off threatening competition.

Although it continued to face competition from other vendors, the 3705 became the mainstay of IBM's communications strategy, and it continues to this day to serve many of the company's largest customers. Situated as it is between the central 370 system and virtually every piece of communications and networking gear that attaches to that system, the 3705 controller is critical. In November 1973, Frederic G. Withington, the highly regarded computer industry analyst quoted earlier, evaluated the 3705 for IBM. In 1977, he testified at length at the government antitrust trial. His expert evaluations confirm that IBM's motives surrounding the 3705 were determined more by commercial aims than by a quest for optimum technical efficiency or for the satisfaction of customer demands.

"The 3705 and NCP will not be completely responsive to user needs," Withington concluded in his 1973 report to IBM. Without enhancements, he concluded, from 30 to 40 percent of IBM's customers would find the product unacceptable.

Four years later, on the witness stand, Withington stated that the 3705 and 3704 controllers, "while performing more functions independently of the central processor than predecessor devices had done, still did not and do not now offer . . . complete independent message switching and network control capability." Withington recalled "no basic change" in the 3705 as compared with the IBM 2700s, since both worked "primarily under the direction of the central processing unit" and neither could switch messages without engaging the central processor. Competitors' stand-alone controllers, he pointed out, could reroute messages from site to site, a common task, "without interrupting or otherwise burdening the general purpose system."[34] Moreover, he stated, non-IBM controllers could insulate the terminal network from failures in the central computer system—the 3705 could not.

Withington noted, too, that the VTAM software was "a product unique to the IBM product line since all other . . . manufacturers use communications processors with stand-alone capability and only IBM requires software of this particular kind. I think, in fact, that I would not regard it as a highly risky or innovative product since it is less in functionality than the previous software offered with the 270X processors."[35] And because of the delay in delivering NCP software, he said, "the user received less functionality or capability or cost effectiveness from the total system."[36]

He recalled telling IBM in 1973 that "users would prefer to see IBM go a step further and provide the complete stand-alone communications processor capabilities," but he noted that even in 1977 those capabilities had not been added to the 3705. All that would be required, he said, would be a disk drive for temporarily storing messages, some means of entering programs into the 3705 directly (instead of only via the central processor, as the 3705 was originally designed to do), and "some output capability for reporting to the operator."[37] Certainly these were not functions beyond IBM's technical capabilities.

Yet a decade after the competition had offered these functions, IBM still had none of them in its 3705, despite its full awareness that customers wanted the functions and despite its reputation for technological leadership and visionary management. Evidently, IBM had commercial reasons for not providing its customers with what they wanted. Asked how IBM might have benefited from the choices it had made, Withington told the Court that "in some cases at least a larger central processor might be needed than if the communications processor were capable of performing the entire function, which might bring more total revenues to IBM."

Furthermore, "It is possible that in terms of future product plans, future general strategies on which IBM has spoken several times of the importance of communications systems, that IBM wishes to retain an involvement of the central processor in the . . . network control process so that should it be necessary to involve the central processor more in the future, they are able to."[38] Withington continued, "By maintaining an involvement of both the communications processor and the central process in the network control process, the two products are brought closer together in terms of software function, and it is more difficult for an outsider or third party competitor to replace" the communications controller.

Although IBM's approach to the complex problem of extending its systems into the interactive environment was fundamentally flawed from a technical point of view, it did the job IBM needed doing. That is, IBM's approach, inflexible as it was and seemingly oblivious to its customers' changing needs and the possibilities presented by changing technology, kept those customers locked in to centralized systems. Against the tide of decentralized approaches pursued by its systems competitors and the many add-on vendors that entered the industry during the 1970s, IBM contrived to keep a major part of the communications function located in the central processor and its operating system, where its hold was most secure.

To have taken any other route would have caused IBM to lose control of the computer industry in a profound way. Repeatedly, therefore, IBM put profits before its customers' needs—they asked for equipment and software products that IBM could easily have provided, but it declined for commercial reasons. Of course, the most-needed products were available from independent suppliers and were used by some of IBM's more adventurous customers, but as the interrelationships between the various components of the sprawling communications networks grew more complex, customers came to view non-IBM communications gear with increasing caution. The relatively tiny communications suppliers that had once found niches to fill in the IBM product line got overlooked, especially as IBM worked on streamlining its ponderous communications offerings. The technical sophistication of its products may be questioned, but the commercial success of IBM's strategy is hard to fault. It has won the interactive computing market hands down—and there's more commercial gain ahead.

18. Extending the Empire

It's something like an Eastern religion.

—IBM press agent, describing
IBM's enormously complex
networking scheme, SNA

IBM's unilateral control of the communications interface gave it great power over the entire network. By functionally cementing the communications controller to the mainframe processor, where its power was the greatest, IBM made it difficult for competitors to attach their controllers and, consequently, all other equipment farther down the network. Through the tight interaction between the constantly revised NCP and VTAM programs, the interface between controller and processor was made complex and unstable. As a result, rivals had a harder time keeping up with IBM than they might have had had stand-alone controllers been the norm. But needless to say, the actual arrangement worked to good advantage for IBM, because its own terminal products were largely inferior to those of its smaller rivals.

The nature of terminal devices changed dramatically during the 1970s, and IBM relied on the same tactics to make trouble for the competition. Repeatedly, other companies would innovate and produce computer devices specialized for a wide variety of customer needs. Their success would proceed apace until the market niche they had pioneered was no longer a niche but was large enough for IBM finally to take notice—and action. For reasons we have seen earlier, the company could not allow any market sector to grow out of its control if that sector neighbored one in which IBM was already involved. IBM's growth objectives propelled it into every sector that offered the potential to earn its normal rate of profits and that could over time threaten some other high-profit sector in which it already had power.

In virtually every case, no matter how late it entered an emerging market sector, IBM quickly won a majority share. Coming late, of course, meant that earning IBM's traditionally high profits was more difficult, for intense competition between its smaller rivals made functional pricing harder. So it was that

IBM resorted to other tactics to ensure itself of high profits and a strong market share.

Primary among IBM's unique strengths was its unilateral control over the communications interface into its dominant mainframes, control that let it split virtually any market in two. In one section were data processing products that were used in isolation—their users had no need to attach them to mainframes. Here competitors could continue to compete on relatively equal footing, almost as if IBM had not yet entered their market.

The other section of the market, of course, was made up of those who needed to connect their devices to a mainframe so that information could be shared between the two. Naturally, IBM had a distinct advantage there. As these users caught on that there would never be a fixed, standard interface for them to use and that without it all non-IBM suppliers remained vulnerable to the monopolist's interface changes, they tended to choose IBM over all others—even if its prices carried a substantial premium. As computer networks stretched into all nooks and crannies of their organizations—into offices, into factories, and into everything in between—it seemed only common sense to cut risks and equip both ends of the network with machinery from the same vendor. As the interaction between terminal device and central mainframe grew more complex, which it inevitably did with the increasing amounts of computing function located at the terminal end of the network—the users were assured that everything would "sing together." It seemed unlikely that IBM would build its own terminals to be incompatible with its mainframe systems.

Once IBM's entrance had bifurcated their once-homogeneous market, the original entrants were left to fight among themselves for the shrinking standalone part of the business.* They might still try to keep their gear compatible with IBM's mainframes and try for a piece of that part of their market, but IBM would hold the upper hand in every case. Meanwhile, IBM would hardly ignore the stand-alone part of the market, and it would usually do well there, too, due to its high-volume production and other economies of scale. Profits from the network-compatible part of the business would help IBM move ahead in the rest of the business. Competition suffered, for it would effectively be impoverished.

All this power, remember, stems directly from IBM's strength in the communications controller market. Functionally, through the intimacy of VTAM and NCP, its 3705 controller was merely an extension of the central 370 processor. Competitors' stand-alone controllers, had they been successful, would have

---

* Over time in each of these bifurcated markets the part that users will want to attach to the mainframe grows, further squeezing those isolated in the "free standing" section. For example, IBM quotes an industry expert that between 1984 and 1989, the proportion of personal computers attached to networks would go from 6 percent to 60 percent of the total number installed.[1]

broken that link and made it possible for some other controller-terminal inter-face—probably a standard one, not under IBM's control—to flourish. A stan-dard interface, of course, would have ensured that all competitors had an equal chance to attach new devices to the network and, by extension, to have those devices interact with application programs running in the central 370 processors. In a competitive market, there would be incentives to all, including IBM, to standardize around simple, even elegant, interface specifications instead of around the contrived interface between the 370 and 3705. Competition would then be free to take place on the basis of product performance and price rather than on the shifting sands of IBM compatibility. Were IBM not a single monop-olist, but if instead its resources were divided among several competing com-panies, standard interfaces would be a natural phenomenon, for customers would find it easier than they do now to take their business elsewhere should any of the mini-IBMs not satisfy their needs. As it is, IBM has been able to ex-tend its reach down the network to market after mainframe-dependent mar-ket—with no end in sight.

Ironically, IBM's public rejection of fixed communication standards relies heavily on the notion that technology is still "evolving" and innovation might be stymied if the industry settled on a networking standard too soon. "Prema-ture standardization is likely to be worse than none at all," Edward H. Sussen-guth, "chief architect" of IBM's own networking scheme, told a reporter in mid-1985 when asked to explain the extraordinary complexity of that scheme (known as Systems Network Architecture, or SNA); industry wags claim SNA stands instead for System for Negative Alternatives.[2] Although at first glance it is an appealing argument, IBM's antistandards stance has clearly given it signifi-cant commercial advantage by narrowing the range of viable competitive offer-ings from which customers can choose. It is clear, too, that in certain situations, the main motivation behind IBM's favoring one technical alternative over an-other has not been maximum system efficiency but rather the company's com-mercial gain at the expense of competitors and its customers.

Worse, today's IBM-dominated computer industry is heavily burdened by its huge, irretrievable investment in 370 systems and other IBM gear that connect through a set of needlessly complex communications interfaces defined by SNA. Having ignored numerous proposals for industry-standard interfaces (it made SDLC a variation on the standard HDLC protocol, chose EBCDIC over ASCII, and so on), IBM itself now struggles hard to make its dozen or so incompatible families of computer systems intercommunicate. Customers, and perhaps the company itself, may soon choke on the complexities of this "tower of babble," as industry pundits call the mess IBM is in from having pursued profit over common technical sense. The task of productively interconnecting what has be-come a proliferation of incompatible IBM systems slowed IBM's business in

1985 and may now be beyond even the giant company's abilities to quickly solve.

MINICOMPUTERS

The largest and most significant market, so far, to suffer the consequences of IBM's control over communications in its mainframes has been the minicomputer market. It offers a prime example of how IBM, once it is provoked into action, can muscle its way into even the most robust, well-developed market and gain control in virtually no time at all.

That the minicomputer market was robust and well-developed when IBM entered it in 1976, there can be no doubt. The first commercial minicomputer, Digital Equipment's PDP-1, was shipped in 1959. For the next seventeen years, the market evolved along quite different lines from the IBM-monopolized mainframe business—and it thus provides a foil against which to compare the structurally flawed mainframe market. In the minicomputer market, the lack of a single, overly powerful supplier let loose a torrent of technical innovation.

"The technological evolution in these systems is even faster than elsewhere in data processing," stated a large IBM study of the "mini" market in 1974.[3] It found that minis "have been, and will continue to be, very close to the state-of-the-art technologically." The result of riding declining cost curves was that "the price of a given function ... has gone down at approximately 10 to 12% per year." Thus, a machine priced at $18,000 in 1965 went for a mere $4,000 in 1973.

Again in contrast to IBM's main market, the lack of a monopolist in the mini market also meant opportunities for many mini suppliers to successfully compete. Over the years, more than a hundred companies took a shot at the market, whose growth was "spectacular": installations grew at 40 to 45 percent a year, according to IBM. These companies had installed about 100,000 mini systems in the United States by the end of 1974, and they were expected to have installed some 175,000 over the next three years. In 1974, IBM found that "at least 35 companies [are] currently producing more than 100 systems. Of these, over 80% of the business is concentrated in ten companies."

The machines were being used by customers for a broad variety of applications, ranging from "basic data collection" to control of other machines in factories to "highly interactive communications systems." They were popular for two reasons. First, minis helped cut costs, especially for manufacturers using them for automation. "Each dollar saved in production costs may yield as much as 50 cents profit," IBM determined, "while additional sales dollars typically yield 5–10 cents."

More important, and increasingly threatening to IBM's power and pricing schemes, was that minicomputers offered customers tremendous flexibility in how they could automate various aspects of their businesses. The mini "brought a modular and low cost electronic solution within reach of virtually every operational department." Modularity meant that a customer needed to install only that amount of gear necessary to solve a particular problem—there was no need to hire a sophisticated and expensive data processing staff, to tend to a gangling operating system like OS, or to get locked in to IBM's price discrimination scheme. It also meant a healthy lack of IBM-imposed barriers to flexible configuration of systems such as bundled memory, changing peripheral interfaces, and needlessly complex communications schemes.

Mini makers, IBM also discovered, made a point of maintaining compatibility between old software and new hardware: minicomputers could "execute programs originally written in the 1960's on newer and more powerful models. [Suppliers] have demonstrated that new function and new technology can be implemented without obsoleting existing programs. As a result, their application base has been self feeding and their sales productivity has steadily increased."

Computing products were naturally extensible, as the leasing companies had proven by upgrading the 360 systems against IBM's many death wishes. But a product's life got extended only if the supplier's commercial interests permitted it—which it did in the competitive minicomputer market.

Mini makers could maintain modularity while still giving their customers all the benefits of improved technology and software compatibility for one simple reason. They provided "friendly" interfaces between peripherals and processors, as IBM put it, and that encouraged the independent peripherals industry to develop a wide range of miniperipherals. Once installed, minicomputer systems often included components from several different suppliers, depending on the application in which they were to be used. Similar modularity was to be found in their operating systems and other software options. "The significant result, and attraction," IBM concluded, "is that a customer selects and pays for only those functions that are required to do his particular applications, thereby minimizing his investment and eliminating the burden of unrequired capability." In contrast to the mainframe market, in which one company dictated most of the important interfaces to its own advantage, free competition in the minicomputer market had fostered stable, well-understood interfaces that provided users with a wider choice of products.

But things were about to change. IBM was growing anxious about the minicomputer's encroachment on its commercial data processing turf. For most of their short but high-growth history, minis had been used primarily in scientific and engineering applications. In the early 1970s, however, the small machines had grown sufficiently powerful and were appropriately programmed to handle tasks that were once relegated only to relatively large mainframes like the 360. IBM forecast that by 1977, two-thirds of the $3.2 billion minicomputer industry's revenues would come from users who used the machines in commercial data processing applications that were, or could have been, handled by IBM mainframes. These applications, a company task force concluded, broke down into two categories, "operationally autonomous" and "distributed systems."

The first category included the "substantial number" of minis that worked alone, without any connection to another computer. But more important, the task force discovered, was that "more than 50%" of current mini users were planning eventually to connect their small computers to some other machine, and that usually turned out to be an IBM 360 or 370 mainframe. "The estimated 140,000 installed minisystems are a tremendous source of information" that could be fed into a mainframe for additional processing, IBM found. "They will contribute heavily to the justification for a S/370-type supporting Host [central mainframe system] when the IBM distributed system solution is available." In many future applications, it seemed, minis would complement, not replace, IBM's dominant mainframes. IBM's customers had indicated that using minis in isolated, stand-alone applications was not inconsistent with their concurrent move to centralize data processing onto large 370 systems. Minis were particularly useful for "capturing" information about transactions in remote locations—at a bank's branch office, say—and storing the information until evening came when telephone rates dropped and it could be sent en masse to the central system for final processing. "A major opportunity is available to the vendors who successfully develop a distributed system product family, which fills the growing information and processing gap between centralized systems and stand-alone mini-systems."

But IBM was not likely to be one of those vendors anytime soon. It found that "the majority of this growth business is currently not attainable . . . because the required product solutions are neither available nor part of the current planned program." Once again, IBM had been blind sided in a key market sector. "The alternative is to abandon this substantial opportunity to the increasing number of vendors who have recognized the requirement for interconnected systems and are marketing 'host' systems to which their own minisystems can be attached." If it did not respond, IBM ran the risk of other vendors' increasingly powerful minicomputers becoming the hosts, or central hubs, of users' computer networks. When it was used as a distributed system, interconnected with other computers, the minicomputer thus threatened the very core of IBM's business. IBM figured that unless it acted fast, it stood to miss out on almost $10 billion worth of minicomputer equipment that could be attached to its central systems over the next eight years.

IBM's response was planned under the name Hierarchical Distributed Systems, which was seen as a "natural extension" of its centralized 370 system, along with its tightly coupled network, "down to the minisystems environment where an increasing amount of valuable data resides. As customers seek to interconnect the tens of thousands of minisystems now being installed annually, they may naturally look to IBM for a systems solution. The rate at which customers interconnect these minisystems and 'funnel' the information into standardized data bases depends largely on the availability of a systems solution from recognized vendors." In other words, minis on a communications network would feed the central system great amounts of data, thereby boosting demand for extra disk storage and processing capacity in the mainframe. IBM saw that demand growing so large through the 1980s as to "help offset decreasing systems prices."

IBM determined that its customers would not continue expanding their central systems with expanded networks, more and larger disk drives and other peripherals, and bigger processors—at least not at the traditional expansion rate—unless they were provided some means of attaching their minicomputers. "As it turns out, more and more of the up-to-date information needed by the DB/DC [database/data communications, i.e., central 370] system is located in minicomputers spread throughout the customer's facilities. Therefore, IBM must provide the means to harness this data in such a way that enhances the usage of the large DB/DC system while protecting the autonomy of the minisystem user."

SNA

And it did. In 1975, just as it was preparing to enter the minicomputer market itself the next year with its Series/1 product, IBM unveiled a grand scheme to organize 370-centered networks. It was the set of communications protocols, or rules of the road, called Systems Network Architecture (SNA). These rules, embodied in software that ran in the 370 "host" system, the tightly coupled 3705 communications controller, and the soon-to-burgeon array of small IBM computers and intelligent terminals, defined the interfaces needed to build hierarchically managed networks. As the term *host* implies, control over the SNA network always resided in the mainframe, where in turn IBM's power remained firmly anchored. All devices in the outlying regions of the network—CRT terminals, minicomputers, and so forth—were forced by SNA's rules to act as slaves to the master central system. How much more hierarchical could a network scheme be than to declare everything attached to the central mainframe a slave?

Software in SNA terminals and related devices is loaded not locally to each device, but instead—as in the technically backward 3705—only from the central 370 host, across the network itself. That's a relatively inflexible approach, but it serves IBM's interest in preserving tight links between host and terminal. In general, moreover, all message traffic in the SNA network takes place under the control of the 370 processor: it alone can initiate links between devices on the network, be they simple terminals or powerful minicomputers. In networks that include several 370 systems, SNA's inflexible logic dictates that one of those machines be declared host to all others. IBM made sure through SNA, which can be viewed as a functional layer of software added to the 100-percent-IBM-controlled OS operating system, that there is always some point in the network where it can apply its power—where it can install a new version of software or microcode that affects the entire network's compatibility and where the data processing manager can be given the famous IBM sales treatment.

Because their products have always been forced to be "slaves" to IBM's hosts, competitors have had problems fighting IBM in the distributed processing arena ever since the SNA saga began. The set of protocols making up SNA has continued to grow—or "evolve," as IBM likes to describe it, ascribing a disarming inevitability to the commercially motivated changes—in size and complexity. Some changes in SNA have indeed been prompted by the continuing technical advances IBM likes to point to, but there can be no doubt that many of the changes work only to the company's commercial advantage and no one else's.

SNA has easily become the most dexterous exploitation of interface control that the company has ever attempted. Periodically, IBM either revises each of the original SNA protocols or adds completely new ones with different functions. Each revision and addition in effect changes one or another of the interfaces that competitors must use to participate in the 20,000 or so SNA networks installed by year end 1985. Only if his product is totally compatible with the latest version of IBM's host SNA software (known as advanced communications function, or ACF/VTAM) can a manufacturer be sure his minicomputer or other network product is as competitive as possible with IBM's comparable device. But as IBM surely foresaw when it cooked up the SNA scheme, maintaining ongoing compatibility with constantly changing interfaces can be turned into a quite costly and time-consuming pursuit for those not privy to future SNA plans. Not only does IBM withhold all but the skimpiest details of each revision of SNA, but it alone can make detailed product plans based on the functions and interface characteristics the next revision will comprise. By virtue of that advance knowledge—the propriety of which it has vigorously defended in several courts—IBM is less likely to implement SNA functions on its various minicomputers and terminals in a way that might interfere with future, as-yet-unannounced functions.

But there is more to the SNA story. The function of SNA is to be the bridge which allows two different pieces of equipment to communicate. The difficulty of its task depends on the particular characteristics of the equipment—the more similar, the easier the communication; the more different, the more difficult.

This simple truth is the basis of much of IBM's technical problems with SNA. Ironically, the same company whose success in computers has often been attributed to the compatibility of its 360 systems today offers a product line riddled with over a dozen incompatible system families, none of which can use the same software. It is this hodge-podge of incompatible systems that SNA has to effectively bring together. IBM's competitors, with fewer incompatible systems to unite, have found hooking theirs together a much less formidable task.

IBM, moreover, was not unaware of the problems these incompatible systems would eventually pose as customers tried to connect them. (See Appendix I for one IBM employee's unheeded plea in 1970 for it to maintain compatibility among all its systems.) Yet, IBM has announced one incompatible system after another while its much smaller competitors have extended the range of their compatible product lines. Why?

The problem posed to IBM by compatible systems and stable, simple interfaces is that they make life too easy for its competitors. That in turn undercuts IBM's ability to safely charge high prices. It was for this reason that the System/3 was made incompatible with the 360. Because it was incompatible, IBM could price the machine aggressively and contain competition without fear that the high-priced mainframe user would move to it. The success of the strategy is seen in the higher market share IBM enjoyed for this system compared to that of the smaller systems which remained compatible with its mainframes. It was a winning strategy, one that IBM has repeated often.

Business Week, when viewing this situation, concluded "IBM will need every bit of ingenuity it can muster to straighten out the mess."[4] Since IBM has benefited for years from segmenting its markets with incompatible systems and the discriminatory prices they make possible, calling it a "mess" seems to miss the point. It intentionally chose the SNA "mess" as a way to meet Watson, Jr.'s instructions decades ago—that the "main aim of this company must be to protect and expand our position in the market place."

Of course from the customers' perspective it was clearly a "mess." They are now burdened with a huge investment in mutually incompatible hardware and software, much of which will have to be abandoned in order for there to be any hope of effectively interconnecting it.

Getting SNA to function effectively will be difficult for IBM, much as a similar problem with OS was decades ago. But then IBM has resources aplenty, and in the end will succeed. Moreover, from IBM's perspective the resulting products will be wonderfully complex and constantly changing, an environment particularly difficult for the competition. It should easily be able in such a world to "protect and expand" its power.

As a result of the complexity of SNA, a minor industry of SNA consultants has grown prosperous by supplying hard-earned SNA expertise to distributed processing system manufacturers that need to play IBM's game of continual catch-up. But even with the experts' help, experience shows that it still takes IBM's rivals a good two years to decrypt a typical new SNA protocol, to design, build, and test a compatible software version for their own machine, and to deliver it to impatient customers. That is, of course, two years after IBM first delivers its own implementation of the protocol, which may not happen until two years after it first tells customers that the protocol is on its way.

In sum, this open-ended complexity and number of SNA protocols provides IBM with ever-changing interfaces that ensure that it *always* has the competitive edge over rival distributed processing suppliers. It is always first to market with new SNA function, and it can therefore reap the high profits that early marketing permits. Its products are always seen by cautious customers as the safest bet in the continually changing, complex data communications marketplace that SNA's changes and advancing technology create. Given their constant need for the latest SNA functions and performance in order to maximize the efficiency and capacity of their 370-based networks—which increasingly affects the efficiency and productivity of their basic businesses—large corporations are less likely to settle for a non-IBM product that is compatible only with a previous, outdated version of SNA and therefore offers less function, especially if their only gain is to save a few thousand dollars with the non-IBM gear. As it did when functionally binding its communications controller to the central 370 processor by making the NCP software dependent on the processor's VTAM, IBM has used the master/slave SNA scheme to favor the attachment of IBM gear to all nodes of its networks. That one-way dependence between SNA terminal and host, it must be emphasized, holds no matter what intervening communications medium is used. IBM does not much care at this point whether a coaxial cable, a long-distance telephone line, a packet-switching network, or a satellite link, to name a few options, is used to connect the two devices. IBM still holds the upper hand by virtue of its monopoly over central mainframe systems and the function and interfaces defined by those boxes' operating system software. And by extension, once it has gained control of both ends of these communications links, what's to say it won't then pursue the business of providing such links itself?

PERSONAL COMPUTERS

The shifting sands of SNA interfaces were key to the company's decisive takeover of the personal computer market, too. Although much has been made of the Charlie Chaplin advertising campaign and other unorthodoxies of IBM's tardy but overwhelmingly successful push into personal computers, that success can be interpreted for the most part as a natural consequence of IBM's short, SNA-driven climb to dominance in distributed processing. Indeed, there is not much difference in power or function between the typical personal computer of today and the minicomputers IBM discovered encroaching on its mainframe turf ten or more years earlier.

As it did in the minicomputer market, IBM divided the PC arena into those machines that were used in isolation and those used, primarily by its most valuable, large customers, in concert with a 370-based network. Customers in the latter category heard repeatedly from IBM that PCs would be most useful when participating in an SNA network: that way, the desktop machines could share information with a large host, deliver messages to other devices on the network, pass the host particularly difficult and time-consuming tasks for speedy execution, and, most important of all, keep their local files synchronized with the corporate data base. There was nothing worse, IBM implied to large customers, many of whom were uncertain about how to deal with the wildfire proliferation of PCs throughout their organizations, than having a group of PC users make plans based on Lotus 1-2-3 spreadsheets that were based on differing assumptions and data. Without some hierarchical management of PCs, preferably through SNA, data processing anarchy might break out. IBM found many eager listeners to this pitch among its most important accounts, for data processing managers often felt that their political standing within the corporate structure was threatened by the PC phenomenon—IBM's plan for corraling these rabbit-like beasts appealed to more than mere technical concerns.

Once again, however, IBM was blowing just so much hot air with all this talk about connecting PCs and hosts. The best it offered in the way of PC communications was a plug-in device that made the PC perform like a 3270 terminal when attached into an SNA network, but that kind of link hardly used the PC's unique qualities to their maximum. In fact, at first (IBM introduced its first PC in mid-1981 and began shipments a few months later), IBM had little commercial interest in equipping its PC with too much SNA functionality, for that would lead its largest customers to install those devices instead of relatively high-profit 3270 terminals and other products. So even though it had no intention of immediately allowing the PC any more than a token role in the SNA network, IBM spoke loud and long of the advantages to be had from connecting PCs into networks. Customers readily complied, no doubt because they had seen how difficult it was for minicomputer makers to keep up with the shifting communications interfaces into the 370 realm. To most of those cautious minds, the IBM PC seemed to be the only intelligent choice. IBM's admonishments were subsequently proven correct when several vendors' clones of its PC were proven incompatible with later releases of IBM's PC-DOS operating system. Before long, IBM had captured an estimated 75 percent of the U.S. corporate PC market.

Meanwhile, the average man on the street, who couldn't care less about connecting his single PC to a mainframe but instead wanted to use it as a word processor or to handle his small business's accounting, was also a sought-after customer for the IBM PC. In this stand-alone sector, where communications interfaces are relatively simple if they are necessary at all, IBM won only a 30 to 35 percent market share. In fact, the company's first attempt to directly tap the home computer market, with the infamous PCjr, ended in great embarrassment for the seemingly invincible IBM: even a fire sale on a reworked version of that deliberately crippled derivative of the standard IBM PC failed to move customers away from their more elegant and satisfactory Apples and Commodores. If nothing else, IBM's almost complete failure with the PCjr actually confirms two contentions of this book: one, when it cannot use the threat of changing interfaces to limit customer choice, IBM's products must stand on their own merits, and those merits often fail them against technically superior products from relatively tiny competitors; two, as a last resort, IBM can always employ price discrimination to move otherwise deficient products. Not only have there been charges by competitors that the PC carried less than the traditional IBM profit margin and that during certain Christmas sales the PCjr was sold at or below cost, but IBM has often bundled hundreds of dollars' worth of software with its PCs to make them more attractive to shoppers off the street. Given its size and profits from markets more under its control, IBM's ability to subsidize such price discrimination can hardly be matched by any other competitor.

THE IBM EMPIRE, SO FAR

Let's see how far IBM has fared in markets that neighbor its central mainframe monopoly. Table 40 shows the relative position IBM held in 1983 in a variety of markets for products that will eventually depend heavily on their ability to communicate with the IBM mainframe.

Table 40
IBM Rank and Market Share in Information Business, 1983[5]

	IBM RANK	IBM SHARE
Mainframes	1	72%
Mass Storage	1	70
Software	1	30
PBX (Rolm)	1	21
Terminals	1	40
Small Business/Microcomputers	2	17
Personal Computers	1	28
Personal Computer S/W	1	10
Word Processors	1	25
Semiconductors (Intel)	3	18

IBM is number one in eight out of ten segments. As a result of its success in the compatible equipment wars, its share is highest in the computer room where mainframe and mass storage devices lie. Over time, the IBM control over the communications umbilical cord will ensure that its share in these interconnected segments rises. Moreover, in at least two of these segments its share is in fact higher than the statistics would indicate.

The reason for the understatement lies in the method used to collect and evaluate these statistics. The clearest example of this commonly found distortion is the semiconductor area, where IBM's vast internal production is ignored by these figures. What IDC shows here are numbers relating to the merchant semiconductor business—those sold from company to company and not produced for internal consumption. Here, therefore, the figures for IBM refer only to its partially owned subsidiary, Intel. Similarly, systems software that comes bundled into certain IBM hardware products is not included in the above software figures. Only in the small business/microcomputer segment does IBM's less-than-first-place number reflect the true market situation, for that is a sector where Digital Equipment remained ahead of IBM. But not for long—IBM is catching up quickly.

This was a remarkable success for IBM. And when the focus is solely on the central core of IBM's installed base, the mainframes, market research data show its share rising. The company's share of the value of 1984 mainframe shipments was 76.8 percent, up from 72 percent the year before:

Table 41
1984 Worldwide Shipments of Mainframes[7]

	VALUE (IN $ MILLION)	SHARE
IBM	$11,600	76.8%
Burroughs	845	5.6
Amdahl	760	5.0
Honeywell	495	3.3
Control Data	460	3.0
Sperry Rand	430	2.8
National Advanced Systems (Itel)	325	2.2
Cray	165	1.1
NCR	25	0.2
Total	$15,105	100.0

The erosion of the market share of the other independent systems suppliers continues as more customers shift to using the IBM architecture. This and their low profit rates (a continuation of the results shown in Appendix E) makes the future prospects for these long-standing competitors dim. According to Mr. Koji

Kobayashi, chairman and chief executive officer of Japan's NEC Corp., "If I were the president of a U.S. computer company, it would be hopeless because of the existence of IBM."[6]

Seeing the writing on the wall, in May 1986, Burroughs and Sperry agreed to merge their operations. Though this will increase their total size it will bring with it additional problems as it attempts to support the two groups of customers using incompatible systems. Its goal will be to move these customers to a future common system family while losing as few as possible to IBM. Some, as with the prior mergers in the industry, will be lost and the combined market share of the resulting customer base will end up less than the sum of the prior two.

Two decades after Watson, Jr., had set out the goal "that IBM should attempt to maintain its market share in the immediate and foreseeable future with the idea that with the industry growing as rapidly as it is, other companies can grow quite rapidly under this general mandate," it has succeeded. Today its share is practically the same as it was when the industry was much smaller.

It has been a very dynamic time with truly amazing technological changes and a continuing and rapid growth in the size and importance of the industry. In each period there has been a different cast of courageous and innovative firms that have attacked IBM, a process that continues today as the fruitful technology offers what appears to be an irresistible chance to gain some of IBM's bloated share and high profits. The result of their efforts are also just as IBM had predicted years ago, their "success or failure will primarily depend on trading shares among themselves," and not with IBM.

Moreover, as the period comes to an end, IBM has more than enough power to insure that its past successes will continue well into the future. Nowhere is this growing power seen more clearly than its increasing rate of profits, profits that will enable it to price discriminate in the future as it has in the past.

Clearly these were years of rapid growth—almost doubling in five years. The true measure of its increasing power is not this increase in size, however, but

Table 42
IBM Revenues and
Profits, 1980–85
(in $ billion)[8]

YEAR	REVENUES	PROFITS
1980	26.2	3.4
1981	29.1	3.6
1982	34.4	4.4
1983	40.2	5.5
1984	45.9	6.6
1985	50.1	6.6

rather its increase in profitability during the 1980–84 period. As competition dropped away, IBM's rate of profit increased. Its return on stockholders' equity increased from 21.1 percent in 1980 to 23.4 percent in 1982 to 26.5 percent in 1984. Not bad, considering that it was still marketing the same basic 360 and 370 architecture that it concluded could not "technically or efficiently" meet its users' needs during these years. (The 1985 results reflect the impact of a poor year for the industry in general and the announcement of a new series of IBM high-end mainframes rather than the effect of competition.)

This increasing profit rate—an increase of over 25 percent—is the clearest manifestation of IBM's consolidation of its power. Absent more effective competition from firms with more equal capabilities—this long-term process will only continue.

Part 4

Just a Beginning

19. The Rest of the World

IBM has to be as good for the United Kingdom as it is for the United States. And for that matter, as good for Japan as it is for Canada or Mexico or France.

—John Akers, President and Chief
Executive Officer of IBM[1]

Having seen the power that IBM enjoys in the U.S. computer market and in most of the markets for equipment that attaches to its mainframes, we can now consider the company's position in the world computer market and see how IBM adversely affects the United States' global competitiveness. The past two decades have seen U.S. producers of steel, automobiles, and consumer electronics thoroughly trounced by foreign competitors, and now U.S. memory chip makers are suffering. With computers so dependent on such chips, it seems fair to ask if the U.S. computer industry might be the next to fall to outside forces—or will IBM's domestic strength save the nation from that fate?

IBM goes to great lengths to have itself perceived as a savior of U.S. competitiveness, but in fact the company is a major source of problems in that area. The company's domestic monopoly is distorting and impoverishing many neighboring sectors of the economy. The chip industry, as we shall see, is only the first that may fall due to IBM's overwhelming market share in computers.

To see that IBM's domestic strength is actually a global weakness for the United States, we must first understand that IBM's international power matches that which it enjoys at home. The company has used the same pricing and interface tactics abroad as it has used at home, and it has achieved comparable results: overwhelming market share in virtually every major computer market in the world. The one big difference is that IBM's success abroad has created political problems that it has avoided at home. IBM is viewed as a foreign company in all other nations, and to have such a foreign company—and an extremely powerful one at that—so firmly in control of as critical an industry as computers is politically unacceptable in most countries. As a result, foreign governments have intervened directly in the competitive process in hopes of containing IBM's power and nurturing domestic computer producers. Yet despite substantial and expensive efforts, such government support has had little if any effect on IBM's power. Rather, the same long-term process of competitors' "trading market share" among themselves has taken place internationally. The winners have been the artificially supported local producers, and the losers have been the non-IBM, U.S. computer companies that are forced to compete abroad without the benefits either of a monopoly or of lavish support from Washington. Ultimately, more of the United States' computer capabilities are becoming concentrated in IBM.

Here we shall investigate two approaches taken by foreign companies in their attempts to counter IBM's power within their borders. First, France and Japan will be considered. A surprise for many in the United States is the role IBM has played in compelling those nations to step in and support their local computer makers against the U.S. monopoly. Their governments, among many others, fear IBM's power, even if Washington does not. Next will be seen the drastic effect IBM has on the U.S. chip industry, an effect that can be best understood in the light of market structures observed in France and Japan.

IBM's foreign business to a large extent reflects what we have seen in the United States. The company sells essentially the same product line throughout the world. Its share of the international computer market is as high as its share in the United States market. Most of its foreign business comes from the largest commercial companies, which have invested billions in software and training that tie them to IBM. The evolution of those customers' computer systems mimics that in the United States, moving from small batch to large, centralized, and finally distributed interactive systems.

FRANCE

The French were among the first to identify IBM as a threat to their country's sovereignty and industrial health. A widely read report to French President Valery Giscard d'Estaing prepared by Simon Nora and Alain Minc in 1978 articulated fears that can now be heard in many European and Asian nations: "IBM's place (60% to 70%) in the world computer market reveals its technical and commercial capacities and explains its financial strength, which supports a policy that holds all the trump cards for penetrating the data-processing market from above and below. No firm, and no government either, has so mastered the chain extending from component to satellite."[2]

IBM's power, Nora and Minc reported, threatened nothing less than the "entire nervous system of social organization." The computer "is not the only technological innovation of recent years, but it does constitute the common factor that speeds the development of all the others."[3]

Similarly, there is no question in the minds of Japanese industrialists as to which company dominates the world's computer markets. "IBM alone controls 70% of the U.S. market and 66% of the world market and thus has unrivaled hegemony," stated a 1972 government report. "No other firm has attained a size one-tenth that of IBM and there results a Gulliver-type economic structure consisting of one giant and a number of Lilliputians."[4]

Governments find it hard to accept their economies' growing dependence on IBM for technology as critical as computers. Yet none of the available remedies seems to be effective. Nationalizing local IBM assets, for example, would gain little. Since most of the company's important research and development work takes place in the United States, any nationalized arm would find it hard to succeed on its own. One of the benefits to IBM of its organization is that it discourages attempts to nationalize the company. Another option that governments might consider when trying to nurture local computer industries is forming a joint venture with IBM, but IBM is usually not interested (although lately it has been making exceptions). IBM has traditionally insisted on total ownership of all its foreign subsidiaries.

Leaning on IBM risks damaging the local computer industry more than leaving the company alone. IBM's trump card against all efforts to limit its power within a particular country or region is to threaten withdrawal from the hostile territory. IBM's leaving France or West Germany, for example, could severely hurt local employment, and it could also affect employment in all other industries that depend on IBM systems to be competitive in their respective markets.

Hence, IBM is essentially unhindered by law, and national governments are left to fund their domestic computer manufacturers in hopes of beating the U.S. giant. The potential benefits of a successful run at IBM this way seem enormous. Unfortunately, the cost of successfully competing with IBM over the long term has taxed even the most determined governments.

Despite the overall losses, there have been some benefits from these heavily funded attempts to counter IBM. Foreign computer makers have succeeded against IBM in roughly the same areas as those in which U.S. competition has done best, namely small and medium-size mainframes. As in the United States, however, IBM abroad now has stronger products in those areas, and the battles have become increasingly difficult. Rather than winning market share from IBM, nationally coordinated computer efforts have more often gained against IBM's traditional U.S. systems competitors. In addition, these nations have been able to assure themselves of local supplies of certain vital computing gear—military computers, for example. Finally, those countries that have aided local computer makers the most have been awarded the biggest local investments by IBM. IBM knows when and where it must spend a little more to polish its image as a worthy corporate "citizen." Especially now, when future economic health seems to depend on strength in "high technology," IBM's favors of a new factory (more jobs) or development facility (better technical skills among the locals) are eagerly sought after.

How well a national computer effort succeeds against IBM depends on a number of factors, but IBM usually holds the upper hand. It generally gains the largest and most important customer base in a given country, and local suppliers remain limited to a small portion of the most critical business. IBM's world market share has remained stable or has increased during the last few decades; any temporary loss in one country is compensated for by a gain elsewhere. IBM has a uniquely large customer base over which to spread research and development costs for new products. Local competitors, no larger than one-tenth its size, are forced to compete with similarly proportioned customer bases, at best. Should competition get too fierce in one country, IBM can always resort to price discrimination between countries, charging prices as high as the competitive climate in different places will allow. This is particularly effective against suppliers whose marketing is concentrated within their home boundaries. Their only reasonable means of competing is to dig deeper into their government's pockets, but IBM can make sure they never show a profit, for its pockets are always deepest.

Thus, the global computer business is a checkerboard. Each country's local suppliers achieve some success at home but not much beyond its borders. In virtually every nation, IBM is by far the biggest computer supplier of all. Its strength is greatest in large-scale commercial computer systems and in those procurements where government does not intervene. IBM is the supplier of choice for companies that run extensive international operations, for it is the only computer maker active everywhere from Buffalo to Beijing. It is the only computer maker truly worthy of the name International. Finally, when profits are considered, its power shows its awesome proportions, especially when compared with its many international competitors, which are marginally profitable at best.

Government support has done little to help foreign computer manufacturers avoid the fate of their similarly narrow-based counterparts in the United States. With relatively small customer bases and low revenues, they have had trouble affording the research and development expenditures necessary to keep pace with IBM and its compatible "helpers." None, either, has been able to establish more than a shaky foothold in the largest and most important market of all, the United States.

As described by Raymond Vernon, France, Great Britain, and West Germany were from the 1960s on particularly active in backing their domestic computer suppliers, known as "national champions." They employed several common forms of aid: "Providing capital on favored terms was one typical device; discrimination in governmental procurement policies was a second; subsidizing research programs a third. Whatever the method, it implicitly or explicitly embodied one important factor: the exercise of public power to discriminate in favor of chosen national champions ... and limiting the role of foreign-owned firms in the country in order to give their own champions greater opportunities."[5]

There is little doubt that these actions were prompted by IBM's looming presence in European markets. "In essence, this firm has come to symbolize the success of American industry and to play abroad the role of the U.S. national champion," observed Nicolas Jequier in a paper presented in Vernon's book, which was published in 1974.[6]

France responded to the U.S. computer industry in general and to IBM in particular in 1967 with Plan Calcul, which sought to compensate for three competitive weaknesses in its domestic industry: French computer companies were too small; the French market was too restrictive; and American firms were subsidized by military and space programs. France formed a "fusion" of small firms and created a national champion, Compagnie Internationale pour l'Informatique (CII), which was to be cultivated into France's own broad-based "IBM." CII was chartered to focus its efforts on small and medium-scale systems and peripherals.

Despite the many millions of dollars spent on Plan Calcul, Nora and Minc found in 1978 that U.S. computer suppliers still dominated the French market. The home country, they found, "satisfies only 20 percent of its needs in office computers and 40 percent in terminals and universal minicomputers." Worse, U.S. companies had done better in France than in other industrial nations: "In 1975 American companies supplied 45 percent of the computer pool in Japan, 60.5 percent in Great Britain, 75 percent in Germany, 83.5 percent in France ... the battle to reduce the position of American industry is already over, a battle aimed first and foremost at IBM because of its dominance of computer manufacturing."*

In the fifteen years following 1967, France pumped more than one billion dollars into its national computer champion, but the company showed a true profit (before subsidies were taken into account) in only two of those years, 1979 and 1980. In 1982, with total revenues of $1.49 billion, CII-HB (so named after its merger with Honeywell) showed a net loss of $249 million, despite close to

---

* In a June 1983 report, the U.S. Commerce Department held up the failed French national champion effort as an example of what other nations ought *not* to do as they struggle to keep up with information technology.[7] It is preferable for other nations to remain dependent on U.S. companies, according to this report, than to try to develop their own computer capability. That seems to be asking for a great deal of trust from those countries in whose eyes the U.S. government and the companies it supports have a checkered record, at best.

$200 million in government subsidies that year. Its president, Jacques Stern, stated that current levels of government support were inadequate and that unless additional funds were made available, the company would go bankrupt. He sought $550 million in government support for 1983 alone but stated that even with that much aid, profitability would be unachievable until 1986.[8] CII-HB's low profits have been matched by a low market share.

As might be expected, CII-HB and other European national champions have successfully increased their shares of the data processing business in their respective government and state-owned enterprises. But CII-HB, now known as Groupe Bull, is hardly competitive outside the public sector, let alone internationally. By 1980 the company not only earned less profits in France than IBM's French subsidiary, but it employed fewer people: only 16,120, compared with IBM's payroll of 20,596. Finally, France's trade deficit in computer equipment had not decreased in the slightest as a result of the CII-HB efforts: it grew from only $19 million in 1976 to $386 million in 1981. Nevertheless, France perseveres. A five-year electronics plan slated to end in 1987 calls for investing a total of $26 billion in electronics, a major part of which will go for computer equipment.

Plan Calcul was no success, but before discarding altogether the notion of government support for local companies battling IBM, we must consider another of its implementations, this one by Japan. The results have been remarkably more positive than those experienced by France.

JAPAN

The Japanese, living on small, crowded islands with limited natural resources and no fossil fuels of their own, are determined to capture a significant share of the computer industry in order to shift their economy away from energy-intensive manufacturing to the cleaner, higher-growth information industry.

"Through its ability to promote the development of systems in other industrial fields," a 1977 Japanese government White Paper stated, "the computer industry also constitutes a strategic tool which assists in the realization of a more sophisticated industrial structure for the nation.... [The] computer industry has an economic effect beyond the borders of the industry itself.... [It] will make a great future contribution to the nation as one of its leading industries."[9] It seemed a straightforward calculation and an appropriate direction for the country to move.

Japan has a long history of interaction with IBM. IBM Japan is the single largest and oldest non-Japanese investment there. Japan Watson Business Machines Company was set up before World War II to market punch card machinery, and in 1949 it became the wholly-owned subsidiary IBM Japan. IBM

Japan first began building products in 1960, and by the 1970s it was building several 370 and System/3 processors, disk drives, and other peripherals. Additional products are built by IBM Japan now, some of them designed in that country primarily for Asian markets.

Beginning in the mid-1960s, the Japanese government set a goal that its domestic electronics companies be internationally competitive in computers. Almost every year, beginning in 1968, the Japan Information Processing Development Center published a report on the state of the Japanese computer industry. These White Papers, as they are known, focused heavily on the perceived threat of IBM (and other foreign suppliers) and the various measures taken to protect the Japanese market and bolster its fledgling industry.

"The Japanese Government, for its part, placed a considerable importance on the information industry from a very early stage and has not only instituted measures for promoting the development of the electronic industry with private capital but has also attempted to protect the industry from excessive external pressures by placing restrictions on the import of capital, equipment and technology," stated the 1977 White Paper. It went on to identify three reasons why Japan and other industrial nations have been compelled to intervene on behalf of their domestic computer industries: "(1) a desire to find wider world markets as a way of escaping from the oppressive influence within the country of IBM and the other U.S. manufacturers. . . . (2) an awareness by the individual countries that it will [be] impossible for them to create adequately informationalized societies without computer industries of their own and (3) a realization that it would be impossible to take advantage of the anticipated sharp demand for computers in the future, as under the previous set-up it was not possible to compete either technologically or financially with the giant IBM."[10]

The first task for Japan, as it was for the French, was to protect its domestic firms. Japan took a different approach to the problem, however, by backing not a single national champion but three. These were actually three pairs of companies, Nippon Electric-Toshiba, Fujitsu-Hitachi, and Mitsubishi-Oki, which were slated in 1971 to compete with each other as well as with IBM and other foreign manufacturers. The idea was that insisting on competition among companies would keep each healthier than if they were merged into a single national champion. That health would benefit Japanese markets by low prices—thereby increasing computer usage and with it the efficiency of all Japanese industry—as well as by giving the entire Japanese computer industry a better chance of battling IBM and its 370 system in world markets.

Just as these three groups were being formed and their activities coordinated "as a means of coping with the impending liberalization of trade and capital," the worldwide recession of 1971 hit—it was severe enough to put a dent even in IBM's growth. IBM at that time was also facing its most active competition in the compatible peripherals market, an arena the Japanese companies had also eyed. The recession, however, made 1971 an "eventful and arduous" year for Japanese computer makers, the 1977 White Paper stated.[11] Those companies were now girding for all-out "combat in rough seas" to defend the penetration of foreign markets that they had won in the "back-yard battles" experienced so far. To help out, their government provided substantial aid. It covered half of the expenses required to develop a new line of computers "fully capable of meeting the challenge of the IBM 370 Series" and related terminal and peripheral equipment.[12]

As the 1970s progressed, the Japanese market officially became more open to computer imports from the United States and other countries. In 1975, the government had faith, however, that its trio of champions could "stand on its own and continue to grow" but that growth would hinge on the [Japanese] industry's ability to secure an appropriate share of the domestic market."

On top of the nagging recession and the continuing pressures from the United States to relax import barriers, the Japanese computer industry faced several other obstacles. It suffered the consequences of the dollar's devaluation relative to gold in 1971, which effectively lowered the prices on IBM and other U.S.-made computers. At the same time, IBM was beginning to ship virtual memory 370s. To compensate, the Japanese were forced to accelerate their own 370-generation development efforts just as they were beginning to ship 360-generation machines. As the decade proceeded, IBM began to make its unprecedented price cuts on many processors and peripherals to fend off the Memorexes and Amdahls of the world. All in all, the Japanese manufacturers were "put in tight circumstances," as the White Paper tells it.

Continuing deficits in the U.S. balance of payments to Japan and pressure from IBM and other domestic suppliers prompted further pressure by the U.S. government on Japan to ease its import restrictions. According to the 1977 Japanese White Paper, the United States "strongly" requested that Japan increase U.S. computer imports, use more imported U.S. machines in government offices, and reduce U.S. import duties on imported mainframes and peripherals. The Japanese began to feel that they were being singled out for particularly harsh treatment and that Washington was leaning on them to open its market to U.S. computer makers to a degree not experienced by any other country. Washington's explanation was that the United States was running a large trade balance deficit with the Japanese due to the latter's massive exports of automobiles, steel, and consumer electronics.

But Washington's position is not without irony, for at the same time as it was pushing for easier imports of computer systems, it was also pushing the Japanese to relax its restrictions on U.S. firms investing in Japan. The result was that goods for the Japanese market would be built by Japanese labor in these U.S.-

owned plants, rather than in the United States and exported to the Japanese market. The most important of these U.S.-owned plants, naturally, were IBM's. Despite the fact that in 1980 IBM had a larger share of the value of installed computers than any of the three state-backed Japanese computer manufacturers, the Japanese government acquiesced to Washington's demands and further reduced restrictions on computer imports. More than the United States, Japan needs international trade to prosper. Access to the large U.S. market is critical. When pushed, and as long as the price is not too high, Japan has yielded to U.S. pressures, at least officially, in order to retain access to U.S. markets.

Despite the many obstacles, Japan has gained a great deal since its three champions stood up to IBM. By 1984, the country could confidently claim that it was "now the only country in the world other than the United States that has its own electronic computer industry. . . . Production of computer equipment has been growing at 15–25% per year. At this rate, the computer industry is expected to grow to become Japan's leading industry."[13] Certainly its industry had fared better than any of those in Europe, particularly that in France, where losses continue to mount each year. (And as we shall see later, Japan's push against IBM in computers enabled it to drub U.S. semiconductor suppliers, whose competitive weakness is largely attributable to the IBM monopoly.)

The top four suppliers in the Japanese data processing market (composed of a wide range of products and services) have roughly equal shares of the business. This contrasts sharply with the worldwide pattern in which IBM gains 60 to 70 percent of each local market and its next nearest competitor has only about a tenth of that. Note also in Table 43 that after 1978, IBM moved from first to second place.

When classified by computer system size, United States suppliers' share of the Japanese computer market is strongest in large-scale systems. In 1981, for ex-

Table 43

Total Data Processing Revenues of Firms in Japan, 1976–84
(in millions of yen)[14]

	1976	1977	1978	1979	1980	1981	1982	1983	1984
Japan IBM	2,755	2,938	3,153	3,242	3,383	4,288	4,849	6,122	7,688
Fujitsu	2,396	2,745	3,030	3,268	3,821	4,484	5,322	6,613	8,573
NEC	1,140	1,376	1,669	2,008	2,404	3,325	4,247	5,203	6,620
Hitachi	1,420	1,600	1,900	2,160	2,500	2,880	3,620	4,430	5,320
Toshiba	592	591	430	504	803	950	1,405	1,830	2,315
Oki	438	444	470	628	788	1,091	1,304	1,648	1,850
Mitsubishi	320	380	450	530	620	730	940	1,300	1,650
Japan Univac	704	678	716	736	786	909	1,037	1,075	1,215
Burroughs	435	450	470	546	505	573	607	667	807
NCR	343	369	343	343	482	496	585	612	696

ample, in the large-scale systems category, U.S. suppliers—led by IBM—had 64.3 percent of the value of systems installed in Japan. In the next three smaller categories, U.S. vendors held respective shares of 42.7, 40.9, and 22.5 percent. And where government intervention in computer procurements was not a factor, IBM's share was even higher. The Japanese effort was most effective only where other competitors to IBM had also been most effective—in midrange and smaller systems.

Most of the growth in computer mainframes has taken place within the large-scale category. Their installed value almost doubled between 1974 and 1976. Here is another pattern found in the United States and other national markets: Where growth is highest, the Japanese have been least effective and have the lowest market share. In 1976, the average large-size system produced by Japanese firms was valued at only 897 million yen, compared with 1,108 million yen for systems made by non-Japanese companies.[15] (Part of the limited Japanese success at the high end was due, of course, to Amdahl, which was backed by and shared technology with Fujitsu; yet Amdahl never would have resorted to Japanese backing had a U.S. company taken interest in its plans.)

As in the U.S. market, the large-scale systems category is the most important in Japan. Though those systems represent only 3.2 percent of the total installed computer units in Japan, they account for 56.5 percent of the total value; the smallest categories make up 56 percent of the units, but account for only 7.5 percent of the total value.

Japan's success to this point has been primarily at home. In 1984, the largest exporter of computers from Japan was IBM Japan. In units of 100 million yen, it exported 2,232, compared with 1,700 for Fujitsu and 1,037 for Hitachi. Using Australia as a nearby English-speaking test market to prepare its assault on the U.S. market, Fujitsu had its Australian marketing arm, FACOM, offer a line of IBM 370-compatible computers there. Even though FACOM has spent heavily during the past decade to win market share, having lost a total of over $50 million by fiscal 1982, IBM's market share in Australia has actually increased. While the share of the wide range of computer products and services held by all Japanese computer companies in Australia rose from 2 to 14 percent in the five years ending in 1984, IBM's share rose from 33.9 percent in 1980 to 34.4 percent in 1982. Other U.S. systems companies, such as Burroughs, Sperry Rand, NCR, Control Data, and Honeywell, lost 6.2 points of market share in three of those years alone, writes William H. Davidson in *The Amazing Race*.[16] Finally, the leading Australian computer maker, Hartley Ltd., failed completely in 1982, filing for bankruptcy.

In the U.S. market, the total shipments from all Japanese companies in 1984—often for inclusion in systems put together by U.S. companies—constituted only 13.8 percent, according to IDC. Sales of Japanese-manufactured central processors in the United States accounted for only 2.8 percent of all mainframe processors in 1984.[17] When Nippon Electric-Toshiba chief executive Koji Kobayashi was asked at the end of 1985 if he could compete with IBM in the United States, his reply was, "Impossible. . . . Capitalwise IBM is gigantic. Japanese companies are very small. It's silly to try to compete with IBM with their huge amounts of money. IBM has established a complete monopoly all over the world. We are only trying to protect ourselves from such a gigantic monopoly company."[18]

In fact, his conclusion is not so different from that of John Akers, president and chief executive of IBM. He claimed several months later that "We're investing for the long term. We don't think anyone [will be able to] touch us," and "I don't care who you are in this industry. No one can compete with the IBM company."[19]

SEMICONDUCTORS

IBM's overwhelming strength in computers, as we have seen, is enabling it to make strong inroads into communications markets because much communications gear attaches in some way to its mainframes. IBM's growing power also threatens businesses that depend on its systems for their competitiveness. But the pervasive effects of IBM's computer monopoly are not limited to those closely related areas. In fact, the company's power has had negative effects in other high-technology markets where it is only minimally involved and where its influence is generally overlooked. The most seriously hurt of these IBM-damaged industries is the U.S. semiconductor industry.

As many people know, U.S. semiconductor companies in recent years have been drubbed by their Japanese competitors. However, their failure has not been adequately explained. The true villain has been IBM, whose computer monopoly has damaged U.S. companies that once enjoyed a wide lead in the fast-paced chip race. In short, Japanese electronics firms, in their drive to establish strength in the all-important semiconductor business, have swung at IBM, missed the computer giant, and ultimately decked U.S. chip makers. Perhaps nowhere can the negative side effects of IBM's ill-gained monopoly be seen so clearly.

Popular explanations for the recent Japanese success in memory chips fall way short of the mark. It has not been the Japanese government's lavish support of native chip makers that has enabled them to win practically the entire memory market. U.S. chip companies have also been showered with government money, usually in the form of military research-and-development contracts.

As the semiconductor business matured during the last ten years or so, there came a radical change in the optimum corporate structure needed to stay economically efficient and globally competitive. Only Japanese chip companies have successfully evolved into this new form, while U.S. companies have, due to IBM's dominance of the computer market, remained in outdated, increasingly vulnerable positions. Initially, semiconductor technology was so fruitful, and the potential applications for it so plentiful, that the freewheeling and innovative independent chip manufacturer was the preferred vehicle for commercial success. Moreover, since creative engineers and managers could capitalize on new areas of unmet demand by leaving one company and forming their own specialty firms, there was an abundance of entrepreneurial activity in such places as Silicon Valley in Northern California. Many millions of dollars were made from chips in the late 1960s and early 1970s by relatively small companies carving out niches for themselves. But then things began to change.

As chip technology improved, the small producers became less viable in relation to companies that were larger and, by necessity, more vertically integrated. The model for success became the producer that sold not just chips but a wide range of chip-based products as well. Only that kind of company could afford the rapidly escalating expenses needed to keep up with the accelerating improvements in chip technology. Before long, most of the easy discoveries had been made, and survival became a matter of investing huge amounts of money in perfecting fabrication techniques and mass producing chips. The chip supplier that operated as part of a larger company could use profits from nonchip products to subsidize these investments. Pure chip markets began to take on the characteristics of a classic commodity market. Memory chips from one company were technically equivalent, for the most part, to those from other suppliers. What primarily distinguished one supplier's chips from another's was price and quick delivery.

The broad-based supplier enjoyed several other advantages over his more narrowly focused competitors. Before long, prices for commodity chips were driven down, chip profits slimmed, and only companies that sold distinct noncommodity items could continue to make the substantial financial investments needed to keep pace. The technology also lent itself increasingly to exploitation by vertically integrated suppliers. As the density of circuits on chips grew, more of the value of chip-based products came to reside in the chips themselves, so much so, in fact, that the very nature of the final product was increasingly determined by the chip's capability. That meant that to keep his final product competitive, a manufacturer needed to gain greater control over the critical chip production process. When the chip and the final product are made by the same company, the maximum advantage can be had from any improvements in the entire production cycle. More important are the speed-to-market advantages that accrue to the vertically integrated chip supplier. The race is to the swift.

The free-standing company, making chips and only chips, is tied to the boom-and-bust cycle of the semiconductor industry. When revenues and profits soften, as they do periodically, broad-based companies enjoy continuing profits from countercyclical markets and can always keep pumping money into research and development in preparation for the next generation of chip technology. Independent chip companies cannot afford to invest comparably. In the end, the chip game is one of resources—the more the better.

Before Japanese chip makers arrived in the United States in force, as they did beginning in the mid-1970s in the commodity memory chip market, the fundamental structural flaw in the U.S. semiconductor industry remained hidden. The Japanese companies were, by design it turns out, more vertically integrated, and they soon gained the upper hand over U.S. suppliers, whose attempts at vertical integration had been severely hindered by the growing IBM monopoly.

The notion that the U.S. chip industry is suboptimally structured flies directly in the face of much conventional wisdom. It is generally thought that free, unfettered market forces will reallocate resources—i.e., restructure the industry—as capital searches for maximum return on investment. This process evidently has not taken place, but why?

The earliest and most important demand for semiconductors has come from the computer industry, where IBM is dominant. What is rarely mentioned in the heated policy discussions concerning the failed U.S. chip industry is that IBM makes most of its own semiconductors—in fact, it is the largest chip maker in the world. By virtue of its computer monopoly and its in-house chip production, IBM has had to itself much of the demand from which U.S. chip makers might have profited during the past fifteen years or so.* All attempts by the chip makers to branch into computers themselves have been thwarted; similarly, demand for their products from the rest of the computer industry, all of which has been stunted by IBM's monopoly, has been severely diminished. If the IBM computer monopoly did not distort their markets, the U.S. chip suppliers would surely have become more vertically integrated and would have been better able to defend their once-substantial lead against foreign competition.

There is more. Not only was the demand foreclosed to them by IBM's reliance on its own chip facilities, but there was much about the nature of the demand that they were denied that has left them chronically vulnerable. At any given moment in the progression of chip technology, there has been a wide spectrum of chips to be made for different applications. Always, mainframe computer

---

* In a memo dated August 9, 1971, IBM's F. T. Cary notified IBM executives that "the Corporation has concluded that to have true leadership in the future IBM must utilize to the fullest, a proprietary FET/LSI technology. To this end the following is effective immediately . . . We will use only in-house FET [Field-Effect Transistor—a type of semiconductor] technology and cease all activities with the merchant semiconductor industry in this area."[20] This was at a time when IBM's costs were "inordinately higher"[21] than these outside suppliers.

processors, of which the System/370 is the most prevalent example, have been the most demanding application of chips, requiring the fastest and densest of chips. Other digital devices, such as toys and even powerful minicomputers, have gotten by with slower and less capable chips, but the mainframe has always been able to use all the performance that chip technology can provide. Only the mainframe has been able to translate excess chip performance directly into economic gain. Therefore, there were great incentives for those wishing to build mainframe computers to push the state of the art in semiconductors as fast as possible.

Yet the structure of the computer industry had dire consequences for the chip industry. Because IBM kept most of the large mainframe business to itself, there was less incentive for chip companies to invest in advanced research and development. Instead, they sought more promising markets, those that were not monopolized but that were less demanding technologically. As a result, when Gene Amdahl decided to build his 370-compatible mainframe, he could not interest U.S. chip companies in helping him—he could not promise them enough volume to make it worth their while to tool up to build his highly advanced chips.

Japanese companies saw things differently, especially after they decided in the early 1970s to take on IBM face to face in the mainframe business. They foresaw that to be successful against the long-awaited IBM FS product line, they would need a timely supply of the most advanced semiconductors possible. "Japan is acutely aware of the urgent necessity to develop an electronic computer capable of meeting the challenge of the FS," a Japanese government report stated. "The basic technological problem in the development of a comparable computer lies in the development of the large-scale integrated circuits having greater density and speed than today's [chips]. It is with this purpose in mind that, starting in fiscal '76, there has been set up a program . . . under which a technological research association participated in by five of the nation's computer manufacturers is given aid to cover 50% of its research and development expenses."[22]

So began the downfall of the U.S. chip companies. They were vulnerable and directly in the path of the accelerating Japan Inc. The heavy expense of advanced chip development and production, half of which was still being borne by the Japanese mainframe makers, could not be totally recouped by using them in mainframes sold against IBM; instead, the Japanese chip costs would be paid off by selling raw chips as well, and that came entirely at the expense of the exposed U.S. chip suppliers. The Japanese were soon building chips that were often better and less costly than those available from U.S. manufacturers, and they soon swept the market.

Today, Japanese companies supply some 90 percent of the world's standard memory chips, those that are most commoditylike and that lend themselves best to high-volume production. Japanese success in the more differentiated logic chips has been less robust, but there is a fear now among U.S. suppliers that the Japanese will do well there, too.

In their conquest of the memory chip market, Japanese companies have engaged in some quite aggressive pricing, and in the process they have stirred up much resentment from U.S. competitors. But from the Japanese perspective, such pricing only makes good economic sense. Since they are not totally dependent on chip revenues—they have broad product lines with many profitable chip-based products—the Japanese companies can afford to price their chips below their average total cost. Since they were compelled to make a large initial investment as part of their computer business, all they had to recoup in their chip price was a small amount above the incremental costs associated with producing the additional chips for the open chip market. In contrast, the exposed U.S. chip makers, limited in the scope of their products, have been forced to charge prices high enough to cover all their costs. In the end, they could not profitably meet the lower price, and they began to drop out of the commodity chip market altogether. All the while, of course, they have complained bitterly that they were the victims of anticompetitive price discrimination.

The attentive reader will recognize the supreme irony in all this. It would appear that not only were the Japanese companies attempting to match IBM's computer offerings, but they had also learned well the value of IBM's favorite pricing mechanism against what economist Carl Kaysen termed "equally efficient short-line competitors."[23] The many specialized U.S. companies that have fallen victim to just such IBM tactics will surely recognize the similarities.

There is more to this story, however. Owing to its control over the mainframe market, which paces chip technology, IBM should also have been able to diversify and begin selling its own raw chips. But that has not at all been the case. For one thing, to sell such basic components as chips would run counter to the company's policy of never selling pieces of its equipment. Recall that in the 1950s IBM would sell its mainframe competitors only complete unit record machines, even when there was strong demand for raw mechanisms. Denying competitors components has been key to tight control over pricing: "IBM has established the value of data processing usage. IBM then maintains or controls that value by various means . . . [including] refusal to market . . . parts," wrote Hillary Faw in his 1969 memo.

Worse, however, was that even as it hogged the demand for pace-setting mainframe-type chips, IBM was anything but efficient in its manufacturing of the devices. Its way of protecting itself against natural market forces has meant that IBM's own chip-making capability could languish safe from the rigors of the competitive market. During most of the 1970s and the early 1980s, IBM's chips were much more expensive and less capable than those available from pure chip makers. That is a major reason why the company was forced to bundle memory (built from chips) with its central processors. It was also IBM's inefficiency in chip production that helped Amdahl remain competitive—his chips, built in Japan, were much less expensive to make and faster than IBM's, to boot. Amdahl passed his savings on to its customers.

IBM's chief scientist, Lewis Branscomb, wondered in a 1975 memo "why our [chip] manufacturing costs are projected to be roughly equivalent to the merchant [chip] industry's selling price. . . . [We] are not in a leadership position."[24] Even as it competed in a business with significant economies of scale and as it garnered most of the business for itself, IBM was unable to match the economies achieved by far smaller chip-only competitors. Having to earn profits without the benefit of a monopoly and having to face the aggressive Japanese chip suppliers, they were always more efficient than IBM.

Even if IBM had had competitively costed chips to sell, IBM would have been unable to earn its traditional rates of profit with the chip market so highly competitive. The company therefore saw little economic benefit. Moreover, entering the chip business would have exacerbated its antitrust problems. Were IBM to drive free-standing chip companies out of the market through aggressive pricing, those companies would most likely have raised a political stink. Better to have the Japanese do that job for IBM, enabling IBM to enter the chip market later as the U.S. savior. Indeed, rumors are circulating that that is exactly what IBM will do shortly.

The upshot of the IBM-inflamed, trans-Pacific chip wars is that trade issues are increasingly tackled as political problems. U.S. semiconductor companies clamor for more support and protection by Washington. Support for advanced research and development gets increased as part of the overall military buildup: "intelligent" weapons need ever-faster and more capable chips. Given this ruse, the support is spread to all companies with the ability to meet Department of Defense requirements. While the Japanese government supported its own electronics companies on the condition that they be commercially viable, and that their domestic market be kept competitive instead of monopolized, the United States doles out money to all that say they can meet Defense Department technical specifications. Naturally, IBM is among those recipients—and the next round of futility begins.

20. Limits of the Empire

We have become a worldwide society of numbers. . . . We define quantity using numbers. We define quality using numbers. . . . We now can reduce everything we do to a number language to be acted upon in machines.

> —Commentary in IBM's Madison Avenue museum of calculating machines

If society continues to perceive itself increasingly in terms of information, "reducing everything" to an intangible but nevertheless valuable stuff that can be produced by machines here, made to flow there, and processed, stored, and sold according to the economic laws of scarcity, the company that controls the technology for performing those tasks stands to gain enormous power over us all. IBM, as the previous chapters have shown, has overcome all competition in the data processing market. The methods that have given it such great commercial success so far will be just as useful in the future for it to conquer the vast array of emerging information-related markets.

Consideration of IBM's growing economic and political power is rare in current discussions of this "information age" we are said to be entering, but a full understanding of this historical moment requires that the IBM phenomenon and its dire implications be grasped fully. Judging by the statements IBM makes to investors and to the public, it sees no bounds to its continued expansion. All that can be defined as "information" seems fair game.

What follows is an informed speculation as to the directions that that expansion is likely to take, and how IBM will exploit its current data processing monopoly to get there. Key to this analysis is the idea that IBM is seeking to capture the high ground in the worldwide communications market, just as it has in computers. From that position, and a further entrenchment in computing, will flow power in potentially every market that depends on interconnected computers—from telephones to robotics, from publishing to genetic engineering, from entertainment to banking, from education to public administration.

IBM, THE GLOBAL TELEPHONE COMPANY

Soon IBM will become the first—and likely the only—worldwide telephone company. Working from its monopoly in computers and its growing strength in telecommunications, it will begin providing telephone services throughout the world and connecting people together on much the same scale as it now connects computers.

IBM the global phone company? Preposterous idea. Impossible. After all, AT&T is the undisputed world leader in communications. And all the nations of the world already have their own politically approved telephone monopolies in place. Besides, IBM makes its money processing data, not selling telephones or moving calls between them.

All true, but given the company's aggressive goals for future growth, its solid ties with virtually every substantial corporation in the world, and its freedom to price discriminate across whatever boundaries it encounters, IBM the telephone company seems much more than just likely—it seems inevitable.

To see how easy it will be for IBM, above all others, to establish the dominant global communications network, we need consider a few basic facts. IBM's business continues to rely heavily on a relatively few large corporations in the world—no more than a few thousand—for most of its growth and profits. These companies' operations are dispersed throughout the world—a factory here, a marketing branch there—and each seeks to maximize its overall efficiency by integrating its international activities through telecommunications networks that carry all sorts of traffic: data, voice, video, and facsimile. Although each and every international office will not get its own mainframe computer, each will have telephones, and most will have Telex terminals and small computers. As the complexities of global-scale business grow, corporate activities come to depend ever more heavily on the different networks of these various communications devices. So much so, in fact, that there comes a point where it becomes economically compelling to combine all networks into one. Costs are reduced, performance and function are boosted, and control is enhanced. An illustration on a recent Citicorp annual report boasts not of bedrock money vaults or of smiling tellers but of the communications satellite that forms the heart of a global Citicorp network.

To be sure, not all transnational companies can justify having their own satellites, but all want to avoid the headaches and expense of linking machines across national boundaries. As things stand today, each of the world's telephone companies is its own empire, a state-approved monopoly company that tightly controls communications within and across its national boundaries. What international telecommunications treaties and agreements there are have done little to erase the differences among each country's pricing, network interfaces, and range of services. Each country's telephone service is unto itself, shielded since its earliest days from technological and regulatory advances elsewhere and purposely kept different from others. In the face of such diversity, IBM the global telephone company would surely be welcomed by large corporations that, don't forget, are already the heaviest users of IBM computers and related networking products.

IBM could conceivably eliminate the hassles of running multinational telecommunications networks by providing much-needed services at prices lower than those charged by local phone companies. If problems arose in a customer's international network, he would have to make only one call, to IBM, rather than hunt down the problems from country to country, vendor to vendor. Transcending national boundaries, as it is already attempting to do with a series of well-placed communications satellites, IBM would become a one-stop shop for all sorts of telecommunications gear and services. It could piggyback voice, video, and other communications channels on its firmly anchored data networks—all types of electronic communications can be reduced to digital form and are thus easily moved from computer to computer.

IBM has already taken many steps toward this goal. It has helped many of its big U.S customers build multipurpose networks on a national scale. There seems to be nothing to stop IBM from helping them expand internationally. In 1984, IBM paid $1.25 billion to purchase Rolm, Inc., a leading maker of small communications switches. Then in late 1985, IBM dropped broad hints that it would soon enter the telephone central switch market as part of an effort to "double" its sales of telecommunications gear in Europe. It also invested heavily in MCI, a long-distance telephone carrier. It has worked closely with Motorola and the Public Broadcasting System to establish a nationwide network of radio links in the United States. Meanwhile, throughout the world, IBM and its agents are lobbying intensely for rapid deregulation of local telephone monopolies.

An international telecommunications network would greatly expand IBM's power. IBM could change network interfaces and exclude competitive computer equipment as it desired, thus limiting other equipment vendors' competitiveness. Once its global network was sufficiently established, there would be an irresistible attraction for even corporations using non-IBM computer systems to attach to it—if only to make efficient links to other companies' computers—and eventually do all their data processing with IBM systems. IBM could bundle communications with data processing into a singly priced service offering, thus once again enjoying the benefits of a lease-oriented business. The possibilities seem unlimited.

And scary, to the world's many phone companies. They rely on the same large commercial enterprises as IBM does for most of their profits, and they don't want to miss out on data communications as a major growth market. Once IBM was able to service those large customers in a way that nationally confined telephone companies could not, the latter would begin to lose that high-profit commercial business while still being obligated to provide telephone service to low-profit residential customers. IBM, of course, would escape all such obligations.

Nora and Minc, the French critics of IBM, coined a new word for the combination of computer and communications technologies—*telematique,* or telematics. They fear IBM's leveraging its way from data processing to communications: "Since the appearance of the first computers, data processing has become a strategic sector in most countries; conscious of the specific character of its raw material—information—governments quickly became interested in this industry. In fact, since 1945 few areas except the atom have received such close government scrutiny; this vigilance was an expression of the wish to limit American domination, stronger here than in any other area. Governments devoted major means to this end, each following a strategy in conformity with its own temperament."[1]

It was, the Frenchmen continue, "a battle aimed first and foremost at IBM because of its dominance of computer manufacturing. Today the challenge is different—IBM is going beyond data processing, and the stakes, the field of battle, and the nature of competition have changed." IBM "dominates the sector expected to undergo the greatest development in the coming decades—data will continue to expand in tomorrow's society, and data processing and later telematics will accompany it. IBM is entrenched, if not alone at least with such reserves of power that it cannot be seriously threatened. Unlike the petroleum groups, it is menaced neither by suppliers who would catch up with it from behind, nor by cartel partners whose solidarity does not exclude rivalry, nor by the uncertainties and hindrances experienced by all the conglomerates."

French national policy, Nora and Minc continue, "has to take into account the renewal of the IBM challenge. Once a manufacturer of machines, soon to become a telecommunications administrator, IBM is following a strategy that will enable it to set up a communications network and to control it. When it does, it will encroach upon a traditional sphere of government power, communications."

To understand the great advantages IBM holds over all the world's telephone monopolies—including the giant AT&T, which was until recently the U.S. telephone monopoly—requires a comparison of its structure to theirs. In most countries, the telephone authority (usually known as a Postal, Telephone & Telegraph, or PTT) is considered to be a "natural" monopoly and either is an arm of the government or is at least held politically accountable through some sort of regulation. But no matter what the method of control is, the purpose of such regulation is to ensure sufficient revenues to cover the necessary costs while at the same time achieving political and social goals. IBM, on the other hand, is not officially perceived to be a monopolist and has avoided all regulation. It is free to do as it pleases.

Once governmental supervision is in place, other interventions are possible. Often there is a belief that by tampering with the natural monopolist's pricing—i.e., by systematically discriminating between different classes of customer—the total value of the service may be improved relative to what would result from purely cost-based pricing. In theory, everyone benefits from such governmental tampering. As the regulators transfer funds from one part of the monopoly to another, its overall profits are kept stable, enabling the average price paid by the majority of subscribers (i.e., residential customers) to be kept low.

This same pricing pattern has been in place throughout the world for decades, although the degree of discrimination varies by locale. In Japan, for example, the prices of long-distance calls in 1985 were forty times higher than underlying costs would dictate, while in the United States the comparable factor was only six. In Europe, to take another example, the monthly rental for a private, 10-kilometer voice circuit, typically used by business customers, varies from $129 in West Germany to only $24 in Sweden.[2] These price differences are the result not so much of different costs but rather of different discrimination formulas being applied to achieve different political goals. Incidentally, politicians have benefited greatly from this price discrimination in communications services, for they can, through manipulation of the regulation mechanism, impose a tax on one set of constituents—often the nonvoting businesses of the country—to improve telephone service for, and win votes from, the much larger set of residential customers.

After decades, this clever system has begun to break down under pressure from rapid advancements in telecommunications technology. Microwave and satellite-based transmission links, to name two important technical developments, offered long-distance communications at costs well below those typical of traditional copper wire, and they increasingly became available beyond the PTTs' monopoly control. Stuck with miles of comparatively costly terrestrial wires and expensive rights-of-ways, PTTs could not match the new equipment's low costs and therefore could not deliver competitively priced services. Yet protecting phone companies from these more efficient competitive alternatives only increased the inefficiency of this basic industry. So movements to remove the PTTs' status as natural monopolies began.

The old order also began to crumble as computers and communications technologies converged, primarily through widespread use of digitization. Market boundaries began to blur. An example of this change was the so-called private branch exchange, or PBX—a minicomputer-based switch to handle telephone calls within a single building or a campus. By off-loading work from the telephone company's large central switches, the PBX has changed the economics of telephone pricing. In obviating the need for making a normal local phone call, PBXs save businesses much of the money that used to go to the PTTs. A host of companies entered the PBX market during the 1970s, including Northern Telecom of Canada, Rolm in the United States, and TIE and Nippon Electric-Toshiba in Japan. Even IBM built a series of PBXs, one of which it marketed (with little success) in Europe.

These technological changes resulted in governments' finding it impossible to oversee the PTTs effectively. Changes began to happen too fast, and the issues were too complex to be dealt with by the established regulatory agencies. Governments had to decide who could compete in this important business, under what conditions, and—if PTTs were to be permitted to compete—at what prices. For example, the PTTs' big central switches were coming to be based on computers, and they could now deliver services comparable to those delivered by PBXs.

These difficult problems were exacerbated by the increasing use by commercial organizations of interactive computer networks. Computers were exchanging messages with other computers, remote terminals, and a broad range of other devices, and that meant added traffic on what were once relatively simple telephone networks. The attractiveness of a particular interactive application was determined not only by the cost of the computer system and terminals but also by the cost of connecting them together. It has been this high-volume commercial usage of its network that was traditionally discriminated against and that therefore earned the PTTs most of their profits. Naturally, those services were most attractive for new competitors to attack.

Meanwhile, so-called value-added networks (VANs) were being built, not only to move data but to process it on the way: incompatible messages could be translated from one vendor's format to another, or stored for later recall, or distributed automatically to many destinations. Constant monitoring by regulators of each price change that PTTs seek in their continual competitive struggles to retain their presences in high-growth, digital communications markets has become next to impossible.

Technological changes and the new service options they have made possible have naturally appealed most to large customers, which pay the most to the telephone companies and are most able to afford the hefty initial investments of purchasing more of their own equipment. Increasing numbers of large U.S. corporations, for example, have begun to unplug from AT&T and its former affiliates and are installing private communications networks. Once the proper equipment became available, large customers were able to bypass all or part of the telephone company's network and, to a large degree, escape its discriminatory pricing. They have brought in their own satellite antennas, communications switches, and even microwave towers—thereby saving bundles, compared with using AT&T, or even one of its long-distance competitors, for all communications.

The existing order in communications has been undercut not only by the technology but also by economic factors. For example, underlying the telephone companies' price discrimination has been the assumption that all commercial organizations should be affected equally. That is, price discrimination in communications had no effect on the competitive process within a country, since the "tax" it imposed was at the same rate for all commercial customers. No customer gained a significant advantage over the other. Once bypass technologies became viable, however, large companies gained a competitive advantage over small ones, for the latter could not afford their own networks and evade the telephone company's price discrimination. The result is that small companies have been gradually forced, unfairly they claim, to cover more than their share of the costs incurred by low-profit, residential customers. Large companies that bypass the PTTs avoid such "taxation."

By the same token, traditional PTT pricing policies threaten to degrade the competitiveness of entire nations as they strive to shift from heavy industry to the information-intensive, service-oriented industries of the future. Services such as banking and insurance depend heavily on communications for their value, and any nation stuck with uncompetitive communications pricing is likely to lose ground in the emerging global services market. A service supplier being charged too much for communications in one country may decide to boost investments in places where communications is priced closer to cost. Yet to reverse decades of history and move to cost-based pricing would mean trouble for the PTTs and their governments. To compensate for lost profits from commercial subscribers, they are forced to raise prices for the subsidized residential subscribers—hardly an attractive path for most politicians.

Into this complex mix of technology, economics, and politics has stepped IBM. It occupies the high ground. Not only is it wealthy and free of regulation, but its main business is to provide worldwide service to high-volume commercial customers. Additionally, communications is of major importance to the company, both in the United States and abroad, for its use encourages hardware and software sales: the more computers can be made to communicate with each other, the busier they can be kept and the more often customers will upgrade them. So it is no surprise to see IBM, along with those large customers it depends on, pressure the world's PTTs either to change their pricing and provide better, lower-priced services for commercial use or simply to let IBM provide communications services as well as computer systems wherever needed.

And IBM will prevail, for it holds significant advantages. It is less constrained by the peculiarities of each country's network and can eventually offer international data communications links that are optimized for use with its 370 computer line. Parochial interests restrict the abilities of the PTTs and prevent them from confronting IBM across the global front. IBM has systems installed worldwide that can absorb great development costs and provide it with functional leverage into new markets. Its largest customers will surely take advantage of its global communications offerings, when they become available, and leave the PTTs to tend to low-profit residential and small business customers.

Ironically, it seems, IBM the unregulated monopolist is becoming the champion of unfettered competition, of more cost-based pricing in communications, and of breaking the power of telephone monopolies everywhere. The ill-fated governments of the world may fight rearguard actions—by putting up obstacles to the free flow of data across their borders and favoring local suppliers with contracts—but they will risk leaving their major corporate customers exposed to more efficient foreign competition in the most important service markets of the future.

Alternatively, foreign nations can accept the inevitable and join IBM instead of fighting it. Not only would that lower the direct expense of supporting their local computer companies, but it would also ensure that local banks and other service suppliers are not burdened with relatively inefficient non-IBM communications. IBM has a wide range of sweeteners with which to placate obstinate PTTs and foreign governments. It can purchase equipment from local suppliers—which it did to the tune of almost $2 billion in 1984[3] from over 50,000 suppliers just in Europe—as well as invest in local plant and make cooperative arrangements with local schools, research centers, and companies.

Of course, no matter what deals it offers the nations of the world, IBM's success in global communications requires that it actually have the necessary productivity-enhancing computer and communications systems its customer-partners need. As we've seen, the company's communications marketing record leaves much to be desired. Besides ignoring customers' desires with its deliberately perverse 3705 controller, it failed several times to build a marketable PBX product. In the end, IBM was forced to shop around for an entire PBX company and ended up paying a premium price for Rolm. Most telling, however, are the company's great difficulties in getting its unreasonably diverse set of incompatible computer families to communicate effectively with each other.

But even if it takes IBM years or even decades to get its communications act together—recall that it took IBM many years to make the OS operating system work properly—it still stands to win the global communications market against all foreseeable challengers. It will continue to monopolize the central hubs of future networks, the large-scale 370 mainframes, and that will give it profits and powerful leverage with which to improve its research and development of communications products (particularly software) and buy whatever else it needs.

IBM can marshal other resources. Simply by publishing more information than usual about certain interfaces, it can invite the rest of the industry to design and offer products that enhance any of its systems that are particularly deficient or that face strong competition. This tactic of making a system's architecture "open" to others was stunningly successful in 1981 when IBM took over the personal computer market from the then-market leader, Apple Computer.

The add-on business that the "open architecture" strategy fosters is not permanently lost to IBM, of course. Once its customers are wedded to the IBM computer system that others have enhanced, and once IBM has designed its own add-on capabilities, it can begin to close the system's architecture to outsiders. A subsequent variation of the original system may be designed to preserve customers' software investment even as it closes the door to others trying to attach products. IBM can begin withholding critical interface information that the outsiders need and limit customers' choices to its own high-priced products.

To be successful in its quest to become the dominant global communications carrier, IBM will, of course, have to best its U.S. rival, AT&T. Even divested of its local Bell operating companies, AT&T remains the largest telephone company in the world, possessing substantial technical and financial resources. Like IBM, it receives most of its revenues from a relatively small number of large organizations. Moreover, of all the world's communications companies, AT&T promises eventually to suffer the least from government interference in its management. The question arises, therefore, as to whether IBM will be able to dominate the all-important U.S. commercial communications market. Only by winning the United States can IBM hope to win the rest of the world.

IBM holds several advantages over AT&T. IBM alone has a strong worldwide presence, cultivated over the years with the world's largest companies. Only since it was divested of its local operating companies has AT&T started to market abroad—and that without much success. IBM had revenues of $46 billion in 1984, compared with $33 billion for AT&T that year. More telling, IBM's profits were $6.6 billion, while AT&T earned only $1.4 billion. IBM, the most profitable company in the world, earned profit at a rate of 14.3 cents per revenue dollar, more than three times AT&T's closer-to-average rate of 4.2 cents per dollar. Worse still, almost half—46.7 percent—of AT&T's profits came from supplying long-distance services, and another fifth (21.7 percent) came from equipment rented to customers. Both those areas are still subject to regulatory scrutiny and are subject to intensifying competition. Profit levels are likely to erode even further. IBM, by contrast, gets about half its revenues from large computer systems, split evenly between processors (with memory) and peripherals; both those areas seem secure against dwindling competition and will show increasing profits.[4] At least as important is the fact that IBM is also free of all governmental scrutiny, so it can change prices and marketing policies quickly. Each of the companies gets about 10 percent of its business from the other's camp, and each may be losing money on those forays, but IBM alone seems far more able to stay the distance and invest what will be needed to win. It may take IBM time, but that's where the smart money is.

Finally, IBM is still free to price discriminate across whatever market segments it chooses to establish through interface manipulation. In direct contrast, AT&T was divested of its operating companies precisely to prevent it from price discriminating and from denying competitors equal access to critical communications services, namely its vast network. Though IBM relies heavily on both anticompetitive tactics, it has no obligation to defend itself in front of government regulators. AT&T must defend itself so and will therefore be relatively incapacitated. (Appendix J contains excerpts from an IBM filing before the FCC in the 1960s that argues these same points. At that time, the claim was that AT&T had unfair advantages, but now and in the future those advantages will be IBM's alone.)

In striving to beat AT&T at home, IBM will likely appeal to its internationally active customers and develop computer and communications products that give it tremendous momentum in international telematics markets. Only if AT&T and the PTTs can provide foreign businesses with function and performance at least comparable to that available from IBM can they stop IBM. To supply such products, of course, would require unprecedented cooperation between the PTTs in unifying their now-disparate networks as well as the ability to deliver product as quickly as IBM and its school of helpers can. Otherwise, customers will increasingly turn to IBM for connection of their IBM computer systems and for an increasing portion of their overall telecommunications needs. Any nation that resists may well lose more than it gains.

Already, it seems, PTTs have seen the handwriting on the wall and are competing with each other to make the best possible deal they can with IBM. IBM has developed a national videotex system and an automatic telephone information service, called Audi, for the West German PTT. It is working closely with British Telecom. And with Japan's NTT, it is building a value-added network for the Japanese market. It will likely attempt to install the same technology in other nations as well.

All the major computer and communications companies in Japan opposed the NTT deal before it went through—understandably, since they saw it forcing them to compete with a local telephone monopoly as well as with the world's computer monopoly. NTT, some predicted, would soon become a major sales agent for IBM. Indeed, one wonders why NTT and the Japanese government agreed to such a deal. It appears that IBM got some help, however. According to one informed observer, such a joint venture would have been unthinkable just a few years ago, but trade frictions between the United States and Japan were so bothersome in 1985 that the government resistance softened considerably.[5] The

U.S. government, pressured by U.S. semiconductor and communications companies at home, lobbied in Japan to have NTT open its equipment procurements to non-Japanese companies in reciprocation for similar openness in the United States. Significantly, when the door opened, IBM was the first in.

Thus is set a pattern we are likely to see repeated for years to come as Washington goes to bat for its own national champion, IBM. Meanwhile, the company is setting its sights on a broad range of other markets that depend directly on computers and communications.

ON THE HORIZON

In Chapter 11, IBM was compared to an electric utility to illustrate the power a monopolist has when it is free to change key interfaces between its products. As computers are deployed in a widening circle of applications throughout the world's economy, it has here been argued so far, the company that controls computer network interfaces wields great power over what types of devices can be attached to its networks. If the interfaces are constantly changing, as they are in the "evolving" SNA scheme that IBM promotes, competitors face the never-ending, impoverishing task of struggling to keep their systems up to date and IBM-compatible. IBM is relying on this strategy to push its monopoly into every profitable sector of the converging computer and communications businesses.

But IBM's power hardly ends with control over the computer and related information processing equipment markets. That very control is now leading the company to enormous power over its own customers, especially those in service industries that depend so heavily on computer and telecommunications gear—indeed, on information itself—for their competitiveness. If current trends continue, banks, insurance companies, all sorts of financial institutions, medical institutions, publishers, and schools, to name but a few potential victims, will all wake up one day to find IBM's expanding monopoly looming over them and threatening their survival. And because IBM's monopoly in information processing equipment girdles the entire world, is there any wonder that foreign nations are so fearful of its power and strive so hard to limit it? Those nations are caught on the horns of a dilemma: whether it is better to let their domestic economies grow inexorably dependent on IBM computers, and thereby retain access to its latest interfaces, networks, and technology, or to limit its power in some way and risk getting cut out of the IBM-defined networks of the future.

Information technology, including the full range of computers, robots, and data communications networks, promises to be the basic industry of the future. Information technology is fast becoming what steel was for the previous industrial era, an essential input for a wide variety of other businesses that use it to produce goods and services. But imagine what the world would be like had a single U.S. company monopolized the worldwide production of steel. Assume for the sake of argument that the basic processes for making steel had been developed and patented by that company and that competitors were denied use of those patents. They would be forced either to produce using an older metal, iron say, or to leave the business.

What, then, would be the implications of such a monopoly over steel—a much-desired raw material for so many dependent industries? At the very least, the monopolist could charge high prices and command all the market, but that is the least of it. The monopolist could choose between selling its unique metal to manufacturers of automobiles, washing machines, and bridges, for instance, or entering any or all of those businesses itself. Naturally, it would hold many advantages over established competitors if it chose to enter their markets with finished goods. The steel-monopolist-turned-automaker could, for instance, price discriminate—high prices on steel sold to rival automakers would provide profits to subsidize low prices on its own cars. Such price discrimination would eventually lead to the steelmaker taking over the auto industry. (This matches the pricing pattern IBM employed when bringing out its first computers, the 701 and 702, even as it supplied rival computer makers with the punch card machinery they found so necessary for survival.) Another alternative would be for the steelmaker simply to refuse to sell its materials to potential customers and leverage its way into their markets. Suppliers of products that depend on the special characteristics of steel would soon be driven out—and once they were gone, the steel company would run a monopoly there, too, and be free to charge exorbitant prices.

Ultimately, of course, no matter what competitive efficiency, innovative products, or more "excellent" management it brought to the market, competition would lose. From pots and pans to automobiles and on to every other neighboring market, the steel monopolist would be unstoppable. If it were smart, of course, it would seek out the most profitable and important of these steel-dependent markets and win them first so as to prevent any major customer from trying to move into steelmaking itself with alternative processes.

And as bleak as this vision might seem to U.S. steel consumers, imagine how foreign companies dependent on the U.S. monopolist would take it. By refusing to sell to the appliance and automakers of Europe and Japan, the U.S. steel monopolist could leverage its power against those companies and take over their markets, too. (Japanese automakers could never have achieved their renowned worldwide success had they not had a dependable source of low-priced steel.) Foreign countries would feel threatened not only by the single, powerful steel company but by the entire U.S. economy as well.

The point is that there is a powerful multiplier effect that benefits that company, or country, that gains a competitive advantage in a basic industry. All companies and markets that rely on that basic industry's output for a major portion of their products' value are affected. But while the effect in our hypothetical steel example is just that, hypothetical, it is quite real in information technology today. IBM's expanding monopoly over information technology is fast giving it the power to enter and ultimately dominate the many service industries of the future that will depend so on that technology.

The single most important component of success in these industries will be superior business tools. Superior computer systems, data bases, telecommunications networks, and the rest will sort the winners from the losers, for the most attractive service industries are information-intensive. As computer-based information tools grow more sophisticated, the value of the service industries' output will be determined increasingly by their ability to apply such tools economically. Not only will computer systems collect and report on information "after the fact," but they will also be used to make decisions autonomously and actually service customers directly. Automatic teller machines at banks are but the beginning of a major trend. Already systems are being used or planned that would track stock market trends and place orders automatically; analyze medical tests and prescribe treatments; watch inventory levels and incoming orders and order new raw materials for factories; and keep track of changing tax laws and advise investors about where to put their money. Over time, these types of systems will provide services more cost-effectively than previous methods, and any company that can master them first has a positive lead on its rivals.

Because it holds such an unassailable monopoly on these vital information processing tools, IBM's current power has frightening prospects for the United States and the entire world. It has a monopoly on the fundamental tools needed to survive in the coming information economy, a monopoly that, by means similar to that in the steel scenario, provide it with a unique range of attractive commercial alternatives. IBM could, for example, choose simply to stay in the "tool" market, providing computer systems and networks to connect them together. That is unlikely, however, because of its massive shift to selling, instead of leasing, this equipment and because the selling price is dropping with each technical improvement. Rather than accept these limits to its future growth, the company is compelled, therefore, to expand its monopoly into new areas, markets where its power in computers and networks will give it a superior competitive position.

To take over a noncomputer market, banking say, IBM could conceivably begin by playing favorites among those institutions that rely on its equipment. Consider what would happen if IBM and a large bank formed a joint venture that involved research and development into ways of improving banking technology (in such a way, of course, as to make IBM banking systems more efficient, but without introducing too much incompatibility with previously installed networks). Since the technology would be developed under a proprietary contract, only IBM's banking partner could use it and reap its benefits in the banking market. If the technology's contributions to efficiency were substantial, and if other banks were denied a chance to use it, that single bank would pull ahead of the others, who would be locked in to their now relatively obsolete IBM systems.

Alternatively, IBM itself could enter the banking industry with these same advantages that no other company could match. In the deregulated banking market of today, which is becoming increasingly dependent on computers and telecommunications for its competitive health, IBM alone would have the latest in IBM-compatible hardware and software. Its lower costs would enable it to compete with a smaller "spread," and therefore it would be able to offer depositors higher interest rates and make loans at lower rates. Other banks would find it impossible to compete successfully, over the long term, as IBM leveraged off its traditional computer monopoly into their business.

By the same means, IBM could maneuver its way into virtually any business in which competitors are heavily dependent on timely processing and communications of information—even if that business were already dominated by another, less powerful, monopolist. Projecting its power even further, IBM could preempt for itself much of the benefit of the move by industrialized nations to information-intensive economies.

Given that it can impoverish and exclude other suppliers of computer and communications gear through its control over key interfaces and that it can leverage its power into any business by allocating future improvements of that equipment to selected suppliers, there seems to be no limit to IBM's economic power or expansion. We have seen many examples of the company's dedicated pursuit of its commercial self-interest at the expense of all other parties—customers, competitors, and government. But can we expect IBM to exploit all these opportunities to their limit? Probably not, but its power has been sufficient to scare many foreign governments into protectionist action. They already fear IBM's most important customers—large United States–based multinational companies—gaining competitive advantages over their domestic suppliers. By applying the latest in IBM computer and networking gear, the U.S. multinationals have expanded their share of foreign markets, particularly in the financial services area. Foreign nations naturally feel frustrated, for they are pressured to satisfy two competing forces. On the one hand, IBM is trying its hardest to dominate their domestic computer markets, and on the other the U.S. multinationals are trying to dominate the local service businesses. For a foreign nation to deny its own financial services suppliers any IBM systems places those companies at a distinct disadvantage relative to U.S. banks and other institutions in the global financial marketplace, but to give IBM a free hand is to damage what's left of a domestic computer industry.

The dilemma is highlighted by the testimony[5] of American Express, the large U.S. company that operates a worldwide network of computers to help it sell financial services. In American Express's business, time saved translates into money earned. The sooner a financial transaction is processed, the quicker money is available for new investments and the greater the return on those investments.

Knowing its exact cash situation at the end of each day, American Express can invest any surplus funds overnight. It behooves the company, therefore, to have the most efficient network possible.

"All our principal businesses must move information across international borders with speed, accuracy, reliability and security. We could not function without rapid, unhindered global communications," said an American Express official in a 1984 Senate hearing. She related how the company processes 350 million credit card slips each year; completes 250,000 credit authorizations a day, each in about five seconds; sells travelers checks in 100,000 outlets worldwide; processes 56 million insurance premiums and claims each year; moves approximately $10 billion a day in international funds; and sends 500,000 daily messages from office to office. "The fact is, telecommunications and data transmission are the lifeblood of my company," she stated.

To be successful, American Express needs full access to global data communications networks that are not only functionally comparable to those available in the United States but are as compatible as possible with its IBM systems at home as well. In fact, most of the many thousands of transactions it processes each day pass through one or another of dozens of IBM computers installed throughout the world. Since its global network is centered on and therefore defined by those mainframes, it behooves American Express to install the latest and most functional IBM equipment wherever and whenever it needs to. Similarly, to remain competitive with American Express, foreign suppliers have little choice but to cast their lot with IBM, too. But American Express and its foreign competitors alike then run the risk that as their common business comes to rely more heavily on IBM computer networks, the U.S. monopolist will cut them out as middlemen and take the financial services business itself.

What other markets besides services can IBM potentially dominate? Predicting the future is no easy task. It is likely that many possible markets to be victimized by IBM are at this point unimaginable, so what follows are only a few obvious examples.

Office of the Future. Office planners are striving to boost white-collar productivity by equipping offices with desktop workstations and eliminating as much paper documentation as possible. For all its flaws, the standard 8-1/2-by-11-inch piece of paper was a communications interface between typewriters, copiers, filing cabinets, and any person who needed to write on it or read it. Once office documents become completely electronic, the standard paper interface will vanish; it will be replaced by a series of IBM-defined conventions on how information is to be represented, communicated, stored, and retrieved. By virtue of its dominance in the office market, IBM alone will have the power to change those conventions to meet its commercial needs.

IBM's dominance in the office will stem from the fact that its mainframe computers are beginning to form the heart of networks to which all word processors, personal computers, copier/printers, and even telephone equipment will be attached. Besides, it already has substantial shares of those individual markets.

Factory of the Future. The automation of factories is proceeding with great speed these days, offering new orders of efficiency. Computers are being applied to all phases of the manufacturing process, from the design of goods to their shipment as finished products. Computers in the factory can cut labor costs—thus allowing successful competition between high-wage and low-wage countries—and provide manufacturers with more flexibility, better quality, faster response to changing markets, and greater dependability. Competence in factory automation is critical to any country that wishes to maintain international competitiveness in manufacturing.

As the totally computer-controlled factory is perfected, IBM stands uniquely poised to dominate all categories of necessary equipment. As their technical names indicate, many small and not-so-small computers will be involved. Goods will be designed using computer-aided design (CAD) systems; engineered through computer-aided engineering (CAE) machines; produced through computer-aided manufacturing (CAM) systems—robots, welders, shapers, and so forth; and assembled by computer-aided assembly robots. At the factory's front door will operate inventory control systems, while at the back will be automated warehousing systems. The market for these different systems is expected to reach $40 billion by 1990.

Although it is already active in all these submarkets, IBM's power will stem primarily from the fact that their overall control and scheduling will take place in a central mainframe computer processing information on incoming orders, work in process, shipments, and everything in between. The mainframe will act as a central repository of computer-coded descriptions of individual parts, their bills of materials, and the instructions for robots that perform the actual production. The mainframe will also perform traditional accounting functions, taking care of billing customers, paying suppliers, and tracking expenses. If different factories contribute to the manufacturing process, each one's mainframe will be connected to the others, and all will be under supervision of a central mainframe complex located at corporate headquarters. The vast number of such corporate mainframes being installed by IBM already means that IBM should do quite well in this business.

Value-Added Networks. These are networks that not only move data from point to point but also process the data in some way before delivering them. Because the world's computer population is growing by leaps and bounds, growth in such networks is expected to be strong in years to come. IBM has already won contracts to supply networks to the insurance industry in the United States, and it is working on networks for home information services and financial information for brokerage houses and other institutions. Corporations in the future are expected to connect their individual computer networks together so that purchase orders, invoices, and other documents can be moved electronically among them.

IBM's supplying of services rather than just equipment should make it easier for IBM to return to its favorite form of pricing. IBM will own the equipment to which its customers—independent insurance agents, for example—will be inextricably tied for the functioning of their business. This means that the service charge can be based on the function rather than the costs of the service, and IBM will regain many of the advantages it enjoyed when most of its goods were leased rather than sold.

Artificial Intelligence. Software techniques designed to give computers humanlike reasoning powers, vision, and the ability to handle free-form, natural language inputs, which, if perfected, will become especially useful to suppliers of computer-based services. Service companies of all sorts are expected to rely on systems that can store and therefore endlessly duplicate expert knowledge. Such "knowledge-based" systems are in their infancy now and are used primarily by the military, but with the cost of computing hardware continuing to fall, banks, insurance companies, and other financial institutions, for instance, could use them to increase sales productivity, make complex decisions, and track market trends. Artificial intelligence also describes systems that can physically manipulate objects. Those capabilities have obvious applications in factories. IBM has no intention of letting such promising technology escape its control.

These are just a few of the broad areas that are ripe for IBM's expansion where it will have the great advantage of its monopoly in mainframe computers. Companies offering stand-alone products in these markets are already scrambling to add IBM-compatible communications. In most cases, their major competitor is IBM. It has entered many neighboring markets with its own products, or it is remarketing others' products where it has to, and it is competing aggressively. Even when it suffers a temporary setback and another vendor's gear gets attached to its networks, IBM still grows, for the network's mainframes must respond to new demand.

21. What to Do

We will see the information industry emerge as the No. 1 industry in the world during this decade—an industry of such magnitude that it will have an enormous impact on the world economy. Thus, it will have to be concerned with its role in society and with public policy.

—Peter L. Schavoir, IBM director
of market research.[1]

"The notion that IBM has some kind of 'stranglehold' on the information industry . . . is just plain wrong," states John Akers, president and chief executive officer of IBM, responding to the question, "Is IBM too big?" Clearly, he disagrees with the central premise of this book. "The idea that IBM controls the industry is simply inaccurate. . . . We believe IBM is good for the United States, and equally good for the other countries where we do business."

There is no question that IBM is "good" for certain individuals—its protected employees, its long-term stockholders, and the many beneficiaries of its philanthropy, for instance. But because it does indeed strangle the computer industry everywhere, IBM is in fact a major problem for practically every country in which it does business, even the United States. By maintaining everywhere a self-perpetuating, lopsided market structure in which it towers over all competitors, IBM has amassed entirely too much power to be considered "good" for any nation as a whole. It will be argued here, therefore, that only by changing the structure of the computer industry, by rearranging its productive capacities and corporate entities, can IBM's power be reduced and competitive vigor be restored. Without effective structural change and a reduction of IBM's power, the problem will only get worse as the company pursues its goal of dominating the expanding information processing market.

How to go about effecting such structural changes is the question. The quick fixes of the past, though offering short-term hope, have in the end all failed. Consent decrees designed to limit IBM's actions and thereby reduce its power have never been successful. The only viable course of action left is to take the ax to IBM and split it up into several equal-sized, vertically integrated companies, which would be forced to compete vigorously with each other.

The problem is not just that IBM is an extremely large corporation, although that in itself is daunting. Given the complexity of modern commercial enterprise, large, vertically integrated companies are necessary, for only they can afford the expense of large and complex tasks and the price discrimination that characterizes this business. No, the problem is not large absolute size per se, but rather IBM's enormity relative to all its competitors. This lopsided market structure and the lack of invigorating competitive pressure it creates is where IBM fails the United States.

Why is it, one might ask, that at any given time the most intense competitive forays against IBM have come not from the largest of its rivals but rather from the smallest? For example, the traditional commercial mainframe systems companies (e.g., RCA, GE, Honeywell, Sperry Rand, and Burroughs), with their technical competence in memory and peripherals and their established sales and service forces, were never major suppliers of IBM-compatible equipment. Why did these seemingly well-positioned companies shy away from direct conflict with IBM and concentrate instead on their own locked-in customers?

The main reason is that they had a great deal to lose. The systems companies were understandably fearful that if they competed for IBM customers' peripherals business, say, IBM would counterattack and use its overwhelming resources to win their systems customers away—they might win a battle only to lose the war. Smaller companies, such as Memorex, Telex, and Advanced Memory Systems, had little or no installed bases of their own and therefore had little to lose and everything to gain. But of course, those small companies had few resources to bring to their fights, which made it all the easier for IBM to smash them. Indeed, their "dying" condition, to use IBM's word, was, despite their admirable courage and tenacity, a foregone conclusion. Is it any wonder that IBM, never having faced a competitor with comparable resources, has been as successful as it has been with such poor performance on its part?

Clearly, what is needed is more intense competition in the computer industry, competition that will compel all firms involved to become more efficient. But how to achieve that competition is the problem. It is naive to believe that present rivals can grow to match IBM. IBM has repeatedly foiled the growth of companies that could have competed effectively with it; the same is sure to happen in the future. Nor will technology, as fruitful and rapidly advancing as it is, solve the industry's structural problems. Many companies have attained commercial success and even substantial size by creatively exploiting computer technology, but they have never even approached IBM's size. A particularly innovative application of some new technology may have a momentary effect on relative market shares, but IBM soon copies the innovation and the situation returns to its previous state. In the long term, successful pioneers such as Digital Equipment in minicomputers and Apple Computer in personal computers inevitably find IBM moving into their territory, exploiting its unmatchable financial resources and its control over the interfaces to its dominant mainframes and using price-discrimination tactics. IBM's stated policy is never to abdicate any major area of growth.

If it were a simple sports match, not a complex industry, under consideration, the problem would be immediately recognizable. Athletes deliver their best performance when competing against other athletes of roughly equal abilities, when each contestant has an equal chance of winning and losing.

Competition in the computer industry can be improved, as it must be, only by a profound restructuring of IBM's assets, which, after all, are but a legal fiction, not a living organism like an athlete. Since IBM exists at the sufferance of the state, all that is required is a political consensus that such a change is in the best interests of all concerned.

Which it is. The only beneficiary of the present lopsided structure is the IBM Corporation. The company's ability to capture most of the computer business, and now neighboring markets, with products that it itself has determined to be competitively deficient and overpriced stems directly from the lopsided market structure that currently exists. For the rest of us, whether in the United States or abroad, there are no benefits sufficient to justify the quite real costs and risks that the present structure demands. With this structure, the state—indeed, all states—risk becoming IBM's slave instead of its master.

IBM would have us believe that it seeks to be a "good corporate citizen" and that we should trust it despite its enormous power. No doubt it has benefited society: its products have helped us boost productivity, increase efficiency, and so forth. But it would be a dire mistake to think that its interests coincide wholly with ours. We've seen repeatedly that the company's unmatched profits derive from its ability to limit customers' choices as they expand their computer systems. Yet according to our traditions, the customer should be king and should have as many options as possible when purchasing vitally important products. That belief holds that the more suppliers that are viable over the long term, the better.

IBM, incidentally, is in this respect no different from any other company. All businessmen would like to control their markets, not let their markets control them—that's a quick way of getting rich. The difference here is that IBM has shown it has the power to do precisely what other companies can only dream of. Combined with the fact that the computer is as critical a tool for the future as it is, IBM's unfettered power has uniquely ominous implications for us all.

Breaking up such a huge enterprise is a frightening prospect for many. Besides the technical complexity of such an action, there would be major, largely unforeseeable disruptions to the computer industry as a whole and profound changes for all those customers who are dependent on IBM systems. For some, it would be somewhat analogous to redesigning the Empire State Building's foundations while keeping the building from falling. With such fearsome implications to deal with, many have chosen simply to ignore the problem. Yet such changes may not be as difficult as we might think. Facilitating a rearrangement of IBM's assets is the fact that the industry is still quite young and still growing rapidly. It can absorb changes more easily than will be the case when growth has tapered or even stopped. This argues for dealing with the problem now, before it is too late. Moreover, structural changes happen with great frequency in our economy—companies merge, divest, and rearrange their components. IBM itself constantly reorganizes its structure. During the course of the 1969 U.S. antitrust case, IBM even volunteered to divest itself of an entire division (the small systems business, which today is a sizable part of the company) as a means of settling the case. (The government rejected this offer as not significantly increasing overall competition.) Moreover, the 1984 breakup of AT&T, although unpopular with residential customers who had benefited from the phone company's price discrimination, is a prime example of the fact that it is possible to carry out such a major restructuring. Now it seems likely that we will suffer under another communications monopolist.

How is it that we have come to be so tolerant of uncompetitive, inefficient markets? There are three main answers to that question, the first being the vested interests of presently dominant companies. Intensely competitive markets are far less comfortable for those involved than are markets where competition is blunted. All-out rivalry puts great pressure on workers and managers—they risk losing their jobs and companies if they do not make the grade. Stockholders, too, prefer less competition, for that ensures them of a higher return on their investments. Finally, organizations with significant market power, and the resulting surplus profits, will fight strenuously to maintain that power. In a participatory democracy, their high profits ensure that their interests are heeded,* while advocates of more competitive markets have no such comparable resources. The result is a favoring of entrenched power at the expense of invigorating competition.

---

* The resources available to IBM to ensure that its position is well heard in the political process are substantial. Consider, for example, the fact that the members of its Board of Directors have also traditionally sat on the boards of the most important other U.S. firms (most of whom are also major IBM computer customers). The following are examples of IBM Board members—past and present—that have served on the boards of major media firms important in defining the political agenda for the nation.

William W. Scranton	The New York Times Co.
Cyrus R. Vance	The Washington Post
Nicholas deB. Katzenbach	Time Inc.
Thomas J. Watson, Jr.	Dow Jones and Co., Inc.
William McChesney Martin, Jr.	Times Mirror Co.

Secondly, many policymakers are now asking if competitive domestic markets are a luxury the United States can no longer afford. The nation's fall from the lofty heights of its postwar industrial supremacy has provoked much introspection along those lines, particularly in the light of Japan's many successes at our expense. Only huge corporations, it is widely thought, can hold the Japanese and other Asian nations at bay. Many are the incantations of jingoistic success formulas from Japan, Theory Z and the lot, but almost completely overlooked is the fact that, all notions of a monolithic "Japan, Inc." notwithstanding, the Japanese themselves firmly believe in competitive domestic markets. Their planners wisely hold to the idea that in the long run, international competitiveness for Japan depends on maximum efficiency for each of its native corporations. Only companies able to produce at the lowest possible cost while still satisfying customers can hope to succeed domestically and internationally. And only robust domestic markets can ensure continued growth, dividends for company owners, and future employment for workers.

Monopolies ultimately frustrate the achievement of all those goals. Though highly profitable in the short term, monopolies such as IBM breed great inefficiency as they earn profits more through excessive power than through streamlined operations. The supposed advantage of permitting a single company to dominate a market is that it can thereby capture more economies of scale. But if economies of scale were as important as their proponents claim, then small companies would never succeed in taking on competitors with high market shares. Similarly, no large company would ever have to resort to the kinds of anticompetitive actions IBM has used—bundling products, capriciously changing interfaces, and so forth—for its costs would be so low as to let it sweep the market fair and square.

Companies that face no effective competition always tend to slip into bureaucratic sclerosis, waste, and inordinate caution. The only goad that can keep such tendencies in check is the continued threat of competitors' gaining commercially whenever the large company rests on its oars. Hence the Japanese approach to automobiles, computers, and other products: no concentration of productive capability in just one firm, but instead a collection of sleek competitors of roughly equal power forced to work hard to survive. Whatever loss in economies of scale may have resulted from this arrangement has been more than compensated for by the high efficiency that Japanese producers have achieved. Now even France has learned this lesson and is backing away from the single-national-champion model used for so many years there in computers.

Even though international competition is heating up considerably, the state of domestic markets still matters a great deal. Local suppliers provide the most intense competitive pressure, for they are closest to the customer and can respond quickest to his needs. Domestic competition, in which one company's loss is another's gain, keeps domestic employment levels relatively stable; losses to foreign companies can mean fewer jobs at home. Even more important, however, are the political pressures generated when the only significant competition comes from foreign as opposed to domestic suppliers. Competition among locals creates no call for government intervention to protect the losers. Protectionist measures such as import quotas and tariffs do little to make domestic companies more efficient—in fact, they do quite the opposite, dooming the protected to inefficiency. Insufficient competition in a domestic market can easily result in a loss of international competitiveness and a long downward cycle of political and economic decline.

If we as a nation are unwilling to structure our domestic markets so as to extract maximum economic and technical potential from them, we will give away significant advantages to our trading partners. Up until the recent past, the U.S. lead over other nations was so overwhelming that we could afford many inefficiencies, but that is no longer the case. There is no better place to begin optimizing market structures than with IBM and the computer industry.

In IBM's case, all efforts to enforce the antitrust laws against it and unleash competitive forces have failed. Had IBM been restructured earlier into several competing companies, as Standard Oil was many years ago, we would not today have to face this difficult problem. With such a change, the data processing industry would hardly have ceased to function—as the petroleum industry did not cease to function following Standard Oil's restructuring. The benefits of IBM's products would not be forgone, computer technology would be exploited at just as rapid a pace (if not faster), and computers would be used just as widely throughout the economy—but commercially the business would have evolved quite differently.

Why have antitrust measures failed against IBM? The most recent antitrust effort was simply cut short before completion by Ronald Reagan's antitrust chief, William Baxter. He ended the case by declaring the government's charges "without merit" rather than allowing the judge to make a decision based on the evidence at hand. Without speculating about Baxter's motives (see Appendix K for a brief discussion of some of the troublesome specifics) it is safe to say that his decision hardly explains everything about why antitrust laws have failed. Antitrust laws are also enforced by private parties, and IBM has faced many private litigations and won most of them. Why?

At the simplest level, it is quite difficult for judges to punish this company, which is so widely admired, unless the evidence against it is overwhelming. Most judges hearing the two dozen or so private antitrust suits filed against IBM in the 1970s found that the evidence failed to meet this demanding test. So IBM was let off. This is no indication that IBM does not maintain and exploit its monopoly, but it shows rather the inadequacy of the historical standards of antitrust enforcement and the failure to update them to deal with a monopolist such as IBM.

Monopolies are problematic because they lock a market to such a degree that commercial success stems not from running a better race but from an exercise of power. Monopolies also damage competitive companies in neighboring markets, often driving them out of business through price discrimination. Monopoly often begets monopoly, leading to a fulfillment of Marx's prediction that competitive markets are only a temporary phase in the evolution of a nation's economy. When the United States adopted its innovative laws designed to prevent monopolies from abusing their power, the thought was that by limiting the kinds of actions that monopolists could use, the competitive process over time would erode their advantages. Moreover, the availability of redress offered by these laws would encourage competition to make the effort. Hobble the monopolist, the theory went, and although unequal, at least some competition would still exist. If the monopolist responds unfairly, then sue him.

IBM, however, is a significantly different kind of monopolist from those against which these laws have proven effective. And the laws have hardly kept up with the times. If nothing else, the computer industry is marked by an extreme proliferation of products—the previous chapters mention only a tiny fraction of the many thousands of products, options, features, and variations that IBM lists in its catalogs, not to mention those offered by all other vendors. For the general observer, say a judge or jury member, the blizzard of model numbers, prices, performance figures, and functional descriptions can easily serve as a smokescreen behind which IBM can hide its true pricing and interface strategies. The always-lengthy litigation process is not particularly adept at dealing with such situations in which facts change so dynamically. Recall IBM lawyer Bruce Bromley's boast of how he could so easily tie up even a simple antitrust case. The inevitable result of this dust storm of changing technology is that by the time a court is satisfied with a set of critical facts, they may no longer be relevant.

Computer technology is also a slippery subject for antitrust cases because prices have tended to drop, not to rise, as is the case in more traditional monopolistic situations. With IBM delivering so much more performance and function for what seems to be a continually declining price, it is difficult to generate and maintain a political consensus for vigorous antitrust action against it.

The pricing issue is in fact the most troublesome area of effective antitrust action against IBM. Courts, lawyers, and economists involved in antitrust work have traditionally relied on pricing as the most telling sign of a monopolist's intentions. If a monopolist sets a clearly profitable price in some contested market, it is hard to impute anticompetitive intent. Alternatively, if the price is below this fully allocated price but above an estimate of the costs directly associated with producing the last unit of output, it becomes a closer call. Some courts may allow such a price, others may not. After all, such a price would contribute at least some, if not all, profits needed to cover the producer's overhead. Only if the price were set below this bottom level, where it would not cover even the direct costs of making the product, would all observers conclude that predatory action had taken place. This has been a simple formulation, and for many industries it has been entirely workable.

In high-technology markets such as IBM's, though, such pricing considerations are, for several reasons, practically worthless. High-technology products generally entail quite high fixed overhead expenses, both for basic research and applied development. Once research and development is completed, actual production costs may be small; in contrast, traditional heavy industries generally show direct costs as a high portion of total costs. In computer software, to take a prime example, initial development costs can be high, while the direct cost of making an additional copy of a program is relatively trivial. Except for the cost of a floppy disk, say, there is no more expense for additional steel, plastic, or other basic material when producing one more unit of the program. That means that a well-heeled company can drop prices to a very low level without being deemed to have misbehaved. This is exactly what Japanese semiconductor companies did with such devastating results against their U.S. rivals.

If, however, such a low price is not enough to do in the competition, the monopolist can fiddle with any of the many important assumptions that underlie its established price. It can give the product a long estimated life or assume that costs will drop unrealistically fast. Later, when the competitor has been driven out of business, the most damaging conclusion to be drawn will be that the monopolist makes poor projections, not that it set out to kill its rivals.

If that is not sufficient to stay the antitrust enforcement, there are ways for a company selling many products to hoke up its accounting procedures so that costs are allocated to protected products while being stripped from those facing effective competition. This leaves a benign trail handy for justifying what would otherwise be a clear case of predatory, below-cost pricing.

Without the ability to examine prices and determine unambiguously the intent of a particular action, the antitrust system fails. A monopolist is free to price as low as necessary to drive out companies that lack comparably deep pockets and avoid all penalty. Marx may turn out to be right after all, not in yesterday's heavy industries, but in tomorrow's high-technology markets.

In sum, due to the nature of high-technology products and their cost structures, the U.S. antitrust statutes have failed. It has become extremely difficult for courts to second-guess a monopolist's pricing actions and decide between predatory and permissible actions. As a result, the only alternative left is for the government to use its ax directly, to restructure companies that hold monopoly power and ensure that intense competitive pressure will compel them to be efficient. The virtue of this solution is that in such a restructured market, pricing would not be a major concern to the government, regulators, or the court, for each company would face rivals of comparable power. A low price by one would be met by these other companies, each of which would be able to withstand the competition. Under such a structure, the temporary winner would be the company selling the best product at the lowest price. That advantage would last only until its competition matches its advantages, resulting in an overall increase in efficiency for all.

Yet although it is highly desirable to have competitive domestic markets, the antitrust laws provide only limited means for achieving that end. Private antitrust plaintiffs rarely seek to restructure the monopolist they sue. Why should they, if their own success stems from exploiting the monopolist's inefficiencies? Better to compete with a bloated whale than a restructured pack of hungry sharks.* Instead, private antitrust plaintiffs seek money—they usually want simply to pick the monopolist's deep pockets. In many private suits against IBM, moreover, plaintiffs have been only too willing to cut a deal with their opponent and get on with business. IBM pays them off with cash or a sizable order of goods and avoids the problem. IBM's customers, although large firms, see their interests in cooperating with IBM rather than attacking it. This means that government must shoulder the burden of correcting the computer industry's basic structural flaw. Although that suggestion seems to run counter to the *laissez-faire* direction of much current policy, the alternative is to give IBM free rein to monopolize an ever-wider portion of the economy. That, of course, would be quite unfortunate in this nation where robustly competitive markets have been so highly valued.

---

* In fact, it is not in the interests of IBM's competitors to admit their vulnerability—that they exist at the sufferance of IBM. This was clearly stated by the executives of several of these firms when, during the *U.S.* v. *IBM* trial, they were asked just such questions. Why? Simply because the ongoing success of these firms comes from convincing customers that they will remain viable alternative suppliers to IBM. This means that a candid admission of their vulnerability is not in their commercial self-interest; it only increases their already-substantial marketing problems. Much better that they assume a more intrepid if less accurate pose—that they, with their superior products and lower prices, can successfully compete with IBM. With all those companies hawking their many wares, the general public is intentionally deceived as to the true extent of IBM's power. With both IBM and its competitors working for the same end—though for very different reasons—it is not surprising that they are successful. Many think that the data processing industry is highly competitive when the very opposite is the case.

The implication for antitrust enforcement of this competitive bravado is that private suits focus on particular aggressive IBM actions rather than on the pervasive underlying IBM power. Yet this course is doomed. Any restrictions on IBM's freedom, given the flexibility of the technology and IBM's creativity in devising new strategies, will be ineffective. The only realistic solution to IBM's power is to break the company up—and that will require acceptance of the unpleasant fact of the weakness of its existing competition.

So while there is much in today's complex international trade arena that is beyond U.S. control, there are significant improvements to be made at home. Government's direct ability to make domestic companies more efficient may be limited—it cannot force managers to manage efficiently, force workers to be more diligent, or force engineers to be more innovative—but it can, and should, optimize the structure of domestic markets. If government is unwilling to do that—either due to a lack of political will to update and enforce antitrust laws or because it is already too late—then we have no one to blame but ourselves when our markets get overrun by foreigners. The United States will never succeed in competition with low-wage nations merely by imitating their production techniques. Only by working more efficiently ourselves can our industries pay the premium wages needed to maintain the differential in our standard of living. We have to capitalize on our two relative strengths: a highly skilled workforce and the mobility of that workforce and of capital. If the computer industry is allowed to remain as rigid as it is under the dominating influence of IBM, innovations will not take hold here but will instead be exploited by our foreign competitors.

Let it be said once more: There is nothing necessarily wrong with price discrimination if it occurs in a competitive market. But the pervasiveness of IBM's price discrimination, taking place in a monopolized market, is the single most important measure of the company's power, and it is the method it uses most to expand its empire. Changing the structure of this industry will solve the problem of its abuse of price discrimination.

IN THE MEANTIME

There are several ways to deal with the problems caused by IBM's excessive market power in the interim. First and foremost is for IBM's major customers to recognize that it is in their best interest to have many, not fewer, suppliers for equipment that is as critical to their daily operations as computers are. These customers must resist the tendency to buy only from other large companies. They should encourage competition by acquiring non-IBM gear when it offers better price and performance than IBM products. IBM should have as much responsibility as its competitors, Amdahl says, to keep today's products compatible with prior systems. If customers want the benefits of competition, they will have to take some risks to ensure that competition can survive.

Meanwhile, the government should more actively limit IBM's freedom to manipulate interfaces. Not that IBM should not change its interfaces at all, but they should be changed in an orderly, competitively fair manner. Rival suppliers must be given necessary interface specs with enough time for them to get their compatible products to market at the same time as IBM. This may well require new laws to be passed. To the degree that a new IBM interface contains true innovation, IBM should be permitted to earn a royalty payment for its use. That would be preferable to allowing it to incorporate the innovative interface into all its products and thereby leverage the benefits into the whole hardware and software business that depends on that interface.

In a similar vein, organized groups of users and national governments should press ahead in their efforts to impose standards on IBM that would limit its ability to continually expand the scope of its power. Standards have the ability to ensure greater choice of equipment and in turn to pressure IBM to perform more effectively.

Ultimately, however, IBM's power will still be quite substantial. It has agreed to several proposals in the past that were supposed to limit its power, and it has evaded them all. Its power runs deep, and the technology it controls is sufficiently flexible to allow IBM great freedom to maneuver. Much is at stake in the IBM monopoly, and there is every reason to believe the company will be quite creative in its search for ways to agree to change while still retaining control over industry prices. It has in the past, even if reluctantly, been forced to give away only the sleeves on its vest.

Finally, efforts must be made to break IBM's hold on the basic information concerning this vital industry. IBM's control over information about itself, the production of computers, and their application helps it pass as only one company in a highly competitive business. (See Appendix L for an example of how it manipulates our view). Perhaps the most frightening aspect of IBM is that its monopoly and power are kept so well hidden, out of sight and mind. Yet refuting IBM's fictional account of itself and attempting to arrive at effective policies to deal with its monopoly power are impossible when the monopoly controls the basic data. Perhaps this is the most telling aspect of the much-ballyhooed Information Age—a monopolization not of heavy industry but of information itself.

This book has attempted to shine a new light on IBM and the evolution of the computer industry, but that would never have been possible had there not been a break—albeit a temporary one—in IBM's control over information about itself. What little I have been able to learn about the company and its power has come primarily from a careful reading of once-confidential IBM documents that it was forced by a U.S. Federal Court and a particularly tenacious judge to supply. That breach of IBM's control came as part of a court case that was initially filed under a most unusual set of circumstances, but had that breach not come to pass, this different view of IBM would still be locked away in company vaults.

The need for information about IBM only grows stronger. Only by keeping a careful eye on its actions, particularly those that affect other companies' ability to compete with it, can we ever hope to restrain IBM. Absent determined scrutiny, the company will see no incentive to keep to its knitting, to improve its products instead of simply earning profits by smashing competition. With this need for scrutiny in mind, an Institute for IBM Documentation to collect further data on the company, its products, its competitive actions, and the computer industry, and to extend the analysis begun in these pages should be established. This book has limited itself to considering only the major IBM products in each period and an initial sketch of the overall pattern of IBM's power. Many other product areas deserve analysis: tape drives, about which much data was revealed during the recent government case, computer-aided design and factory automation (CAD/CAM), and value-added networks, to name a few.

The institute should seek to flesh out the present analysis in several ways. One is to collect the personal experiences of those involved with critical decisions at IBM—people who used functional pricing as part of their job or who were responsible for segmenting markets in order to make price discrimination effective. Such people can confirm what has already been done and bring a new richness of understanding to the public. The Institute could also help private litigants in their efforts to sue IBM for redress of its actions against them. The Institute's files would be available to those who can use them, in exchange for information that they generate in their court battles. No longer would IBM have a monopoly on historical records, and no longer would each new plaintiff have to rediscover what the last one has done. The less expensive it is to sue the company, the greater the incentive there will be for IBM to use its power responsibly. IBM no doubt saves all court-related memos, briefs, and other documents. Why shouldn't others?

The Institute would operate as a nonprofit organization whose only purpose would be to document IBM's actions and inform the debate over important public policy issues. It would be neither a market research house nor a stock picker, although it would welcome the information such organizations might like to contribute.

It is my sincere hope that this book and any ongoing efforts of such an Institute will also provide a basis upon which IBM's 400,000 employees can better understand their jobs, their responsibilities, and the implications of their employer's position in the world. Often these people are expected to devise strategies to achieve a corporate goal, yet the technical complexity of such efforts often precludes understanding the moral implications of those strategies. Only through a broader view of The IBM Company, as they call it, and of what actions are clearly exploitative of its power can IBM employees act responsibly.

It is sobering to recall that throughout history, great concentrations of power have not tolerated much criticism, but in the end the resulting repression of freedoms have weakened the very societies that permitted the power to be concentrated in the first place. If we wish to preserve our freedoms, we should use them. It would be tragic, given the rapid growth of the computer industry and the many markets it will enhance, if in the face of even greater IBM power than exists today, a political consensus to deal with that power were finally to emerge and then fail because of a lack of the necessary documentation.

Appendix A
The 1956 Consent Decree—Rules for IBM's Game.

The final judgment in the *United States of America* v. *International Business Machines Corporation* (Civil Action No 72–344 in the Southern District of New York) was entered January 25, 1956. The thirty-seven-page document, consisting of twenty sections, ended the antitrust proceeding prior to any evidence being taken. The order was signed for the Court by District Judge David N. Edelstein (the very same judge who would preside over the next Department of Justice case against IBM a decade later), and for IBM by, among others, Bruce Bromley.

The decree was designed to limit IBM's freedom. It not only forced IBM to sell its equipment and no longer exclusively lease it, but also tried to open up competition in the maintenance of that equipment. The government, as part of the agreement, was given substantial enforcement power. It could, for example, inspect IBM's books and demand additional information from the company to ensure that the agreement was not being frustrated.

Naturally, one of the government's biggest concerns was the prices IBM would establish for its equipment. If purchase prices were set high enough, IBM could effectively discourage purchases and encourage leasing. This was dealt with as follows:

> It is the purpose of this Section IV of this Final Judgement to assure to users and prospective users of IBM ... data processing machines at any time being offered by IBM for lease and sale an opportunity to purchase and own such machines at prices and upon terms and conditions which *shall not be substantially more advantageous to IBM than the lease charges,* terms and conditions for such machines. (Emphasis added.)

Moreover, in order to insure that IBM did not discourage its salesmen from selling instead of leasing equipment, Section IV (c) (4) of the decree stated that IBM must

> afford to its salesmen compensation for selling ... electronic data processing machines which shall be not less favorable to them than their compensation for leasing the same machine.

Since IBM had the power to discriminate between purchase and lease customers not only with prices, but also with providing different amounts of services, Section VI called for IBM

> (a) to offer to render, without separate charge, to purchasers ... the same type of services ... which it renders ... to leasees of the same type of machines;

(b) to offer, ... to maintain and repair at reasonable and nondiscriminatory prices ... for the owners ... provided that, if any such machine shall be altered, or connected by mechanical or electrical means to another machine, in such a manner as to render its maintenance and repair impractical for IBM personnel having had the standard training ... then IBM shall not be required by this Final Judgement to render maintenance and repair service for such IBM machine.

In addition to limiting IBM's ability to set discriminatory prices for service, the agreement tried to limit IBM's ability to tie together two products and foreclose competition. Section XV (b) states

IBM is hereby enjoined and restrained from conditioning the sale or lease of any standard ... electronic data processing machines ... upon the purchase or lease of any other standard ... data processing machine.

The Consent Decree also hoped to encourage other firms to compete with IBM for the business of maintaining the equipment and to offer service utilizing it. Thus it required that IBM provide the necessary training and detailed information on the design and operation of its machines. Therefore Section IX stated "IBM is hereby ordered and directed:

to afford to any person (other than ... a manufacturer of ... electronic data processing machines) who is engaged ... in the repair and maintenance or distribution of IBM ... electronic data processing machines the opportunity to obtain training in the repair and maintenance of such IBM machines. ...

(b) Upon written request to furnish ... to any owner of an IBM ... electronic data processing machine ... copies of any technical manuals, books of instruction, pamphlet, diagrams or similar documents, which it furnishes generally to its own repair and maintenance employees. ...

In addition to training and documents, competitive maintenance firms needed access to parts. Therefore IBM was ordered:

to offer to sell at reasonable and nondiscriminatory prices and terms, to owners of IBM ... electronic data processing machines ... and to persons engaged in the business of maintaining and repairing such machines ... repair and replacement parts and subassemblies. ...

Another concern was that IBM might use its power as the major supplier of data processing equipment to dominate the business of providing service to customers that did not wish to install their own equipment—the service bureau business. These firms process other people's data for a fee. It would be only too easy for IBM to supply its own service bureau with discounted equipment while charging its competitors a high price and thereby driving them out of business. In order to prevent such a tactic, the Consent Decree first called for IBM to establish a separate service subsidiary:

IBM is hereby ordered and directed to transfer, within one year ... all its contracts for service bureau business to a corporation (hereinafter called the Service Bureau Corporation), which may be wholly owned by IBM, and IBM shall thereafter be enjoined and restrained from engaging in the service bureau business. ...

Next, in order to prevent unfair price discrimination in favor of its own Service Bureau and against competitive bureaus, IBM agreed to maintain, in accordance with good accounting practice, separate and complete corporate records and accounts which shall be audited annually by independent public accountants and (2) charge for services rendered by its prices based upon rates which shall fairly reflect all expenses properly chargeable thereto. . . .

The government was also worried about IBM's patent position. Therefore, the decree forced IBM to make these available to its competitors.

IBM is hereby ordered . . . to grant to each person making written application therefore an unrestricted, nonexclusive license to . . . use . . . any, some or all IBM existing and future patents. These were to be made available without "any restrictions whatsoever. . . ."

Finally, IBM agreed to "furnish a true and complete copy" of the Consent Decree "to each of its officers, directors and employees at the policy level, its engineering personnel, [and] its employees engaged in selling . . . electronic data processing machines." One result of that provision was IBM's publication of the booklet, *Business Conduct Policies: Responsibilities and Guide.* (The January 1, 1962, version, referred to in the text of this book, contains a complete copy of the 1956 decree. Updated versions of the guidelines continue to be distributed to all IBM employees.)

It was only by accepting these conditions that the Department of Justice agreed to not pursue its case against IBM. The terms of this agreement would set some limits on IBM's use of its power and compel it to do things that it might never have done on its own. One example is the provision that required it to educate its employees. This has had some clear benefits—to IBM, to its employees, and to the customers and competitors with whom it deals. By clearly explaining what is expected, IBM encourages its employees to act in a legal and ethical way. This, in turn, has enhanced IBM's already lofty public image. Often overlooked, however, is that the Antitrust Division of the Department of Justice deserves at least some of the credit.

It must be said that many of these provisions were strictly adhered to by IBM. The problems for IBM, as this book attempts to document, would come when abiding by one of these provisions could lead to competition eroding its monopoly.

Appendix B
Procedure for Estimating the Cost of Memory Used on the 1401

Montgomery Phister, Jr., in *Data Processing Technology and Economics,* presents data on the cost of producing one thousand units of core memory in 1955 and 1960. He estimates that in 1955 they cost $64.00 to produce and that in 1960 the comparable cost had dropped to $37.00.[1] Assuming this drop in cost was uniform over these five years, in 1959, when the 1401 was announced, the cost would have been approximately $42.40 per thousand.

IBM's actual costs, however, were probably much lower than this figure. Many of the 1401 systems were built in 1960–62, when production costs had fallen even lower. For example, Phister estimates that by 1965 costs for comparable memory had fallen to almost one-half of this estimate—$24.45 per thousand. In addition, given the popularity of these systems and the resulting large volume of IBM production, its economies of scale may have driven the costs down even faster than Phister's estimate.

There are, of course, additional costs besides production costs that IBM's price had to cover. Assuming that the direct costs are only about 20 percent of the total price, this estimate of $42.40 is multiplied by 5, resulting in the $212 estimate of total costs per thousand core used in the text.

Appendix C
IBM's 360 Systems

The underlying data for the summary statements on the 360 systems found in pages 71–72 follow. The data presented are for the most active years of the 360—1966 to 1968 (or 1970, where data is available). The four tables show: (44) the percent of bidding situations where IBM systems won after facing a competitive bid, (45) the IBM ratings of its 360 systems compared with those offered by competitive systems companies, (46) the percent of time IBM systems actually faced competition, and (47) the number of IBM systems replaced by competition. Tables 44, 45, and 46 come from the IBM Quarterly Product Line Assessments*; Table 47 comes from IBM's Data Processing Division product charts.

EFFECTIVENESS

Table 44 (see following page) shows data on what IBM called effectiveness. This is defined as the percent of the time that IBM was successful in those bidding situations in which it faced a competitive bid. These statistics aggregate IBM commercial and noncommerical systems together according to the following size-based groups: very large systems—360/85; large systems—360/75, 67, and 65; large-medium systems—360/50; small-medium systems—360/40 and 44; intermediate systems—360/30 and 25; and small commercial systems—360/20.

IBM's systems on average only won one-third of the bidding situations in which it faced a competitive bid.

* These are the QPLAs that provided sources for the data in Tables 43–45.

Period	Date	Exhibit Number (PX)
Third Quarter 1967	10/26/67	2125
Year-end 1967	2/7/68	2183
First Quarter 1968	5/9/68	2238
First Half 1968	8/29/68	2308
Third Quarter 1968	11/27/68	2360
Year-end 1968	2/20/69	2388
First Quarter 1969	5/26/69	2437
First Half 1969	9/69	2482
Year-end 1969	4/3/70	2567
First Half 1970	8/14/70	2627
Third Quarter 1970	Undated	2606
Year-end 1970	Undated	2644
First Half 1971	8/71	2679
Year-end 1971	2/20/72	2685

The same or similar data are presented in an IBM Marketing Report, PX 3360-B.

Table 44

Percent of Times That IBM Won the Order When It Faced Competition in a Bidding Situation, 1966–68

SYSTEM GROUP	1966	1967	1968	1966–68
Very Large	48%	14%	21%	28%
Large	20	37	25	28
Large-Medium	28	32	35	32
Small-Medium	29	23	24	25
Intermediate	29	34	35	33
Small	29	36	37	35
Average	29	33	34	32

SYSTEM EVALUATION

Table 45 presents the summary evaluations for the IBM commercial 360 systems contained in the QPLAs, 1967–70. The notations used in this table are as follows: + means superior, 0 means equal, and $\div$ means deficient, in relation to systems offered by competitors.

On average, IBM considered its systems only equal at best to those offered by its systems competitors.

Table 45
IBM'S Evaluation of Its 360 Systems, 1967–70
(at year end)

SYSTEM	1967	1968	1969	1970
360/20	—	—	—	—
360/25	0	0	0	—
360/30	0	0	0	—
360/40	0	0	0	—
360/50	+	0	—	—
360/65	0	0	0	0

COMPETITIVENESS

Competitiveness is an IBM measure used to describe the percent of the times that each IBM system encountered a competitive bid when bidding for an order. Table 46 shows this data by system size and year.

On average, IBM's systems faced competition during these years on only about one-third of the order situations.

Table 46
Competitiveness of IBM Systems, 1966–68

SYSTEM GROUP	1966	1967	1968	1966–68 Average
Very Large	77%	64%	45%	58%
Large System	69	44	33	45
Large-Medium	16	16	11	14
Small-Medium	38	46	39	41
Intermediate	37	39	30	35
Small	38	44	32	37
Overall average				36

REPLACEMENT OF IBM SYSTEM BY COMPETITION

Table 47's data from a 1971 IBM report show how often, from 1967 to 1970, each particular commercial IBM system was replaced by a competitive system and the total number of these IBM commercial systems installed.

Very few—between one-half and one percent—of the IBM systems, once installed, were replaced by a competitive system during these years.

These data show that IBM's success came from an absence of effective competition. This insufficient competition sprang from two sources. First, software lock-in kept competitors from bidding for existing users' additional systems business, and second, IBM's low entry-level system pricing undercut its competitors' ability to win the new and uncommitted users' systems business.

Table 47
IBM 360 Systems Replaced by Competition, 1967–70

SYSTEM	1967	1968	1969	1970
360/20	14	41	68	108
360/25			2	7
360/30	37	26	47	30
360/40		8	10	18
360/50	2		1	6
360/65	2	1	1	1
Total Number Replaced	55	76	129	170
Total Number Installed	10,137	14,137	17,458	18,127
Percent Replaced	0.5%	0.5%	0.7%	0.9%

Appendix D
IBM Greybooks

The primary source of data used here is a series of detailed financial studies of the 360 performance made by IBM during the 1960s known as the Greybooks. These studies were initially used to establish the prices for products and later to monitor the products' financial performance in relation to the initial projections. IBM's method in these studies is to establish an initial price and project forward the number of months a particular product would be on rent and the volume of sales, in order to calculate total expected revenues. Next, total costs, both direct and indirect, are estimated and overhead is allocated down to each specific model of product. The result is a profit estimate in dollars and an estimate of profitability in percentage of revenues. In addition, IBM separately calculates the profitability of leased equipment and sold equipment.

The major difference between the early 360 studies, done at the time of introduction, and the ones that followed was that the latter employed much actual—as opposed to projected—financial data. As such, the early studies were reflections of what IBM expected, while the later studies measured what had actually been accomplished.

The most important single Greybook is that dated December 15, 1966, PX 1962A. This 548-page document is the most valuable for understanding the IBM 360. In its statistical appendixes, each important box attached to each model of system is analyzed both as to its financial results up until then and into the expected future. Incidentally, the earlier versions of this document—PX 1962—are incomplete and lack many of the statistical tables contained in the later and larger document.

There are additional Greybooks entered into the record of the trial. These usually deal with a single system or a particularly important device as follows:

	EXHIBIT NO.	EQUIPMENT	DATE
PX	1001	1401	Jan 1960
	1002	7070	Feb 1960
	1003A	7080	Mar 1960
	1004	1401	Jan 1961
	1009	7040/7044	Jul 1962
	1030	1401 CPU	Jun 1963
	1195	1440	Sept 1964
	1570	360/20 CPU	Aug 1965
	1888	1400/7000	Sept 1966
	2207A	360/85	Apr 1968
	2208	360/75	Apr 1968
	2209A	360/25	Apr 1968
	2210	2420-7 Tape	Apr 1968
	2211A	Tapes	Apr 1968
	2212	Disk	Apr 1968

EXHIBIT NO.	EQUIPMENT	DATE
2223A	360/30	Apr 1968
2224A	360/40	Apr 1968
2225A	360/50	Apr 1968
2226A	360/65	Apr 1968
2227A	360/67	Apr 1968
2228A	360/20	Apr 1968
2229A	360/44	Apr 1968
2415	360/50	Apr 1969
2416	360/75	Apr 1969
2417	360/40	Apr 1969
2418	360/67	Apr 1969
2419	360/44	Apr 1969
2432	360/30	May 1969
2435	Tapes	Apr 1969
2444	360/25	Jun 1969
2459	System 3	July 1969
2460A	360/65	July 1969
2473A	360/20	July 1969
2583	360/summary	May 1970
2619	370/155	Aug 1970
2620A	370/165	Aug 1970
2639	Plan 25	Sept 1970
2645	370/165	Oct 1970
2662	3360 Storage	Oct 1970
2672A	370/145	May 1971
2684A	System 3/Md 6	Nov 1971
2686	370/135	Feb 1972
2682	3830/3330/3336	Aug 1971

Appendix E
Profit and Loss from Data Processing Operations, 1960–72

Estimating the profit and loss of just the data processing part of the systems competitors' business is no simple task. Using a variety of accounting records supplied in response to subpoenas of the Court and relying on estimates where data were unavailable resulted in the following total for the years 1960–72.

While IBM was making in excess of $7 billion in profits during the twelve-year period, the other firms were in total losing almost $1 billion.

While IBM was earning in excess of $9 billion in profits on U.S. operations during this twelve-year period, competitors were losing a combined total of almost $1 billion.

The data below show clearly why several of these major firms chose to leave the business, the attraction of IBM's high profits notwithstanding. The largest losses were suffered by NCR, losses that it could cover from its lucrative cash register business. Moreover, NCR could not afford to leave, for increasingly these cash registers were being threatened by point-of-sales terminals connected directly to computers. Losses or no, NCR had no place to go, and stayed in the business.

The next largest losers were RCA and GE—both of which left the business. These were large, technically sophisticated firms and IBM expected them to play an important role in the computer business. GE, IBM concluded, had "the potential to become a much more potent force in EDP in the 1970s."[2] And "RCA could evolve into one of IBM's strongest competitors in the 1970's."[3] Yet both saw only continuing losses ahead: GE predicted it would take an additional $800 million in losses on its computer business between 1970 and 1975 before it would begin to break even.[4] RCA, in 1971, projected that it would have to invest an additional $700 million into its computer systems business between 1971 and 1976 to achieve its first year of break-even operations.[5]

Faced with such losses, both chose to invest their resources into other more promising parts of their diversified businesses. GE concluded that computers were too hazardous in part because of IBM's "aggressive counter-punches to competitive threats".[6] RCA concluded that its efforts in computers would not be successful due to the "uniquely entrenched competition" in the business, first and foremost, of IBM.[7] Upon leaving the business, RCA wrote off an additional $412 million.[8]

Xerox's story was a similar one. Using its position in copiers, it purchased Scientific Data Systems in 1969 for about $918 million worth of stock. Xerox then attempted to broaden the capabilities of SDS's system to compete in the commercial market. The efforts resulted in the substantial losses seen in Table 48. In 1974, Xerox concluded that further efforts would increase annual losses by $20 million to $25 million per year, increasing projected total losses through 1979 to $200 mil-

Table 48

Before-Tax Profit or Loss From Domestic Electronic Data Processing Business for Various Firms, 1960–72

(in $ billions)

	1960	1961	1962	1963	1964	1965	1966	1967	1968	1969	1970	1971	1972	TOTAL
IBM	290.6	362.5	415.4	518.6	615.4	588.4	589.8	804.7	1,248.2	1,073.3	894.6	846.6	973.3	9,221.7
Burroughs	-8.8	-14.6	-18.0	-14.4	-12.1	-10.8	-12.2	-4.3	8.0	10.1	20.1	14.2	17.0	-25.8
Control Data Corp	-1.8	2.9	5.7	10.6	14.3	6.2	7.2	25.7	39.1	32.2	-43.5	-14.8	10.8	98.2
Digital Equipment Corp	N.A.	1.0	2.2	2.2	1.5	2.2	4.8	6.5	10.2	15.6	17.0	12.7	17.6	93.6
General Electric	-6.6	-13.7	-18.0	-20.2	-23.9	-36.0	-50.8	-31.1	-18.4	-12.9	-22.5	N.A.	N.A.	-254.1
Honeywell	-6.8	-11.8	-13.1	-8.4	-9.8	-16.4	2.6	1.8	10.2	24.1	57.0	15.6	6.0	51.0
NCR	-12.5	-19.4	-22.2	-24.2	-22.1	-22.1	-36.8	-43.3	-43.9	-30.7	-44.8	-65.9	-65.8	-453.8
RCA	-23.4	-31.9	-27.9	-16.6	-7.3	-11.1	-26.8	-39.2	-37.0	-34.9	-36.1	-54.0	N.A.	-346.1
Singer Corp	N.A.	N.A.	N.A.	N.A.	N.A.	N.A.	N.A.	N.A.	N.A.	N.A.	N.A.	N.A.	1.2	1.2
Sperry Univac	-15.6	-15.6	-24.2	-28.2	-21.8	-20.2	-5.5	-12.1	-1.2	-4.2	-11.1	-2.3	3.4	90.3
SDS/Xerox	N.A.	-.1	-.5	2.3	4.4	5.4	7.8	12.6	19.6	24.5	-32.8	-38.3	-47.3	-42.5
Total w/o IBM	-71.9	-103.3	-115.9	-96.9	-76.8	-102.0	-98.8	-59.2	-11.0	32.3	-74.5	-132.7	-57.1	-968.5

lion. There was seen little or no possibility of profits until the mid-1980s.[9] Xerox in 1975 therefore decided to call it quits. Upon leaving, it wrote off an additional $166 million.[10] Xerox went back to its copier business, in which IBM by then had became increasingly active.

Frederic G. Withington of A.D. Little testified that in the mid-1970s it would take at least $2 billion for a new firm to enter the business successfully against IBM absent a "technological miracle." He foresaw no such new full-line entry.[11]

Appendix F
IBM Warnings to PCM Customers[1]

International Business Machines Company Limited

5 Place Ville [illegible]
Montreal 2, Quebec
Canada
Area Code 514
874-6123

February 12, 1969

Mr. H. Murphy
Director of Information Services
Canadian Lady-Canadell
140 Cremazie Blvd. W.
Montreal, Quebec

Dear Harry

Concerning your intention of including non-IBM disk drives on your on-order Model 25 System, I would like to bring to your attention a number of points that should be seriously considered and evaluated before a decision is made. I will not repeat the facts established in our Multiple Supplier System Bulletin which you have, but will elaborate on the significance of our policies to the multiple supplier system user.

1. The MAI drive was designed to be compatible with System/360. You must assess the risk in assuming that the drive will continue to be compatible at all times in the future, when engineering hardware and programming software changes will be made to our systems.
2. Engineering changes are continually being sent to our users of System/360. There is a real possibility that such changes, similar to a number made to the IBM 2311 last year, could render the MAI drive incompatible for a period of time. EC's are designed in conjunction with total system characteristics and software features. Even though the MAI drive is compatible at this time, the effectiveness of the drive in a changing 360 environment is a question mark.
3. If Canadian Lady chooses to delay EC level installation to ensure MAI drive effectiveness, any increased maintenance on the IBM portion of the system that can be attributed to the delays can be billed to you on a per call rate. In addition, Canadian Lady cannot indefinitely delay engineering changes, for IBM retains the right to maintain its equipment at the latest performance level.

4. In the area of software, major changes are continually being made to our operating systems which are designed to function in conjunction with our hardware characteristics. New releases of DOS could jeopardize the operating effectiveness of the MAI drive since hardware changes to our 2311's have been made in the past to take advantage of improved software features. Canadian Lady could delay implementation of any release of DOS to maintain compatibility, but at the risk of losing Type 1 program support. IBM will support the second last release of DOS up to one month after the availability of the latest release. Thereafter, Sales, Systems Engineering and Customer Engineering support of the software will not be available.

5. If at any time IBM determines that the maintenance of your Model 25 System is higher than it normally should be without competitor's disk drives attached, such maintenance will be charged to you at the per call rate.

6. Since MAI service people cannot touch the IBM portion of your system, there will be times when apparent disk problems will require the presence of an IBM Customer Engineer. If the problem was with the MAI drive, Canadian Lady would be charged for the maintenance call of our CE. In your own experience, you will know that the necessity of complete system coverage on a disk problem is not unlikely.

7. In the event of immediate back-up requirements due to non-IBM device failure, Canadian Lady will be charged Datacentre rates for usage of one of our systems installed in our offices.

8. IBM disk and tape drives have complete data checking and error detecting capabilities. This is extremely important since even one undetected error could result in serious reconstruction or rerun problem. It is a fact that different competitors' tape drives, which were somewhat cheaper than our own, have transmitted completely invalid data that was rejected 100% of the time by IBM drives. Tape drives have been competitive for some time, whereas disk drives have become so only recently. It is advisable to evaluate the error checking facilities of the MAI drive in comparison to those of the 2311.

9. In an earlier conversation, you stated that the MAI drive processed sequentially faster than the IBM 2311. This is in fact not the case, for the MAI drive actually processes slower than the 2311 in sequential mode. This is caused by the longer head settling time required by the MAI device, once the access arm has reached the required track. This fact should be evaluated in view of the volume of your present sequential jobs.

10. In the case of back-up requirements necessitated by failure of the IBM portion of a multiple supplier system, we will provide required machine back-up for the IBM devices on the system. If competitors' disk drives are on your system, the use of IBM 2311's for back-up will be charged at Datacentre rates.

Yours very truly

T. C. Trecarten:ns
Marketing Representative
Data Processing Division

Appendix G
Friends in High Places

At all times during the late 1960s and early 1970s, when the peripherals battles were at their fiercest, IBM had great access to the banking and investment community. The clearest manifestation of this was the many senior IBM people who sat on the boards of major financial institutions and commercial corporations.

Consider: Thomas J. Watson, Jr., while IBM chairman and chief executive officer, was a director of Bankers Trust Co. of New York and a trustee of the Rockefeller Foundation. A. L. Williams, IBM director and member of the executive committee, sat on the boards of First National City Bank of New York, Mobil Oil, General Motors, and General Foods. While IBM president T.V. Learson, was a director of Chemical Bank and Standard Oil of New Jersey. Arthur K. Watson was, while serving as IBM vice chairman, a director of the Federal Reserve Bank of New York. Frank T. Cary, then senior vice-president of IBM, served as a director on the boards of both Morgan Guaranty Trust Co. of New York and the J.P. Morgan Bank. IBM senior vice president and chairman of IBM World Trade, G.E. Jones, was a trustee of the United States Trust Co. and a director of Continental Oil.

These personal connections, along with the quite substantial business IBM could offer the financial community, were of major concern to peripherals competitors and leasing companies as they attempted to raise vital capital. Several of these competitors ended up filing antitrust suits against IBM, alleging, among other things, that IBM exerted improper influence on potential sources of finance and discouraged them from investing in IBM's competition.

Specifically, IBM was alleged to have concluded in late 1967 that one of the principal constraints to the growth of computer leasing companies was their access to capital. At IBM's request, Morgan Guaranty's research staff conducted financial studies of the leasing companies in February 1968, January 1969, and December 1969. IBM itself used these studies in a report entitled "Viability of Systems Leasing Companies," but the studies were also distributed among Morgan Guaranty's many member banks. These reports offered a subtle way, as IBM's top financial man T. P. Papes observed, to "send information to the investment banking community that would cast doubt upon the future of the leasing company industry." Not surprisingly, these reports showed that the leasing companies were a poor investment, in no small part due to actions IBM might take against them.

In another allegation, T.V. Learson, IBM president, learned that DPF&G, a leasing company, owed Ford Motor Credit Co. $30 million and had no bank credit available. In November 1968, Learson asked Arthur K. Watson to use his friendship with Henry Ford II to harm DPF&G's credit relationship with Ford Credit. Watson responded later that month that he would look into the matter.

In May 1970, Continental Illinois National Bank and Trust Co. issued a report stating that the computer leasing companies were making a comeback. Learson late that month shot off a memo to John R. Opel, then senior vice-president, asking that Opel "get someone to talk to the Continental Bank." Opel directed IBM treasurer Henry Sibley to handle the matter. Evidently, as noted on the memo, the issue was "settled" with the bank being put straight on the risky future of the leasing companies.

Memorex became critically dependent on funding for its ambitious plans for expansion into new computer markets. In the process, it approached the Morgan Guaranty, First National City, Chemical, and Manufacturers Hanover banks, among others. Memorex claimed that J. J. Forese, IBM data processing group director of finance, discussed Memorex's financing with bankers, accountants, and business executives at a New York meeting of the Financial Executives Institute. David Brillhart, vice president of Morgan Guaranty, admitted in court on November 27, 1970, that he had discussed the Memorex financing with Forese. Morgan Guaranty, along with other major banks, eventually refused to lend Memorex any money.

Appendix H
Standards for Avarice

(reprinted from *ComputerWorld,* September 1980)

Back in the days when users were first learning they could save money by hanging plug-compatible peripherals on their IBM mainframes, IBM took umbrage at such acts of disloyalty. Its reaction came in the form of intimidation, according to many users who claimed to be on the receiving end.

Although not officially sanctioned by Armonk, sales representatives, branch and even regional managers were reportedly leaning—very hard—on deserters from the fold. Most of those deserters were too frightened to speak out in print, fearing further retribution.

Aggrieved DP directors claimed that when they decided to farm out some business to a plug-compatible manufacturer (PCM), the computer goliath started its strong-arm tactics. The user was told maintenance on remaining (and there was usually plenty) IBM equipment would suffer if they bolted.

If this friendly advice was ignored and the user strayed, IBM allegedly brought in higher level executives whose job it was to pressure the DP director's boss, who may or may not have known anything about computers.

Playing on that weakness, the ploy called into question the validity of the peripheral selection process and, more importantly, the competence of the DP director who played an integral role in it. This meant he was raked over the coals without a chance to defend himself.

After a few years of this behavior, things seemed to calm down. PCMs had become a reality IBM was forced to accept, albeit grudgingly.

So, just when everything seemed aboveboard again, *ComputerWorld* received a spate of letters and phone calls complaining of the same old tactics. We conducted a survey of DP directors who had selected PCM mainframes over the past year and discovered nearly one-third of them had experienced some form of retribution.

What goes on here? IBM quarterly earnings in July reflected a 14% increase over the same period last year. Despite the emergent threat from Japanese shores, the company still has a virtual hammerlock on worldwide computer trade.

These latest methods used to maintain that control have done little to enhance IBM's image, and the crude and craven attempts by some of its employees to retain business at all costs have set new standards for avarice.

IBM sets high standards on a corporate level, and it's time it started enforcing them in the field.

Appendix I
A Voice Crying in the Wilderness

The most important problem that IBM and its customers face today is how to enable its diverse and incompatible product line to communicate easily. If each of the dozen or so product families had from the beginning been designed to be compatible with each other, SNA could be much simpler and IBM's problems far less daunting than they are. One who saw it all coming in 1970, and vainly tried to stop this proliferation of incompatibility, was IBM's W. S. Humphrey, of the Systems Development Division's Endicott, N.Y., laboratory. He addressed the question of[1]

> whether a compatible product line should be our [Data Processing] Group objective. This is such a fundamental issue that I have taken some time to prepare an answer. . . . Compatibility is a major and growing requirement of our customers. Compatibility is most essential for the advanced and highest-potential applications environment. . . . I strongly recommend that the DP Group adopt as its strategic goal the achievement of an operationally compatible product line. Each of our system and product strategies should be measured against this goal, our planning and testing should be so directed, and our organization and management system should be established towards this end.[2]

Humphrey's concern was that even then IBM's product line had too many layers of incompatible systems. His objection to this approach was that it made it difficult and expensive for customers to move their application programs from one system to another as their processing needs grew. That the existence of incompatible systems was segmenting the market was not in doubt. He continued:

> In any case where growth is blocked by an incompatible barrier, we find that the customers are either slow to move or reassess their IBM decision versus competition. In the first case, the growth of [360] Mod 20 customers into the DOS environment has been almost completely stopped by the incompatibile nature of these two systems. Similarly, the transition from DOS to OS/360 is difficult and represents a serious impediment to customer growth out of the [360/] Mod 40 marketplace. . . . It is clear that smooth growth is an absolute requirement. That is, growth within a product line and growth between generations of a product line. In each case, our customer is concerned with his ability to install a new system smoothly without expensive conversion.

Humphrey could see what was coming—that these systems would soon be hooked together into large networks.

> I believe that interconnected systems, as well as interconnected networks of systems will be of growing importance in the 1970's and a major factor in the 1980's. This being the case, we should recognize this requirement for [370] and System 3 exten-

sions. It is an absolute requirement for FS which will be introduced in the late 1970's and will be operational in the marketplace through much of the 1980's. Operational compatibility in that timeframe will be required across a complete product line. It will, for instance, be completely unacceptable to introduce systems like the [360] Mod 20 . . . Similarly, the introduction of the System 3 with an architecture that precludes any significant upward growth would be recognized as limited to the small single installation customer and unacceptable to the large customer with many small operations. . . . [By] the end of the '70's and into the 1980's we must offer a completely compatible line from the terminal and device to the smallest and the very largest of our processing systems.

Moreover, as early as 1970 Humphrey felt that it was a technically achievable goal. "There is a large body of technical opinion that it can be done." And, in fact, today other firms such as DEC have managed to accomplish just what he was advocating.

Thus, based on the goal of "a completely compatible line" for the 1980s, IBM's present offerings have to be considered a monumental failure. In spite of the technical capability to do so and the knowledge that customers wanted it, IBM's incompatible products do not allow its customers the freedom to move easily from system to system or to connect different systems into a communicating network easily.

Appendix J
What's Good for the Goose

Beginning in the late 1960s, there was some question in the computer and communications industries as to whether such a huge monopoly as AT&T should be permitted to enter competitive arenas outside its regulated business. The Federal Communications Commission (FCC) began an inquiry into the issue and invited interested parties to comment. Dr. James McKie submitted this statement as part of a larger memorandum on IBM's behalf.

(Briefly, the term *carrier services* here refers to the regulated communications companies, of which AT&T was the biggest. *Teleprocessing services* are data processing services offered remotely over phone lines, either by data processing vendors [IBM et. al.] or by common carriers [AT&T, General Telephone & Electric, et. al.])

"The economic relationships that are developing between teleprocessing and the common carriers would not involve special problems if the spheres of operation of the carrier utilities and data processors were separate and distinct. But when communications utilities offer teleprocessing services for sale, problems inevitably arise from the fact that they have a monopoly of common-carrier communications services while other data processors are dependent on the carriers for these services. Relative prices and other terms of availability for common carriage will then affect the conditions of competition in the (unregulated) data processing services themselves.

"A public utility operating a complete system under a monopoly umbrella can adjust particular rates to conditions of demand for the service. It can set varying prices for the same service for different quantities, different classes of customers, etc. and fix price differentials for different services which in no way correspond to specific cost differences. . . .

"This system of utility pricing under regulations need present no difficulty to users as long as rates are fair, reasonable, and nondiscriminatory among users in the same class or industry and as long as the overall rate of return is not excessive—until the utility itself also engages in an unregulated business, in actual or potential competition with other firms who are users of its services. In a competitive market, the rules and standards are quite different from those applying to a franchised public utility. Competitive sellers could not for long meet below-cost prices that were subsidized from monopoly earnings by a hybrid utility enterprise that used common plant for both regulated and competitive activities. Such a firm could easily defeat the purposes of regulation and undercut its competitors by implicitly transferring revenues across the line through its price policy while the relevant costs were lost to sight in the labyrinth of internal accounts. A hidden subsidy would be paid by captive consumers of its monopoly services. The utility might not even intend to mix its revenues or to depart from competitive standards of price, but the danger would always be there. . . .

"What cost allocations do is to prevent the generation of excess revenues in the regulated sector to subsidize unduly low prices in the utility enterprise's competitive business activity. They prevent an excess allocation of current common costs against utility revenues. Cost allocations are admittedly imperfect, but they can greatly reduce the magnitude of the internal-subsidy problem."

There is concern here not only about the potential for anticompetitive price discrimination to drive those firms lacking monopoly power from the business but also about preferential terms and access to the market that the competitive parts of the communications carrier might enjoy against nonintegrated competitors. The statement continues:

"A closely related problem is preferential terms, meaning simply that the utility may wittingly or unwittingly prefer its own customer to that of outsiders when setting prices and other conditions of sale of the regulated monopoly service. If the utility set higher rates for common-carrier services to data processing competitors than it charged to its own data processing divisions, for example, it could make competition in data processing very difficult. Regulated tariffs are supposed to forestall discriminatory effects among competitors, but equal treatment demands an arm's length purchase of services by the utility's data processing division under exactly the same tariffs as those applying to independent data processors who wish to purchase communications. There must be no combination of services at preferential rates not available to independents. Special tariffs must not be custom-tailored to the special mix of services that the carrier wants to offer. There must be no sharing of circuits at preferential rates by the carrier's data processing customers unless independent teleprocessing firms have the same privileges. All services and modes of access to central processing offered to the carrier's data processing customers must be made available to other processors for their customers. There must be no non-price discrimination in favor of the carrier's own data-processing customers, such as preference when a shortage of peak-load condition occurs, special back-up services, better technology for dedicated facilities, more solicitous repair and maintenance service, etc.

"These conditions of equal treatment would be impossible to guarantee without some safeguards. The best safeguard against deep-pocket subsidies, preferential rates, and discriminatory service would be a separately organized teleprocessing division or unit for the common carrier that would be subject to the following rules. (1) It should purchase all common carrier services under published tariffs which offer the identical service to all independents. (2) When a data processing unit uses the same facilities as the common carrier services, such as a computer, the common facilities should be subject to formal cost allocation, as advocated above."

McKie thus lays down rules to limit the ability of, in this case, a regulated monopolist to leverage its power into neighboring markets where competitive firms are active but could not long survive against such tactics. If these same rules had been applied to IBM—in its dealing with competitors needing its unit record equipment, in its low-priced scientific systems, in its allocation of common costs of attracting new users to existing users, in its low-priced entry-level equipment—its success would have been much less. There is no disagreement between this analysis of potential abuses of market power by a regulated communications monopoly, AT&T, and the present analysis of IBM's market power: price discrimination enables a monopolist to circumvent the competitive process, to win not through superior products, lower prices, better management, or other societally beneficial characteristics, but rather because of power.

Price discrimination by a monopolist enables it to achieve two usually contradictory goals—high market share and high profits. Such tactics by a monopolist lock the structure of the market. Competitors are powerless, despite the monopolist's high prices, to erode its position. As this last passage makes clear, its author thinks that such advantages are unfair, and even scrutiny by governmental regulators of the monopolist's actions may still not be sufficient.

IBM, it would appear, has different rules for other companies with monopoly power from those it has for itself. But, of course, IBM has never admitted to having a monopoly.

Appendix K
U.S. v. IBM

The history of the *U.S.* v. *IBM* antitrust case begins with the commencement of the preliminary inquiry in 1964, when Nicholas DeB. Katzenbach was Deputy Attorney General.* In the fall of 1968, IBM was informed that a complaint was being recommended to the then Attorney General, Ramsey Clark. To allow IBM a hearing with the Attorney General, the DOJ delayed filing the case until January 1969.

In early 1972, the new head of the Antitrust Division, Richard W. McLaren, sent the complaint and supporting data to the Council of Economic Advisors for review and opinion as to whether it was in the public interest to proceed with the litigation. When a favorable reply was received from the Council, preparation for trial accelerated in early 1972—leading, in May 1975, to the commencement of trial.

On January 8, 1982, after all the evidence for the case had been completed and the only remaining tasks were submitting of briefs and the judge's decision, Assistant Attorney General William F. Baxter, in charge of the Antitrust Division, ordered the case to be dismissed. This decision particularly troubled the former Chief of the Division's Special Litigation Section, Lewis Bernstein, who had been responsible for the development and trial of the case and who had participated in it from the preliminary inquiry through the completion of the affirmative case:

> [I]t does not seem to be in the public interest for an Assistant Attorney General to dismiss a matter which had been initiated thirteen years earlier after it had been reviewed by two Assistant Attorney Generals, the then Attorney General and after IBM had an opportunity to make a presentation to each of them respectively setting forth the reasons why the case should not be filed. Each succeeding Assistant Attorney General thereafter reviewed the matter as well as the Council for Economic Advisors. Each came to the conclusion that the theory of the case was sound and that it was in the public interest to continue the action.[1]

In all, the case was prosecuted under the supervision of nine Assistant Attorney Generals—Donald F. Turner, Edwin Zimmerman, Richard W. McLaren, Walker B. Comegys, Thomas E. Kauper, Donald I. Baker, John H. Shenefield, Sanford J. Litvack, and William F. Baxter. The last of these withdrew the case as being "without merit."

Ordinarily, under Department of Justice procedures, the Assistant Attorney General in charge of the Antitrust Division would make a recommendation to dismiss an important pending case to the Deputy Attorney General, who would then review and forward it to the Attorney General. In this case, the Attorney General and Deputy Attorney General had both withdrawn from participation so that Baxter remained the final decision maker.

In his testimony before the House Subcommittee, Bernstein testified that it would have been in

* Mr. Katzenbach subsequently played an important role in the defense as Vice President and General Counsel of IBM.

the public interest for Baxter to have allowed the case to be decided by the presiding judge so that the decision could be made by one who never had any previous connection with IBM. And, he said, if that decision were in favor of the Government, then if Baxter, after reviewing the opinion, felt strongly enough that it was incorrect, he could have recommended to the solicitor general that the Government confess error on any subsequent appeal that IBM might bring. If this procedure had been followed, Bernstein said, the public would have had the opportunity to review the court's opinion and the solicitor general would have had the opportunity to review Baxter's different analysis.

Because there was no review process, and Baxter was the final arbiter, despite the views of the previous nine assistant attorney generals, the whole effort failed. In the end, this is not so surprising. Though Baxter purported to review the record of the case, evidence later surfaced that he had in fact made up his mind on the worth of the case long before taking the job. He had written several years earlier in a memo to the then incoming Carter Administration transition team, the following:

On the basis of what I now know, including the evidence which has been introduced so far, I think that the I.B.M. case should never have been brought.[2]

When later given the power to act on his earlier conviction, he did just that.

There is evidence in the record before the House Subcommittee that shortly after the case was filed, Baxter had been retained by IBM to review some aspect of it. Later, there were some communications between IBM's counsel and Baxter seeking to retain him for advice in some aspect of one or another of the private damage actions brought against IBM. Nonetheless, the House Subcommittee made no further inquiry about them.

Appendix L
IBM's Lawyers' Advice to Its Executives Re: Department of Justice Investigation[1]

The following is a list of points to be kept in mind when reviewing long range plans and other internal IBM documents, or proposed business decisions. These relate to our current thinking on how to deal with the Department of Justice investigation, and supplement the more obvious matters we have all been on the lookout for, over the years. None of the suggestions is absolute, but before approving a course of action or document which is inconsistent with any of the following, you should check with the Antitrust section of Corporate Legal.

I. Market Structure and Market Share
  (a) Don't restrict IBM's market, e.g., by statements that military computers are in a separate market.
  (b) Don't restrict discussions of IBM computer manufacturer competitors to the eight major companies ("Seven Dwarfs" plus SDS); at the very least, include a reference to the existence of many other manufacturing competitors.
  (c) Expand on the classes of IBM's competitors, e.g., leasing companies and other owners of IBM machines, manufacturers of peripheral equipment.
  (d) Avoid loose, inaccurate or unnecessary documents which talk about IBM's market share, either as a whole or in any segment of the market.
  (e) Don't understate the capabilities of present competitors or potential competitors; don't discount the possible entry of new competitors.
  (f) Don't predict a slowdown in the growth of the data processing market or in the rate or change of its technology; conversely, take the opportunity to point to continuing growth and technological change.
  (g) Avoid predictions of a stable or increased market share for IBM.
  (h) Avoid references to large customer investments in programming or any other factors which might point towards a "lock in" of IBM's installed customers.
  (i) Avoid references to the inexperience or naivete of IBM's customers, or to their dependence on IBM.
  (j) Avoid discussion of economies of scale in any part of IBM's operation.
II. Performance
  (a) Don't make unnecessary comparisons of profit levels among different IBM products.
  (b) Emphasize the data processing industry's past history of rapid innovation and decreasing costs to the customer.

III. Behavior

(a) Avoid post-mortems, case studies and other discussion of the System/360 announcements or subsequent price changes.

(b) Avoid pricing and related actions which are designed to maintain or increase market share at the expense of profit.

(c) Do not permit pricing of individual machines at a loss, even if a profit is expected on the System as a whole.

(d) Take occasion to record any "fall out" from the Model 90 or its technology.

(e) Don't boast about any superiority IBM enjoys in the technology or manufacture of its components, or about any unique advantages IBM enjoys by making its own components; where appropriate, acknowledge any technical or price advantages of components manufactured by our competitors or by suppliers like Texas Instruments or Motorola.

(f) Don't offer separately priced services which overlap or extend from parts of the "bundle," e.g., non-hardware emulators, education or systems management services.

(g) Don't market free programs that compete with programs already being offered by others for a price.

(h) Don't concede, even indirectly, an ability on the part of IBM to protect its investment in programs, e.g., distribution of programs on the basis of an agreement to keep confidential.

(i) Take the opportunity to emphasize the sales support activities of IBM systems engineers, and avoid references to their customer service activities.

(j) Don't link IBM's lease/purchase multipliers to leasing companies.

(k) Avoid statements indicating that IBM's systems engineering capabilities or services are unique, or superior to those of others, even in the eyes of the customer.

(l) Don't relate IBM's educational allowance, or changes in the allowance, to market conditions.

(m) There should be no value received or buy-back arrangements unless they are totally divorced from sales of IBM equipment.

(n) Don't define "normal support"; avoid any indication of differing levels of support for different customers or different installations, even if the differences are unrelated to getting the order.

(o) Don't discuss the advantages of having IBM's multiple access offerings made through DPD, or any resulting handicaps faced by our customers/competitors. Avoid the imposition of any unnecessary price or other handicaps on our multiple access customers/competitors.

Notes

INTRODUCTION

1. Rex Mallik, *And Tomorrow . . . the World: Inside IBM* (London: Millington, 1975), p. 5.
2. Thomas J. Peters and Robert H. Waterman, Jr., *In Search of Excellence: Lessons from America's Best-Run Companies* (New York: Harper & Row, 1982).

PART I: IBM MAKES THE RULES—A GAME OF POWER
1. THE EDUCATION OF T. J. WATSON

Watson senior's early experience at NCR and later at IBM have been written about in many books. Included among these are:

- William Rodgers, *THINK: A Biography of the Watsons and IBM* (New York: Stein and Day, 1969).
- Thomas and Marva Belden, *The Lengthening Shadow* (Boston: Little Brown, 1962).
- Robert Sobel, *IBM: Colossus in Transition* (New York: Times Books, 1981).

1. Rodgers, p. 44.

2. A MATTER OF TRUST

1. This incident was told to me by Mr. Dan Hosage, who during the 1960s was in charge of marketing IBM's middle-sized computer systems.
2. From Federal Rules, 23 F.R.D. 319, p. 417.
3. The relationship between Barr and Bromley is described in James Stewart, *The Partners* (New York: Simon and Schuster, 1983), pp. 56–59.

3. ENTER THE COMPUTER

1. PX 4794 (PX means Plaintiff's Exhibit in the trial record of *US* v. *IBM;* DX means Defendant's Exhibit; JX means Joint Exhibit, TR. refers to the transcript page of witness testimony.)
2. IBM's economists prepared an extensive culling of the evidence from the trial record called a Historical Narrative (DX 14972). This they represent as "a detailed economic history of IBM and the industry." A revised version was published (Fisher, Mancke, and McKie, *IBM and the U.S. Data Processing Industry: An Economic History* (New York: Praeger, 1983)). This quote is from DX 14971, p. 7.
3. DX 14971, p. 127.
4. "Thomas J. Watson Jr. of IBM—Winning the race, Lessons of Leadership part XCIII" in *Nation's Business,* February 1973, pp. 41–45.

5. PX 5035A.
6. PX 1001A.
7. Just such an explanation is offered in DX 14971, pp. 125–26.
8. IBM Business Conduct Policies: Responsibilities and Guide (IBM-BCP), January 1, 1962. Part II, 24.
9. IBM-BCP: Part I, pp. 5–6.
10. PX 5035A.
11. PX 1.
12. PX 5035A.

4. THE FIVE-YEAR GENERATION

1. "Is IBM Good for America?", *Business and Society Review,* Winter 1986, No. 56, Warre, Gorham & Lamont, Inc. "Big Blue Responds," a response by John Akers, president and chief executive officer of IBM, pp. 14–15.
2. IBM-BCP, p. 19.
3. PX 1888A.
4. PX 1888A.
5. PX 1888A.
6. PX 2508A.
7. PX 1001A, p. 14.
8. From IBM's price lists.
9. PX 1888.
10. PX 1001A, p. 4.
11. Tr 19908-10.
12. PX 2717.
13. IBM-BCP, Part II, p. 26.

5. RUSHING THE 360s

1. PX 1225.
2. PX 1684.
3. PX 3446, p. 86.
4. PX 4284.
5. PX 1630.
6. PX 2483A.
7. PX 6221.
8. PX 4285, p. 240.
9. PX 1877.
10. PX 3647.
11. "IBM's $5,000,000,000 Gamble" and "The Rocky Road to the Marketplace," by T. A. Wise in *Fortune,* September and October 1966.
12. Statement made in IBM pre-trial brief in *US* v. *IBM* antitrust case, p. 306.
13. PX 6671 and 6675.
14. PX 1630.
15. PX 3641.
16. PX 3641.
17. PX 2009.
18. PX 1900.
19. PX 3425.

20. PX 6220.
21. PX 1805, p. 6.
22. IBM-BCP, Part I, pp. 5–6.
23. PX 1856.
24. IBM-BCP, p. 26.
25. PX 4005.
26. PX 2126, p. 9.
27. PX 2126, p. 11.
28. PX 1630, pp. 1–2.

6. DIVIDE AND CONQUER

1. PX 4794.
2. The record of the case is replete with statements that competition traditionally has to price its equipment 5 to 20% below IBM equipment of comparable capability. The following are just some of these: Withington of A. D. Little, Tr. 58533, 58463, 58797-98, 58830, 58423, 56566; Beard of RCA, Tr. 8493-96; McCollister of RCA, Tr. 9269-73; Bloch of Honeywell, Tr. 7599-7601, 7596-97; Hangen of NCR 6350-52; McDonald of Sperry-Univac, Tr. 2883-86, 4150-56, 4178-9, 4217-9; Norris of CDC, Tr. 5653-54; Lacey of CDC, Tr. 6570-73; Palevsky of SDS 3149-50, 3165, 3176; and Wright of Xerox, Tr. 12182-84.
3. PX 4285.
4. PX 1983, pp. 10–11.
5. PX 4285.
6. PX 1983.
7. PX 1962A.
8. PX 1962A.
9. PX 1962A.
10. IBM Blue Letters and PX 1962A.
11. PX 1962A.
12. PX 1962A.
13. PX 1962A.
14. PX 4216.
15. IBM-BCP, p. 19.
16. PX 5310A.
17. PX 1962A.
18. PX 5310A.
19. PX 6449 p. 11.
20. PX 1962A, pp. 532, 534, 535, 537.
21. PX 5310A.

7. DIFFERENT STROKES

1. PX 1063.
2. PX 1043, 1044.
3. PX 1205.
4. PX 1962A.
5. PX 1962A.
6. PX 1563, 1564, 1565, 2825, 6212.
7. PX 2856, p. 8, PX 1582.
8. PX 1952.

9. PX 1626.
10. PX 1993.
11. PX 2418A.
12. PX 5735, 5758.
13. PX 1044.
14. PX 1144B.
15. PX 4079A.
16. PX 2731.
17. CDC 1965 Annual report, p. 5—DX 14214.
18. PX 5132.
19. PX 5132.

8. AND THE WINNER IS . . .

1. Buck Rodgers, *The IBM Way* (New York: Harper & Row, 1986). p. 222.
2. PX 1962A & QPLA.
3. PX 4655, PX 3451.
4. Column 1—PX 5637; Column 2—PX 5527, a study done by Dr. L. Weiss and presented at the trial; Column 3—PX 5550, from *The Economic Report of the President*, 1978, Table B-84, p. 355.
5. Op. cit., *Nation's Business.*
6. PX 4827A, 7350, 2032B, 2932, 5523, 4933, 4936, 5445, 5448

9. FACTS AND THEORY

1. PX 1962A.
2. John Z. DeLorean and J. Patrick Wright, *On a Clear Day You Can See General Motors* (New York: Avon, 1979), p. 211.
3. Quoted in "Predatory Price Cutting: The Standard Oil (N.J.) Case" by John S. McGee in *The Journal of Law and Economics,* p. 137.
4. Fisher et al., *Folded, Spindled, and Mutilated: Economic Analysis and U.S.* v. *IBM*, (Cambridge: MIT Press, 1983), pp. ix–xiii.
5. Fisher et al., op. cit., p. 346.
6. Carl Kaysen, *United States* v. *United Shoe Machinery Corporation: An Economic Analysis of an Anti-Trust Case* (Cambridge: Harvard University Press, 1956), p. 52.
7. Kaysen, op. cit., p. 126.
8. Northrop Tr. 82232, 82247.
9. Fisher et al., op. cit. pp. 512–52.
10. Kaysen, op. cit., p. 74.
11. Kaysen, op. cit., p. 78.
12. Weiss Tr. 69891-93. PX 5528.
13. Fisher et al., op. cit., p. 346n.

PART 2: THE GAME CHANGES
10. THE MARKET SPLINTERS

1. PX 5085.
2. PX 1311, 5296, 5298.
3. Statement by Walter Misdom of IDC in a presentation to the New York Society of Security Analysts, November 3, 1970.
4. PX 2308.

5. PX 2567, p. 201.
6. PX 3908A, pp. 5, 24.
7. PX 2152A.
8. PX 2308, p. 197.
9. PX 3908A, p. 24.
10. PX 2152A.
11. PX 3958.
12. PX 3096A, pp. 2–3.
13. PX 3201A.
14. PX 2472A, p. 1.
15. PX 3829.
16. PX 2276.
17. PX 2112, 2294, 2369.
18. PX 2883, p. 13.
19. PX 2414A, p. 63.
20. PX 3082, p. 62.
21. PX 3908A.
22. PX 1232.
23. PX 1225.
24. PX 3158A.
25. PX 2308, p. 220.
26. PX 2508A quoted in the rest of the chapter.

11. IBM RESPONDS

1. PX 3993, pp. 20–21.
2. PX 3236, pp. 6–7.
3. PX 3365.
4. PX 3483, p. 48.
5. PX 2125, pp. 48–49.
6. PX 2459.
7. PX 2684A.
8. PX 1962A.

12. THE DISK DRIVE MARKET

1. John R. Opel, Chairman, IBM; Remarks before American Chamber of Congress in the United Kingdom, May 31, 1984, p. 7.
2. IBM product description; PX 1962A.
3. PX 1962A.
4. PX 1962A.
5. PX 2377A.
6. IBM's Statistical Response in its cases against C.A.C. & Greyhound, December 10, 1971.
7. PX 2392.
8. PX 3117.
9. PX 6748A.
10. PX 6747A, 6753A, 6754.
11. PX 3930.
12. PX 6227, 6228.

13. PX 912—*Transamerica* v. *IBM* case.
14. PX 4151.
15. PX 3965.
16. PX 3966.
17. PX 4162.
18. Hochfeld Tr. 34617–20, 3211A, p. 6.
19. Ashbridge Tr. 23821–31.
20. James Tr. 35078.
21. PX 4201, pp. 6–7.
22. PX 4202.
23. Butters Tr. 43738–54.
24. PX 3851, p. 18.

13. SMASHING THE DISK DRIVE PLAYERS

1. PX 2508A, p. 2.
2. PX 5148, 5149.
3. PX 3154.
4. PX 4120.
5. PX 3158A.
6. PX 3158A.
7. PX 6388.
8. PX 2674, PX 4145.
9. PX 4095.
10. PX 4095.
11. PX 3749A.
12. PX 4130.
13. PX 4125.
14. PX 2680.
15. PX 5561.
16. PX 3985.
17. Much of the material dealing with Memorex's activities in the disk area comes from a memo prepared by Memorex titled "The Madrid Story."
18. Memorex filings.
19. The calculations were presented to the Court in the case IBM EDP Devices Antitrust Litigation MDL No. 163-Rm (PTO 5 Material Deleted) in a memorandum in support of a motion for a preliminary injunction.

14. THE BIGGER THE BETTER

1. IBM-BCP, Part II, p. 17.
2. Awedia Tr.
3. Faw, PX 5143.
4. From filing in *Itel* v. *IBM*.
5. The case filed February 10, 1972, in San Francisco was *Advanced Memory Systems, Inc., and Itel Memory Equipment* v. *International Business Machines,* C-72-245.
6. On January 31, 1973, the German District Court (Reg. no. 3 KfH 0 4/73 (Kart)) issued its opinion of IBM's refusal to maintain its 360/30 CPUs.
7. PX 6630.

8. PX 2574A.
9. PX 6630, p. 23.
10. PX 4403.
11. PX 4191.
12. PX 3271B, pp. 3–4.
13. IBM price lists.
14. IDC Study—McPherson Deposition Exhibit—TS 11, p. 13, 7, 70.
15. PX 6431.
16. McPherson Deposition exhibit—TS 26.
17. PX 5565.
18. PX 7314, p. 38, 7316, p. 24.
19. PX 4822.
20. PX 2260.
21. PX 2262B, p. 7.
22. Throughout the trial there were meetings between IBM and the Department of Justice, both parties looking for an agreeable solution to the case. In the fall of 1974, IBM made a series of presentations about computation and the industry. These were made on IBM's side by Messrs. Phypers, Bertram, Gold, Gomory, Low, Evangelista, and deB. Katzenbach. As part of that process, the mentioned IBM-FS memo was produced, p. 12.
23. IBM-FS memo, p. 12.
24. IBM-FS memo, pp. 16–17.
25. Case TR. 78511–13.
26. DX 14971, pp. 341, 345.

15. THE FUD FACTOR

1. Rodgers, op. cit., p. 225.
2. PX 4840.
3. PX 6453
4. DX 12690, p. 35.
5. PX 2685.
6. Amdahl Filing with Commission of the European Communities, vol. 1, dated Dec. 20, 1978.
7. PX 7314, 7316.
8. PX 6446, p. 113.
9. PX 6431.
10. PX 7314, p. 38, PX 7316, p. 24.
11. PX 6449.
12. PX 4839, p. 12.
13. PX 6431.

PART 3: BIGGER AND BIGGER
16. EVER OUTWARD

1. Peter L. Schavoir, *Future Without Limits,* published in IBM employee newsletter.
2. PX 2679, p. 66.
3. PX 2388, p. 66.
4. IBM-FS memo, p. 14.

5. PX 1192.
6. PX 2388, p. 66.
7. PX 2650, p. 8.
8. PX 2567.
9. PX 2567, pp. 269, 270.
10. PX 2567.
11. PX 1983.
12. PX 2685.

17. REACH OUT AND CRUSH SOMEONE

1. PX 4794.
2. PX 2167.
3. PX 4060.
4. PX 2659A.
5. US Brief p. 160.
6. PX 4046.
7. PX 4046.
8. PX 4046.
9. PX 4046.
10. PX 2167.
11. PX 2606.
12. PX 2606.
13. PX 2167.
14. PX 4069.
15. PX 2766.
16. PX 4060.
17. PX 2167.
18. PX 1662.
19. PX 4060.
20. PX 2766.
21. Op. cit., December 20, 1974 Statistical Response.
22. PX 2685.
23. PX 2482.
24. PX 3484.
25. PX 2627.
26. Memo prepared by J. M. Keefe, Corporate Counsel to R. C. Sanders, Jr., outlining the Anti-trust Claim against IBM, March 14, 1974.
27. PX 6450.
28. Cowen/Datamation Survey, February 1985.
29. Op. cit., IBM, December 20, 1974, Statistical Response.
30. PX 2679.
31. PX 2685.
32. PX 2685, p. 145.
33. Much of this material comes from a memo prepared by Memorex titled "Memorex vs. IBM Communications Issue Summary."
34. Withington Tr. 58480–81.
35. Withington Tr. 58917.
36. Withington Tr. 58503.

37. Withington Tr. 58496.
38. Withington Tr. 58500.

18. EXTENDING THE EMPIRE

1. I.B.M. E.H.Q. News, Nov.–Dec. 1985, p. 10.
2. *ComputerWorld,* April 18, 1983, p. 1.
3. PX 6444.
4. *Business Week,* April 21, 1986, p. 62.
5. *ComputerWorld,* December 31, 1984, p. 124. Data from Technical Financial Services, Inc.; IDC.
6. *ComputerWorld,* December 9, 1985, p. 59.
7. *ComputerWorld,* December 31, 1984, p. 124. Data from Technical Financial Services, Inc.
8. IBM 1985 Annual Report, p. 44; 1984 Report, p. 44.

PART 4: JUST A BEGINNING
19. THE REST OF THE WORLD

1. *Business and Society Review,* p. 15.
2. Simon Nora and Alain Minc, *The Computerization of Society: A Report to the President of France* (Cambridge: The MIT Press, 1980), pp. 69–70.
3. Nora and Minc, op. cit., p. 3.
4. *Computer White Paper—1972 Edition: A Summary of Highlights Compiled from the Japanese Original* (Originally published by Japan Computer Usage Development Institute), p. 20.
5. Raymond Vernon, ed., *Big Business and the State: Changing Relations in Western Europe* (Cambridge: Harvard University Press, 1974), p. 12.
6. Chapter 10—"Computers" by Nicolas Jequier in Vernon, *Big Business and the State,* p. 214.
7. *French Government Assistance to its Domestic Computer Industry: Lessons and Implications,* U.S. Department of Commerce, Bureau of Industrial Economics, June 1983.
8. Quoted in *French Government Assistance to its Domestic Computer Industry,* p. 10.
9. 1977 White Paper, p. 12.
10. 1977 White Paper, p. 4.
11. 1977 White Paper, p. 14.
12. 1977 White Paper, p. 30.
13. 1977 White Paper, p. 8.
14. 1976–83 Data from Computopia, December 1984; 1984 Data *ComputerWorld,* December 9, 1985, page 58.
15. Computopia, December 1984.
16. William H. Davidson, *The Amazing Race: Winning the Technorivalry with Japan* (New York: John Wiley & Sons, 1984), pp. 251–55.
17. *ComputerWorld* 12/9/85.
18. Quoted in *ComputerWorld* 12/9/85, pp. 58–59.
19. *Business Week,* April 21, 1986, p. 62.
20. PX 6779.
21. PX 5565.
22. 1977 White Paper, p. 5.
23. Kaysen, op. cit.
24. PX 6306.

20. LIMITS OF THE EMPIRE

1. Nora and Minc, op. cit., p. 68.
2. Jim Rohwer, "The World on the Line," *The Economist,* November 23, 1985, p. 18 of Survey.
3. "Remarks by John R. Opel, chairman IBM." American Chamber of Commerce (United Kingdom) 31 May 1984, p. 5.
4. *The Economist,* November 23, 1985.
5. From a Statement of Joan E. Spero, senior vice president, International Corporate Affairs and Communications, American Express Co., New York, N.Y. in the Hearings Before the Subcommittee on International Trade of the Committee on Finance of United States Senate, September 12, 1984, p. 119–34.

21. WHAT TO DO

1. Peter L. Schavori, *Future Without Limits,* IBM newsletter.
2. *Business and Society Review.*

APPENDIX B

1. Phister, Montgomery, Jr., *Data Processing Technology and Economics* (Santa Monica Publishing Co., 1974).

APPENDIX E

1. PX 5112.
2. PX 3222, p. 7.
3. PX 3221, p. 3.
4. Bloch Tr. 7,680–8,003; Ingersoll Tr. 8,421; PX 362.
5. Conrad Tr. 13,909-10, PX 208, 301, 349.
6. PX 371A, p. 72.
7. PX 209, 216.
8. PX 341, Conrad, Tr. 14,145-6, 14,147-91.
9. PX 390.
10. Weil Tr. 7,016-019, 7,054.
11. Withington, Tr. 56,015.

APPENDIX F

1. PX 4057.

APPENDIX I

1. PX 2659A.

APPENDIX J

1. Part of IBM response to Federal Communications Docket 16979, dated 3/5/68, nr. 16979 entitled "In the Matter of Regulatory and Policy Problems Presented by the Interdependence of Computer and Communications Services and Facilities."

APPENDIX K

1. The testimony of Mr. Lewis Bernstein before the Subcommittee on Monopolies and Commercial Law of the House Committee on the Judiciary, February 4, 1982, p. 19.
2. *New York Times,* March 10, 1982.

APPENDIX L

1. PX 5055.

Index